Relocating Britishness

Published in our
centenary year
~ **2004** ~
MANCHESTER
UNIVERSITY
PRESS

STUDIES IN POPULAR CULTURE

General editor: Professor Jeffrey Richards

Relocating Britishness

EDITED BY
STEPHEN CAUNCE
EWA MAZIERSKA
SUSAN SYDNEY-SMITH
JOHN K. WALTON

Manchester University Press
Manchester and New York
distributed exclusively in the USA by Palgrave

Published by Manchester University Press
Oxford Road, Manchester M13 9NR, UK
and Room 400, 175 Fifth Avenue, New York, NY 10010, USA
www.manchesteruniversitypress.co.uk

Distributed exclusively in the USA by
Palgrave, 175 Fifth Avenue, New York,
NY 10010, USA

Distributed exclusively in Canada by
UBC Press, University of British Columbia, 2029 West Mall,
Vancouver, BC, Canada V6T 1Z2

British Library Cataloguing-in-Publication Data
A catalogue record for this book is available from the British Library

Library of Congress Cataloging-in-Publication Data applied for

ISBN 0 7190 7026 0 hardback

First published 2004

13 12 11 10 09 08 07 06 05 04   10 9 8 7 6 5 4 3 2 1

Typeset
by Northern Phototypesetting Co. Ltd, Bolton
Printed in Great Britain
by Biddles Ltd, King's Lynn

STUDIES IN POPULAR CULTURE

There has in recent years been an explosion of interest in culture and cultural studies. The impetus has come from two directions and out of two different traditions. On the one hand, cultural history has grown out of social history to become a distinct and identifiable school of historical investigation. On the other hand, cultural studies has grown out of English literature and has concerned itself to a large extent with contemporary issues. Nevertheless, there is a shared project, its aim to elucidate the meanings and values implicit and explicit in the art, literature, learning, institutions and everyday behaviour within a given society. Both the cultural historian and the cultural studies scholar seek to explore the ways in which a culture is imagined, represented and received, how it interacts with social processes, how it contributes to individual and collective identities and world views, to stability and change, to social, political and economic activities and programmes. This series aims to provide an arena for the cross-fertilization of the discipline, so that the work of the cultural historian can take advantage of the most useful and illuminating of the theoretical developments and the cultural studies scholars can extend the purely historical underpinnings of their investigations. The ultimate objective of the series is to provide a range of books which will explain in a readable and accessible way where we are now socially and culturally and how we got to where we are. This should enable people to be better informed, promote an interdisciplinary approach to cultural issues and encourage deeper thought about the issues, attitudes and institutions of popular culture.

Jeffrey Richards

Contents

List of illustrations

Notes on contributors

Charles Barr is Professor of Film Studies at the University of East Anglia. His publications on British cinema history include *All Our Yesterdays: 90 Years of British Cinema* (1986: editor and contributor), *English Hitchcock* (1999) and a monograph on Hitchcock's *Vertigo* (2002).

Jonathan Black has recently published essays on the work of C. R. W. Nevinson and Eric Kennington, and curated an exhibition of the latter's work at University College, London. His first book is *The Sculpture of Eric Kennington* (2002). He is working on a major survey of Vorticism, to be exhibited in London and Manchester, and a monograph on Nevinson's prints between 1916 and 1931.

Stephen Caunce is Senior Lecturer in History at the University of Central Lancashire. He works on regional networks and identities, with special reference to the North of England, and his publications include *Amongst Farm Horses: Farm Servants in East Yorkshire* (1991) and *Oral History and the Local Historian* (1994).

James Chapman is Senior Lecturer in Film and Television History at the Open University. His publications include *Licence to Thrill: A Cultural History of the James Bond Films* (1999) and *Saints and Avengers: British Adventure Series of the 1960s* (2002).

Jon Cook is Senior Lecturer in English at the University of East Anglia and Director of the Centre for Creative and Performing Arts. His interests focus primarily on Romantic and post-Romantic literature and culture, and his publications include *Romanticism and Ideology* (1981) and *William Hazlitt: Selected Writings* (1991).

Matthew Hilton is Senior Lecturer in History at Birmingham University. He is the author of *Smoking in British Popular Culture, 1800–2000* (2000), *Consumerism in Twentieth-Century Britain: The Search for a Historical Movement* (2003) and co-editor with Martin Daunton of *The Politics of Consumption* (2001). He is a Phillip Leverhulme Prizewinner (2002).

Christine Kinealy is Professor of History at the University of Central Lancashire. She currently holds a visiting fellowship at Drew University, New Jersey. Her books include *A Death-dealing Famine: The Great Hunger in Ireland* (1997) and *A Disunited Kingdom? England, Ireland, Scotland and Wales, 1800-1949* (1999).

Jim McGuigan is Reader in Cultural Analysis in the Department of Social Sciences, Loughborough University. His books include *Cultural Populism* (1992), *Culture and the Public Sphere* (1996), *Modernity and Postmodern Culture* (1999) and the forthcoming *Cultural Policy*. He received financial support from the AHRB for the project on 'The Meanings of the New Millennium Experience' of which his chapter in this volume is a product.

Cahal McLaughlin is Senior Lecturer in Media Arts at Royal Holloway College, University of London. He is a documentary director and producer who has broadcast on Channel 4, BBC and RTE. He is researching the recording of audio-visual testimonies about political conflict.

Ewa Mazierska is Senior Lecturer in Film and Media Studies at the University of Central Lancashire. She has published four books and many articles in Polish, dealing with Polish and world cinema. Her publications in English include (with Laura Rascaroli) *From Moscow to Madrid: European Cities, Postmodern Cinema* (2002) and *The Cinema of Nanni Moretti: Dreams and Diaries* (2004), as well as several journal articles.

Jeffrey Richards is Professor of Cultural History at Lancaster University. He is series editor of Studies in Popular Culture (Manchester University Press) and Cinema and Society (I. B. Tauris). His many books include *Films and British National Identity* (1997) and *Imperialism and Music: Britain 1876–1953* (2001).

Andrew Spicer teaches in the Faculty of Art, Media and Design at the University of the West of England. He has published widely on aspects of British cinema, including *Typical Men: The Representation of Masculinity in Popular British Cinema* (2001). He has recently completed *Film Noir* (2002), and his biography of Sydney Box is in press.

Susan Sydney-Smith is Senior Lecturer in Film and Media Studies at the University of Central Lancashire and author of *Beyond Dixon of Dock Green: Early British Police Series* (2002).

John K. Walton is Professor of Social History at the University of Central Lancashire. He has published widely, especially on regional identities, seaside resorts and tourism in England and Spain. His most recent book is *The British Seaside: Holidays and Resorts in the Twentieth Century* (2000).

Val Williamson teaches media, communication and cultural studies at Edge Hill College and Liverpool John Moores University. She has published several chapters in edited collections of essays, and her forthcoming Ph.D. thesis deals with the Liverpool saga novels and novelists between 1974 and 1997.

General editor's foreword

For several decades after the Second World War, the issue of class dominated historians' discussions of modern British history. It became unfashionable to talk about national identity because of its nineteenth-century overtones of race, empire and hierarchy. But the sociological and ideological impact of eighteen years of Thatcherism, crystallized in the widely supported old-style colonial war in the Falklands in 1982, changed all that. National identity replaced class at the top of the historians' agenda.

The academic interest has been sharpened, widened and enhanced by Britain's failure to engage fully with Europe, the continuing struggle over the status of Northern Ireland, the emergence of multiculturalism, the rise of nationalist and home-rule movements in Wales and Scotland and the chorus of criticism of traditional institutions such as the monarchy, the law and the Church of England. This has stimulated a stream of conferences, articles, books and television programmes on Britishness, Englishness and national identity in general.

The present volume resulted from one of those productive and illuminating conferences that sought to take the debate forward. It examines the idea of British national identity from a variety of perspectives, political, social and cultural. In particular it explores the complex of meanings embodied in a series of key cultural icons, among them the Millennium Dome, the seaside holiday, Association Football, cricket, the Orange Order, First World War British Tommies and the television police series. The result is a rich, thoughtful and stimulating mix of interpretations and analyses.

Jeffrey Richards

Introduction

John K. Walton

This book is the product of an interdisciplinary conference on 'Relocating Britishness', held at the University of Central Lancashire in June 2000. It is a themed selection of contributions, offering a distinctive array of perspectives on the historical roots of problems of identity that are endemic to the concept of the United Kingdom. They continue to break out prolifically in new directions, as the constituent parts of this strange hybrid state assert their own identities in new and changing ways, and the legacy of Empire acquires new vital forces of its own, in the globalizing (if we may still use this much-abused word) and post-colonial (or at least post-*British* colonial) setting of this demanding new millennium.[1] This introduction identifies the distinguishing features of the book and the neglected niche it fills in a proliferating literature, before situating the chapters in wider context and suggesting some ways of reading them and setting them to work on a wider stage.

The interestingly problematic nature of the book's title, and therefore its subject matter, is indicated by the red line that appeared under 'Britishness' as it appeared on the computer screen, indicating a word that was absent from the machine's internal dictionary.[2] Tom Nairn's entertaining coinage of 'Ukanian' met the same fate.[3] As Peter J. Taylor notes succinctly, this absence of established or acceptable terminology for the state of being a British or United Kingdom citizen (or subject) indicates that, 'We live in a state without an inclusive term for its citizens'.[4] The all-embracing term 'United Kingdom' is seldom used. The English tend to deploy 'English' and 'British' interchangeably, as if there were no difference. The Welsh, Scots and Northern Irish, along with Britons whose identity (for themselves and others) is inflected through skin colour as well as (for example) accent, language and religion, negotiate their perceptions of self through flexible and changing ideas about relationships between Britishness and alternative but overlapping collectivities. Confusion is compounded by the residues of empire (the enthusiastic reception accorded to the Commonwealth Games in Manchester in 2002 should provoke interesting contemporary research in this area) and by changing relationships with, and within, an expanding European Community.[5]

All this highlights the lack of a clear overarching sense of British identity, as such, and by implication the existence of a general preference, most of the time, for geographical definitions of the self in society that focus on entities nearer to home. This applies not only to the 'nations without a state' within the United Kingdom, with varying and changing quasi-national systems of government, language and culture, but also to regions, counties, cities and localities, in a layering of allegiance which, at levels closer to the grassroots, has its counterpart in every society with horizons beyond the immediate and the local.[6] Such geographical self-identifications are, of course, endlessly flexible, as attachments to one level of identity can coexist and interact with others in harmony or conflict; and Doreen Massey argues that space is better imagined subjectively, in terms of the changing ways in which people use and populate it, rather than as an imposed shape on the ground or as a reified political or economic entity with firm administrative boundaries.[7] This perception slots in alongside older and still fruitful formulations about imagined communities.[8] But what is clear is that ideas about what it is to be British have been, and are being, relocated along a variety of axes and in several dimensions. They are also the objects of intense discussion, as hardly a day passes without serious comment from journalists and cultural critics on questions of Britishness and the 'nations without states' that the concept both contains and antagonizes.

Historians have contributed to these discussions, often in accessible idioms. But it is surprising how recently issues of Britishness, as opposed to Englishness, have pushed their way to the fore, even in sophisticated treatments of patriotism and national identity. The three-volume History Workshop collection in 1989, for example, routinely conflated 'British' with 'English' as the signifier of national identity and character, and even the chapter on 'Britannia' tended to collapse this potentially unifying figure into an incarnation of Englishness doing duty for the wider entity.[9] By this time the importance of looking at the genesis of the United Kingdom as something encompassing Scotland, Wales and Ireland was engaging early modernists, especially those who felt the need to understand the civil wars of the mid-seventeenth century 'in the round', and during the 1990s this was passing into an orthodoxy in the field.[10] But it took Linda Colley's *Britons*, published in 1992, to bring to the fore an argument about the emergence of Britishness as an expression of national identity created in a 'long' version of the eighteenth century, between the Act of Union in 1707 and the accession of Queen Victoria in 1837.[11] Colley expressly distanced herself from earlier interpretations of Britishness put forward by Keith Robbins and Michael Hechter: 'Great Britain did not emerge by way of a "blending" of the different regional or older national cultures contained within its boundaries . . . nor is its genesis to be explained primarily in terms of an English "core" imposing its cultural and political hegemony on a helpless and defrauded Celtic periphery.'[12] Her own argument emphasized the crystallisation of a British identity founded on Protestantism and the military virtues, on conquest and Empire, on commerce and respect for the monarchy, and on reactions to the perceived 'otherness' of the French, the emergent United States of America and foreigners more generally. All of Colley's bastions of British unity came under challenges which ebbed and flowed through her period and beyond it, of course, while the 'others' against which it is defined have remained powerful although ambiguous and confusing. Indeed, the declining currency of several key aspects of this historic vision of Britishness since the Second World War has contributed very significantly to the crisis of identity that this book investigates. Colley has set a strong agenda, to which the contributors respond both explicitly and implicitly; but alongside her contribution Norman Davies' compendious reinterpretation of British history on a genuinely British stage, and Richard Weight's massive and provocative work on national identity in Britain since Dunkirk and the Blitz, demand to be read attentively alongside the present book.[13]

Despite the loss of Empire, the limited resonance of the Commonwealth (sport, apparently, aside), and the failure of a heartfelt identification with Britain-in-Europe to extend beyond a small group of articulate enthusiasts, most recent studies of the roots of Britishness have not been uniformly introspective. Indeed, their gaze has been much more strongly directed towards the living legacy of Empire than to the regional (as opposed to nation-without-a-state) and local dimensions of identity. Most of the swelling historical output has looked outwards rather than, or as well as, inwards, emphasizing the enduring importance of the Empire, and of imperial pasts both tangible and imagined, for contemporary perceptions and complications of what it is to be British. Such concerns are, above all, a product of the 1990s, in eventual response to (among other things) John Mackenzie's influential assertion (in his significantly-titled *Propaganda and Empire*) of the powerful influence of imperial motifs in late Victorian and Edwardian popular culture, and more generally to Edward Said's telling and controversial coinage of 'Orientalism'.[14] Despite such stimulating contributions between the late 1970s and the mid-1980s, however, Robert Colls and Philip Dodd could still complain in 1986, in their important and pioneering edited collection of essays on Englishness at the turn of the century, that: 'Because we could not find a suitable and willing contributor, there is no account of what "the Empire", or a part of it, thought of the English'.[15] Nor, it might be added, was there a chapter on what the British thought about the Empire, and the Irish were presented as 'marginal Britons'. Sixteen years later, Colls' substantial study of English identities now contained well-documented chapters on 'Colonials' and 'Imagined Nation', which addressed the renegotiations of English and British identity that followed the post-war settlement of large numbers of black citizens from the former colonies, although the Irish still received episodic treatment, mainly in a section labelled 'Celts'.[16] Indeed, the book could still have said more about the ways in which Britons' own perceptions of Englishness or Britishness were defined in relation to the 'otherness' of colonial peoples (including the Irish), and about perceptions of the 'mother country' and its salient characteristics when viewed from 'peripheral' imperial vantage-points redefined as the projectors rather than the targets of an appraising, labelling gaze. The key point is that the intervening years had produced historical interpretations in abundance, through (for example) the 'Studies in Imperialism' series edited by John Mackenzie and the work of (among others) Catherine Hall, Wendy Webster and Antoinette Burton, each of whom brings important gender perspectives to this task.[17]

This draws attention to the multitude of ways in which Britishness can be relocated. This book addresses some of the dimensions that have featured less strongly in recent literature, but which remain important to our understanding of the problem as a whole. The focus is on the components of the British state itself, examining aspects of England, Scotland, Wales and Ireland and taking on board questions of region, class, and especially gender and (mainly popular) culture, in an broad sweep that embraces political science, literature, art history, anthropology, and film and television studies as well as work from those who identify themselves as owing their primary allegiance to the historical profession. One of the key objects of this exercise is to draw together a range of perspectives that would normally be kept in the separate compartments that notions of the hermetic sanctity of the academic discipline perpetuate, and to encourage the sharing of a common pool of perspectives and insights in a truly interdisciplinary (possibly even post-disciplinary or transdisciplinary) spirit.[18] We can, and should, borrow and learn from each other, adopting transferable ideas and crossing academic borders in pursuit of enhanced understanding of the phenomena we seek to apprehend.

We lack a chapter with an entirely Scottish focus, although there are Scottish dimensions to several of the contributions. Scotland's importance to the problem of Britishness has been enhanced by developments since 1970. These include the rise of political nationalism to become a major and enduring force, the insertion of nationalist or at least devolutionary perspectives into the other major parties, the referendum on devolution in 1977, the debate over to whom North Sea oil belonged and what should be done with it, the widening discrepancy during the 1980s between a Thatcherite metropolitan political culture and a disintegrating Conservative political presence in Scotland, and most recently the referendum of September 1997 which led to the election of the first modern Scottish parliament in May 1999.[19] This story runs parallel to the Welsh developments analysed by Carwyn Fowler in chapter 11, and an awareness of Scottish developments will also provide a helpful context for Christine Kinealy's treatment of the Orange Order in chapter 12. But the essential distinctiveness of Scottish economic, social and cultural history, from law and social policy through the Scottish diasporas and the Scottish role in empire, the contrasting and traumatic economic experiences of (for example) Clydeside, the Highlands and the east coast, the peculiarities of Scottish Protestantism and its sudden eclipse in the late twentieth century, and the relationships between sport, literature, the arts and senses of Scottish identity, underlies the political issues. It also subverts any easy perception that this is an extension of the English regions or an alternative version of Wales with the same issues coming up in different forms and relative strengths. 'Red Clydeside', for example, as myth and history, was more than just another 'Little Moscow'; Scottish football fans cannot be equated simply with English 'hooligans'; and the intersections between politics, culture and national identity are as complex in the Scottish setting as elsewhere in the United Kingdom.[20] The fashion for comparisons between Scotland and Quebec, Catalunya or Flanders has a validity of its own, and the European dimension to changing perceptions of Scottish identity is of the utmost importance, but internal comparisons between the component parts of the United Kingdom should also be worth pursuing.[21]

Stuart Hall's definitions of how national communities are formed through cultural practices and representations are highly relevant at this point. He identifies five key themes, which emerge in various guises in the course of the following chapters: (1) telling of stories indicating common experience, triumph, struggle; (2) construction of a 'timeless' national character; (3) invention of ritual, pageantry and symbolism; (4) the construction of foundation myths and legends to affirm quasi-sacred distinctive character for the imagined nation;

and (5) ideas of common breeding or racial purity.[22] Ideas of Britishness, like other overarching concepts and identifications, are cross-hatched by differences of class, gender/sexuality, generation, race/ethnicity, location (metropolitan, urban, suburban, rural, for example), culture, region/nation without a state, and political affiliation (including attitudes to the monarchy and the constitution), which may both challenge and confirm, and confirm by challenging, the 'national' project. What Britons do have in common, of course, is the status of being constitutionally subjects rather than citizens, an enduring anomaly that seems to feel particularly pressing in the United Kingdom outside England, and that sets the British apart from Western European neighbours and from the United States alike.

Jon Cook's scene-setting chapter 1 builds on these ideas (though not without challenging aspects of them) through an examination and elaboration of the ideas of Tom Nairn, Homi Bhabha and Slavoj Zizek, who are taken as representative of constitutional, narrative and symbolic approaches to the problems entailed in imagining Britishness and encompassing its relocation. Zizek's work does not deal directly with the British case, but Cook argues convincingly that it provides transferable ideas and is relevant by analogy. Presenting these approaches side by side is itself a novel undertaking, and (for example) film historians will find that his insertion of post-colonial theory into debates on cinema and nationality breaks new ground and opens out fresh research strategies. Although the present book's gaze is directed predominantly within the four kingdoms rather than outwards to Empire or inwards from it, Bhabha has as much to offer to it as Cook's other authors, and not only from his advocacy of a 'performative' narrative that disrupts boundaries and questions inherited accounts. His emphasis on the nation as a site of cultural differences rather than a unity embracing subordinate diversity is in tune with what follows. So is Zizek's concern to highlight diversity, plurality and contrasting forms of collective identity, while paying due attention to the power of names and labels to shape and order the solidarities of the imagination. Particularly arresting is Cook's suggestion that British identity could eventually be relocated in the positive celebration of diversity and plurality.

This was supposed to be part of New Labour's agenda for the Millennium Dome, which is the subject of Jim McGuigan's chapter 2. McGuigan points out that the Dome, as inherited and spun by the Blair government, was supposed to lay claim to global cultural leadership on behalf of a confident, adventurous, forward-looking Britain, whose nationalism paid no heed to the past and took very little interest in cultural diversity. For McGuigan, the salient feature of the

Dome was its celebration of neo-liberalism through public/private partnership, and he offers a highly critical analysis of the role of corporate sponsorship in the presentation of most of the exhibits. This was a business-led, and decidedly Anglo-American, vision of Britishness; but in so far as visitors were well-disposed to the Dome, they welcomed the diversity of images and viewpoints presented in the self-portrait zone, and the non-sponsored Millennium Show, bringing a degree of agency to their evaluation of the experience, and valuing the populist rather than the corporate aspects of what it had to offer.[23] This was, perhaps, a failed attempt to relocate Britishness from the top down, further hampered by a geographical location in Greenwich (chosen ahead of Birmingham), which made access difficult from beyond the economic forcing-house of south-east England. Above all, as Weight points out, the Dome failed to convey any sense 'of what it meant to be English, Scottish, Welsh or Northern Irish', and in the spring of 2000 'the *Daily Record* gleefully reported that fewer than 400 tickets had been sold in the whole of Scotland'.[24]

Chapter 3, on Blackpool and Britishness, presents a sharply contrasting picture, despite the first working-class seaside resort's historic affinity with the business culture of popular entertainment, and its political embrace of New Labour in the 1990s, an affection that was not reciprocated by the party's governors. Where the Dome might be presented as metropolitan and even transatlantic, Blackpool offers a perspective from 'the provinces' that embraces Scotland, Wales and Northern Ireland, and it also recruits large numbers of visitors from the Republic. Above all, it retains historic affinities with the old working class of manufacturing industry and with the North of England, which probably helps to explain New Labour's uneasy relationship with it at party conference time. Here, the significant 'others' include the metropolis itself and the romantic idealisation of English countryside. All this reminds us of elements of internal colonialism, within England itself as well as within the British Isles; and in Bhabha's terms it might be argued that Blackpool provides a performative narrative of Britishness, with emphasis on the narrative. Visions of the past are important here, in contrast with the present-mindedness and futuristic aspirations of the Dome, but (in adapting in pursuit of survival) Blackpool has continued to welcome 'other' versions of Britishness, most obviously a profit-led orientation with a pedigree of more than a century here, and perhaps therefore a stronger claim to British authenticity than the bland corporate commercialism that dominated the Dome, although not without its own lacunae and ambiguities.[25]

Ewa Mazierska's treatment of family and class in three films by Mike Leigh in chapter 4 returns us to the metropolis, but to a London of neglected estates and sterile suburbs. The core of her argument is that during the 1980s and 1990s (if not before) representations of the working class as a key component of Englishness ceased to be viable, and that the fragmentation of communities culminated in the family, with all its inherent tensions and flaws, becoming the defining component of what had been working-class identities. Not only do Leigh's films express (without in any sense endorsing) the way in which Thatcherite policies became self-fulfilling prophecies, destroying the solidarities whose existence, or at least legitimacy, she had denied. They also show a shift towards an acceptance on Leigh's part that relative wealth need not be incompatible with virtue, which Mazierska identifies as potentially congruent with an identification with the politics of New Labour (although not, presumably, in their Millennium Dome guise). The contrast with Ken Loach's very different representation of beleaguered Northern working-class communities is sometimes made explicit, and it would be interesting to extend the agenda of the chapter to cinematic representations of similar environments in Scotland, Wales and Northern Ireland. Where Leigh's work (and Mazierska's interpretation of it) stands, in relation to Cook's suggestion that a relocated Britishness might come to be characterized by diversity and plurality, constitutes a stimulating question.

In chapter 5 Jeffrey Richards' highly original reinterpretation of the relationship between football (at once the 'national' and the 'people's' game) and Britishness begins with Tom Nairn on the break-up of Britain, but moves on rapidly to argue that the rize of football hooliganism is a symptom of a retreat from a distinctive and civilized version of what it was to be British, which evolved in the eighteenth century, became dominant in the nineteenth and has been on the retreat since the 1960s.[26] In Bhabha's terms, what he presents is a pedagogic narrative, featuring an overarching vision of a dominant British culture that transcends class divisions; but it is presented as the history of a myth by which people lived, and (in many cases) continue to live.[27] Richards equates Harold Perkin's concept of a 'moral revolution' of the early nineteenth century with the hegemonic triumph of a civilized, decent, imperial 'Britishness' over a loutish, uncouth, insular 'Englishness', which in turn has begun to reassert itself with the decline of the old working class and the rise of the new media and the cult of the self.[28] This time, aspects of 1960s counter-culture join Thatcherism as the agents of damage and decline; but Richards ends by suggesting that elements of the civilized Britishness of industry and Empire have survived the retreat from empire and the collapse of Protestantism: the problem is how to harness them. Here, too, diversity, plurality and tolerance are central to the agenda.

In chapter 6 Charles Barr writes about the other aspirant to the title of 'the national game' – at least, that of England – although he begins by arguing that cricket, with its Welsh and Scottish players for British Test Match teams with an 'England' label, has a stronger claim to Britishness than what is overwhelmingly English rather than British cinema. His examination of cricket as unifier of British diversity, conducted through cinematic representation, J. B. Priestley and the socio-geographical analysis of the composition of Test Match sides, resonates well with Zizek's conjuring of the imaginative power of names and symbols, as well as his emphasis on the incorporation of local communities into a larger national unity. As Barr remarks, the very specific cricketing allusions whose recognition could be taken for granted in the England of 1940 now require explanation; and cricket's relationship to myths of Englishness has changed since the 1960s, and especially since 'Botham's Test' of 1981, in ways that might be thought to intersect with the trajectory of Richards's pedagogic narrative on football. Barr's portrayal of cricket and myths of Englishness also engages with myths of Empire, especially through discussion of Basil D'Oliveira and C. L. R. James; and it will benefit from being read alongside the recent, complementary contribution by Cronin and Holt on English cricket and decolonisation.[29]

Questions of Britishness and masculinity haunt the chapters by Richards and Barr; and the contribution by Chapman and Hilton in chapter 7 brings these issues to centre stage, as they present four phases of representations of masculinity in British popular adventure fiction, from Sherlock Holmes to James Bond by way of Bulldog Drummond and 'The Saint'. They emphasize the enduring importance of the ideal of the gentleman amateur, coupled with a strong drive to autonomy and independence, and a rejection of subordination and routine; and they demonstrate the ways in which, also enduringly, notions of patriotism, loyalty and duty are cross-cut by celebrations of singularity and difference. Official narratives are set against subversive ones, but the former predominate (especially in the political sphere, where socialism gets short shrift in these stories); and extended comparison with the chapters on football and cricket would bear interesting fruit. So would further exploration of the roles of Scotland, the United States and empire in this literature, which can only be hinted at in Chapman and Hilton's firmly-themed chapter, along with the relationships between novels and other media and the development of other aspects of gender and sexuality.[30]

J. A. Black's chapter 8, on representations of the military through sculpture and painting, extends discussion of masculinity in additional directions and dimensions. He identifies, in First World War and war memorial art, a preference among commentators, critics and commissioners of monuments for portraying the British soldier as either weak and pathetic, or as perfectly proportioned on classical Greek lines of masculine beauty. That minority of artists who depicted soldiers as strong, powerful, grim and efficient faced angry criticism, even though artists like Jagger and Nevinson were coming from the Kipling tradition of representing the ordinary soldier as tough, long-suffering and capable of bearing the burden of Empire on behalf of those at home. How representative the critics were, and of whose aesthetic of English masculinity, remains an interesting question; but treading the line between effeminate sentimentality and unacceptable storm-trooper toughness must have been a difficult task for artists with an eye to commissions and esteem. Black emphasizes recent reassessments of the English, as well as the Scots, Irish, Welsh and 'Dominions' soldier, as a tough and efficient fighter; and the resistance to accepting this portrayal sits curiously alongside the acceptable toughness of Chapman and Hilton's adventure heroes, although Bull-dog Drummond and 'The Saint' were hardly likely to be leaders of a post-war proletarian revolution of the kind that seems to have preoccupied Black's commentators. Black's chapter should be read alongside the work of Joanna Bourke on the First World War, the technologies of killing and the vulnerability of the masculine body; and its subject matter hints at issues around male sexuality, homoeroticism and ideas of Britishness, which also rear their heads implicitly in the novels examined by Chapman and Hilton, and indeed in some of the cinematic material discussed by Barr.[31]

Contested portrayals of the British military also form the central focus of Andrew Spicer's chapter 9, which returns us firmly to the realm of popular consumer culture. Spicer points up the coexistence, through the 'long' 1950s, of contrasting, competing and complementary cinematic representations of the Second World War. His analysis of the 'alternative' version to what might be imagined as the pedagogic narrative of selfless courage, duty and sacrifice brings to centre stage a sequence of comic, irreverent, carnivalesque, 'worm's eye view' 'service comedies' that celebrated the 'skiver', the individualist who subverted oppressive military machines and the 'bullshit' that went with them. There were at least two wars here, the second being a form of class conflict; but the 'battle of the sexes', celebrating female agency, energy, appetite and high spirits, was also an occasional feature of the genre. Spicer concludes, however, that both the celebrations of wartime virtue and the 'service comedy' parodies were popular with overlapping audiences and met overlapping needs, and that these conflicting but complementary versions of the war were central to the evolution of British identity in what he sees as the important transitional decade of the 1950s. Here again, the relevance of Bhabha and Zizek, as represented here in Cook's chapter, is very much in evidence.

Gender interacts with class and region as the main organizing concept of Val Williamson's chapter 10 on the working-class domestic 'saga' novel in north-west England, especially Liverpool. Williamson establishes this genre as a major publishing phenomenon of the late twentieth century. It is the product of female authors drawn from the cultures they describe, who represent working-class women as having agency and strength, and recover (and celebrate) for their readers the craft skills of the (mainly) pre-1960s 'housewife' and the strategies for survival and the protection of 'respectability' that were adopted. In terms of readership numbers and accessibility of text, these novels are far more influential in constructing popular views of 'people's history' than the works of professional historians or even the reminiscences of successful autobiographers such as Robert Roberts and Bill Naughton. However, the recent best-seller status of William Woodruff's Blackburn-based autobiographical novel *The road to Nab End* (a book covering seemingly similar ground, but with very different origins, and written by a male academic) raises interesting questions about readerships and marketing in this context. It is interesting that Woodruff's book went through three publishers and titles before 'taking off' as a best-seller: it shifted from the very particular, being the 'story of a Lancashire weaver's son', through 'a Lancashire childhood', to eventual success with an appeal to a broader constituency as 'an extraordinary Northern childhood', perhaps suggesting the greater difficulty this kind of book faces in finding a niche.[32] Even when academic offerings take the form of 'history from below', deal with domestic themes, make use of oral history and are sympathetically and accessibly written, they are unable to tap into the same markets.[33] The saga phenomenon also exists alongside the 'official' histories of academics and museums, drawing its sources from interview and reminiscence, and sustaining a mutually validating dialogue between writers and readers. Here we examine the construction of identities in the domestic sphere, within gendered collectivities which are defined in terms of single towns (especially) and of wider industrial regions, relocating important dimensions of lived Britishness at the level of locality and popular culture. Every aspect of this dimension has been neglected in most existing work on the Britishness theme.

In chapter 11 Carwyn Fowler seems, at first glance, to return us to the constitutional agenda associated with Tom Nairn, as he seeks to provide a dynamic vision of Welsh national identity through the political process, with sustained awareness of the importance of the European context and especially of the 'new regionalism' within the EU. But his sensitivity to cultural variations within Wales as well as to change over time, his attention to Welsh language movements as expressing a vision of sovereignty founded in people and culture rather than the UK conventions of the Crown in parliament, and his insistence on the nebulous nature of the theoretical link between nation and state in this setting, provide connections with all the authors and approaches presented in the Cook chapter. The emphasis on the lack of 'ultimate' goals, in terms of a separate Welsh nationhood, and on the perpetuation of Welshness as a strong component of Britishness, with its own cultural and linguistic identity, link up in particularly interesting ways with aspects of Cook's representation of Zizek.

Christine Kinealy takes up questions of regional identity and political culture in a Northern Irish context in chapter 12, exploring the historical relationship between the Orange Order's claims to loyalist Britishness and the recurrent tensions between it and the British state. Here, questions of the 'break-up of Britain' obtrude more strongly. As Kinealy points out, Orange identity is founded in a Protestant vision of the British state that (for example) would withhold allegiance to a non-Protestant monarch. It is defined as much in reaction to the threatening 'otherness' of Catholicism, and the perceived need for protection from it, as by positive identification with notions of Britishness that would be recognized elsewhere in the UK. A dissection of the invented nature of Orange history and traditions, and of the Order's recurrent historical willingness to defy the British government when its perceived interests are being challenged, prompts the conclusion that even 'Ulster-Britishness' will have difficulty in coping with current trends towards secularisation, an 'ecumenical monarchy' and devolution. The contrast with Wales, as represented by Fowler, is particularly striking, and the precipitate decline of the Catholic Church's influence in Ireland will presumably complicate matters even further.[34]

Cahal McLaughlin's chapter 13, dealing with representations of British–Irish conflict on film, also emphasizes the ambiguity of 'loyalist' attitudes to the British state in a Northern Ireland where 'the country' can mean either the six counties or the United Kingdom, but where UK politics, as is so often apparent in Kinealy's presentation of the history of the Orange Order, seem to threaten the nature or even the persistence of the Union. But McLaughlin's central focus is on the ways in which the ceasefire of the mid-1990s, together with new developments in the funding and organization of film-making on both sides of the border, opened out opportunities to explore and represent the nature of the conflicts over Ireland and their relationships with individuals. Gender reappears as an important theme, as mothers are seen being drawn into political conflict in Northern Ireland. Alongside this, McLaughlin emphasizes the limited development of social and economic context and political nuance that is imposed (especially) by United States funding and expectations about what the market wants to see, while hoping that these initiatives will prove a stepping stone towards more satisfying representations of these complex conflicts in future years. Here again, an agenda that clearly contributes to debate over the 'break-up of Britain' can also be related to the Bhabha and Zizek components of Cook's introductory chapter.

In chapter 14 Susan Sydney-Smith makes explicit connections with the Bhabha agenda in her treatment of the emergence of the 'northern' police series in the early 1960s, through Z Cars and its immediate precursors, and the new incarnations of the genre in the more complex and competitive broadcasting environment of the late 1990s, especially The Cops. She points up the uneasy negotiation between ideas of national cultural unification and the expression of regional diversity in British broadcasting history, and the ways in which the imagined North, a subordinate regional identity within Britain rather than a 'nation without a state', has been abstracted from geography or topography in the essentialist representations of metropolitan programme-makers. This colonial, orientalizing gaze is evident in Z Cars, and the regional press and BBC archives provide evidence of the angry reactions of northern viewers both to the elision of localities and the damage done to the reputations of identifiable places, together with the perceived misrepresentation of regional cultures (including that of the police themselves). The 'grassroots', working-class regional identities presented here, however over-generalized and lacking in genuine local understandings, have not been exportable in police series form. The international success of The Full Monty seems to have been another matter, subtitles or not. It has fallen to Heartbeat, with its focus-group origins and soft-focus celebration of a pastoral, bucolic, nostalgic alternative to the industrial, inner-city, working-class northern England, to gain acceptance and commercial success beyond Britain. Here is a further reminder of the complex variations in landscape, society, image and representation within a single regional sub-division of England, which could be replicated, of course, for each of the components of the United Kingdom and a fortiori the British Isles.[35]

No volume of this size could hope to cover all the angles along which Britishness has been, is being and might be relocated, or to give equal weight to all the internal dimensions of the phenomenon. We regret the loss of a promised essay on Scottish identity, the limited engagement with representations of the working class over the years between Hoggart, Williams and the 'affluent worker' studies and the recent ruminations of Darcus Howe[36] and the absence of chapters offering a direct focus on (for example) race, ethnicity, the citizenship question and the changing place of the monarchy.[37] But we do lay claim to have provided a distinctive, novel, interdisciplinary set of perspectives on a set of problems that will continue to preoccupy politicians as well as cultural commentators in Britain for the foreseeable future, as well as having obvious analogues wherever national identities are cross-cut and problematic.

Notes

1 Stuart Christie, review of Naomi Klein, *Fences and Windows: Dispatches from the Front Lines of the Globalisation Debate* (London, 2002), in *Guardian: Review*, 9 November 2002, p. 15. David Morley and Kevin Robins (eds.), *British Cultural Studies* (Oxford, 2001) appeared too late for the interpretations of its contributors to be considered here, but it should be read in parallel with this book.

2 Significantly, 'Englishness' was entirely acceptable on the same criterion.

3 Tom Nairn, *The Enchanted Glass: Britain and its Monarchy* (London, 1988).

4 Peter J. Taylor, 'The meaning of the North: England's "foreign country" within?', *Political Geography* 12 (1993), p. 136.

5 For a succinct introduction to some of these issues, see Selina Chen and Tony Wright (eds.), *The English Question* (London, 2000).

6 For example, Patrick Joyce, *Visions of the People* (Cambridge, 1991); Robbie Gray, *North and South Revisited: Locality, Nation and Identity in Victorian Britain* (Portsmouth, 2000); L. Castells and J. K. Walton, 'Contrasting identities: north-west England and the Basque Country, 1840–1936', in E. Royle (ed.), *Issues of Regional Identity* (Manchester, 1998), pp. 44–81.

7 Doreen Massey, 'Places and their pasts', *History Workshop Journal* 39 (1995), pp. 182–92; Linda A. Craig, 'Identity and belonging, 1850–1945', Ph.D. thesis, University of Liverpool, 2002.

8 Benedict Anderson, *Imagined Communities* (London, 1983), continues to haunt all these discussions.

9 Raphael Samuel (ed.), *Patriotism* (3 vols., London, 1989).

10 John Morrill (ed.), *The Scottish National Covenant in its British context, 1638–1651* (Edinburgh, 1990); Brendan Bradshaw and John Morrill (eds.), *The British problem c. 1534–1707: State Formation in the Atlantic Archipelago* (Basingstoke, 1996); Austin Woolrych, *Britain in Revolution, 1625–1660* (Oxford, 2002).

11 Linda Colley, *Britons: Forging the Nation 1707–1837* (New Haven and London, 1992).

12 Colley, *Britons*, p. 6, citing Keith Robbins, *Nineteenth-Century Britain: Integration and Diversity* (Oxford, 1988) and M. Hechter, *Internal Colonialism* (Berkeley and Los Angeles, 1975).

13 Norman Davies, *The Isles: A History* (Basingstoke, 1999); Richard Weight, *Patriots: National Identity in Britain 1940–2000* (London, 2002). See also J. K. Walton, 'Britishness', in Chris Wrigley (ed.), *A Companion to Early Twentieth-Century Britain* (Oxford, 2003), pp. 517–31.

14 John M. Mackenzie, *Propaganda and Empire* (Manchester, 1984); Edward Said, *Orientalism* (London, 1978).

15 Robert Colls and Philip Dodd (eds.), *Englishness: Politics and Culture 1880–1920* (Beckenham, 1986), unpaginated preface.

16 Robert Colls, *Identity of England* (Oxford, 2002), chapters 6 and 10.

17 This literature can be approached through Stuart Ward (ed.), *British Culture and the End of Empire* (Manchester, 2001), and the themed issue 'At home in the Empire', *Journal of British Studies* 40 (2001). See also, for example, Catherine Hall (ed.), *Cultures of Empire* (Manchester, 2000); F. Driver and D. Gilbert (eds.), *Imperial Cities: Landscape and Display* (Manchester, 1999); F. Driver, *Geography Militant: Cultures of Exploration and Empire* (Oxford, 2001); Catherine Hall, *Civilising Subjects* (Cambridge, 2002); Wendy Webster, *Imagining Home: Gender, 'Race' and National Identity, 1945–64* (London, 1998); Antoinette Burton, *Burdens of History* (Chapel Hill, N.C., 1994).

18 The Université Neuf Avril, Tunis, was already organizing 'transdisciplinary' seminars on art, architecture, planning and policy in the mid-1990s, and the concept deserves encouragement.

19 Christopher Harvie, *Scotland and Nationalism: Scottish Society and Politics 1707–1994* (London, 1994), Part II, remains the essential introduction to these and related issues up to the mid-1990s. For devolution and the Scottish parliament, see Lindsay Paterson, *A Diverse Assembly: The Debate on a Scottish Parliament* (Edinburgh, 1998); John McCarthy and David Newlands, *Governing Scotland* (Aldershot, 1999); Brian Taylor, *The Scottish Parliament* (Edinburgh, 1999); Alex Wright (ed.), *Scotland: The Challenge of Devolution* (Aldershot, 2000). See also, moving beyond political systems themselves, Murray G. H. Pittock, *Scottish Nationality* (Houndmills, 2001); Christopher Harvie and Peter Jones, *The Road to Home Rule: Images of Scotland's Cause* (Edinburgh, 2000); Jonathan Hearn, *Claiming Scotland: National Identity and Liberal Culture* (Edinburgh, 2000); Catherine Di Domenico et al. (eds.), *Boundaries and Identities: Nation, Politics and Culture in Scotland* (Dundee, 2001); and the return to the fray of three established stalwarts of debate and polemic: Alasdair Gray, *Why Scots Should Rule Scotland 1997: A Carnaptious History of Britain from Roman Times Until Now* (Edinburgh, 1997); Tom Nairn, *Faces of Nationalism. Janus Revisited* (London, 1997); Neal Ascherson, *Stone Voices: The Search for Scotland* (London, 2002).

20 See, for example, William Ferguson, *The Identity of the Scottish People: an Historic Quest* (Edinburgh, 1998); Ian Donnachie and Christopher Whatley (eds.), *The Manufacture of Scottish History* (Edinburgh, 1992); David McCrone, Steve Kendrick and Pat Straw (eds.), *The Making of Scotland: Nation, Culture and Social Change* (Edinburgh, 1989); Carl Macdougall, *Painting the Forth Bridge: A Search for Scottish Identity* (London, 2001); Ray Ryan, *Ireland and Scotland: Literature and Culture, State and Nation, 1966–2000* (Oxford, 2002).

21 For example M. Keating, *Nations against the State: The New Politics of Nationalism in Quebec, Catalonia and Scotland* (Basingstoke, 2001).

22 Stuart Hall, 'The question of cultural identity', in S. Hall, D. Held and T. McGrew (eds.), *Modernity and its Futures* (Cambridge, 1992).

23 Compare Julian Barnes, *England, England* (London, 1998).

24 Weight, *Patriots*, pp. 692–5.

25 J. K. Walton, *Blackpool* (Edinburgh, 1998), provides additional supporting material and argument.

26 In some ways this runs parallel to Norbert Elias' concept of the 'civilizing process', which has itself been applied (but in unsatisfactory ways) to the question of football hooliganism: see the exchange between Eric Dunning *et al.* and Robert Lewis in *International Journal of the History of Sport* 13 (1996) and 15 (1998).

27 Cf. R. Samuel and P. Thompson (eds.), *The Myths We Live By* (London, 1990).

28 For strong images of the 'old' working class see especially E. J. Hobsbawm, *Worlds of Labour* (London, 1984).

29 M. Cronin and R. Holt, 'The imperial game in crisis: English cricket and decolonisation', in Stuart Ward (ed.), *British Culture and the End of Empire* (Manchester, 2001), pp. 121–37. See also Jack Williams, *Cricket and England: A Cultural and Social History of The Inter-War Years* (London, 1999).

30 See also Weight, *Patriots*, pp. 398–9.

31 Joanna Bourke, *Dismembering the Male: Men's Bodies, Britain and the Great War* (London, 1996); idem, *An Intimate History of Killing: Face-to-Face Killing in Twentieth-Century Warfare* (London, 1999); see also Jay Winter, *Sites of Memory, Sites of Mourning: The Great War in European Cultural History* (Cambridge, 1995).

32 Robert Roberts, *The Classic Slum: Salford Life at the Turn of the Century* (Manchester, 1971); idem, *A Ragged Schooling* (Manchester, 1976); Bill Naughton, *On the Pig's Back* (Oxford, 1987); idem, *Saintly Billy: A Catholic Boyhood* (Oxford, 1988); idem, *Neither Use nor Ornament* (Newcastle, 1995); William Woodruff, *Billy Boy: The Story of a Lancashire Weaver's Son* (Halifax, 1993); idem, *The Road to Nab End: A Lancashire Childhood* (London, 2000); idem, *The Road to Nab End: An Extraordinary Northern Childhood* (London, 2002).

33 Andrew Davies, *Leisure, Gender and Poverty: Working-Class Culture in Salford and Manchester 1900–1939* (Buckingham, 1992), is one example among many.

34 See also Robert Pope (ed.), *Religion and National Identity: Wales and Scotland, c. 1700–2000* (Cardiff, 2001).

35 See especially N. Kirk (ed.), *Northern Identities* (Aldershot, 1999).

36 See, for example, the controversial work of Jeremy Seabrook: among others, J. Seabrook and T. Blackwell, *A World Still to Win: The Reconstruction of the Post-War Working Class* (London, 1985); J. Seabrook, *Landscapes of Poverty* (Oxford, 1985).

37 Jeffrey Richards has dealt with aspects of the monarchy elsewhere: see J. Richards *et al.* (eds.), *Diana: The Making of a Media Saint* (London, 1999). But this is a part of Nairn's agenda with which this book engages only intermittently.

Relocating Britishness and the break-up of Britain

Jon Cook

The study of nations and nation states is always comparative and, whether admitted or not, theoretical. In what follows I want to compare three ways of thinking and imagining the nation – the constitutional, narrational and symbolic – incorporating a commentary on the perceived current crisis in British or English national identity. Each of these can be identified initially by reference to three writers who have made significant contributions to thinking about modern nations. Tom Nairn's work is a major example of constitutional-ist thought. The title of his influential book, *The Break-Up of Britain*, first published in 1974, is echoed in the title of this essay, as is the work of Homi Bhabha who epitomizes thinking about the nation as narrative. Slavoj Zizek, unlike Nairn and Bhabha, has not written extensively about the British nation. But his reworking of Marxist and psychoanalytic ideas about the fetish is relevant to an analysis of how nations act symbolically. Between them Nairn, Bhabha and Zizek offer different and sometimes overlapping accounts of what nations are made of and how they are best understood. Each marks out a significant con-text for the analysis of contemporary Britain. In Nairn's case it is devolution; in Bhabha's the question of post-colonial ethnicities; and in Zizek's the problem of globalization.[1]

These comparisons are driven by more than an interest in theories for their own sake. Each account identifies the fundamental question of nationhood dif-ferently. Each offers different historical stories about the modern nation state. Taken together they raise two important questions about 'relocating British-ness'. Is 'relocating Britishness' a synonym for the break-up of Britain or for its renewal? And is talk of break-up or renewal itself a symptom of a compulsive narrative drive to imagine nations in just these terms of rise and fall, persistence and dissolution? The emotional investment in this narrative drive is evident and powerful. In Britain it can produce an endless mourning for something lost, or sustain a sense of betrayal, or celebrate a new diversity, or turn the nation into an archaeological site, or become the occasion for continuous and low-level complaining. The moods sustained by narratives can be as important politically as the more obviously political disagreements about devolution or the European single currency. The latter would not possess their peculiar blocked intensity without the former. Hence another question: is it possible to imagine nations otherwise, as the subject of a story whose terms are not dictated by either decline or renewal?

Certainly media interest in the question of British and, more particularly, English national identity is widespread. By this I do not just mean the standard rhetoric of the *Sun* or the *Daily Mail* with their attacks on 'bogus asylum seek-ers', 'gypsies' and 'Eurocrats'. These presume a national identity that exists in the face of perpetual threats of invasion: the guarantee of national identity lies in what opposes it. This kind of rhetoric has a long history. It invites us to unite in the face of increasingly implausible enemies.

But there has been more reflective commentary: Jeremy Paxman's best-selling book, *The English*, is one example, as is Julian Barnes's novel, *England, England*, or Michael Wood's *In Search of England*.[2] Tom Nairn's recent book, *After Britain*, provides a valuable revision and up-dating of the arguments in *The Break-Up of Britain*. There is a sense of low-key emergency in much of this work. Something that has existed for a very long time is felt to be coming to an end. Its immediate political circumstances refer to devolution, Europe, and post-war immigration. The Blair administration has started a process of devo-lution whose consequences are far from clear. New institutions have been cre-ated – the Scottish parliament, the Welsh assembly, the re-creation of the Northern Irish assembly on the basis of power sharing between Protestant and Catholic communities – and this has produced new configurations of power. What applies to the internal politics of Britain has its external correlative. Whatever its caution over the Euro, the Blair administration is more favourably disposed towards the European Union than its Conservative predecessor. The Eurosceptic wing of the Conservative Party has gained one kind of ascendancy but lost another. Until recently it dominated the Conservative party but no longer has any direct influence on the conduct of government. The political disagreements sparked by the linked questions of devolution and Europe mark an important historical moment. Perhaps Britain has reached the end of the end of Empire. This ending coincides with another: the unravelling of that United Kingdom which was the origin and the metropolitan basis for the British Empire.

A recent series of Channel 4 television programmes, written and presented by Darcus Howe, anticipate and circle around the possibility of Britain and England's disappearance as defining cultural realities. Howe adapted for television a well-established literary form as a basic structure: he made a journey through the kingdom.[3] In his travels he encountered England in its regional and social differences. He visited a sink estate, bristling with surveillance cameras, in the Northeast. He talked to affluent workers in Birmingham and discussed national identity in a Peterborough strip club where Afro-Caribbean men took off their clothes for white women. He met a prosperous group of Francophile English patricians. One question framed all of his encounters: what does it mean to be English? 'We're all American now' was one recurrent answer. What the English do, in this view, is what the American do: go shopping in malls, dance in lines, and watch basketball matches – even if they do it in an English way. Or, it marks a freedom from constraint: being American is being free from traditional English modesty and reserve. Another, more abashed, answer came from the Francophile patricians. They expressed some embarrassment about their attachment to another country, but their preference was clear: living in the Dordogne was better than living in England. The French countryside was quieter, more beautiful, less threatening. An unconscious historical irony was at work. Another idyll, the arcadia of the Home Counties, had been relocated in south-west France.

Howe's strange meetings identified at least some features of contemporary English national identity. One of these repeats what Paxman and other commentators have noted about the relation of England to Britain: the tendency of the English to live out their national identity by means of some surrogate. The difference is that it is no longer an imperial Britishness which acts as this vehicle, but the United States or France. Another feature of contemporary Englishness, and one that is not just true of the English, links identity to leisure. Leisure time, for those who have it, comes branded with connotations of national identity. And, if this is true, the imperative character of national identity changes. Loyalty is no longer to institutions, histories, or destinies. Instead it becomes a matter of consumer preference. Being 'American' or 'English' or 'Italian' becomes a matter of style preference.

Howe's journey through England included at least one more significant encounter: a visit to Scarborough to hear Norman Tebbitt address the local Conservative association. After the displacements of English national identity by way of the United States or France, Tebbitt offered an assertive English nationalism. Its dominant emotion was resentment: about devolution (giving the Scots a parliament denied to the English); about immigration (foreigners crowding the island, taking jobs, living off the welfare state); about Europe (a European super-state threatening our sovereignty and its main emblem, our currency). Tebbitt was in urbane and articulate mood when interviewed by Howe, but the underlying vision was clear: a sovereign England of leafy sub-urbs, concentration camps and prisons – the first the home of white comfort, the last two its necessary guardian against foreigners and criminals.

England, in Howe's imagination, was a country united by one thing, its loss of a common culture. The core of this common culture had been a working class with high levels of skilled and unskilled male employment. An emigrant to England in the 1950s, part of the Windrush generation, Howe had discovered in this working class a national way of life. Its disappearance had produced a hedonistic excess of leisure on the one hand and an infernal scarcity of work on the other.

The familiarity of Howe's diagnosis raises a question of method in thinking about national identity. The encounters in his journey were presented as evidence in support of a specific historical claim. Yet the claim itself has the status of rhetorical trope as much as an empirical induction. In 1957 Richard Hoggart had diagnosed a similar crisis in English working class identity in *The Uses of Literacy*. If we accept Hoggart's argument, the working class Howe encountered in the mid-1950s was itself already threatened by Hollywood culture, the 'candyfloss world' of television quiz shows and pulp fiction. In Hoggart's history the authentic English working class – and it is important for Hoggart that it is a national, a specifically *English* class – existed before the Second World War. As with Hoggart, so with Howe: integrity is always back-dated to a point within the living memory of the observer. And before Hoggart there were others: George Eliot, for example, in her 1846 review of Riehl's *Natural History of German Life*, where the loss of a peasantry, not a working class, seems to threaten the substance of English national identity. There is a pleasure in all this mourning: nations become fascinating just as they are felt to be disappearing, and England's disappearance has been around for a long time.[4]

Howe's programme, like Hoggart's book, has its own obligations and imperatives. Both perceive a crisis. Both set out to diagnose its causes and consequences. Neither is concerned to reflect on how nations are thought about or imagined. Clearly specific histories, case studies and texts are all important to any understanding of the questions brought together by the fact or possibility of the break-up of Britain or relocating Britishness. But the method of this essay is based upon the assumption that this activity needs to be complemented by another: identifying the assumptions that guide different ways of thinking about nations in general and Britishness in particular.

The analysis of nations and nation states in Nairn's work contrasts with Howe's angry and melancholic imagination. Like Howe, Nairn addresses the question of national decline that has dominated thinking about Britain since the end of the Second World War. But this prospect of decline does not produce a brooding meditation on a vanished working class. As far as Nairn is concerned the British working class does not provide the ground of an authentic national identity. It is simply an aspect of a wider problem, the persistence of a nation-state form, the United Kingdom, beyond its sell-by date. Its persistence in decline offers possibilities and political choices. Identities held in check or deformed by the British State and its national culture can shake themselves free. The central example of this new emergence in Nairn's work is Scotland, but this understanding is informed by comparison with the other 'peripheral' nations of the British Isles.

Nairn's account of the condition of Britain has developed over a number of years. The arguments presented in the 1974 edition of *The Break-Up of Britain* had been published earlier as contributions to debate in the *New Left Review* about the origins and prospects of the British state. Nairn's colleagues in this work included Perry Anderson, Anthony Barnett and Benedict Anderson.[5] While it would be false to suggest that they simply shared a common position, their diagnosis of Britain's malaise converged on a set of political questions. In their view the late twentieth-century United Kingdom was a busted flush, no longer capable of providing effective governance. The required political response was thoroughgoing constitutional reform. This would include devolution, but would extend beyond that to the creation of state forms whose sovereignty had their source in a citizenry, not in the doctrine of the crown in parliament. The British state's archaisms, notably the continuing attachment to the hereditary principle, must be removed in a process of modernization whose hallmark would be the gathering together of enlightened citizens to create a written constitution.

Nairn's analysis of the current crisis of the British state is based upon an historical argument about its origins. Its archaisms, and the configuration of its class relations, are due, paradoxically, to Britain's emergence as the first modern nation. The threshold events of this emergence include the English Civil War, the Glorious Revolution of 1688, and the 1707 Act of Union with Scotland. Its central historical processes include an agrarian and then an industrial revolution, both unprecedented in their scale and intensity, and the creation of an overseas empire whose development was overseen by British naval dominance.

Its key political elements included the transfer of a royal prerogative to a parliamentary institution and to its governing party (the doctrine of the crown-in-parliament), the absence of a written constitution, and the persistence of feudalism in the parliamentary system, notably in the idea that birth-right should bestow access to the state's legislative body. In economic, political and cultural terms the result was one of the most successful modern nations. One sign of this success in the eighteenth and early nineteenth centuries was Britain's reputation in Europe: it was the country to visit not for its heritage but because the future was being created there.[6] Britain's expansionism was evident from an early stage, but unlike France and, later, Germany, this was not directed towards mainland Europe. The political consolidation of Empire was based on a maritime global network established by trade and exploration. Britain's emergence as a state claiming to represent its constituent nations in a single United Kingdom was coterminous with and, at times, hardly distinguishable from its emergence as an imperial power. The very uneven loyalty of the constituent nations to this state form increasingly depended upon its success as an imperial as well as a national state.

The very scale of this success made the experience of decline more difficult. According to Nairn the history of twentieth-century Britain has been dominated by stratagems for evading this difficulty. The faltering competitive strength of Britain's industries, evident from the late nineteenth century, has been mitigated by the City of London's success as a centre for finance capital. The result was that the problems of the British industrial economy could always be postponed even when they were ostensibly being addressed. The waning of Britain's international influence was muffled by the persistence of its empire into the middle of the twentieth century; the emergence of the Commonwealth out of the old empire; and the tenacious myth of Britain's 'special relationship' with the United States. Britain could still be on the winning side in major wars, while shuffling aside the extent of its dependence on the United States or the Soviet Union for military success. The projects of modernization or renewal embarked on by successive administrations over the latter half of the twentieth century are, for Nairn, similarly implicated in a collective act of self-deception. The post-war history of British government has been that of a corner always about to be turned, of problems identified but only partially or precariously solved. The Suez crisis in 1956, the rise in oil prices in the 1970s and the continuing erosion of Britain's manufacturing base all testified to a persistent political and economic vulnerability which no amount of bravura or spin could conceal. What was repeatedly being postponed, in Nairn's view, was the necessary transformation of the British constitution, the underlying cause of Britain's failure to adapt to its post-imperial condition. Captured by the 'enchanted glass' of monarchy and tradition England's, if not Britain's, dreaming could continue unabated. Sentimental attachment to beliefs about a national working class and its disintegration are part of the same dream world.

Confronted with this decline in the practical and symbolic efficiency of the British state, the 'peripheral' nations have found the arrangement of the United Kingdom less and less to their liking. The result has been a resurgence of nationalist movements in Scotland, Ireland and Wales. Different histories and demands have marked the character of each of these nationalisms. In Scotland the primary demand was for the recovery of a nation state autonomy subordinated at the time of the 1707 Act of Union. In Wales the language question became a focus for nationalist aspirations, leading to the creation of a Welsh language television channel and the restoration of Welsh as part of the school curriculum. Northern Ireland has been marked by a violent struggle between forces demanding the completion of Ireland's independence from Britain on the one side, and the fierce counter-assertion of the rights of a Protestant population to remain British on the other. This struggle acted as a reminder of old links between religion and nation and their continuing force in the constitutional arrangements of the United Kingdom.

The refusal of peripheral status by Scotland, Ireland and Wales is for Nairn a key episode in the post-war history of the British State. At once a major symptom of political crisis and a means to its resolution, these new or renewed nationalisms have already had a significant impact on British political and cultural life. The British government has renounced any 'special interest' in Northern Ireland. A power-sharing assembly of a kind that had earlier been destroyed by Protestant working-class militancy now sits precariously in Stormont. In Scotland a new parliament has asserted itself by pursuing different policies to the Westminster-based government on education funding. The Welsh assembly has refused to be led by a candidate imposed by the Labour Party machine. Obviously it is too early to say what the future will be for these different states of devolution. One key question for the relocation of Britishness is whether they will remain within the current British nation-state form or effectively mark its demise.

Nairn's analysis finds significant echoes and variations in the work of other theorists and historians. In Linda Colley's *Britons*, the 1707 Act of Union between England and Scotland is identified as a key moment in the making of modern British identity.[7] Colley analyses the interplay of economic, political and cultural conditions that sustained this constitutional settlement. An energetic civil society in both England and Scotland discovered more benefits than hindrances in this state form. It created opportunities for Scottish as well as English commercial and political ambitions and was cemented by dynastic marriages amongst the aristocracies of both countries. Nor were these arrangements exclusive to the union between England and Scotland. Britain offered opportunities and advantages to Wales and Ireland as well, although these were unevenly distributed and often confined to social elites. But, in the conclusion to her argument, Colley recognizes that the internal and external conditions that gave dynamism and unity to modern Britain have largely passed away. As with Nairn, a sense of an ending hangs heavily:

> [W]e can understand the nature of the present crisis only if we recognise that the factors that provided for the forging of a British nation in the past have largely ceased to operate. Protestantism, that once vital cement, has now a limited influence on British culture, as indeed has Christianity itself. Recurrent wars with the states of Continental Europe have in all likelihood come to an end, so different kinds of Briton no longer feel the same compulsion as before to remain united in the face of an enemy from without. And, crucially, both commercial supremacy and imperial hegemony have gone. No more can Britons reassure themselves of their distinct and privileged identity by contrasting themselves with impoverished Europeans (real or imaginary), or by exercising authority over manifestly alien peoples. God has ceased to be British, and Providence no longer smiles.[8]

Benedict Anderson's study of nations and nationalism, *Imagined Communities*, has no direct concern with the break-up or re-invention of Britain. But his analysis of the nineteenth-century emergence of 'official nationalisms' has important implications for thinking about the end of Britain or its continuation. Anderson's account of official British nationalism is part of a wider comparison that finds parallel developments in several nineteenth- and twentieth-century imperial states, including Russia and Japan. What makes these nationalisms 'official' is the increasing involvement of the state in promulgating a form of national culture. Anderson summarizes the intent of official nationalisms thus: it was a way of 'stretching the short tight skin of the nation over the gigantic body of the empire'.[9] The metaphor implies the ultimate impossibility of the task, which was nonetheless undertaken purposefully. In the British case, it involved making a version of English the official language of the empire. This in turn required an education policy. Thomas Babington Macaulay's 1835 'Minute on Education' is exemplary in its tone and assumptions. Referring to India, Macaulay set out an ambition to create 'a class of persons, Indian in blood and colour, but English in taste, opinion, in morals and in intellect', and invoked the authority of orientalists to support the view that 'a single shelf of a good European library was worth the whole native literature of India and Arabia'.[10] Variations on this theme of an imperial *Bildung* continued through the nineteenth century and into the twentieth. Its products included the dissemination of versions of the English public school through the British Empire, and the creation of a volatile combination of cultural inferiority and ambition that characterized the attitude of the subject nations to the metropolitan centre. It created a feedback loop which readily sustained the view that the British way of life, whether in its daily culture or in its literary achievements, was superior because so widely admired, desired and imitated. More than a national way of life, it became a model for humanity in general.

But this assertion of the superiority of the 'British way' was fraught with risk and contradiction. According to Anderson, the adoption of the official culture in the subject countries of the Empire carried with it a promise of power. If it was to work, it had to create a sense of opportunity. But these opportunities in many cases proved either limited or illusory. No Indian became Prime Minister of Britain, nor did an Australian, Canadian or New Zealander. There was no repetition of the success of Scottish or Welsh born politicians in the metropolitan nation. Access to intellectual and cultural elites in Britain was possible in theory, but in practice severely restricted. An Anglicized culture might be found throughout the Empire, but in variants that often confined those who adopted it to their native, colonized nation. The disillusionment this produced helped fuel anti-colonial movements. Official nationalism helped unpick the very thing it was intended to maintain.[11]

To say that, in Britain, official nationalism has crumbled under the force of its own contradictions is too neatly dialectical. But the conditions that sustained it have largely disappeared. Obviously there is no longer an Empire to be shaped by official nationalism. These external changes are matched by changes within the metropolitan nation. Imperial culture was not just something that happened abroad. It shaped the metropolitan culture as well: whether in the elusive sense of a participation in 'greatness'; or in the more palpable institutions of a national literature and history; or in the existence of cultural and political elites whose horizon of expectation was shaped by an imperial Britain. Other forces have come into play: the attractions of another imperial American culture as a source of pleasure, allegiance and identity; the resurgence of popular nationalisms with values and idioms very different from the official version; the creation of a new Europe; the ending of the national monopoly in television and radio; and, of course, the emergence of cyberspace and the internet. Popular as well as elite experience now routinely goes beyond the national horizon, redefining the nature of the nation from within.

Taken together, the work of Nairn, Colley and Anderson suggests three arcs of development: a state form, the crown in parliament, created in the late seventeenth century; a civil society created in the eighteenth; and an official culture created in the nineteenth. All have come to an end within fifty years of each other. Even if we retain the name Britain, or the United Kingdom, to refer to the union of England, Scotland, Wales and Northern Ireland, the cultural, economic and political substance of that union has irrevocably changed. For Nairn the bit of old Britain called England has the greatest difficulty acknowledging this change. From the legislative centre of the old state, devolution is seen as a way of preserving Britain, another episode in a long history of conservation by way of reform, the hallmark of the nation's political wisdom. But the new constitutions taking shape in Scotland, Ireland and Wales have as yet no English equivalent. This English inertia is the major problem confronting the new constitutionalism. According to Nairn the break-up of Britain, anticipated in the 1970s, has become a political reality, but the old state form lingers on, not least through its frantic attachment to projects of modernization.

Linda Colley finds arguments about British exceptionalism less convincing. She argues that Britain's historical experience matches that of other European imperial states including France, Germany, Portugal and the Netherlands. She is also more sanguine than Nairn about England's capacity to learn from neighbouring nations about the value of political reform. These important differences of emphasis do not prevent them from agreeing that making and reforming constitutions is fundamental to modern national identity. For both of them, modern nationhood for Britain is involved in an active participation in the supra-national institutions of Europe. In 'Old Britain' what lay beyond the nation was the Empire, confirmation of the nation's power and exceptional status. Europe was the locus of rivalry and alliance, but also an imagined place of lesser nations. In 'New Britain' what lies beyond the nation is Europe, a complex and expanding partnership of nation states that also calls into question established nation state forms. And this Europe, or parts of it, has developed the uncomfortable habit of doing important things, like developing transport systems and health care, better than Old Britain. The 'lesser' European nations have impertinently become 'greater' or appear that way. The comfort blanket of Empire has been withdrawn and with it Britain's place in a particular imaginary geography.

Nairn's constitutional arguments depend upon narrative. The 'Break-Up of Britain' is a story that might be included in a genre of end-of-Empire stories which have pervaded English culture in the second half of the twentieth century.[12] The same underlying narrative informs Nairn's most recent book, *After Britain*. Its context and intellectual dramaturgy draw on the eighteenth-century Enlightenment. The old British nation state is the source of superstition and decay, its inhabitants deluded by the 'enchanted glass' of monarchy, its statecraft dedicated to the preservation of secret and arbitrary powers. The new devolution is an assertion of enlightenment values: a renewal of rationality in politics, the creation of a state whose bedrock is not monarchy but free citizens working in political institutions that enable them to deliberate freely on their collective future. In *After Britain* this basic context is modified but not transformed. Nairn presents himself as agent and witness of historical change as much as enlightened and exasperated satirist of a decaying state. But the basic conflict between enlightenment values and archaic superstition persists.

To recall the importance of narrative in Nairn's analysis of the British nation state may underline the obvious. The very idea of national identity seems to depend upon the stories a nation tells about itself to itself and others. If we think of national identity as the organization of differences of class, gender, region and language into a supervening unity, then stories about a shared past provide cognitive and affective maps that maintain a sense of collective identity. These stories have different generic forms and different forms of permanence and authority. Histories and novels, cinema, television and newspapers, banknotes and postage stamps, sport and ceremony can all become vehicles of national narrative, working on a major or a minor scale, through the grandest gestures or the smallest hints.

There are at least two ways in which to understand this relation between nation and narrative. One is that a nation pre-exists its narratives and is mediated more or less adequately by them. Arguments about what is more or less adequate will move back and forth between notions of obligation to national ideals and claims for realism, telling things as they really are. The other is that narratives constitute nations. Stories bring them into being and sustain them.

The argument that nations are constituted by acts of narration is central to the work of the post-colonial theorist, Homi Bhabha. According to Bhabha a major subject and audience for national narratives is the 'people', imagined as the bearers of national identity. Allegiance to a legally binding constitution is not the decisive condition of national identity. To be British is, according to this view, to be one of the British people and hence to be involved in the national story: at one moment identified as the subject of the story, at another as its audience, at other times as both. The 'people' are a narrative invention as much as a sociological entity, patch-worked together out of diverse individual and collective experiences.

But the popular identity created by narrative is itself divided. In his analysis of the forms of national narrative Bhabha identifies two modes, the 'pedagogical' and the 'performative'.[13] Both have the people as their subjects and audiences, but presented and addressed in radically different ways. The 'pedagogical' narrative is historical in a familiar sense. Its stories derive their authority from their capacity to explain the present in terms of the past: to provide, for example, an account of national characteristics which have evolved over time, or to point to a future which can be imagined as a fulfilment of potential contained in the past. Examples might include the Condition of England novels of the 1840s, Grote's History of Britain, E. P. Thompson's essay 'The Peculiarities of the English', or, in an elegiac mood, Michael Wood's recent book, *In Search of England*.[14] The pedagogic narrative binds the nation together and sets its boundaries. It stipulates the conditions of a particular national identity, its modes of inheritance or physical appearance, its beliefs and primary allegiances.

The 'performative' narrative displaces or, in Bhabha's word, 'erases' the 'pedagogic'. It gives shape to a present that is not authorized or predicted by an understanding of the past. The 'people' are no longer the bearers of a national tradition as they are or have to become in the pedagogic narrative. They are a source of vitality that erupts in the present. Bhabha cites Franz Fanon's account of 'the fluctuating movement that the people are just giving shape to'. The 'performative' narrative disrupts boundaries and questions inherited accounts of national character.

How might these distinctions test the presuppositions that shape an understanding of Britishness? Bhabha proposes something other than a familiar way of thinking about the nation in terms of an ongoing dialectic of unity and division. The framing of the terms of division and unity – class, gender, ethnicity, region- and their resolution is the work of 'pedagogic' narrative. The 'performative' narrative disrupts these categories and operations. In Bhabha's metaphor it is imagined as 'casting a shadow' across the clear demarcations established by the 'pedagogic', obscuring and estranging distinctions between 'us' and 'them', 'black' and 'white', the 'English' and whatever enemy opposes and defines them. Bhabha invokes another way of imagining the national space in his account of the 'performative', not as something to be fortified and defended against invasion, but as a state of transition encompassing the spaces between self and other, 'here' and 'there', 'us' and 'them'. For Bhabha national identities are constituted by difference, whose logic cannot be grasped by concepts of contradiction or opposition. National identity emerges in the fluctuating space between 'us' and 'them', 'native' and 'immigrant'. It is necessarily 'impure', although this necessity can produce its violent counterpoint in the desire to produce the ethnically pure nation.

Bhabha's theory has specific historical sources and references, relocating Britishness in the experience of diaspora, the great movements of people from the Caribbean, Africa and Asia that have shaped the history of colonial and post-colonial Britain. One of his key quotations comes from the stuttering S.S. Sisodia in Salman Rushdie's *Satanic Verses*: 'The trouble with the Engenglish is that their hiss hiss history happened overseas, so they don't know what it means.'[15] The emerging narratives of British or English identity reverse a standard trope of the colonial imagination. Instead of stories about the British going out to encounter the exoticism, seduction or recalcitrance of the colonies, Bhabha's work reminds us of other narratives about the journey from the colonial home to an exotic and recalcitrant Britain. It is these 'foreign' stories that are now significant for imagining Britishness. Britain becomes part of a global narrative about diaspora.[16] The meaning of that narrative is not principally about imperial greatness and decline but about the migration of people from Africa and Asia provoked by different empires. This is how the history of the 'Engenglish' happened overseas. It happened in the work of slaves on the sugar plantations or in the Indian mutiny. Its stories take as their primary material the experiences of the colonized not the colonizers. The typical orderings of foreground and background are reversed. Figures from the shadowy backgrounds and margins of stories by Conrad, Forster or Paul Scott now take centre stage. Franz Fanon's terse comment – 'Europe is literally the creation of the Third World' – provides a forceful summary of this transformation of perspective.

One context for these stories and the historical experience they summon is a heightened awareness of ethnicity. In Britain, as in other post-colonial European nations, a new white ethnicity, fuelled by resentment, has emerged. Its most obvious manifestations include Enoch Powell's 1968 Rivers of Blood speech; the by-election in Smethwick the same year which included the slogan 'If you want a nigger for a neighbour vote Labour'; the sabotaging of the Stormont agreement by Protestant Trade Unions in 1974; the obsession with English soccer hooligans and the ethos of newspapers such as the *Daily Mail* and the *Sun*. In her reflection on modern nationalism Julia Kristeva describes the psychological structure of this form of ethnic assertion as a 'hate reaction':

> *Hatred of others* who do not share my origins and who affront me personally, eco-
> nomically and culturally: I then move back among 'my own'. . . . in spite of the
> petty conflicts those family members so often, alas, had in store for me . . . *Hatred*
> *of oneself,* for when exposed to violence, individuals despair of their own qualities,
> undervalue their achievements and yearnings . . . and so they withdraw into a
> sullen, warm private world, unnameable and biological, the impregnable 'aloof-
> ness' of a weird primal paradise-family, ethnicity, nation, race.[17]

Kristeva's quartet of terms – family, ethnicity, nation, race – are the basis for
a tightly-drawn set of conditions: no nation without a common ethnicity, no
ethnicity which is not modelled on the blood-link of the family, no true nation
without racial homogeneity. The nation becomes a tribe, driven to turn in
upon itself in the face of external threat. The constructive and expansive idea
of the nation as a process that brings people of different ethnic and linguistic
backgrounds into a new solidarity is abandoned, perceived as yet another
failure of politics and politicians. The persistence of white ethnic nationalism
in Britain and elsewhere is a source of continuing embarrassment to those who
like to think of fascism as a thing of the past.

But the idea of the ethnic nation has more than one manifestation and
inflection. Britain has always been a multi-ethnic or 'multi-cultural' nation
state. The same holds true for many other modern nation states. They have
been created from the imposition of a national order on pre-existing ethnic
identities. What is less obvious is the reconsideration of the very notion of ethnicity itself. In 'New Ethnicities' Stuart Hall describes a complex change in
black cultural politics in Britain. The struggle to represent black experience, to
overcome its banishment to the margins of cultural life or its containment in
oppressive and negative stereotypes, is now joined by a new questioning of the
notion of black experience itself, resulting in the emergence of a contemporary
politics of identity emphasizing the numerous factors – class, gender, sexuality
– that situate people in cultures. The shared ethnicity that might seem the most
primordial and natural fact about people, something given at and by birth, is
now understood as 'without guarantees in Nature'. Hall's argument seeks to
give a new political connotation to the idea of the ethnic. In contrast to the
white backlash politics of 'family, ethnicity, nation, race' centred on the ideal of
a cleansed, ethnic nation state Hall proposes 'the beginning of a positive conception of the ethnicity of the margins, of the periphery':

> . . . a recognition that we all speak from a particular place, out of a particular his-
> tory, out of a particular experience, a particular culture . . . We are all in that sense
> *ethnically* located, and our ethnic identities are crucial to our subjective sense of

who we are. But this is also a recognition that this is not an ethnicity which is doomed to survive, as Englishness was, only by marginalising, dispossessing, displacing and forgetting other ethnicities.[18]

Hall identifies 'Englishness' as the paradigm case of an ethnic identity dependent upon imperial violence. The idea of new ethnicities in Hall's argument occupies an equivalent position to Bhabha's performative narratives. The equivalent to the pedagogic narrative is Thatcherism, described by Hall as the 'embattled, hegemonic conception of "Englishness"'. The relevance to the question of relocating Britishness is clear. The Britain of the new ethnicities is a nation without nationalism. What is proposed is another kind of devolution: not necessarily that which gives independence to Scotland, Ireland and Wales, but a devolution away from binding intellectual and imaginative attachments to an idea of Britain as the essential imperial state. If the loss of empire is one way of maintaining an attachment to it, it is this loss that must now be given up. For Bhabha, at least, this is something much more than an acknowledgement of a new cultural diversity within the existing geographical and cultural boundaries of Britain. It means imagining the nation not in terms of a unity that embraces diversity but as a place of cultural difference. To imagine the nation as a unity in diversity assumes a perspective that overlooks and measures from on high the different cultures that compose a national unity. Cultural difference lives in the midst of different cultures, their abrasions, antagonisms, and hybrid growth. It acknowledges that the world can look very different from the perspective of another diasporic culture, and makes the migrant into the vital part of the nation, precisely because this is the part that does not fit.

Nations manifest themselves in signs: flags, food, clothes, ways of talking, distinctive styles in literature, theatre, film and television. The list can seem endless. One way in which the sign character of nations becomes evident is in the customary and enduring belief that they have characteristics that mark out their individual members. Once these are recognized the differences between nations become clear, as do their distinctive identities. National characteristics usually take the form of a list of qualities. The historian Paul Langford has identified some 'major supposed traits of Englishness'.[19] They include Energy, Candour, Decency, Taciturnity, Reserve, Eccentricity. William Hazlitt, writing in the early nineteenth century, came up with a different picture, not so much to do with the listing of traits as with the manifestation of a dominant characteristic: '. . . they [the English] would all rather use force to gain their point . . . and regard good-will and complaisance as perfectly insipid and out of character . . . A true

Englishman, on coming into a coffee-room, looks round to see if the company are good enough for him, to know if his place is not taken, or if he cannot turn others out of theirs'.[20]

What is at issue here is not whether Langford's list is more accurate than Hazlitt's description – one, we might think, is the necessary obverse of the other – but how these attributes come to be representative in the first place. The answer to that question depends upon complex and sometimes unconscious assumptions about what a nation is. For ethnic nationalists national characteristics are an expression of the distinctive traditions that have evolved in the history of a nation. They are the qualities that make a nation like a family, the expressions of a common bond and affinity. From a more sceptical perspective, national characteristics are a kind of fiction, not something deep-rooted in the natures of English, French or Chinese people. But if they are a fiction their power to command allegiance and shape identity needs to be understood. If we understand national characteristics as manifestations of national identity, then we also need to understand how these signs work on and through us.

Slavoj Zizek provides an analysis of these issues. He has not written any sustained commentary on Britain, but his work turns repeatedly to questions of nationalism and national identity. On the one hand Zizek understands nations in terms of a broad historical overview. They are born out of intertwined economic and political imperatives. According to Zizek, the coercion of local communities into a larger national unity goes hand in hand with capitalism's need to develop new modes of production and consumption. Nations are Janus-faced, *seeking* to affirm their often fragile unity by appeals to tradition while committing themselves to forms of economic development that repeatedly undermine what tradition seeks to affirm. One way of managing this tension is to identify economic activity with national pride. Hence the calls to 'Buy British' or to re-brand Britain as 'UK PLC'. But these marketing ploys betray the very anxiety they seek to conceal. We are exhorted to 'Buy British' exactly because we can buy French, Italian, American, Japanese and so on. The interests of the consumer and the patriot are by no means identical. Economic globalization makes the connection between national and economic life ever more tenuous.[21]

Zizek's historical overview looks at nations and nation states from the outside and sees them as transitory rather than eternal forms. He is enough of a Leninist to agree with Lenin that 'national states' meet the 'requirements of modern capitalism' and enough of a Marxist to agree with Marx that the 'bourgeoisie has through its exploitation of the world market given a cosmopolitan character to production and consumption in every country'.[22] But this account of a nation state determined by economic forces is paralleled by another line of thought in Zizek's work: his analysis of different forms of collective identity. This is sustained by two related propositions. One is that identity is vested in signs and does not have an existence outside them; the other is that collective identities, such as nations, appear to be greater than the individuals who compose them. Moreover, this greatness takes on a law-like and demanding character. It has the capacity to call for sacrifice, or require reform, or oblige us to live in particular ways if we are to be properly a part of it. If that is the case, how might something made up of signs take on these peculiar powers?

Zizek's answer is complex. He asks us to set aside the assumption that all signs simply represent pre-existing realities. The example of national characteristics would be a case in point. Zizek discerns three steps in the process of attributing characteristics of this kind. In the first stage a series of attributes are *encapsulated* in an idea of English character (whether Energy, Candour, or force, suspicion, hostility to goodwill). In the second the series is used to *interpret* the meaning of the English character (to have an English character means to have possession of Energy, Candour, and so on). In the third stage another kind of summation occurs: the English have this series of attributes *because* they are English. What starts as a name ends as a cause. As a result a virtual or fictional entity is created, an enigmatic ground or foundation of a set of attributes that become its expression. And these changes correspond to different moments in the relation between a sign and what it stands for. Initially, the sign simply points to the series it summarizes. But once we take 'Englishness' to be the cause of English national characteristics what we have, according to Zizek, is a '*signifier* that performatively establishes the series in its totality'.[23]

Zizek's analysis here draws on two philosophical contexts. One from Hegel, the German Idealist philosopher, concerns the logic of names and has to do with Hegel's distinction between the use of a name to introduce a definition or set of attributes: 'An English person is likely to display characteristics of Energy, Candour, Eccentricity . . .'; and the use of a name to bestow an identity: 'This is an English person', or 'I'm English'. The other comes from J. L. Austin, the philosopher of language, and his distinction between two kinds of linguistic behaviour: the 'constative' when we use language to make statements about the world that can be judged true or false – 'the car was travelling down the road at thirty miles an hour' – and the performative, when utterances in an appropriate context are themselves actions of a special kind: 'I pronounce this couple man and wife', or 'I name this ship the Queen Elizabeth'.[24]

This analysis reminds us of something obvious: 'England' and 'Britain' are signs that are also names of something. If asked to explain what these names refer to, the answer might have to do with identifying a group of islands of the coast of mainland Europe that have a shared history, a sovereign government and (broadly) a shared set of laws. This answer could be extended in all sorts of ways, specifying what those laws are, how they have become laws, elaborating the narrative of the shared history and so on. But for Zizek that would constitute only half an answer. However painstaking and detailed an historical account of the evolution of Britain or England might be, it does not exhaustively explain the imaginative and identifying power vested in the nation's names.

Zizek's fascination with the imaginative power of names is connected to their power to sustain illusions that take on the force of practical necessities in our lives. Our social experience, and, by implication, our experience of national identity, rests on such a constitutive illusion:

> An individual experiences his society not as a mere collection of individuals but as an order which transcends these individuals and forms the substance of their lives – and it is this very substantial In-itself which is purely virtual, a symbolic fiction, since it exists merely as the *presupposition,* by each of the individuals, of the already-existing co-ordination of all other individuals.[25]

Zizek is not writing explicitly about nations, but his analysis can be readily applied to them. His account of how we experience collective identity revises the argument that nations are forged out of a consensus of the kind defined by Renan in the nineteenth century as 'the clearly expressed desire to live a common life . . . a daily plebiscite'. Zizek's virtual order is not based upon a contract, or an agreement about shared interests, or a form of government. It is an assumption that we make in order to make sense of the social world and our place in it. This 'symbolic fiction' is endowed with a powerful agency. It becomes the condition of having an identity. To be 'outside' it is to be in a state fraught with fear and anxiety.

Born out of a shared presupposition, this order – an order notably exemplified by the nation – cannot be directly experienced as such. It is not an empirical fact or event, but something made manifest in signs. One property of these signs is their constitutive and causal power. Another is their capacity both to be part of an order and lay claim to represent it in its entirety. Until recently, at least, the monarchy has played this role in Britain for over a century. In a more diffuse and transient way many other signs can take on this role of representing the nation whether in nostalgic images of cricket pitches, country houses, and the sound of church bells or in the more vitriolic signs of mad cow disease and a crumbling railway system. In each case a sign is read as a symptom of the condition of an underlying order, 'the state of the nation'. But, in the case of the nation understood as a symbolic order, the signs are more than symptoms; they make up the order itself.

Zizek's analysis invites us to think of a nation as a paradoxical entity. The nation is a substantial fiction, something that is felt to be more than any of its representations. But that 'something more' is like a *trompe l'oeil* effect, creating an illusion of depth where none really exists. And the illusion is sustained, according to Zizek, by a distinctive kind of belief. It is inter-subjective in a way that carries a quite precise meaning. Phenomena like the nation are sustained not simply by the assumption that one person's belief is shared by many, but by the existence of what Zizek describes as a 'subject supposed to believe'. This subject can be summoned by a typical sentence, as in coverage by the *Daily Mail* of the Queen Mother's death: 'The nation comes to a standstill to remember'. The 'nation' here is something more than a convenient shorthand for 'lots of people'. It identifies a subject who believes, or mourns, or 'comes to a standstill' on our behalf, such that the possibility of my belief depends upon an assumption of the existence of people who believe the same thing.

What bearing might Zizek's analysis of collective identity and belief have on the relocation of 'Britishness'? One implication of his analysis is that nations are like ciphers. The belief that they have a core identity that endures through change is a powerful collective illusion, but an illusion nonetheless. Nations survive because they can be so thoroughly transformed. According to Zizek, these transformations are not simply random. They depend upon what was once regarded or reviled as subordinate becoming a central and governing principle. In the case of Britain the very diversity and plurality that from one perspective threatens the core of British identity could itself become what defines that identity. This may already be taking place.[26]

These questions of identity are not independent of political power. The decline in the political autonomy of the British State remains one of the most important facts about its history in the twentieth century. Whereas it was once the symbolic and political centre of an international order, it now depends upon its incorporation in orders that are defined elsewhere. These go by various names: 'Europe', 'The United States', 'Globalization'. 'We are all Americans now' can be understood as the slogan of a contented colonialism. Meanwhile the actions of the British political elite seem guided by an assumption that caution about union with Europe is a means of asserting a special kind of difference or autonomy in relation to the threat of an over-mighty power.

Britain will best direct the future of Europe by maintaining a distance from it. It would be entirely in character for a Zizekian analysis to discern in this a kind of political masquerade: asserting autonomy in relation to one order as a diversion from an ever increasing servitude to another, that of the United States. By this stratagem at least the British political state retains its pretensions to being a 'significant player on the world stage'. The old imperial pretensions die hard.

Notes

1 The following works by Nairn, Bhabha, and Zizek will be referred to: Tom Nairn, *The Break-Up of Britain* (London, 1977); idem, *After Britain* (London, 2000); Homi Bhabha, *The Location of Culture* (London 1994); Slavoj Zizek, *The Metastases of Enjoyment* (London, 1994); idem, *The Indivisible Remainder* (London, 1996); idem, *The Plague of Fantasies* (London,1997); idem, *The Ticklish Subject* (London, 1999).

2 Jeremy Paxman, *The English* (Harmondsworth, 1999); Julian Barnes, *England, England* (Basingstoke and Oxford, 1998); Michael Wood, *In Search of England* (Harmondsworth, 2000).

3 Darcus Howe, *White Tribes*, Channel 4, February 2000.

4 Richard Hoggart, *The Uses of Literacy* (Harmondsworth, 1958); George Eliot, 'The natural history of German life', in T. Pinney (ed.), *The Essays of George Eliot* (London, 1963). See also Patrick Wright, *On Living in an Old Country* (London, 1985).

5 Amongst the important texts are Perry Anderson, 'Origins of the present crisis', *New Left Review* 23 (1964), pp. 26–53; idem, 'Components of a national culture', *New Left Review* 50 (1968), pp. 3–57; Tom Nairn, 'The British political elite, *New Left Review* 23 (1964), pp. 19–25; idem, 'The English working class', *New Left Review* 24 (1964), pp. 43–57.

6 Ian Buruma, *Voltaire's Coconuts: Or Anglomania in Europe* (London, 1999).

7 Linda Colley, *Britons, The Forging of a Nation* (London, 1996).

8 Colley, *Britons*, p. 395.

9 Benedict Anderson, *Imagined Communities* (2nd edn., London, 1991), p. 86. Anderson acknowledges his indebtedness to Hugh Seton Watson for the phrase 'official nationalisms': H. Seton Watson, *Nations and States* (Boulder, 1977), p. 148.

10 For an edited version of Macaulay's minute, see W. T. de Berry (ed.), *Sources of Indian Tradition* (New York, 1958), vol. 2, pp. 44–9. Macaulay's condescension needs to be put in context. The Bengali reformer Rammuhan Roy argued a similar case a few years before Macaulay.

11 David Cannadine's *Ornamentalism* (London, 2001) provides a different account of British imperial culture from Anderson's, stressing the importance of equivalences of status and hierarchy across ethnic and cultural differences.

12 See, for example, Paul Scott, *The Jewel in the Crown* (London, 1966).

13 Homi Bhabha, *The Location of Culture* (London, 1994): the distinction between 'performative' and 'pedagogic' is elaborated in chapter 8.

14 See, for example, T. B. Macaulay, *History of England* (10 vols., London, 1849–61); E. P. Thompson, 'The peculiarities of the English', in *The Poverty of Theory* (London, 1978), pp. 35–92; for Michael Wood see footnote 2.

15 Salman Rushdie, *The Satanic Verses* (London, 1988), p. 343.

16 For some examples of diaspora narratives especially relevant to Britain see Samuel Selvon, *The Lonely Londoners* (London, 1979: first published 1956) and *Ways of Sunlight* (London, 1973: first published 1957).

17 Julia Kristeva, *Nations Without Nationalism*, trans. L. S. Roudiez (New York, 1993), pp. 2–3.

18 Stuart Hall, 'New ethnicities', in J. Donaldson and A. Rattansi, *Race, Culture and Difference* (London, 1992), p. 258.

19 Paul Langford, *Englishness Identified* (Oxford, 2000).

20 William Hazlitt, 'English characteristics', in Jon Cook (ed.), *William Hazlitt: Selected Writings* (Oxford, 1991), p. 157.

21 Zizek, *Ticklish Subject*, pp. 213–15.

22 For Lenin's argument, see 'The right of nations to self-determination' (1914) in *V. I. Lenin: Selected Works* (Lawrence and Wishart, London, n.d.), vol. 4, p. 251; for Marx, 'The Manifesto of the Communist Party (1848)', in *Marx/Engels: Selected Works* (London, 1968), p. 38.

23 For a comparable analysis of the logic of Jewish identity, see Zizek, *Metastases* (London, 1994), pp. 47–50.

24 J. L. Austin, *How to Do Things with Words* (2nd edn., Oxford, 1976).

25 Zizek, *Indivisible Remainder*, pp. 139–40.

26 Ibid., pp. 128–9.

2

A shell for neo-liberalism: New Labour Britain and the Millennium Dome

Jim McGuigan

Rebranding Britain

In its 1999 survey of worldwide attitudes to Britain and Northern Ireland, the British Council noted, 'On balance people were more inclined to think of the UK as a traditional than as a modern society.'[1] The command centre for what used to be the largest and most powerful empire in the world was still perceived abroad as 'an old country'[2] in spite of Tony Blair's declared aim, a few years earlier, of projecting New Labour Britain as 'a young country'.[3] Shortly after coming into office in 1997, Blair had sought to associate his 'modernizing' government with cool and youthful culture by inviting Brit Pop celebrities from design, fashion, film, music and television around for drinks at Downing Street. No longer 'Rule Britannia' but, instead, it was supposed to be 'Cool Britannia'.

At the time of the Funeral (of Diana, Princess of Wales) in September 1997, a key moment for New Labour's political theatrics,[4] the young policy advisor Mark Leonard's pamphlet *BritainTM* was published by the think-tank Demos and endorsed by the Design Council. It offered a diagnosis of Britain's enduring image problem, recommending a solution that involved taking stock at the turn of the millennium. *BritainTM* applied the principles of corporate promotion and public relations to the task of rebranding what Raymond Williams had named prophetically, in the early 1980s, 'Yookay PLC'.[5] Leonard insisted that rebranding Britain would not require falsehood and distortion. The task was to distil the modern strengths of Britishness and, in place of reiterating traditional myths, publicize them globally with greater boldness than hitherto. These strengths were summed up by the following set of slogans: 'Hub UK – Britain as the world's crossroads', 'Creative island', 'United colours of Britain', 'Open for business', 'Britain as silent revolutionary' and 'The Nation of fair play'.[6]

Leonard argued that the turn of the millennium afforded the opportunity for repositioning British identity and, therefore, British business in the world at large. This might be achieved, at least partly, by 'building a model "living museum of the future"'. It would become 'a real global village or "Millennium City" in Greenwich, to act as a showcase of the future of health, learning, retailing and democracy, and to situate the UK as a laboratory of future ways of living'.[7] Leonard's suggestion was not original. He was jumping on a bandwagon already rolling into the deeply toxic dust of Greenwich Marsh, the site of industrial dereliction and a former coal-fired gasworks on a southern peninsula of the Thames in East London, where the Prime Meridian cuts across the tip of the peninsula like a circumcision.

Plans for a Millennium Festival and its centrepiece of an exposition on the Greenwich peninsula, funded by the National Lottery through the Millennium Commission, had been set in train under the last Conservative government. The incoming Labour government could have cancelled the exposition in Summer 1997 at little financial cost (less than £200 million of tax revenue for buying and reclaiming the site) in comparison with its eventual and controversial drain on Lottery money (escalating to £628 million during 2000).[8] There had already been much sceptical comment on the potential wastefulness of the project, not only in the news media but also amongst front-bench Labour politicians and on the Left generally. Blair himself, however, was persuaded of its value by leading Conservative advocates. Six weeks after the May 1997 landslide election, Labour decided to adopt the previous government's scheme on the grounds that it would articulate a moment of national renewal, in effect, symbolizing New Labour Britain. In June, a budget was agreed which seemed to make sense at the time but subsequently proved to be quite inadequate, especially with regard to the exposition's projected visitor number of 12 million. Of the 6.5 million who did visit the Dome, over a million entered free, and many others had cut-price tickets due to various promotions by sponsors such as Boots and Tesco.

Blair appointed his close associate, Peter Mandelson, to oversee preparation of the exposition as sole 'shareholder' – in effect, 'Dome minister' – in the New Millennium Experience Company (NMEC). Symptomatic of the vogue for 'public-private partnerships', NMEC had evolved from a private company, registered originally by the design firm Imagination, into a non-departmental public body at 'arm's length' from government while retaining inappropriately but significantly the business terminology of 'shareholding'. As Minister without Portfolio, it was Mandelson's job to manage the favourable presentation of government policy. Responsibility for the Dome fitted into his general brief for orchestrating public opinion. Mandelson's maternal grandfather, Herbert

Morrison, had been in charge of the post Second World War Labour government's Festival of Britain in 1951, which was preoccupied with the question of national renewal. For Mandelson, the New Millennium Experience was to be not only of national but global significance, an instantly recognisable icon around the world. In the face of enduring public scepticism about the Dome, Mandelson embraced the role of its chief spokesperson until his first forced resignation from the government over a loan scandal in December 1998. While still in charge, Mandelson talked up the project extravagantly: 'Greenwich is the home of time. The meridian line runs through the exhibition site. It is a great chance for Britain to make a big statement about itself and the rest of the world'.[9]

New Labour rhetoric on the Dome enunciated an extraordinary hubris that was certain to attract persistent sniping in a country once described as 'rotten with criticism'.[10] The government would inevitably be blamed for its failure. Defending the ill-starred project against critics and calls for its abandonment, Blair made a famous speech on the announcement of some of the Dome's contents in February 1998:

> Picture the scene. The clock strikes midnight on December 31st 1999. The eyes of the world turn to the spot where the new Millennium begins – the Meridian Line at Greenwich. This is Britain's opportunity to greet the world with a celebration that is so bold, so beautiful, so inspiring that it embodies at once the spirit of confidence and adventure in Britain and the spirit of the future in the world. This is the reason for the Millennium experience. Not a product of imagination run wild, but a huge opportunity for Britain. It is good for Britain. So let us seize the moment and put on something of which we and the world will be proud.
>
> Then we will say to ourselves with pride: this is our Dome. *Britain's* Dome. And, believe me, it *will* be the envy of the world.[11]

According to Blair, then, the purpose of the Dome was to reposition Britain – to relocate Britishness – in the eyes of the world, as a virtual leader in global affairs. This involved 'bring[ing] the nation together in a common purpose'. The exposition would be an instructive guide to conduct, particularly for children: 'I want today's children to take from it an experience so powerful and memories so strong that it gives them that abiding sense of purpose and unity that stays with them through the rest of their lives.'[12] It has been argued that the Great Exhibition of 1851 was, in a Foucauldian sense, about the education of conduct for an industrial age, articulated through spectacular display of machinery, commodities and patriotic scenarios.[13] The idea, however, that its putative successor might function similarly a century and a half later in the information age of time-space compression, when everything is said to be instantly available to view at the press of a button, was no longer viable.

In its politics and its Dome, New Labour abolished the past. 'Old Labour' was the catch-all binary opposition and ideological repository for all that the Blair government was to relinquish from the social-democratic project so as to prove itself business-friendly. The Millennium Dome also turned away from the past towards a vaguely imagined future, but it was not merely propaganda for New Labourism despite the inflated rhetoric. Irreversible decisions concerning purpose, funding and location were taken under the Conservatives before the 1997 election. That the Millennium project remained substantially unchanged when the incoming government adopted the outgoing government's plans exemplifies a broader thesis concerning the post-Thatcherite identity of New Labour.[14] This general observation must be qualified, though, with reference to the mediating role of Michael Heseltine, the Conservative politician largely responsible for overthrowing Margaret Thatcher herself.

Selling our country

Heseltine's dramatic though overstated break with Thatcherism was motivated not only by his ambition to become leader of the Conservatives but, allegedly in principle, by Thatcher's lack of economic patriotism and solidarity with Europe. He resigned from her government in the late 1980s over the refusal to privilege British and European companies when issuing governmental defence contracts. Thatcher's neo-liberalism – put simply, unrestrained free trade denying any kind of protectionism, however nationally desirable – amounted to an Atlanticist bias, in Heseltine's estimation. When Heseltine's challenge to Thatcher for the Conservative Party leadership failed, the way was opened, instead, to John Major as the compromise candidate. Heseltine's reward was the deputy premiership in Major's government.

As the leading politician on the Millennium Commission, Heseltine took a special interest in the Greenwich exposition. He had a ministerial record for promoting urban regeneration schemes in de-industrialized localities. In his autobiography, Heseltine mentioned his regret that Greenwich had been neglected during the Docklands regeneration of the 1980s,[15] the most prominent aspect of which was the Canary Wharf office complex, across the Thames from the peninsula where the gigantic fibre-glass tent of the Dome was eventually built. By supporting the choice of Greenwich rather than Birmingham for the Millennium Dome and related developments, including housing, hotel accommodation and retail outlets, Heseltine sought to make amends for this earlier neglect.

News media blamed a succession of individuals for the 'disaster' at Greenwich: Mandelson and his successor as Dome minister, the disingenuously populist Lord Charles Falconer, as well as Blair himself and a vast array of advisors, managers and variously interested parties. The journalists' game of naming and shaming the culprits was far too simplistic a means of accounting for a very complex and multidimensional phenomenon. Nevertheless, there is a case for arguing that Heseltine was indeed the key figure in the politics of the Dome as symbol of the post-Thatcherite makeover of neo-liberal Britain. He stated the project's purpose most sharply and used his influence to make sure it survived the switch from Conservative to Labour government. Heseltine said in 1996:

> I want millions of visitors to the visit the country, share in the festival and go away deeply impressed, much excited by British achievements. The excellence of UK companies, the pre-eminence of the City of London as a financial centre, the technological prowess, the innovative genius will leave an indelible impression.
>
> We can do that only in partnership with our leading companies. It is not a bureaucratic concept of central government, or a whim of the Millennium Commission. It is about selling ourselves and our country.[16]

This patriotic capitalist rationale for the Millennium Festival and Dome was reminiscent of a tradition of universal expositions since the nineteenth century in that host countries had typically sought aggrandizement in the eyes of participants from other countries.[17] Heseltine's conception of the project, however, had two distinctly contradictory features. First, the Millennium exposition coincided with the legitimate successor to the international tradition, Hanover 2000. It was presumptuous to stage such a nationalistic exposition in the same year and expect the world to be impressed. Similarly beholden to corporations in many respects, Hanover 2000 nevertheless represented a world of nations – minus the USA – whereas the Millennium Dome represented a nation of corporations. Second, the 'partnership with our leading companies' included American companies, such as Ford, McDonalds and Manpower, but none from continental Europe.

Strenuous efforts were made to bring 'British' businesses on board. No private company would agree to run the project: hence the formation of the New Millennium Experience Company, which was staffed by public-sector administrators rather than business managers in the first instance. Lack of private-sector expertise in running a visitor attraction – before the former civil servant Jennie Page was replaced by the ex-Disney employee P-Y Gerbeau as

CEO in February 2000 at the instigation of a group of sponsors disgruntled by bad publicity – became the official explanation for its early troubles. The fact that it had proven so difficult to attract corporate sponsorship strengthened the negotiating position of sponsors. Moreover, a number of them had not even finalized contracts by the time the Dome opened on 1 January and some were apparently reluctant to pay up at all. Payments were delayed until as late as October 2000. In addition to NMEC depleting its contingency fund in order to meet the escalating costs of an immovable deadline, the reticence of sponsors was as important a cause of the instant financial crisis that erupted as the early shortfall in visitor numbers. The government had to bail out the Dome from bankruptcy on four separate occasions throughout the year by requiring the Millennium Commission to release extra grants from the National Lottery in February, May, July and September.

Consideration of the role of corporate sponsorship is at the heart of explaining how the Millennium Dome turned out. Sponsorship eventually amounted to less than one-fifth (around £150 million at the highest estimate) of the amount of public money spent on the New Millennium Experience (in excess of £800 million, including £628 million of Lottery money). Yet corporate sponsors had a decisive impact on the exposition's focal concerns, design and management. Sponsors were associated with particular thematic zones: for instance, BT's Talk, Ford's Journey, Manpower's Work, Marconi's and BAe Systems' Mind, Marks & Spencer's Self Portrait. A few zones failed to attract sponsorship, such as Living Island and Play. Living Island was critical of environmental pollution. Play lost its sponsor, BSkyB, because the designers, Land, were not prepared to redesign the zone in order to publicize that company's products.

The most obvious motive for sponsorship was not philanthropy, to be sure, but commercial promotion to the public. This was manifestly evident in the case of BT's Talk Zone and Ford's Journey Zone. Both these companies negotiated 'turnkey' contracts with NMEC, which meant they were allowed to design, build and run their own zones, with minimal interference from NMEC. The only motor vehicles in the Journey Zone were Ford. BT and Ford spent a great deal more on their zones than NMEC spent on the zones ostensibly under its control. On the other hand, several sponsors quite evidently paid less than the official tariff for association. 'Value in kind' – equipment and so forth – was often supplied rather than hard cash, such as Coca Cola's ice rink.

NMEC had editors who oversaw the design of zones and a 'Litmus Group' of luminaries from the cultural industries advising on representational aspects of the exposition. NMEC did much hiring and firing of designers. Even in these cases, however, it is apparent that it was willing to give up a measure of control to sponsors. Some sponsors brought in designers they had worked with on product launches and trade fairs. In fact, many of the designers came from the world of corporate communications rather than public museum design. Also, for example, the American employment agency Manpower was permitted to put up screens of jobs on offer through the agency in its Work Zone, which was dedicated to extolling the brave new world of flexible labour in general.

Left-wing critics of the Millennium Dome attacked its promotional culture.[18] Jonathan Glancey said, 'The Millennium Experience, its entrance flanked by a branch of McDonalds, proved to be an exhibition of corporate sponsorship.'[19] As well as the largest McDonald's in Europe in front of the main entrance there were two McDonald's eateries inside. McDonald's also hosted Our Town Stage, with its distinctly American connotation, where groups of schoolchildren from around the country had their day performing at the Dome. This was a notable feature of the National Programme for articulating nationwide activities with the central attraction in London. McDonald's copyrighted performance recordings. Involvement in the National Programme facilitated its incursion into schools across Britain. In January 2000, an advertisement appeared on television, asking 'What's in the Dome?' The answer: 'McDonalds.'

Undoubtedly, the Millennium Dome was an artefact of promotional culture in which commercial speech framed national-popular meanings. However, that is only half the story and perhaps not the more significant half. The troubled Dome was the biggest news story in Britain during the year 2000 in terms of column inches and broadcast time. It was a soap-operatic saga with elements of situation comedy and, more seriously, scandalous revelation, such as BBC Television's reporting of sponsors' complaints about mismanagement. Journalists, however, rarely tried to penetrate the deeper motives for sponsorship.[20] It is easy enough to see why Boots promoted pharmaceutical products at the Body Zone but harder to see why BAe Systems put money into the Mind Zone, the most intellectual of zones, designed by deconstructionist architect Zaha Hadid. One of the largest armaments manufacturers in the world, BAe Systems does not sell Hawk jets directly to the public.

Mind did not blatantly promote BAe's core business. Instead, the declared purpose of the zone was to represent modern engineering and encourage the education of engineers. Were there ulterior motives indirectly to do with promotion? On coming into government in 1997, New Labour promised to pursue an 'ethical' foreign policy, which might have meant not sanctioning weapons sales to dictatorships like the Suharto regime in Indonesia. Soon, this 'unrealistic' policy was quietly dropped, since the production of armaments is one of the few remaining buoyant sectors of British manufacturing for export in what is said to be a predominantly 'weightless' informational economy. The government's U-turn on foreign policy – unrestrained issuing of export guarantees to armaments manufacturers and conduct of diplomacy on their behalf – was of more than incidental benefit to BAe Systems. That was of greater significance than the much-discussed allegation that Peter Mandelson had sold British passports to the Hinduja brothers for a modest and tax-exempting donation to the Faith Zone, which won the journalists who broke the story the journalism of the year award.

The Hinduja passports-for-sponsorship scandal, which brought down Mandelson for a second time in 2001, was only the tip of an iceberg, the greater part of which the news media largely ignored. As the former marketing director of one corporate sponsor remarked in interview, everyone had a political deal. This was evidently true of the Work Zone's sponsor Manpower, which handled human resources for NMEC, hiring, training and relocating employees on closure. In association with Ernst & Young, the government's favourite accountancy firm, Manpower won nine out of fifteen contracts for the management of employment zones around the country, a little remarked upon feature of New Labour's privatization of public agencies. This may just be coincidental.

There are several other coincidences. The supermarket chain Tesco – sponsor of the Learning Zone and heavily involved in promoting its business through computing in schools – must have been pleased when the government decided to withdraw proposed legislation for taxing out-of-town car parks at retail estates. BA and BAA (British Airports Authority) – co-sponsors of Home Planet, the closest thing to a ride at the Dome – must have appreciated the government's sanctioning of Terminal 5 at Heathrow in face of popular local environmental protests against its building. It seemed surprising that Camelot – sponsor of Shared Ground – had its National Lottery contract renewed by a Labour government that had vowed to replace its profit-making operation with a not-for-profit operator. Rupert Murdoch's BSkyB – sponsor of the 'Baby Dome', Skyscape – has benefited from the government's light-touch policies on broadcasting and digitalization, not to mention its relaxed press policy. There are other examples. It may all just be coincidence. However, it is reasonable to infer that the New Millennium Experience was more than a relatively expensive promotional exercise as a proportion of annual PR budgets for participating corporations.

Something completely different?

How the Dome turned out is inexplicable without reference to the role of sponsorship, supported by massive public subsidy for business promotion. However, the meanings of the New Millennium Experience are not entirely reducible to corporate propaganda and the opaque effects of governmental machinations behind the scenes. It is a truism of cultural analysis that production does not inevitably legislate for meaning at the point of consumption. Visitor research at the Millennium Dome demonstrated that in whole and in parts the exposition meant different things to different people. There is abundant quantitative evidence of high levels of visitor approval and, also, qualitative evidence of generous and reflexive visiting modes that put the media's damnation of the Dome into question.[21] Generally, people made the best of what was there and had a good day out. For many, the whole amounted to more than the sum of its many tainted parts. The sponsorless Millennium Show in the Central Arena, which told an allegorical story of the rise and fall of industrialism, was the most consistently popular feature of the exposition. A distinction needs to be drawn, then, between attractions that were and were not sponsored at the Dome. For instance, artworks scattered in and around the Dome – such as Antony Gormley's *Quantum Cloud* out on the River Approach and Ron Mueck's *Boy* placed in the otherwise inhuman Mind Zone – were counterpoints to corporate representation. There were also significant differences of message construction and scale of intrusiveness in sponsored zones, ranging from the crude propaganda of the Work Zone through the subtle ideology of Mind to the relative detachment of the sponsor from the zone's design in Marks & Spencer's Self Portrait.

The approach taken here is that of a critical and reflexive cultural policy analysis. It differs from more instrumentally oriented research by interrogating the assumptions of prevailing policy and administrative practice from an independent and academically 'disinterested' point of view. Questioning and unconstrained by pragmatic imperatives, such analysis is not necessarily negative, however, since it may seek to engage governmental agencies either directly or indirectly in dialogue over policy options. It is not unusual, of course, for such agencies to resist any criticism at all, however constructive in intent, and to defend themselves typically through public relations and self-validating research with performance indicators and the like. In itself, that is sufficient reason for asking awkward questions as a matter of critical witness. Calling a public cultural artefact like the Dome into question, albeit after the event, obliges dialogical critique to explore alternatives both actual and potential so as to establish grounds for debate. Quite different ways of marking the Millennium from that of the Dome's transient exposition of corporate power were no doubt possible. Other projects supported by the Lottery, moreover, have been judged of greater success than the Millennium Dome. Cornwall's unbranded and enduring Eden Project is frequently cited in this regard. If the exposition in the Dome at Greenwich is seen as a reasonable undertaking, admittedly a debatable proposition, it is still worth speculating, even in retrospect, on different contents. These might have contributed to public debate and social learning rather than officially prescribing amazement at the wonders of technology, such as a critical War Zone instead of the ideological obscurantism of Mind.[22]

It is also important to appreciate that heterogeneity of zone-sponsor relations at the Millennium Dome was symptomatic both of a tension over sponsorship within public-sector culture and a transition occurring from *associative* to *deep* sponsorship.

Associative sponsorship is the standard form of supporting arts and cultural provision in the public sector. Sponsors may acquire prestige by association with artistic culture but are not supposed to influence content. This is not necessarily so in practice. Sponsorship exerts all sorts of subtle pressure on editorial decision-making, programme selection and so on.[23] Yet the norms of associative sponsorship continue to be asserted in the public sector, however unconvincingly, to protect cultural integrity.

Deep sponsorship is a constitutive feature of the cultural marketplace where the interests of corporate business in the production of culture and its circulation are ubiquitous. The cultural form itself may become a vehicle designed for advertising, merchandizing and public relations as much as for pleasure and knowledge. Disney was a pioneer in this respect. Corporations' ideological construction of culture not only in entertainment but also in education is increasingly widespread. Under-funded public education is now an eager host for corporate intervention. In the USA, educational television, as a means of reaching young consumers, most notably K-111's Channel One, is gratefully received. The free gift of the ZapMe! Browser in schools is a device for customer surveillance and marketing.[24]

Tesco's computing in schools programme is an instance of deep sponsorship, as was its Learning Zone at the Dome. Corporate 'social responsibility' of this kind encroaches upon public spaces that are no longer safeguarded from commerce. A number of other sponsor-zone relations can similarly be categorized as deep sponsorship such as the City of London's Money Zone, Manpower's Work, BT's Talk and Ford's Journey. The Dome was a site of tension over public and corporate control, that is, regulation. Residual evidence of associative sponsorship and even absence of sponsorship at the Dome indicates the tensions in play.

An example of associative sponsorship was Marks & Spencer's support for Self Portrait, which addressed the vexed question of British national identity. Self Portrait was housed in a huge drum, with an illuminated photographic collage, 'Andscape', of celebrities and objects chosen by the general public on the glass-panelled outer wall. A striking feature of this zone was voluntary queuing on the way in. Since Self Portrait was one of the less crowded zones, visitors were not usually obliged to queue before entering, unlike at Boots' highly publicized Body Zone. As a signification of Britishness, however, voluntary queuing there was in itself meaningful. Visitors stopped to read postcards on the entrance ramp. Thirteen thousand individuals and groups had replied to the question, 'What one thing best represents Britain to you, something which you would like to take into the future?' Selected replies were presented in uniform typography with illustrative photographs on postcards along the wall. Topics included: graffiti, Vivienne Westwood, Sgt. Pepper's Lonely Hearts Club Band, the red double-decker bus in London, the Football Association crest, Sooty, Liquorice Allsorts, municipal parks, Imam Khoesi Islamic Centre, tea in bone china cup and saucer, lollipop ladies and gentlemen, the countryside and its hedgerows, socks and sandals, Michael Caine, a game of conkers, the *Beano*, a miner's safety lamp, the White Cliffs of Dover, the British weather, the British letter box, sarcasm ('It is distinctly British'), Talvin Singh, imagination ('Because it is the start of everything'), Speaker's Corner, spirit, Padstow, the Angel of the North ('It combines all that I feel about Britain. It conveys a sense of solidarity. It acknowledges the industry that made our country what it is whilst at the same time being overwhelmingly beautiful and graceful'), Morecambe and Wise ('They are so funny, and so British'), David Hockney ('The most well known British artist'), Sunday lunch, the Irish Peace Agreement, Blackpool Tower, golf, Tony Benn ('A thorn in the side of the Establishment for over forty years').

The wall of the circular space inside was covered by the 'National Portrait' collage, put together by David Mach from a selection of the quarter of a million photographs sent in by members of the public. It also incorporated images from the work of Constable and Gainsborough in the background. In front of Mach's collage were tall placards extolling the virtues of Britishness – creativity, diversity, fair play, humour, inventiveness and so on – much of it in the tone of Leonard's *BritainTM* pamphlet. Read in isolation, these placards were self-congratulatory;

yet juxtaposed with them were Gerald Scarfe's satirical sculptures representing another side of Britishness that punctured the inflated boasts. For instance, a quote from Jeremy Paxman – 'You don't need to be a white Anglo-Saxon to be British' – could be read alongside Scarfe's hideously respectable *Racist*. There was a 'couch potato' about to be engulfed by vomit from his TV set, a notice beside the sculpture observing: 'British culture – > How many of us sit lazily in front of our televisions, letting them spew sub-standard culture all over us? This chap has been sitting in his armchair for so long, with his beer and remote control, that the upholstery is taking him over.' This could be viewed from one angle against the placard for Creativity and from another against the Inventiveness placard. Similarly, *Bootman*, the thug with a boot for a head, stood menacingly in front of the Fair Play placard.

Gerald Scarfe's *Bootman* in Marks & Spencer's Self Portrait Zone

Self Portrait set up a series of contradictions regarding Britishness past and present. In my experience of observing responses to its contents, it offended very few visitors yet pleased and challenged most to reflect upon a problematical identity. A wickedly subversive eye was thus cast upon New Labour Britain. Scarfe's *Traditional Cool Britannia* – Elizabeth II as the Lion and the Prime Minister as the Unicorn – had a notice saying, 'The Queen and Tony Blair preside over the joys of traditional Britain: warm beer and cricket, Beefeaters and mad cows, late trains and leaves on the line'.

It would have been surprising, to say the least, if this zone had commented on what was happening to its sponsor, Marks & Spencer. A 'quality' and erstwhile 'patriotic' retail chain, currently losing custom precipitately, Marks & Spencer was laying off workers in Britain and closing stores on the continent, while newly outsourcing product from cheap labour markets around the world in order to alleviate its crisis of profitability. Nevertheless, the sponsor did not prevent a questioning of Britishness and a potential opening up of popular debate over national identity from being articulated in its zone; and did not promote its own products there as a number of other sponsors did in their zones. Self Portrait exemplified the residual norms of associative sponsorship at the Dome in contrast to the corporate appropriation of public discourse through deep sponsorship in several of the other zones.

Giving it away

Opposition politicians and right-wing newspapers, such as the *Daily Mail*, depicted the Dome as profoundly symbolic of the New Labour regime, its wastefulness and its lack of substance. The most trenchant attack from the Right was launched by former Tory minister for higher education George Walden in his book of 2000, *The New Elites – Making a Career in the Masses*. According to Walden, the New Labour elite and its associates are characterized by a dumbing-down populism that is actually, though secretly, contemptuous of the masses. This was especially manifest in the Millennium Dome, 'a godsend illustration of the thesis of this book', in Walden's estimation. He went on to say:

> The psychology that led to its construction could hardly be more revealing of our ruling caste's state of mind. Priggish, hollow, self-aggrandizing, vapidly jokey, mincingly patriotic, cynically populist, massively patronizing, mediocre to its soul and curiously provincial – the Great White Wen of Greenwich is a monument to the new elites.[25]

Stephen Bayley, who was briefly design advisor to NMEC, had already denounced, in his book *New Labour Camp* of 1998, how the Dome was likely to turn out. For stylistic vacuity and tastelessness, he claimed, it was symptomatic of New Labour's cultural policy in general.[26] These criticisms of New Labour's Millennium Experience were exclusively cultural and, therefore, limited in consequence. No doubt there are cultural populists who would be inclined to counter such criticism by celebrating the Dome as a misunderstood site of people's pleasure, active consumption or resistance on similarly exclusive cultural grounds. Neither cultural criticism of the old school nor apologetic populism of the new school, however, is capable of providing a satisfactory account of how the Dome turned out, since they both tend to neglect the material determinations of political economy and, specifically in this case, neo-liberal ideology.

New Labour's 'Third Way' politics, described by its leading exponent Anthony Giddens as 'the renewal of social democracy',[27] has embraced rather than resisted the neo-liberalism bequeathed by the previous regime, further developing what George Monbiot calls 'the corporate takeover of Britain'.[28] Privatization of public assets, public-private partnerships and private finance initiatives are the main planks of New Labour governmental policy in the public sector, originally touted as 'reinventing government' in response to US tax revolts of the 1970s.[29] The Millennium Dome was not a simple reflection of this political and economic reasoning. It is often argued that private enterprise is needed in order to make the public sector work efficiently and prudently. Yet, the Dome swallowed up a great deal of public money in order to aid private enterprise, to promote corporations and to demonstrate business friendliness. In that sense, it was an inversion of the official ideology, functioning revealingly as a government-sponsored exercise in the corporate violation of public culture. The Dome was not the site for a cultural public sphere – an entertaining space for popular disputation over meaning and purpose – that it might have been, with the possible exception of Self Portrait and the sponsor-free elements. Instead, it became the object of what has sometimes been described as a 'pseudo' or 'phantom' public sphere, where controversial issues are rendered inconsequential, for a scandalized news media that somehow missed the real scandal. With its corporate agenda and touchy-feely rhetoric, the Dome was a costly shell for neo-liberalism[30] and a huge embarrassment to New Labour.

In the end, New Labour had trouble giving it away. Although the contents were sold off at knockdown prices in February 2001, shortly after closure, the site continued to be a public cost for maintenance until it was literally given away in July 2002. A number of failed attempts were made to sell off the Dome and its extensive site. Had the Dome been demolished, the land would have been more valuable for developers. This, however, might have been construed as a final admission of failure for its flagship project that the New Labour government was not prepared to countenance. Rather than do that, the government gave the place to the Meridian Delta consortium for nothing up front, in the vague hope that it might eventually receive a share of profits, to be derived from use of the Dome as a sports and entertainment venue by the American Anschutz Corporation and property development around it by Quintain Estates and the Australian Lend Lease Real Estate Group.

Notes

1 British Council, *Through Other Eyes: How the World Sees the United Kingdom* (London, 1999), p. 2.

2 P. Wright, *On Living in an Old Country: The National Past in Contemporary Britain* (London, 1985).

3 T. Blair, *New Britain – My Vision of a Young Country* (London, 1996).

4 J. McGuigan, 'National government and the cultural public sphere', *Media International Australia Incorporating Culture and Policy* 81 (1998), pp. 68–83; idem, 'British identity and "the people's princess"', *Sociological Review*, 48 (2000), pp. 1–18.

5 R. Williams, *Towards 2000* (London, 1983).

6 M. Leonard, *BritainTM – Renewing Our Identity* (London, 1997), pp. 50–5.

7 Ibid., p. 7.

8   See J. McGuigan and A. Gilmore, 'Figuring out the Dome', *Cultural Trends* 39 (December 2001), pp. 39–83, for a detailed breakdown of facts and figures pertaining to the New Millennium Experience.

9   Quoted by L. Harding, 'Lift-off for £750 million Dome', *Guardian*, 27 June 1997, p. 3.

10 R. Williams, 'A Lecture on Realism', *Screen* 18 (1) (May 1977), p. 73.

11 T. Blair, 'Why the Dome is good for Britain', people's palace, royal festival hall, 24 February 1998, p. 1.

12 Ibid., p. 4.

13 T. Bennett, 'The exhibitionary complex', in *The Birth of the Museum – History, Theory, Politics* (London, 1995 edn.), pp. 59–88.

14 S. Driver and L. Martell, *New Labour – Politics After Thatcher* (Cambridge, 1998).

15 M. Heseltine, *Life in the Jungle – My Autobiography* (London, 2000), pp. 509–14.

16 Quoted by A. Nicolson, *Regeneration – The Story of the Millennium Dome* (London, 1999), p. 2.

17 P. Greenhalgh, *Ephemeral Vistas: The Expositions Universelles, Great Exhibitions and World's Fairs, 1851–1939* (Manchester, 1988).

18 A. Wernick, *Promotional Culture: Advertising, Ideology and Symbolic Expression* (London, 1991).

19 J. Glancey, *London: Bread and Circuses* (London, 2001), p. 26.

21 MORI's polls of visitors for NMEC are summarized and commented upon in McGuigan and Gilmore, 'Figuring out the Dome'. J. McGuigan and A. Gilmore, 'The Millennium Dome – sponsoring, meaning and visiting', *International Journal of Cultural Policy* 8 (2002), pp. 1–20, reports upon conversational interviews conducted independently by the authors and presents a typology of generous and reflexive visiting for interpreting the data. It also outlines a multidimensional methodology used to analysis the Millennium Dome for the Arts and Humanities Research Board project, 'The Meanings of the New Millennium Experience'.

22 For fuller discussion of critical and reflexive cultural policy analysis, see J. McGuigan, *Cultural Policy* (Buckingham and Philadelphia, forthcoming).

23 R. Shaw (ed.), *The Spread of Sponsorship – in the Arts, Sport, Education, the Health Service and Broadcasting* (Newcastle, 1993).

24 N. Klein, *No Logo: Taking Aim at the Brand Bullies* (London, 2000).

25 G. Walden, *The New Elites: Making a Career in the Masses* (London, 2000), p. 142.

26 S. Bayley, *Labour Camp: The Failure of Style Over Substance* (London, 1998).

27 A. Giddens, *The Third Way: The Renewal of Social Democracy* (Cambridge, 1998).

28 G. Monbiot, *Captive State: The Corporate Takeover of Britain* (London, 2000).

29 D. Osborne and T. Gaebler, *Reinventing Government: How the Entrepreneurial Spirit is Transforming the Public Sector* (Reading, MA, 1992).

30 Here I am adapting Perry Anderson's observation that the Third Way is an 'ideological shell of neo-liberalism': 'Renewals', *New Left Review* 1 (2nd series), January–February 2000, pp. 5–24.

3

Blackpool and the varieties of Britishness

John K. Walton

I t is often assumed that seaside resorts are peripheral to Britain and British-ness, and to the component parts of this entity and identity. This applies especially to those that have historically served 'the provinces', beyond the usual field of vision of the dominant metropolitan gaze. Indeed, from this vantage point such places are often not so much seen as peripheral, as not seen at all. Jon Cook, in his paper at the conference on which this book is based, remarked on how even a relatively successful and enduring resort like Scarborough might be represented as being peripheral to Britain: not only in the literal, physical sense that it was a long way from London, the great cities and the motorway network, at the dead end of a long spur of the surviving railway system and with no outlet to Europe, but more so because of the kind of place it was, an end-of-millennium seaside resort and in many people's eyes therefore representative of an older, declining popular culture and of cantankerous, conservative, 'Little England' retirement, for those who resist or cannot afford the Mediterranean and more exotic alternatives.[1] This perception does scant justice to Scarbor-ough's capacity for adaptation and survival, which has left it as one of the most successful of Britain's old resorts at the turn of the millennium. I have argued elsewhere that the British seaside resort has been more resilient than most met-ropolitan and transient commentators allow. The place of the sea in British national mythology is strong and enduring. Even Blackpool, the most popular resort of all (and historically one of the most vigorous and inventive in resist-ing decline), still derives some of its allure from its position on an exposed and exciting shoreline, even if most of its visitors do little more than breathe in the sea air from the promenade or kick a ball on the beach. It is also coming to be perceived as being nearly as peripheral as Scarborough, despite its (small) airport, direct motorway access and proximity to the West Coast main line. These contradictions and cross-currents raise important issues.[2]

Firstly, positive associations between the sea itself and ideas about Britishness do indeed abound, expressed in (for example) the words and especially the chorus of 'Rule Britannia'; the mythology of Drake and the Spanish Armada; Nelson's Column, the commemoration of the Dunkirk evacuation, and the Royal Navy more generally; the celebration of fish and chips as 'The Great British Dish'; the much-anthologized John Masefield poem about the tramp steamer; the persisting mystique of the QE2; the heroics of lifeboat crews and the high visibility of the RNLI as a collecting charity; and the occasional recognition, usually in the immediate aftermath of tragedy, of the risks fishermen run in their daily avocation. The loss of empire and of the merchant marine, and the demise of the transatlantic liner routes with their 'Blue Riband' competition, together with the collapse of shipbuilding and the decline of the great trawler fleets, have pushed these associations from the centre stage they formerly held; but they remain pervasive in the culture of at least the immediate post-war generation. And this is a genuinely British set of associations, embracing Harland and Wolff at Belfast, Cardiff's Tiger Bay, Scottish fishing communities, Aberdeen as one of the main trawler ports, and the traditions of Clydeside and the Glasgwegian ship's engineer, which were international enough to be incorporated into *Star Trek*. Much of this is naval and post-imperial, running in line with Linda Colley's central theses in *Britons*; but there is a civilian side to this perception of a positive national affinity with the sea, which should be extended to seaside pleasures, and even to the British seaside holiday.[3]

Accounts of the displacement and decline of the 'traditional' seaside holiday have been a seasonal staple of the British broadsheet press for a quarter of a century, although reports of the patient's death have been much exaggerated and more credit should be given for the resilience and adaptability of all but the most ill-favoured of British resorts.[4] But the seaside has remained newsworthy because, from its origins as a British invention in the early eighteenth century, the seaside holiday has become part of the cultural baggage of Britishness: it is assumed that the annual pilgrimage to the sea is integral to British (especially English) identity, adding associations of leisure, escape and relaxation (but also of difficulties involving travelling constraints, taboos and consciousnesses of class, status and gender) to the other ways in which the self-proclaimed island race claims a special relationship with the azure main. So the reported decline of the domestic seaside holiday habit and industry appears part of a wider traumatic transition away from older certainties about what constitutes national identity, towards what might appear a less grounded, more fragmented, kaleidoscopic and uneasy future. The seaside holiday, as affectionately remembered, conjured up, represented in literature and film and handed on to the next generation, has been a particularly evocative (and contradictory) element in perceptions of the relationship between the sea and Britishness.[5]

Despite the importance of the seaside holiday as a taken-for-granted aspect of Britishness, perceptions of the resort as a peripheral location, a 'place on the margin' far removed from the real and active concerns of government and wealth creation, an opposite pole to the vibrant agenda-setting of the metropolis, have predominated in both journalistic and academic readings. Rob Shields' presentation of seaside resorts as marginal places has put an academic gloss on this, although Shields' direct and exemplary focus on Brighton has its ironic aspects, as it has been (since the days of the Prince of Wales of the late eighteenth century) the most metropolitan of all British resorts, 'London by sea' in cultural and sometimes political terms (especially with the regular visits of the party conferences in the second half of the twentieth century).[6] Resorts in other countries which acquired the status of 'summer capital', especially through royal residence (San Sebastián until Spain's Second Republic began in 1931, or Ostend under Leopold II) but also (as with Scotland's North Berwick) as gathering-points of choice for the political classes, spent at least part of the year as anything but peripheral places.[7] We may be sceptical of Soane's argument that resort environments and cultures offered a vision of the civilized, relaxed life to their residents and consumers which formed a model for wider social improvement, a kind of 'civilizing process'; but such an argument at least brings the resort back from the periphery to the centre, with an influence based on regular usage and widespread shared experience. The resort as miniature capital city in another sense, that of concentrating and displaying new fashions and disseminating them through the provinces and down the social scale, is a more plausible variant on this theme, as the seaside holiday experience promoted the nationalization of culture and consumption patterns (though it might also promote their internationalization, as in the debates over the alleged Americanizing influence of Blackpool which were emerging in the 1930s).[8]

Shields also argues for the seaside experience as productive of feedback into the wider society, bringing to mind the argument that national identities may be constructed more tellingly on the 'periphery' than at the 'centre', partly through defining them the more sharply in direct confrontation with otherness; but his argument contrasts with Soane's vision of constructed and communicated civility. He argues for seaside resorts as classic sites of liminality and the carnivalesque: gateways between the controlled and the anarchic, the cultured and the natural, the civilized and the unrestrained; safety-valves which allowed the frustrations of the rest of the year to be vented harmlessly in a setting where the consensus about acceptable behaviour was more relaxed and tolerant; even places where the world could be turned upside down, with celebrations of the grotesque and the excessive, and the removal of the veneer of everyday civilization which covered the beast within. He cites Brighton's reputation for freedom from the sexual constraints of everyday life, from the Prince of Wales's circle in the late eighteenth and early nineteenth century to the 'dirty weekend' and the concoction of adultery evidence for the divorce courts in the 1930s (an ambiguous illustration, as chronicled by Evelyn Waugh, with no direct sense of sexual liberation about it), through (he might have added) to the post-war beatniks and squatters and the proudly and ostentatiously gay dimensions of the Brighton of the late twentieth century.[9]

In fact, the sheer diversity of the British seaside, with scores of resorts catering for the broadest possible spectrum of tastes, niches and social strata, has meant that most generalizations about its role as an expression of versions of national character apply to some places rather than others, or to some parts of individual resorts, or even to different seasons, dates or times of day. Those in search of tranquillity and a Britishness of order, restraint, tidiness and litter-free lawns (or 'greensward') can go to Frinton; those who prefer a proletarian version with abundant alcohol, easy-going physical contact, singing and horseplay can look for its stereotypical Cockney version at Southend (but not Westcliffe), Margate (but not Cliftonville); or its big-hearted Northern incarnation in Blackpool (but not Lytham St Annes). Very British conflicts have been, and are, fought out over issues of 'social tone', where contrasting preferences in enjoyment (all, in principle, equally 'British') come into contact and conflict (as in Frinton's enduring, well-publicized and ultimately unsuccessful efforts to exclude first a fish and chip shop, then a pub).[10] Even in the most permissive of locations, moreover, notions of liminality or the carnivalesque have had to be qualified, as Shields is aware, by awareness of internal and external boundaries and constraints, as people brought their own inhibitions with them and were aware of the possibility of censure by neighbours, workmates or other arbiters of propriety, while local authorities imposed their own grids of regulation and enforcement. At Blackpool the holiday crowds of the 1930s (and long before) went to and fro according to the timetable of the factory day, which they had internalized and brought with them.[11] But seaside environments could be tightly regulated, as local government from the Victorians onwards introduced strictly enforced by-laws, although obsessive attempts at control might themselves be a response to a setting that was perceived to be conducive to high jinks and unseemliness, and the Home Office tried to keep a tight rein on the more out-landish attempts at restriction.[12] The British seaside has been important as a site where assumptions about proper behaviour are challenged and, in response, articulated and reasserted: so seaside resorts can be good places to look for the strengths and weaknesses of core values and the fault-lines running through them. The best way to take a provisional section through the relationships between Britishness and the seaside entails a strongly flavoured case-study. Blackpool, firmly located at the proletarian (or at least popular) and permissive end of the spectrum, stands out as an appropriate setting.

Blackpool's reputation as proletarian playground is long-established, origi-nating with its popularity among Lancashire millworkers at the dawn of the working-class seaside holiday in the later nineteenth century. It had developed a genuinely national catchment area by the inter-war years, including Scotland and Wales if not yet Ireland, while continuing to celebrate Lancashire and more broadly northern identities in popular culture, associated especially but not exclusively with George Formby and Gracie Fields. For Jeffrey Richards it was 'the Mecca of the North' at this time. In the early post-war years of paid holidays and growing popular purchasing power it pulled in unskilled workers, and even young families and pensioners in the troughs of the poverty cycle, to make a sea-side holiday open to almost everyone. Visitor numbers ran at around 4 million annually in 1913 and 7–8 million in the late 1930s. Ready accessibility and cheap, basic accommodation were central to this unique success, which stood up well against competition from the Mediterranean and then the longer-haul package holiday in the late twentieth century, as successive reinventions rein-forced old loyalties while creating new ones. Blackpool remains one of the largest and by far the most popular of British seaside resorts. It is therefore, of course, wildly untypical; and in the late twentieth century it turned its back on a polluted sea to become a pleasure resort whose maritime location was increas-ingly incidental to its attractions; but its popularity and visibility are such that it has carved out its own relationships with some of the most important com-ponent identities within Britishness. Above all, it is indelibly associated with the industrial working class, that fascinating and frightening 'other' which was indispensable to older Englishnesses and Britishnesses without being incorpo-rated into the dominant discourses, except as an indigestible element whose habits and customs were mysterious, but whose virtues became apparent in wartime, although it remained suspect in time of labour dispute and related civil strife.[13] This identity, always complex, has been and is only part of the story:

Blackpool has never lost its middle-class visitors, clustering at either end of the promenade and going forth to enjoy its more raucous delights (if only as *flaneurs* and observers) when it suits them, while the town has been run by entertainment, drink and building employers in sometimes uneasy coalition with the petty bourgeoisie, and the dominant tone of its local press has usually reflected this through the assertive language of populist Toryism, especially since the demise of the Liberal *Blackpool Times* in 1933. The eventual triumph of 'New Labour' in first local, then parliamentary elections during the 1990s, coupled with the highly-charged symbolism of the party's temporary but telling rejection of Blackpool as a conference venue, has confused this picture dramatically, even as the 'traditional' identification with a disappearing industrial working class has faltered towards dissolution at the end of the millennium. The historical roots seem more clearly defined than the current circumstances.[14]

As well as being predominantly proletarian (or, perhaps, in Patrick Joyce's term 'popular', in the sense that it pulled together a set of tastes and preferences which extended beyond wage-earners or manual workers, to express the communitarian values of broad cross-sections of local societies), Blackpool might also be represented (as the journalist William Holt did in 1934) as the epitome of a northern English identity: '[Paris] is as essentially a part of French life and France as is, say, Blackpool a reflection of the spirit of North English mill-land'.[15] Tony Bennett elaborated an argument around this theme in the mid-1980s, suggesting that Blackpool as holiday and entertainment centre stood for a northern English identity which offered an assertive alternative pole to metropolitan and southern versions of Englishness which were, from this perspective, decidedly 'other'. It expressed the principle of working and playing hard, laying claim to vitality, enterprise, and the earthy enjoyment of the fruits of manufacturing enterprise, as opposed to (in the view from the Tower) the limp-wristed snobbery of the exploitative financial manipulators of the corrupt metropolis and effete Home Counties. As Joyce elaborated for the pre-1914 period, the northern culture Blackpool distilled took pride in bluntness, common sense and deflation of pretensions, sharing a sense of humour which could be bawdy as well as effervescent, but which bounded the acceptable with both self-respect and an awareness of the limits of shared tolerance. The society gossip columnist Charles Graves, more accustomed to Cannes or Biarritz, confirmed that Blackpool was too much for southern aristocrats or plutocrats:

> Yes, Blackpool is flabbergasting. You are like a cheerful straw in an organised whirlpool of ridiculously inexpensive gaiety. Blackpool takes off its jacket to give you a good time ... It has been described as a pleasure factory. But what a factory!

... Blackpool is overpowering. Its air is so strong, its places of amusement so gigantic, its enjoyment of life so terrific ... that you grope for phrases to describe it adequately. But this is certain. Blackpool is no place for weaklings. The flabby pulse of Continental resorts only begins to beat at 11 p.m. At Blackpool by that time everyone is in bed. The pace is too tremendous.[16]

Bennett's treatment of these issues is sometimes short on context or heavy-handed, as when he presents the Tower as a phallic expression of the heroic virility and fecundity of the physically-productive North; and this rendering of Blackpool has proved vulnerable to the de-industrialization and loss of manufacturing identities and solidarities in the late twentieth century. But that is, above all, a salutary reminder that Blackpool's relationship with national and sub-national identities has changed over time; and these ideas deserve a hearing.[17]

Alongside them, however, is the vision of Blackpool as underminer rather than celebrant of these proud northern virtues. Late Victorian commentators remarked, usually admiringly, on its American vigour, enterprise, pushiness, informality and sheer rapidity of growth, and the Pleasure Beach fairground which developed from the turn of the century was an avid importer of American amusement technology, drawing on spectacle from American history to feature the Monitor and Merrimac Civil War naval battle show. Coney Island was a key influence here.[18] Critical comments about Blackpool as a vector for the Americanization of British popular culture were gathering momentum by the 1930s. J. B. Priestley complained in 1934 that, 'Its amusements are becoming too mechanized and Americanized ... It has developed a pitiful sophistication – machine-made and not really English – that is much worse than the old hearty vulgarity.'[19] A few years later, however, the idiosyncratic anthropological investigations of Mass-Observation found little specifically American to highlight in Blackpool's eclectic and eccentric array of idiosyncratic amusements, and despite its early embrace of the jukebox, and a fleeting visit from Frank Sinatra, its live entertainments of the 1950s and after continued to be dominated by British performers and frames of reference. Here is a representative comment from Mass-Observation's portrayal of Blackpool in the late 1930s: 'Blackpool culture means the old waltz, stars falling out of heaven and dream-boats, and Reg Dixon's Mighty Wurlitzer organ. Even in the ballrooms there is little enthusiasm for the hot American stuff.' George Formby satirized American song-writing conventions, and it was, perhaps, the coming of rock 'n' roll that heralded the big breakthrough. Long after that, however, Bill Bryson found nothing here in the mid-1990s to make him think of the United States: his verdict was that it was 'ugly, dirty and a long way from anywhere . . . its sea is an open toilet, and its attractions nearly all cheap, provincial and dire'.[20] Worries about Blackpool, in particular, acting as a Trojan horse for creeping Americanization smack more of moral panic than of considered appraisal. Interestingly, Blackpool's current attempt to pull itself out of a turn-of-the-millennium crisis by embracing casino gambling on the grand scale has conjured up comparisons with Las Vegas (Atlantic City would be a better analogy), rather than the Continental pleasure resorts that would have provided the obvious analogy in previous generations; but the 'casino culture' is represented as generally problematic (but necessary in the eyes of an overwhelming majority of local councillors) rather than essentially American.[21]

On an older, subversive reading, Blackpool might indeed be thought to stand for a quasi-Continental denial of British respectability of the stiff upper lip variety. The Carnivals of 1923 and 1924 presented the most serious challenges. They were marketed, outside the standard pattern of the industrial holiday calendar, as an opportunity to set aside British reserve, forget about the work ethic and adopt the pleasure principle; and they borrowed, overtly, from Mediterranean festivities which involved disguise, hedonism and the temporary dissolution of the social order. They owed more to the vital forces that bubbled just below the surface of northern industrial repression than to genuine borrowings from Catholic southern Europe, however, despite the giant papier-maché heads that were imported, as a concept, from Nice. Playing with these fires was dangerous, and the Carnivals were too subversive to be allowed to continue, despite careful policing which marched in step with the ritual mockery of individual officers and of figures representing constituted authority (an enduring theme of music-hall and stage shows, reaching its apotheosis in the anarchic posturings of Frank Randle in the immediate post-war years). Their demise, to be replaced by the return of the more sedate and carefully choreographed autumn Illuminations, indicated the limits to which Blackpool's core of respectable Britishness could be challenged on this front. Drawing on the foreign 'otherness' of Catholic Europe, in these northern climes, was a step too far, despite the growing inter-war popularity with Lancashire and Yorkshire holidaymakers of (for example) Ostend.[22]

A more acceptable form of 'otherness', the popularization of Empire, expressed a potent variety of extended Britishness in and through Blackpool, with its exotic aspects displayed and celebrated at the Raikes Hall pleasure gardens of the 1870s and 1880s, through the Tower's circus and themed exhibitions here and at the Winter Gardens from the 1890s onwards, to the fascination with the 'Orient' in various guises which Mass-Observation elevated into a theme of the late 1930s, drawing on the Pleasure Beach and Golden Mile to do so. But these were exploitative gestures rather than informative exhibitions, reinforcing stereotypes and equating difference with inferiority. Britishness here was promoted as a contrast with the lesser breeds from the outposts of Empire, rather than as something to integrate and invigorate the whole vast familiar stain of red that covered the schoolroom maps.[23]

Where parts of Blackpool (itself a town of many identities) did step over boundaries was in the space it provided for the enjoyment, and display, of alternative sexualities and sexual behaviour to the official ideal of the chaste heterosexual marriage and nuclear family. This is now most obvious in the rise to visibility and acceptability of 'Gay Blackpool' at the end of the twentieth century, building on an earlier reputation and drawing in the most obviously international of Blackpool's visiting publics. Basil Newby has not only opened a highly-profitable (and therefore, to some degree, acceptable) chain of gay night-clubs, but also, through his cabaret bar 'Funny Girls', brought the overwhelmingly heterosexual culture of the established holiday market into cheerful (if sometimes uneasy) contact with the 'otherness' of drag queens and high camp. But this celebration of excess and innuendo again taps into deeper roots in Blackpool's holiday entertainment, where the content of stage acts was already bubbling through the veneer of respectability in the 1930s and earlier. Mass-Observation's interest in representations of sexual ambiguity in the sideshows of the 'Golden Mile' ('Colonel Barker', for example, the woman who posed as a male army officer), coupled with the camp aspects of some of the music-hall and variety shows of these years (in which male cross-dressing was endemic), might be viewed as indicative of a genuinely subversive set of challenges to normative monogamous heterosexuality, which could be enjoyed vicariously by Blackpool's working-class audiences, and constituted an alternative brand of Britishness, a celebration of excess and 'otherness', which was able to flourish in the liminal interlude of the popular seaside holiday.[24]

Blackpool was certainly conducive to a distinctively British brand of sexual humour, expressed most obviously through comic postcards, although the firm most strongly associated with their manufacture and distribution was based in Holmfirth, West Yorkshire, and any claim to a British monopoly on the humour of postcard innuendo would have to reckon with the parallel developments in Belgium.[25] Blackpool challenged expectations about gender, power and domestic authority through the conspicuous and legendary figure of the landlady, presiding assertively over her boarding-house and dominating husband and guests alike; although this challenge brought its own response through the debunking humour of sketches in comic papers, music-hall gags and indeed the postcards themselves.[26] But the authoritarianism ascribed to the landlady was also a protective response to what some saw as the rampant sexuality of the Blackpool holiday: the antithesis of more orthodox, privileged Britishness ('No sex, please . . .') and, of course, a contested image which is almost impossible to pin down. Anthony Burgess' recollections of Blackpool in the 1930s had even boarding-house life seething with sex, although he and the maid with whom he dallied were shamed and (in her case) sacked when caught.[27] The Blackpool interviewees for Stephen Humphries' *A secret world of sex* offered broadly supportive reminiscences, but may have gilded the lily. Mass-Observation's efforts to test the validity of the already well-established assumption that Blackpool was a hotbed of cheerful promiscuity came to disappointingly foggy conclusions, though by an enjoyably ludicrous route. How far innuendo (as in George Formby's memorable 'Little stick of Blackpool rock') was matched by action must remain inscrutable; but Blackpool's version of Britishness, as it developed from the inter-war years, contained a much stronger dose of active sexuality than most, and this was to be developed further in the late twentieth century as the resort catered for 'stag' and 'hen' parties as well as for the pink pound. As Club 18–30 and the rise of the Ibiza scene showed, sex and British identity could be willing bedfellows, especially at a youthful and popular level. Blackpool was in at the beginning of this development as a twentieth-century phenomenon.[28]

All these incarnations of Blackpool's alternative Britishnesses swirled like a kaleidoscope, shifted over time and varied within the resort, just as they would be different at any given time within Southend or Hastings or (later) Benidorm or Torremolinos.[29] Cutting across them are the differing dimensions, within the greater 'Britishness', within which identities express themselves in terms of geography, class and lifestyle. We now try to make provisional sense of all this by charting Blackpool's changing and varying incarnations and orientations over time.

It remains important that Blackpool's first dominant resort identity was provincial and middle-class. Until the mid-nineteenth century its visitors came overwhelmingly from the northern, and especially the Lancashire, middle classes: people whose increasingly pivotal role in an emergent world economy did not require them to have a broader cultural outlook beyond the advancement of free trade as practically a secular religion, the active propagation of which was left to the leaders of the Anti-Corn Law League. What they sought and celebrated was the emergent Northern English version of the sublime in a seaside setting (the tumbling sea, great open spaces with ranges of hills on the skyline, sumptuous sunsets), rather than the softer southern version of the picturesque. This would require a separate essay to pin down in practice, and what mattered more was the unpretentious sociability of one's peers and the pursuit of health through the accessible rituals of sea-bathing and airy promenading. In these beginnings, Blackpool's separate identity was of little weight, and what it represented was confined to the local and regional stages, despite the stirrings of international economic upheaval in its hinterland.[30]

It was in the early railway age (Blackpool's first station opened in 1846) that the developing town became visible as the playground of the world's first industrial working class. As their numbers swelled, their economic importance increased and their familiarity with surroundings and expectations gave them enhanced social competence in the eyes of their 'betters', while local government took a tighter grip, so external commentary on their behaviour shifted in tone. Early and mid-Victorian perceptions, from developers and respectable tradespeople in the resort as well as censorious outsiders, emphasized inappropriate aspects of the working-class presence, insufficiently civilized, noisy, scruffily dressed, literally unwashed, and generating demand for street vendors and touts who further challenged that combination of genteel refinement and acceptable incarnations of the picturesque that made up the preferred vision of the British seaside resort. The trippers threatened the dominant Britishness of the respectable family, and therefore, until perhaps the 1880s, the resort's economic prosperity. As rising living standards and longer (unpaid) holidays in the late nineteenth century enabled the working-class presence, spread over a season from early July to early September, to dominate the town centre, so it became more acceptable. From being dangerously 'other', noisy savages redolent of the discourse of moral panic associated with the 'slum', with their chokers, clay pipes and tin trumpets, the working-class visitors began to gather praise for their orderly, unthreatening demeanour. The beach stalls and street traders that catered for them began to seem picturesque and distinctive. This transition from fear to celebration was part of a wider process of assimilating the 'respectable' working class (or the working class when it had its respectable head on) into an image of British decency and self-control (shown, for example, in the thrift needed to save for the holiday) that corresponded on the national stage to the reinvention of the private soldier as 'Tommy Atkins'. Strikes and demonstrations might still be another matter, but this was the working class at leisure, and it was increasingly a matter for anthropological amusement rather than fear or dismay. This positive reinvention of the

Lancashire working class at play contrasts with the image of the raffish Cockney or loveable rogue portrayed in *Ally Sloper's Half Holiday*, and the dialect literature of Lancashire and Yorkshire does offer alternative readings which approximate more to this disreputable London/Brighton/Southend representation; but the incorporation of the working-class Blackpool holidaymaker into 'respectable' Britishness was still an important change. Within Blackpool itself, of course, it helped that there were enclaves to north and south in which the 'better classes' could still take refuge.[31]

This integration of the working-class Blackpool visitor into an acceptable set of images of the decent British working man (and, especially here, woman) was consolidated and sustained through the first half of the twentieth century. It reached a climax in the 1930s, when both local and external newspaper accounts celebrated the decency and likeable ordinariness of visitors who were arriving from all over the country, braving early starts and spending hours on the train to enjoy the innocent pleasures that Blackpool had to offer. Journalists and novelists saw the crowd as an organism, a collective entity, marvelling at its placidity and the ease at which a few policemen could keep it in order, and rejoicing in the spectacle of the 'masses' happily at play. The Carnivals of 1923–24 were founded on the local authorities' confidence in these characteristics of the crowd; and the behaviour that allegedly brought about their abandonment fell far short of anything really threatening. Mass-Observation, determined to avoid romanticism, was keener to point up undertones of tolerated drunkenness and back-street sex; and the mid-1930s are also the backdrop for Carolyn Steedman's father's tale of escape from northern commitments to south London, using the Blackpool Tower ballroom and an alleged intrigue with 'the organist's woman' as the confused rationale for his passage through a wormhole from one universe to another. This is tellingly anarchic, and reminds us of other Blackpools; but the dominant image was that of the respectable working class at play, not exactly decorously, but in a relaxed, unchallenging atmosphere of shared democratic enjoyment: the happy holiday multitude, unthreatening because it contained within itself a set of built-in disciplines, controls and timetables.[32]

It was even possible to include Blackpool among the counter-revolutionary influences that sustained the Britishness of political moderation and acceptance of the status quo, which was so self-interestedly peddled as a core element of national character during the inter-war years (and afterwards). The town planner T. H. Mawson quoted an unnamed Lancashire businessman, who was unusually explicit about Blackpool's role: once a year his workpeople 'must either burst out or go to Blackpool; and there they go, and after a fortnight they come back quietened down and ready for work again . . . Blackpool stands between us and revolution. May it long continue as the protector of social order.'[33] Blackpool itself was a bastion of Conservatism, to the extent that even a solitary Labour councillor was seen as unnatural; and local working-class solidarity in support of the General Strike had no echoes at the ballot box.[34] The town and all it stood for was attacked, from the 1890s onwards, by representatives of the alternative Britishness that exalted the romantic socialisms of the Ruskin of *Unto this last*, William Morris and the Clarion Cycling Clubs. If true Britishness was to be found in an idealized countryside, in a dream of egalitarian smallholdings and the arduous joys of 'back to the land', then Blackpool's commercialized democracy of manufactured leisure seemed a corrupting and distracting sham. Indeed, it became an 'other' against which this self-consciously virtuous alternative British identity could see itself in sharp relief.[35]

This remained a minority position, easily represented as snobbish and out of touch. Middle-class, 'middlebrow' and 'highbrow' takes on Blackpool tended rather to adopt postures between the condescending and the contemptuous, while accepting that it represented an acceptable if not a laudable phase of popular Britishness, which improved education and the Reithian BBC might eventually render outmoded. But the post-war years, when paid holidays were newly available across the board, opened the existing Blackpool menu to practically the whole of the working class, right across the spectrum of age and skills, and still sharing the mobile democracy of public transport as romanticized for the 1930s by Mass-Observation and for the 1950s by Richard Hoggart.[36]

This was not 'mass' holidaymaking, despite huge numbers and strongly-defined traffic flows, and despite widely-shared tastes in (for example) films, dancing and humour, and widely-shared constraints of time and destination. It cries out for deconstruction. Individual holidaymakers and families chose in widely divergent ways from the menu on offer, interacted with the shows according to personal perceptions and preferences, and were capable of rejecting or being indifferent to particular offerings. Frank Randle, for example, a comedian whose humour was very much of its place and time, did not 'travel' beyond Lancashire in his cinematic incarnation, but attracted ecstatic (and tolerant) audiences of his own people to a show that invariably challenged a wide range of taboos.[37] And Blackpool's own identity, as opposed to that of its visitors (invariably the basis for the generalizations), was flickering and elusive: it still had a considerable middle-class presence, whose numbers were increasing as residential retirement and commuter Blackpool continued to spread; its footloose show-business population, including a noticeable Jewish presence, added strong and distinctive flavours which could easily be stigmatized as unBritish (there are overtones of this in D. L. Murray's novel *Leading Lady*); and its own working and small business classes were migrant, drifting and had difficulty in sustaining a shared voice or even accent. There were always fragmentations and tensions.[38]

This was exacerbated in the last third of the twentieth century, when the consensus about the virtuous, unified Britishness of Blackpool's working-class visitors was shattered by interrelated transformations. As Albert Gregory, whose photographs of Blackpool in the 1960s juxtapose the generations so tellingly, commented:

> A new era was in the making, an era centred on youth. The innocence which had accompanied the earlier part of the '60s was blown away on the winds of change, which brought a certain sound from the Cavern in Liverpool. Inhibitions were breaking down and a permissiveness and sexual freedom were starting to emerge and although everything took a little longer to reach the North, the signs were evident; young lovers felt free to kiss and cuddle in broad daylight on the beach and teenagers assumed a dominant role of their own.[39]

This could be criticized, using arguments which (perhaps) locate the war as alternative watershed, or look back to Blackpool's earlier reputation, or pick out the Teddy Boys rather than the Beatles as the key markers in the emergence of a new youth culture. But there was a marked divergence of the new, separate youth culture from the shared enjoyments of earlier generations, and this combined with additional changes that threatened Blackpool's older versions of Britishness, eventually displacing its identification with the decent working class on well-earned holiday, and introducing a pathological reading of the resort which, however, remained compatible with adaptability to new markets and continuing success in pulling in enormous numbers of visitors. Most of the locally-based entertainment companies of the late nineteenth century, including the Tower and the Winter Gardens, were taken over by metropolitan and then multi-national conglomerates, and Blackpool's identity as innovative centre of a British live entertainment industry was undermined by competition from television (radio on its own had helped it, by stimulating the desire to see invisible performers in the flesh). The winter poverty endemic in seaside resorts became visible during the season, occupying central bedsitters cheek by jowl with cheap holiday accommodation in declining Victorian streets, and attracting tabloid labels such as 'Costa del Dole', and moral panics (with some statistical backing) about drugs and crime. Above all, the visiting public came to seem less innocent and more unattractive, as the old working class and its (by now) traditional town holidays crumbled under the impact of decline in manufacturing employment and economic restructuring, and competition from new destinations in south-west England (importantly) and abroad made inroads into all but the oldest and most conservative of the established visiting publics. As with other old-established resorts, Blackpool's visiting public came to seem deeply unfashionable, identified with poverty, old age, cheapness, distended stomachs and the unflattering and ephemeral clothing fads of the discount stores. A new discourse of revulsion and disgust began in the 1970s and was making rapid headway at the end of the century. These were attributes no positive vision of Britishness would want to claim.[40]

And yet there were two sides to this coin. Blackpool might have seen its traditional dimensions of Britishness eroded (without being terminated), but it was also responding positively to the diversity of the new post-industrial Britain. The subaltern and the marginal (fittingly) were making their presence felt, and indeed celebrating it on film, although aiming at segmented rather than mass audiences. Thus Blackpool's gay identity emerged into the limelight of the late twentieth century, enjoying the kitsch aspects of the town's dated popular holiday trappings (including bingo), which it was now beginning to exploit. Here Basil Newby, a landlady's son, gave a new twist to older celebrations of the British virtues of the self-made local man, in the context of a Blackpool entertainment industry in which precursors like W. H. Cocker and John Bickerstaffe had received conventional homage in the local media. Exclusively gay or gay-friendly boarding-houses gave new life to Victorian back streets, especially at the North Shore, and a clutch of films responded to these developments and gave them further impetus. By the end of the century this was becoming an increasingly affluent and international scene, featuring (especially) American and Dutch visitors. At the other end of the spectrum British Asians, especially from the (by the 1970s) former 'cotton towns' of Lancashire which had been Blackpool's original suppliers of working-class visitors, were visibly augmenting the holiday throng: elements of what had been (from a metropolitan viewpoint) the exotic periphery of Empire, the objects of the tourist gaze as represented in shows depicting the far-flung 'other', were now themselves the customers of a leisure environment which had always looked exotic in itself to London journalists and was increasingly peripheral in most discourses. The film *Bhaji on the beach* (1993) celebrated this in relation to Hindu women from Birmingham, with fantasies appropriate to the enterprise. Attempts were also being made to attract visitors from beyond Britain; but the

Irish Republic was the most prolific source, supplemented by the international gay contingent and (allegedly) by gamblers from the Gulf. Blackpool as a place of residence and business remained inhospitable (or unattractive) to the British Asian and Afro-Caribbean populations who had rooted themselves in the town's old hinterland, despite the arrival of Jews and Italians in earlier generations. Blackpool did respond to the cosmopolitanism of the new Britain; but only up to a point.[41]

Blackpool in the late twentieth century was thus embracing new kinds of Britishness, if rather uneasily, while important parts of its economy continued to depend on older working-class versions of provincial Britishness which arouse an uneasy mixture of nostalgia, condescension and dismay among contemporary media commentators. Its politics are problematic, too: how far has it really moved from Baldwinite Toryism (the abrasively Thatcherite variety associated with Coronation Street's Mike rather than the misleadingly avuncular inter-war 'One Nation' image projected by or attributed to Stanley) to the embrace of New Labour? How far would it need to move? Pubs, night clubs and hen parties bridge these cultures, bringing together an affluent international gay market with a keen sense of kitsch and irony, and a more literal-minded new generation drawn from the old visiting public, but familiar with Ibiza and the Greek islands as well as Talbot Road. As we take a section through Blackpool's resort identity over the last century or so, however, we find recurrent problems in pinning down the identities which might be attached to it or to which it might be made to correspond: Lancashire, northern English, British, working-class. These are compounded by the declining role of the sea itself, both in Blackpool's presentation of itself and in images of British nationhood; but there is nothing new about Blackpool's amorphousness/polymorphousness. New Blackpool is, in fact, as complex a phenomenon as new Britain, and examination of its complexities provides a useful window on to the wider society, especially that great majority for whom it is the metropolis that is remote, daunting and 'other'.

Notes

1 J. K. Walton, *The British Seaside: Holidays and Resorts in the Twentieth Century* (Manchester, 2000); Nigel Morgan and Annette Pritchard, *Power and Politics at the Seaside* (Exeter, 1999).

2 P. J. Waller (ed.), *The English Urban Landscape* (Oxford, 2000), pp. 274–7.

3 Linda Colley, *Britons* (New Haven, 1992); John M. Mackenzie, *Propaganda and Empire* (Manchester, 1984).

4 Walton, *British Seaside*, p. 198.

5 Ibid., pp. 1–26. F. Inglis, *The Delicious History of the Holiday* (London, 2000), chapter 3, is very untrustworthy on historical interpretation and detail.

6 R. Shields, *Places on the margin* (London, 1991), chapter 2; Clifford Musgrave, *Life in Brighton* (London, 1970), part II and p. 421.

7 J. K. Walton and J. Smith, 'The first century of beach tourism in Spain: San Sebastián and the "playas del norte", from the 1830s to the 1930s', in M. Barke *et al.* (eds.), *Tourism in Spain: Critical Perspectives* (Wallingford, 1996), pp. 35–61; J. K. Walton, '"The Queen of the Beaches": Ostend and the British, from the 1890s to the 1930s', *History Today* 51(8), August 2001, pp. 25–31; and information about North Berwick from a conversation with Professor Christopher Harvie.

8 J. V. N. Soane, *Fashionable resort regions: their evolution and transformation* (Wallingford, 1993); J. B. Priestley, *English journey* (London, 1934), p. 267.

9 Shields, *Places on the Margin*; Musgrave, *Life in Brighton*, pp. 430–7; K. Meethan, 'Place, image and power: Brighton as a resort', in T. Selwyn (ed.), *The Tourist Image: Myths and Myth Making in Tourism* (Chichester, 1996); Evelyn Waugh, *Vile Bodies* (London, first published 1930).

10 For 'social tone', see H. J. Perkin, 'The "social tone" of Victorian seaside resorts in the North-West', *Northern History* 12 (1976 for 1975), pp. 180–94; L. Chase, 'The creation of place image in inter-war Clacton and Frinton', Ph.D. thesis, University of Essex, 1999.

11 William Holt, 'I watch the North on holiday', *Daily Dispatch*, 3 August 1934.

12 J. K. Walton, *The English Seaside Resort: A Social History 1750–1914* (Leicester, 1983), chapter 8.

13 J. K. Walton, *Blackpool* (Edinburgh, 1998), chapter 7; Jeffrey Richards, *Films and British National Identity: From Dickens to Dad's Army* (Manchester, 1997), p. 258; G. Cross, *Worktowners at Blackpool* (London, 1990); Geoffrey Moorhouse, *Hell's Foundations: A Town, its Myths and Gallipoli* (London, 1992).

14 Walton, *Blackpool*, chapter 6.

15 William Holt, 'Under the night lights of Paris', *Daily Dispatch*, 27 August 1934; P. Joyce, *Visions of the People* (Cambridge, 1991), pp. 165–71; J. K. Walton, 'Tradition and tourism: representing Basque identities in San Sebastian and its province, 1848–1936', in N. Kirk (ed.), *Northern Identities* (Aldershot, 2000), p. 87.

16 Charles Graves, *And the Greeks* (London, 1930), pp. 189–91.

17 Tony Bennett, 'Hegemony, ideology, pleasure: Blackpool', in T. Bennett, C. Mercer and J. Woollacott (eds.), *Popular Culture and Social Relations* (Milton Keynes, 1986), pp. 135–54.

18 P. Bennett, *A Century of Fun* (Blackpool, 1996), chapter 2; J. F. Kasson, *Amusing the Million: Coney Island at the Turn of the Century* (New York, 1978).

19 Priestley, *English Journey*, p. 267.

20 Cross, *Worktowners*, p. 134 and passim; Bill Bryson, *Notes From a Small Island* (London, 1995), pp. 268–9.

21 *Guardian*, 18 July 2001, p. 9; *West Lancashire Evening Gazette*, 9 May 2002, pp. 10–11.

22 J. K. Walton, 'Popular entertainment and public order: the Blackpool Carnivals of 1923–4', *Northern History* 34 (1998), pp. 170–88; Jeff Nuttall, *King Twist* (London, 1978); Walton, 'Ostend and the British'.

23 Cross, *Worktowners*; Walton, *Blackpool*, pp. 88–96; Mackenzie, *Propaganda and Empire*.

24 Cross, *Worktowners*; Nuttall, *King Twist*; Roy Fuller, *Souvenirs* (London, 1980), pp. 164–5.

25 Benny Green, *I've Lost my little Willie: A Celebration of Comic Postcards* (London, 1976); P. Florizoone, *James Ensor: les bains à Ostende* (Brussels, 1996), p. 19.

26 J. K. Walton, *The Blackpool Landlady: A Social History* (Manchester, 1978), pp. 1–12.

27 Anthony Burgess, *Little Wilson and Big God* (London: Penguin edn., 1988), pp. 126–34.

28 S. Humphries, *A Secret World of Sex* (London, 1989); Cross, *Worktowners*.

29 Charles Wilson, *Benidorm: The Truth* (Valencia, 2000); Harry Ritchie, *Here We Go: A Summer on the Costa del Sol* (London, 1993).

30 Walton, *Blackpool*, pp. 14–19; J. K. Walton, *Lancashire: 1558–1939* (Manchester, 1987), chapters 6 and 7.

31 Walton, *Blackpool*, chapter 4; Walton, *Blackpool Landlady*, chapter 7; A. Mayne, *The Imagined Slum* (Leicester, 1993); Peter Bailey, *Popular Culture and Performance in the Victorian city* (Cambridge, 1998), chapters 2 and 3.

32 James Laver, 'Blackpool', in Yvonne Cloud (ed.), *Beside the Seaside* (London, 1934), pp. 148–84; Carolyn Steedman, *Landscape for a Good Woman* (London, 1986), pp. 51–2; Walton, *Blackpool*, pp. 122–3; Walton, 'Popular entertainment and public order'; Cross, *Worktowners*, p. 236.

33 T. H. Mawson, *The Life and Work of an English Landscape Architect* (London, 1927), p. 344.

34 Walton, *Blackpool*, pp. 114–16.

35 Harvey Taylor, *A Claim on the Countryside* (Edinburgh, 1997).

36 Cross, *Worktowners*, pp. 55–62, 226–7; R. Hoggart, *The Uses of Literacy* (London, 1957); Walton, *British Seaside*, pp. 58–63, 83–5.

37 Nuttall, *King Twist*; Jeffrey Richards, *Stars in our eyes* (Preston, 1994), pp. 22–32.

38 D.L. Murray, *Leading Lady* (London, 1947); Fuller, *Souvenirs*, pp. 91–2.

39 Alfred Gregory, *Blackpool: A Celebration of the '60s* (London, 1993), p. 22.

40 J. Demetriadi, 'The golden years: English seaside resorts 1950–1974', in G. Shaw and A. Williams (eds.), *The Rise and Fall of British Coastal Resorts* (London, 1997), pp. 49–74; J. Urry, 'Cultural change and the seaside resort', in Shaw and Williams (eds.) *The Rise and Fall*, pp. 102–13; Walton, *Blackpool*, pp. 152–61.

41 Walton, *Blackpool*, Chapters 1 and 6. For an (ultimately) optimistic presentation of a recognizably working-class and 'national' Blackpool, bringing together London-ers, 'scousers' and 'Brummies' (at one point very literally and thoroughly), see John King, *The Football Factory Trilogy* (London, 2000), pp. 413–29.

4

Family, social class and politics in the films of Mike Leigh

Ewa Mazierska

In this chapter I will consider how social class and family life are portrayed in three films by Mike Leigh: *Meantime* (1983), *High Hopes* (1988) and *Secrets and Lies* (1995). By discussing the issues of class and family I attempt to engage with the problem of English identity and more precisely, with the question of its fragmentation and 'relocation' during the 1980s and 1990s. The premise of my discussion is the assumption that the discourse on nation cannot be separated from several others, including that on class. Moreover, it is often argued that in the case of Englishness the connection between nationhood and class is particularly strong, as frequent attempts have been made to equate 'national way of life' with that of a particular class. Jon Cook refers to the idea that there exists (or existed, as it is often consigned to the past when presented in print) a specifically English working class, an epitome of an important reading of Englishness.[1] Cook regards this as only one of many possible approaches to defining an English nation, moreover one beset by numerous difficulties. Nevertheless, he regards it as an important national myth whose very endurance deserves attention. Through my reading of Leigh's films as portrayals of England during the 1980s and 1990s I will assess the viability of attempts to sustain the myth that equates working class with Englishness.

This period covers some momentous changes in English (and British) history, driven primarily by Thatcherism, including a shift from Fordism and Keynesian social democracy to post-Fordism and monetarism, as well as a decline of socialism and the birth of the 'third way' as the dominant ideology of the re-formed Labour Party. It appears that in the 1980s the importance of class decreased in official, political discourse, while that of family increased. The ideologists and politicians representing the New Right, which in the 1980s dominated political thought both in the UK and in the United States, including Margaret Thatcher herself, often talked about policies which should serve 'individuals and their families', as opposed to particular classes.[2] Similarly, New Labour openly distanced itself from the problems of class, suggesting that the old class divisions do not matter any more and claiming to construct political programmes which serve all sections of society equally.[3] This was empty rhetoric. For example, Thatcher's policies were no less class oriented than those of her predecessors (if not more so) and the majority of them had a detrimental effect on families, even if one takes into account the narrow and moralistic definition of 'family' favoured by Tory politicians, as a unit consisting of a married couple with children.[4]

Mike Leigh is renowned for his preoccupation with and sensitive rendering of both class and family life. His films are labelled 'small time dramas', set amongst the members of one or two families living on the same suburban street or housing estate, and mostly lacking sensational events, instead showing, as Michael Coveney puts it, 'pop-up toasters and cups of tea, fake-fur coats and rugs, pink bobble carpet slippers, bad haircuts and domestic arguments on leatherette sofas'.[5] Andy Medhurst adds that Leigh's favourite area of exploration is 'that fractious, disputed zone where upper-working-class meets lower-middle'.[6] Although Leigh utilizes such non-realistic devices as caricature and irony, when his films are discussed critics typically emphasize presentation rather than representation. They concentrate on what the director shows us, rather than the ideology he conveys in his films, generally praising his ability to depict the lives of ordinary English men and women as they really are.[7] For example, Andy Medhurst confesses: 'When it comes to making moving (in both senses of the word) pictures that evoke the horrors and humours of being English over the last 20 years, Mike's my boy.'[8]

I disagree with the view that Leigh's films simply show 'English people as they really are', believing that, as Claire Johnston puts it, 'there is no such thing as unmanipulated writing, filming or broadcasting'.[9] Accordingly, I will suggest that by representing certain people in a certain way, they convey a distinctive ideology drawn from the British Left, particularly that part of the Left which is represented by and identified with the Labour Party. I chose *Meantime*, *High Hopes* and *Secrets and Lies*, in preference to other contemporary Leigh films such as *Life Is Sweet* (1990) and *Naked* (1993), because here the issues of class and family are brought to the fore. Moreover, characters in these films are constructed in a similar way (with two related families at the centre of the story) and they follow a similar narrative structure (with a family crisis at the end). Comparing shifting representations of people, placed in the same position on Leigh's 'map' of families and social classes, will be the main method of establishing the shifts in message conveyed in the films.

The central characters in *Meantime* are two sisters, Barbara Lane and Mavis Pollock, who live in different parts of London. Barbara went to university and used to work in a bank, and now lives with her husband in a neat, middle-class, West London suburban semi. Her sister Mavis, an uneducated housewife, shares a council flat on a housing estate in the East End with an unemployed husband and two jobless adult sons. The film starts at the end of a visit by the Pollocks to the Lanes. The atmosphere is awkward; the families barely talk, as the brothers-in-law detest each other. Moreover, Mavis criticizes her sons, Colin and Mark, for not 'behaving themselves' and bringing mud into the house. In Mark's case his behaviour expresses mild rebellion against the middle-class values of Barbara and her husband, John, while myopic and slow-witted Colin is simply clumsy. The Pollocks have no car, and John drives them home. The tenement blocks on their housing estate look shabby and dilapidated, with litter blown everywhere and colourless, anaemic grass on the public square. Not far from the Pollocks' house bulldozers destroy some blocks, described by a council worker as 'development work'.[10] What the Lanes' and Pollocks' estates have in common is their anonymity, greyness and marginality. The same melancholic atmosphere can be found in their respective homes, which are dominated by browns and faded greens. On one occasion Barbara even comments that her bedroom is 'depressing'. The only difference lies in the age and quality of the furniture and wallpaper – in the Pollocks' home everything, from the windows to the washing-machine, is either old or poor quality; the greyness of the Lanes' house, complete with an L. S. Lowry print, seems to result primarily from their inability to break the suburban norm.

Most of the film is filled with images of the Pollocks' life on the dole, with occasional cuts to the Lanes' house. The Pollocks' lives consist of queuing for unemployment benefit, the menfolk occasionally visiting their local pub and Mavis playing bingo, and most of the time they all watch television. Lack of money and an abundance of time, exacerbated by 'natural disasters', such as the breakdown of their new washing machine, lead to frustration, aggression and low self-esteem. Leigh's representation of the psychology of the unemployed perfectly conforms with the diagnosis provided by sociologists researching this problem. For example, David Ashton writes: 'In the absence of work, time becomes a problem, because alternative ways of structuring it have to be devised . . . Mental health suffers as the stress of daily living increases.'[11]

Mavis and Frank feel uncomfortable in the presence of Barbara and John, revealed in the nervous way in which Mavis takes a cigarette whenever Barbara says something which hints at the difference in their material status and lifestyles. Yet Mavis, feeling ashamed about her situation and being less articulate than her sister, never talks back to her. Barbara's attitude to her sister's family is somehow ambivalent. On one hand, she is sympathetic to their hardship and takes their side in arguments with her husband, who is very critical of the Pollocks. On the other hand, she is exasperated by their passivity and disregard for their material surroundings, in a way which is reminiscent of Tory politicians who tended to regard the British underclass as victims of their own laziness and lack of enterprise.[12] Barbara ridicules Mavis's addiction to bingo, reproaches the Pollocks for 'living in squalor', and forbids her sister from touching her immaculate kitchen. Her greatest sympathy is for Colin, and her desire to help him manifests itself in an offer to pay him for renovating their bedroom, which arouses no enthusiasm among the Pollocks. Frank regards the wages Barbara offers as miserly and Mavis points out the danger of Colin losing his unemployment benefit, if anybody finds out about the job. Mark is the most critical, regarding Barbara's proposal as insulting not only to Colin, but to the whole family. 'Charity, as Mark knows, is hard enough to take from the servants of the Crown, let alone from one's own family', explains John Pym.[13] Yet Colin accepts Barbara's offer and visits her in her suburban home, only to be dissuaded by his brother, who also finds his way to the Lanes' house.

Mark regards Barbara as patronizing, but it is he who treats her with superior disdain, rather than the other way round, mocking his aunt's posh accent and self-contentment and jokingly comparing her to Princess Anne. Mark suggests that, by moving up the social ladder, Barbara has betrayed her family and even her true identity. He also reproaches Barbara for her childlessness, implicitly assuming that (in contrast to her sister) she did not fulfil her potential as a woman. Again, it seems as if Barbara herself accepts this analysis, through her quasi-maternal interest in Colin and her embarrassment when Mark questions her childlessness. Mark's attitude to Barbara is strongly reminiscent of British 'New Wave' films, in which the cruel attitude of a working-class lad to an older, middle-class woman was often regarded as a sign of his angry rebellion against materialistic society.[14] Although we do not see Barbara spending any money on herself, and her style in clothes and interior design is rather modest and dull, the Pollocks accuse her of extravagance. Her employment in a bank, on which she reminisces with pride, is presented as symbolic of her supposed love of money.

The Lanes lead an isolated life, in tune with the grey melancholy of their suburb. We do not see them chatting with neighbours, and the only connection outside the family they mention in conversation is a party they organized for John's boss and his wife. Barbara does not like them, and it is suggested the relationship is based on John's professional interest rather than genuine friend-ship. Even more striking, considering that the term 'community' in English academic language has been so closely associated with 'working-class', is the fact that the Pollocks seem to be almost as isolated as the Lanes, lacking virtually any connections with people in a similar position to their own. We never see Frank meeting his old work pals, or Mavis chatting with the neighbours. Even in the local pub or the bingo hall they sit by themselves and make no attempt to communicate with other customers. They might belong to the working class, understood as an abstract group of people, sharing the same cultural background or even have a working-class consciousness, but they are aloof from any actual working-class community.

Terry Lovell, referring to the famous socio-ethnographic texts of the 1950s, *The Uses of Literacy* (1957) by Richard Hoggart and *Culture and Society* (1958) by Raymond Williams, comments on the shift in British working-class culture, which they perceive as taking place between the 1930s and the 1950s:

> Traditional working-class culture, as characterized by writers such as Hoggart, was forged out of material hardship in communities where the individual's most valu-able resources were collective: family, community, and a shared culture of resist-ance and mutual support . . . As families were moved out of the inner city slums into new housing estates which isolated them, the ties of community were, it was feared, being broken.[15]

The proponents of the 'affluent worker' or working-class embourgeoisement thesis hold similar views, arguing that from the 1950s the bulk of the working class in the 'First World' has enjoyed middle-class living standards, which has far-reaching implications for working class culture. As the working class has ceased to be distinctive in terms of its economic position, so its distinctiveness as a cultural entity is also steadily diminished.[16] Yet, the empirical research done in the 1950s and 1960s by such authors as Goldthorpe *et al.*, and Michael Young and Peter Willmott (who conducted their investigation in East London, where *Meantime* is also set), undermines the embourgeoisement thesis and the claim that by the 1950s distinctively working-class lifestyles and traditions had disappeared in England. Goldthorpe writes: 'Our findings show that in the case of the workers we studied there remain important areas of common social experience which are still fairly distinctively working-class; that specifically middle-class social norms are not widely followed nor middle-class life-styles consciously emulated; and that assimilation into middle-class society is not . . . a desired objective.'[17] Young and Willmott argue that com-munal life, based on kinship, living in physical proximity and sharing a common past was the norm amongst working people in London's Bethnal Green in the middle of the 1950s.[18]

Contemporary films endorse these views. For example, in contrast with *Meantime*, the characters in films belonging to the British New Wave, as well as in the early episodes of the British soap opera, *Coronation Street* (1960–), on which Lovell comments, still have a significant sense of community.[19] Most importantly, they work together and play together. There is no doubt that the crucial factor in the Pollocks' isolation from people of similar socio-cultural background is their unemployment, which was the most obvious and painful consequence of the monetarist policies introduced by Thatcher's government, and the onslaught on institutions representing the workers, particularly trade unions.[20] Those in work would meet more people in a similar position and have greater opportunity to develop an after-work social life. Leigh also hints at additional factors that reduce the Pollocks' opportunities for participation in public social life, such as the high cost of out-of-home entertainment and expensive and inadequate public transport (tube fares forms a substantial part of the 'wage package' that Barbara offers Colin). Having no car and unable to pay the tube fares, the Pollocks are condemned to stay in their own neighbourhood. These factors, as Franco Bianchini and Hermann Schwengel note, were direct or indirect consequences of Thatcherite urban policies.[21] Paradoxically, although inevitably, the young Pollocks, who have never worked, but spent their lives on the housing estate, have more of a social life than their parents. Never having had a respectable, working life, they are also probably less ashamed to share their misery with people in a similar position. Their principal friend, a skinhead named Coxy, is an even more disaffected, angry young man than Mark.[22]

Against the background of the Pollocks' distance from their own social class, the family ties, although deeply unsatisfactory, are relatively firm and genuine. The family seems to be the only institution that remains when working-class people lose their social bonds and the focal point of their old class culture. In this respect Leigh differs strongly from Ken Loach (with whom he is often compared), who in his films expresses an opinion that family life is the first casualty when the material conditions of working-class people worsen, and suggests that the breakdown of the working-class community typically parallels the disintegration of working-class families.[23] Leigh shows how the fiasco of renovating Barbara's house brings the Pollocks closer together, or at least facilitates their communication. After the incident, Colin, known to everyone as 'Muppet' or 'Kermit', resolves to speak out and stand up for himself, thus gaining some respect from his parents and his brother. Paradoxically, at the same time as criticising Thatcherism for creating a situation in which the old connections and loyalties are destroyed, and families become divided, Leigh, as John Hill observes, conforms to Thatcher's often repeated view that 'there is no such thing as society, but only men, women and families'.[24]

Although Leigh is far from glorifying the working class in *Meantime*, his film gives an impression that the working-class family is more cohesive and genuine than its middle-class counterpart. The Lanes lack children and love, they share no common interests, they do not even watch television together or read the same newspapers, as the Pollocks do; it feels as if being together only increases Barbara and John's solitude and alienation.

Class and financial differences in *Meantime* create psychological and ideological barriers between family members. Guilt on the part of well-off, gentrified and successful Barbara, and shame and envy in the Pollocks, make communication between them increasingly difficult, in spite of continuous attempts to build bridges. In *High Hopes* ideological and psychological differences between members of the family lead to class/financial divisions between them, rather than the other way round. *High Hopes* was made in 1988, five years after *Meantime*; and Leigh acknowledges, poignantly, the differences between these moments. In particular, in 1988 it became clear that Thatcherite policy had produced an economic polarization of British society unknown since the end of the Second World War.[25] The principal winner in the Thatcherite revolution became the private sector, especially in the south-east of England; the losers were the working classes and those employed in the state sector. There was also a shift in public opinion and official ideology, promoting individual consumption and egoism as principal vehicles to ensure economic growth and the country's wealth.

At the centre of Leigh's narrative is a couple in their thirties, Cyril and Shirley. Cyril is from a working-class background; his widowed mother, Mrs Bender, is the last council tenant on a street, which became 'gentrified' as a result of the sell-off of all the other houses to private owners.[26] The absence of working-class people amongst Mrs Bender's neighbours is a powerful symbol of the marginalization and transformation of the working class during the Thatcher years. Cyril works as a despatch rider, delivering parcels on his motorcycle, while Shirley works for the council as a gardener. Leigh suggests that it is due to their socialist principles, rather than lack of education or resourcefulness, that their flat is modest, they own no car and have what seem to most people like lowly occupations. This high moral position is particularly espoused by Cyril, an ardent admirer of Marx, whose principal dream is, as he puts it, to live in 'a world in which everyone has enough to eat, a place to live, a job'. Cyril somehow assumes that his noble objective will be jeopardized by any attempt he makes to climb the social ladder. Although not expressed overtly, this conviction is congruent with the changes that took place during Thatcher's 'reign', when the social advancement of some sections of British society was accompanied by the relative impoverishment of millions of others.[27]

If it were not for their worries about the starving millions all over the world (the root of Cyril's unwillingness to have children) and their disappointment at the state of British society under Thatcher, Cyril and Shirley could be described as a model happy couple. They like their jobs, which suit their characters and interests. It amuses Cyril to visit the tall, claustrophobic offices of banks and business corporations, where people live in constant stress and hurry and have no time to look at each other. For Shirley, who loves flowers and plants, her work is an extension of her hobby. Moreover, in spite of living together for ten years, they still show each other affection and enjoy each other's humour. Gilbert Adair describes Cyril and Shirley as 'one of the most poignantly loving couples . . . that our cinema has produced'.[28] Cyril and Shirley also try to live up to their social-ist values in their relations with others. The clearest testimony to their selfless-ness is the shelter they provide for a complete stranger, Wayne, an unemployed young man who came to London looking for his sister and got lost. They also care for Cyril's ageing and increasingly demented mother, Mrs Bender.

Leigh contrasts Cyril and Shirley with Valerie Burke, Cyril's sister, and her husband Martin. They are well-off thanks to Martin's business as a 'Burger Bar' owner and second-hand car salesman – a byword for unscrupulousness (and the 'profession' of one of the most unpleasant characters in British New Wave cinema, Peter in Tony Richardson's *A Taste of Honey*, 1961). Valerie is a house-wife who spends her days shopping, doing aerobics and looking after her Afghan hound. They have two cars, one a Mercedes, and live in a spacious, detached, tastelessly embellished house in an affluent London suburb. Even their house number is lit in neon. Valerie and Martin represent a very different set of values to those of Cyril and Shirley. They are hedonistic, selfish and greedy to the point of caricature. Martin's idea of work is 'to have people work-ing for you and you only collect the dosh'. The Burkes are obsessed with sex. Valerie wants her husband to emulate in bed the style of Michael Douglas; Martin, on the other hand, prefers to indulge in extra-marital affairs. They have crude manners and quarrel almost continuously, with Valerie constantly asking her husband for money and Martin complaining about the quality of her cook-ing. They are also insensitive towards Mrs Bender.

Although the Burkes aspire to be middle class, their tasteless furnishings and shiny clothes betray them as upwardly mobile nouveaux riches. This is particularly true of Valerie, who is an uncritical, poor imitator, trying in vain to reproduce the perceived elegance of her mother's rich and snobbish neighbour, Laetitia Boothe-Braine. The result of these attempts is an impression of neurosis and lack of self-confidence. The Burkes' inability to overcome their poor taste recollects the characters in some of Leigh's earlier productions, particularly *Abigail's Party* (1977).[29] However, in *High Hopes* the gulf between the Burkes' 'high-society' ambitions and their flashy lifestyle is much wider. Cyril and Shirley detest Valerie and Martin's values and lifestyle. The ultimate crisis in the relationship between the siblings and their respective families, as well as between Mrs Bender and her daughter, takes place at a birthday party, which Valerie organizes for her mother. The meeting is a scene of multiple discords and embarrassments. Eventually Cyril and Shirley depart, taking Mrs Bender with them, so distressed that she has to spend the night in their flat. This is also a night when Shirley and Cyril make love without using contraception. After the fiasco of the family gathering at the Burkes, family attitudes and feelings eventually triumph: there is a chance that Mrs Bender will move in with Cyril and Shirley and also become a grandmother. As Pym observes, 'Perhaps after all families are worth something; and perhaps in these acquisitive times, and despite the present ascendancy of the appalling Burkes and Boothe-Braines, there are worthwhile duties: the care of the old, the nurture of children.'[30] Yet, it must be emphasized that in *High Hopes* it is only the working-class family that has these noble, redeeming features. The other families are the locus of greed, insensitivity and lack of authenticity.

As in *Meantime* the working class depicted in *High Hopes* is also fragmented, but this has less to do with financial and geographical barriers to communicating with people in a similar situation, than with cultural and ideological differences between members of the working class. Leonard and Barbara Quart observe that Cyril 'is a very marginal, bohemian member of the working class and a very English sort of socialist. His socialism derives more from his moral revulsion with capitalist greed and upper-middle-class living styles than from an adherence to a set of ideological positions.'[31] Indeed, Cyril is too intelligent and sophisticated to identify wholeheartedly with ordinary builders and factory workers. His political perspective bears a resemblance with the early English socialists as presented by Chris Waters.[32] But Cyril's moral radicalism and political detachment can also be identified as a post-1968 phenomenon, when as Stuart Hall observes 'to be "radical" meant ... to be radically against *all* parties, party lines and party bureaucracies'.[33]

Cyril's attitude is exemplified in his and Shirley's relationship with Wayne, the simple man previously mentioned. They care for him, but also cannot hide the fact that they belong to different worlds, that Wayne is a cultural stranger to them. For example, they giggle in bed when Wayne is lying in his sleeping bag in the next room, listening to loud music on his ghetto blaster. Nor does Leigh spare caricature to depict Wayne – his character wears trainers and a sheepskin jacket and walks like a duck. Being slow-witted and clumsy, Wayne resembles Colin in *Meantime*, but does not have the earlier character's dignity. In common with Cyril and Shirley we can pity Wayne, but cannot respect him or identify with him.

Cyril and Shirley also disagree with their radical and politically active neighbour, Suzi. Cyril dismisses her talk about the coming revolution in England, and the need for international cooperation on the left, as pure nonsense. He also accuses Suzi, who plans to have a stall on the market, of hypocrisy – having working-class views, while wanting to live as a small-time capitalist. Moreover, Shirley scorns Suzi for her pro-choice views on abortion. For Shirley, who yearns to have a child herself, abortion means killing an unborn child. Differences in manner of speaking (Suzi's language is driven by Marxist clichés) and body language (she is hyperactive and neurotic) increase the impression that there is little in common between Suzi on the one hand, and Cyril and Shirley on the other. Leigh exploits Suzi's inadequacies to enhance the viewer's identification with Cyril and Shirley. Yet, they do not present any alternative to Suzi's utopia. Cyril admits that he is completely passive himself, doing nothing to change his country or the world; he is not even a trade union member. This might be the consequence of the isolating nature of his job, which is outside the trade union mainstream.[34] Yet Leigh also suggests that joining trade union or a party would not suit Cyril's individualistic taste. On the whole, as in *Meantime*, Leigh shows disapproval and distaste towards the Thatcherite values of individualism, entrepreneurship and greed, without suggesting any viable socio-political alternative to them. Unlike in *Meantime*, however, where passivity was regarded as the main weakness of the working class, in *High Hopes* it is excused, even extolled as virtuous – the attitude of the wise and mature 'Cyrils', who withdraw from an active politics into the space of their own homes. Such an attitude was much more convenient for Thatcher's government than an active resistance against its policies, as shown in the strikes against mine closures, or riots in inner cities against introducing the Poll Tax. Leigh's portrayal of the fragmentation and impotence of the working classes encapsulates the state of the British Left in the second half of the 1980s.[35] Again, albeit in a different way, 'family' in this film proves more cohesive and robust than 'social class' or 'community', seeming to endorse Thatcher's previously quoted claim that society is non-existent, only individuals and families exist.

Viewed against the background of these two films, the 'family portrait' Leigh creates in *Secrets and Lies* is somewhat different, although the class structure changes little. As with *High Hopes*, we see a brother and sister who belong to different social classes. This time the sister, Cynthia, is poor and working-class, while her brother, Maurice, who owns a photographic studio, is affluent. Cynthia is unmarried and lives with her adult daughter Roxanne in a terraced house in a drab part of London, while Maurice lives with his wife Monica in a spacious house in a pleasant suburb and they have no children.

In spite of the similarity in their social status, Maurice has little in common with the cold John in *Meantime* or the primitive and greedy Martin in *High Hopes*. He is sensitive, selfless and caring. For him money is not so much a way to acquire material goods or advance his social status as a way to help those whom he loves and who are in need. Most importantly, he supports his sister and niece financially and offers them practical help. We see him promising to deal with the damp in his sister's house and organizing a birthday party for Roxanne. Maurice also has a different work ethic from the male entrepreneurs in Leigh's earlier films. He does not like to have people working for him while only 'collecting the dosh', as Martin once put it, but as a true craftsman, prefers to perform all the important tasks himself. This way, he claims, he makes sure that his work is of a high standard and his clients are satisfied – something which was of no concern to Martin. It is revealed that when Maurice bought the business from his partner, it was completely run down and it took him years of hard work to make it flourish. Maurice's method of work, marked by discreet and friendly interest in his clients, suggests that he also treats his job as a social service and a means of communication. His assistant, Jane, does not feel exploited in the least. She is happy to work for him and says that she does not know a 'better man than Maurice'. He, on the other hand, treats her not so much as an employee as a member of the family, inviting her to family gatherings. Maurice is played by Timothy Spall, who is associated with the roles of chubby, cuddly and generally good men. Such casting enhances Maurice's credentials as a respectable and friendly businessman.

Monica is also presented in a better light than middle-class women in Leigh's previous films. In common with them, she is a social climber, house-proud, who likes shopping and spending money, but she is also generous, encouraging her husband not to spare any expense for Roxanne's birthday and taking the trouble to prepare a party for her niece. She is also serious and honest, being the only person in the family who is prepared to tell Roxanne that she is not Cynthia's only child, but has a sister, whom Cynthia gave up for adoption. Monica's positive attitude to her niece is particularly worthy of respect, as Roxanne is not her blood relative. Leigh also hints at Monica's other features, which arouse sympathy and solidarity, such as her inability to have children, her menstrual pains and her Scottishness, which makes her an outsider in London.

In contrast to *High Hopes*, in which Leigh treated the work of Cyril and Shirley with attention and even tenderness, and the jobs of middle-class characters were hardly shown at all, only talked about in derogatory terms, in *Secrets and Lies* more attention is paid to the tasks undertaken by the middle-class characters and they are presented in a favourable light, as a valuable service to others. The labour of working-class Cynthia, on a production line in a box factory, and Roxanne, who works for the council as a street sweeper, is portrayed as repetitive, boring and humiliating. Although they are deeply unsatisfied with their situation, unlike the working-class characters in the previous Leigh's films, they do not complain about their circumstances. There is still no sense of working class community or consciousness; neither Cynthia nor Roxanne have any friends amongst their fellow workers, and the notion of politics is completely alien to them. The relationship between Roxanne and her boyfriend seems empty of anything apart from hasty sex. On the whole, the working class is portrayed in this film as a cultural wasteland.

In common with Leigh's other families, there are conflicts between Maurice and Monica on the one hand, and Cynthia and Roxanne on the other, as well as between those who share the same house. For Maurice, visiting Cynthia's dilapidated house, which he once shared with her and their parents, is a source of guilt and embarrassment. Another source of the siblings' discord is Cynthia's dislike of Monica and her suspicion that the feeling is mutual. The reason for Cynthia's antipathy towards her sister-in-law is Monica's apparent selfishness, by which she means her unwillingness to have a child, which according to Cynthia, is a wife's ultimate duty towards her husband. It is worth noting that in the light of Cynthia's own attitude to children, particularly the fact that she gave away her own child for adoption, this stance seems completely unreasonable and only reflects badly on her. In spite of Cynthia's attempts to please her daughter, Roxanne is always very rude to her. This may result from her frustration at having a low-paid, low-status job and a monotonous life, or from deeper misunderstandings. The tensions between Maurice and Monica result from their childlessness, which is a problem over which they have no influence, so they really cannot be blamed for not being able to overcome it. Again, this contrasts with Leigh's previous films, where the problems between the middle-class couple were caused not by their childlessness (although none of them had children), but by their selfishness, disrespect for their partners or promiscuity.

During the course of the film, a new member joins the family – Cynthia's daughter, Hortense, who was given away for adoption and is black. She was brought up by a middle-class family, went to university and now has a good job as an optometrist. Leigh shows us her tasteful and comfortable (although slightly sterile)[36] flat and new car. In contrast with Roxanne, Hortense has good manners and, in common with some characters in Leigh's earlier films, most significantly Cyril in *High Hopes*, she is looking for a deeper meaning in life and searching for her identity; this seems to be the main reason why she contacts Cynthia. Moreover, in contrast to female characters in Leigh's earlier films, Hortense pays little attention to men, exploring her femininity by reading *The Wild Swans* and talking about men with her girlfriend. Hortense is the first black character to have a prominent part in a Leigh film – there were black people in *Meantime* and *High Hopes*, but their roles were intermittent. When I interviewed the director in 1997 and asked him why Cynthia's daughter is black, he answered simply 'Why not?', refusing to discuss any ideological reasons for his decision. It is possible that including a black character was motivated only by his desire to extend the range of his characterizations to reflect a multicultural society. However, this decision perhaps affects the ideology of the film. I suggest that that being black, and thus belonging to a part of British society which generally has a worse economic and social position than the white majority, Hortense is somehow more deserving of being middle-class and well-off than if she were white. Her belonging to the middle class, and perhaps even the very condition of being affluent, appears more agreeable (at least in the eyes of viewers and critics on the Left) as a result of her colour. In common with Maurice, Hortense is also tolerant; although she has many reasons to resent Cynthia, she shows understanding of the circumstances of her adoption. Soon they become close friends and after some time it feels as if Hortense has become Cynthia's favourite daughter. Not only does she find her behaviour more pleasant than that of Roxanne (Hortense takes her out to restaurants and drives her home), but she is also proud of Hortense's material achievements, which she contrasts with the situation in which she and Roxanne live. 'She has a mortgage and everything', she comments.

First Cynthia tries to keep the rediscovery of her lost child a secret, but eventually she decides to introduce Hortense to the family at Roxanne's birthday party. Yet, contrary to *Meantime* and *High Hopes*, where family gatherings end in disaster, after initial anger and recriminations *Secrets and Lies* ends with a family re-union. Maurice and Monica tell Cynthia about their anguish at not having a child, Cynthia reveals to Roxanne who her father was and eventually everybody declares love and devotion. Thus, the old differences are overcome as a result of abandoning secrets and lies and the large family, encompassing Cynthia, Maurice, Monica, Hortense and Roxanne becomes a paradigm of love and cultural unity. In the last scene of the film Hortense and Roxanne sit in their mother's old garden, pondering on finding each other.

In *Secrets and Lies* we find generosity, good manners and a willingness to help going hand in hand with an affluence which itself is a testimony to responsibility, ambition and hard work. On the other hand, there is nothing virtuous in not having money – its absence leads only to frustration, low self-esteem, resentment and selfishness. Lack of money also suggests a certain irresponsibility, self-indulgence and laziness: all of those in *Secrets and Lies* who are poor have demonstrated major weaknesses in their own lives. Cynthia is promiscuous, irresponsible and lazy, symbolized by her overgrown garden and dilapidated outhouse, as well as her repulsive clothes and uncombed hair. Maurice's previous work partner is a lazy and arrogant drunkard, while Roxanne dropped out of school and follows her mother in indulging in hedonistic, promiscuous sex. Such a division of 'vices and virtues' differs from the other films, previously discussed, where prosperity was associated with greed, corruption and disregard for others, and poverty with either being a victim of political circumstances, or with a conscious refusal to participate in the materialistic, individualistic Thatcherite 'dream'.

This moral respectability, associated with money, contrasting with Mike Leigh's earlier films, where money was regarded as the root of social conflict and misery, does not indicate Leigh's endorsement of Thatcherism, but a reflection of new attitudes to individual wealth, characteristic of New Labour. At the time of the film's premiere in summer 1996, John Major's Conservative government was still in power, but New Labour was flourishing, both as an ideological and political reality – the majority of British people supported it and expected it to win the next general election, which happened the following year. Amongst other features, New Labour was already defined by friendliness to business and entrepreneurship, and relatively little respect for the public sector, manual work and trade unions.[37] I argue that, consciously or subconsciously, Leigh embraced this element of the ideology of New Labour, trying to justify and promote it. Moreover, in contrast to the earlier films, in *Secrets and Lies* class does not constitute an insurmountable social barrier. It is secrets and lies, not money and attitudes to wealth, which divide families, making brothers and sisters mutually hostile. Once the secrets are revealed and lies overcome, there is nothing to keep families apart. The differences in wealth can even help to forge friendships, particularly when those who have money want to help their less fortunate relatives. Again, this is very much in tune with the conciliatory vision of society, promoted by New Labour, epitomized by the 'cuddly businessman' who by the very fact of creating wealth helps those at the bottom of the social ladder and society as a whole.

It could be argued that the ideology that Leigh conveyed in the three films discussed here, followed (or was concurrent with) changes in the British Left. It is also worth noting that amongst both film critics and ordinary viewers *Secrets and Lies* has been Mike Leigh's most successful film so far; its appeal was much broader than his previous films, which at best achieved success in arthouse cinemas. The reasons for that might include style and the artistic quality of this film. However, I suggest that one of the main causes of the popularity of *Secrets and Lies* was that in his diagnosis of British society, Leigh captured a popular mood, or more precisely, conveyed a hegemonic ideology[38] in British society.

To sum up my reading of Leigh's films, I will conclude that during the 1980s and 1990s it became impossible to equate working class with Englishness, due to its socio-political fragmentation and marginalization. However, at the same time as revealing the impotence of the working class, Leigh shows that the middle class is also heterogeneous and fragmented. Instead of any coherent groups, we have only individuals and families, more united than ever. Hence, if we are to believe Leigh, Englishness was relocated from class, and its new site became the family.

Notes

1 See Jon Cook, chapter 1 in this volume.
2 See Christopher C. Harris, 'The state and the market', and Pamela Abbott and Claire Wallace, 'The family', in Philip Brown and Richard Sparks (eds.), *Beyond Thatcherism* (Milton Keynes, 1989).
3 In practice New Labour under Tony Blair, like its predecessor in government, tends to privilege the interests of employers over employees. See Eric Shaw, 'The abandonment of Keynesian social democracy, 1987–1995', in his *The Labour Party Since 1945* (Oxford, 1996).
4 See Abbott and Wallace, 'The family'.
5 Michael Coveney, *The World According to Mike Leigh* (London, 1996), p. 5.
6 Andy Medhurst, 'Beyond embarrassment', *Sight and Sound*, November 1993, p. 7.

7   This does not apply to *Naked*, which is typically discussed in the context of Leigh's sexual politics. See Claire Monk, 'Naked', *Sight and Sound*, November 1993, pp. 64–5, and Leonard Quart, 'Naked', *Film Quarterly*, Spring 1994, pp. 43–6.

8   Medhurst, 'Beyond embarrassment', p. 7. It is worth noting that Medhurst shows the previously mentioned tendency to equate Englishness with a particular class and consequently, an accurate or convincing representation of that class with an accurate rendering of the whole nation.

9   Claire Johnston, 'Women's cinema as counter cinema', in Bill Nichols (ed.), *Movies and Methods* (Berkeley, 1976), p. 213.

10 The images of the Pollocks' estate are reminiscent of Patrick Wright's portrayal of London's East End in *A Journey Through Ruins* (London, 1991). See in particular 'Down in the Dirt', pp. 31–6.

11 David N. Ashton, 'Unemployment', in Brown and Sparks, *Beyond Thatcherism*, p. 26.

12 The opinion that the unemployed are responsible for their own plight was encapsulated and made famous by Norman Tebbitt's call for the unemployed to 'get on their bikes'. For a detailed discussion and critique of the New Right's attitude to unemployment see Ashton, 'Unemployment', and Jeremy Seabrook, 'Aspects of the new poor', in his *Landscapes of Poverty* (Oxford, 1985), pp. 88–108.

13 John Pym, 'Dole life', *Sight and Sound*, Winter 1983/84, p. 62.

14 See John Hill, 'Working-class realism II', in his *Sex, Class, Realism* (London, 1986), pp. 145–76.

15 Terry Lovell, 'Landscape and stories in 1960s British realism', in Andrew Higson (ed.), *Dissolving Views* (London, 1996), pp. 159–60.

16 See John H. Goldthorpe *et al.*, *The Affluent Worker in the Class Structure* (Cambridge, 1968), pp. 8–10.

17 Ibid., p. 157.

18 Michael Young and Peter Willmott, *Family and Kinship in East London* (London, 1957).

19 It must however be acknowledged that some films of the 1950s and 1960s challenged the rosy image of working-class communities, presenting them instead as boring and stifling, as places from which one wants to escape, examples being *Billy Liar* (1963), directed by John Schlesinger, and Ken Loach's television play, *Cathy Come Home* (1965).

20 See Harris, 'The state and the market', and David N. Ashton, 'Unemployment', in Brown and Sparks, *Beyond Thatcherism*, pp. 4–5.

21 Franco Bianchini and Hermann Schwengel, 'Re-imagining the city', in John Corner and Sylvia Harvey (eds.), *Enterprise and Heritage* (London, 1991), p. 213.

22 The character of Coxy perfectly suits Jeremy Seabrook's description of 'the new poor' living in rich countries, who live 'a life of recklessness and spontaneity . . . a here-today-gone-tomorrow fatalism; a saga of feuds and passions . . . lawlessness, excitement . . . and boredom'. Jeremy Seabrook, 'Aspects of the new poor', pp. 91–2.

23 Examples are Loach's *Cathy Come Home* (1965), *Poor Cow* (1967) and *Raining Stones* (1993).

24 John Hill, 'Class, politics, and gender: *High Hopes* and *Riff-Raff*, in his *British Cinema in the 1980s* (Oxford, 1999), p. 198.

25 Particularly worthy of attention in this context is the 1988 budget: Kay Andrews and John Jacobs, *Punishing the Poor: Poverty under Thatcher* (London, 1990).

26 A detailed discussion of Thatcherite housing policy can be found in Sarah Monk and Mark Kleinman, 'Housing', in Brown and Sparks, *Beyond Thatcherism*, pp. 121–4.

27 See Andrews and Jacobs, *Punishing the Poor*, and Brown and Sparks, *Beyond Thatcherism*.

28 Gilbert Adair, 'Classtrophobia', *Sight and Sound*, Winter 1988/89, p. 64.

29 Hill, 'Class, politics, and gender', p. 194.

30 John Pym, '*High Hopes*', *Monthly Film Bulletin*, January 1989, p. 10.

31 Leonard and Barbara Quart, '*High Hopes*', *Cineaste* 2 (1989), p. 57.

32 See Chris Waters, *British Socialists and the Politics of Popular Culture* (Manchester, 1990). The books covers the period 1890–1914, but raises more current issues.

33 Stuart Hall, *The Hard Road to Renewal: Thatcherism and the Crisis of the Left* (London, 1988), p. 181.

34 The diminishing power of trade unions during the Thatcher years largely resulted from the disappearance of thousands of full-time jobs in manufacturing, which either perished for ever or were replaced by part-time jobs in the service sector where it was very difficult for trade unions to set up and operate. See Ashton, 'Unemployment', p. 23.

35 An important factor in the fragmentation and impotence was the Thatcher government's onslaught on trade unionism during the 1980s, its exploitation of conflict between various sections of the working class, particularly between those who were unemployed and those who remained in employment, as well as divisions within the Labour party during this period. See Hall, *Hard Road*.

36 Sterility is a typical feature of the surroundings of childless women in Leigh's films, which can be regarded as a testimony to his conservative attitude to women.

37 On the whole, there are few meaningful differences between Labour under Blair and the Conservative Party, particularly in reference to the economy, as both parties reject Keynesian Social Democracy. See Shaw, 'The Abandonment of Keynesian Social Democracy'.

38 My use of hegemony is indebted to Antonio Gramsci, who defined it as the consensual basis of an existing political system within civil society and contrasted with the concept of 'domination': the state's monopoly of the means of violence and its consequent role as the final arbiter of all disputes. See Walter L. Adamson, *Hegemony and Revolution: Antonio Gramsci's Political and Cultural Theory* (Berkeley, 1980), pp. 170–1 and Stuart Hall, 'Gramsci and Us', in his *Hard Road*.

5

Football and the crisis of British identity

Jeffrey Richards

I t is a commonplace that Britain is experiencing an identity crisis. From Tom Nairn's *The Break-Up of Britain*, first published in 1977, to such recent offerings as Peter Hitchens' *The Abolition of Britain*, commentators of both left and right have argued that the United Kingdom is on its way out and that Britishness has disappeared or is disappearing.[1] Norman Davies, in his overrated *The Isles*, claims that Britain will have disappeared by 2007.[2] The once United Kingdom, it is argued, is dissolving into its constituent parts, England, Scotland, Wales and Ireland, and that provides a particular problem for the English because they have been so extensively identified with Britishness: so much so that unlike Wales, Scotland and Ireland, the English have no national costume and do not celebrate their national day. But England existed long before the United Kingdom was invented. What was the English identity then?

It has been said, 'Since the concept of national character arises out of the comparison of nations one with another, the best self-portrait is likely to be less valid than the pictures painted by foreign observers.'[3] How have foreigners seen the English? Some foreign commentators admired their qualities of energy, candour, practicality and independence of mind.[4] But the darker side of Englishness was also much remarked on.

'The English are great lovers of themselves, and of everything belonging to them; they think there are no other men than themselves and no other world but England', wrote the Venetian Ambassador in 1497.[5] 'The (English) people are bold, courageous, ardent, and cruel in war . . . but very inconstant, rash, vainglorious, light and deceiving and very suspicious, especially of foreigners, whom they despise',[6] was the verdict of Dutch merchant Emmanuel van Meteren in the early seventeenth century. 'An innumerable quantity of Englishmen are still more corrupt in their morals than in their religion. Debauch runs riot with an unblushing countenance. It is not the lower populace alone that is addicted to drunkenness: numbers of persons of high rank and even of distinction are over fond of liquor.'[7] So wrote Frenchman César de Saussure in 1725. 'Englishmen are mighty swearers and I consider this another of their defects. Not only the common people have this unfortunate habit but also officers and what are termed beaux, swear when they are youths to give themselves airs, and continue afterwards from habit', wrote Saussure.[8] This was nothing new. During the Hundred Years War the French christened the English 'Les Goddems' because of the English soldiers' habit of continually swearing. William Hazlitt wrote sadly in 1821, 'The English (it must be owned) are rather a foul-mouthed nation.'[9] C. F. Henningsen, the son of Swedish immigrants, wrote in 1848: 'Any place thrown open to the English was sure to exhibit traces of their visitation in the initial names and ribaldry carved on every piece of woodwork, and scratched on every pane of glass, or to be marked by the mutilation and destruction of pictures and statues, furniture, flowers, shrubs, beasts and trees.'[10] The medieval French chronicler Froissart's comment on the English was: 'The more blood they shed, the crueller and more ruthless they become . . . They're fiery and furious, they quickly grow angry and take a long time to calm down.'[11] These examples could be multiplied many times over.

In this composite pen portrait, the English in the years before the nineteenth century emerge as violent, cruel, drunken, profane, foreigner-hating, self-loving. Then there is from the *Observer* newspaper (9 April 2000) this account of the violence in Istanbul preceding the match between Leeds United and Galatasary, which led to the deaths of two Leeds supporters but was only the latest in a series of violent episodes which have attended the forays of English football supporters onto the Continent and include such extensively reported episodes as the Heysel Stadium disaster, the 'battle' of Marseilles, the 'battle' of Copenhagen and the riots in Belgium, Sweden and Switzerland. The *Observer* reports the violent scuffles and the 'Raki-fuelled raucousness', and goes on, 'The swearing was constant. Passing women were insulted. Glasses were thrown. Trousers were dropped. And then in full view of passing traffic, at least one fan – and probably two – lowered their Y-fronts and wiped their backsides on the Turkish flag.'

This is the year 2000, not 1497 or 1725. So are the English as a breed exactly the same as they were before the Industrial Revolution? Has there been no change in several centuries? There has, in fact, been a remarkable one. As Harold Perkin wrote: 'Between 1780 and 1850, the English ceased to be one of the most aggressive, brutal, rowdy, outspoken, riotous, cruel and bloodthirsty nations in the world and became one of the most inhibited, polite, orderly, tender-minded, prudish and hypocritical.'[12] So what happened to them? The simple answer is: the English became British.

Britain only became a nation as such in the eighteenth century. It was the Act of Union of 1707 that linked England, Wales and Scotland and created a single geographical entity – the United Kingdom of Great Britain. Ireland was only incorporated in 1800 and most of it was unincorporated in 1921.

In her *Britons* Linda Colley demonstrated how a sense of *Britishness* was forged in the eighteenth century, based on a shared Protestantism, the acquisition of a vast overseas Empire, and international trading pre-eminence, on a cherished tradition of parliamentary democracy and on a succession of wars against France which had the effect of consolidating the feeling of being British.[13]

But during the nineteenth century there remained considerable diversity within the Union. Scotland retained its own legal, educational and banking systems. The Anglican Church was the established church in England and (until 1920) Wales; the Presbyterian Church in Scotland. Even within England, there was a north–south divide, as indeed there still is, and London remained a huge, unique, separate entity. Nevertheless a British unity emerged which was perfectly compatible with that diversity. Local, regional, civic and provincial identities not only survived but flourished, and were perfectly consonant with pride in the British nation and Empire, because of the shared Britishness of its key elements. The political system and political parties were national. The railways unified the country, making possible a national standard time and national newspapers. The Empire transcended national differences and became supranational, with the English, Irish, Welsh and Scots serving in the imperial army, providing governors and viceroys and working as merchants and missionaries. The monarchy was constructed as British rather than English, and Queen Victoria ostentatiously paraded her love of Scotland.[14]

A genuinely British culture emerged in which all parts of the British Isles revered Dickens, Shakespeare and Scott. Alongside this developed a strongly structured and regulated society – orderly, law-abiding and deferential. Several factors contributed to this: the growth of the factory system which instilled punctuality, regularity and discipline, and of large-scale organizations like the railways and the post office which enforced military-style regimes and uniformed their employees; the work of the police force and the courts; the general improvement in the quality of life (health, housing, transport, civic amenities); the socializing effects of the schools and Sunday schools on the young, and of chapels, trade unions and adult education movements on their elders; and above all, the pervasive doctrine of respectability at all levels of society. Some put respectability on and off like a Sunday suit, but for many it was a cast iron, rock solid, life-long commitment. 'I've always kept myself respectable' was a working-class mantra.[15]

All of this was reinforced and underpinned by the idea of a British national character, new and distinct from that of the English. What is interesting is how much of it derived from the basic elements of British national identity as defined by Colley: from parliamentary democracy came the values of tolerance, compromise and law-abidingness; from Empire a sense of superiority; from Protestantism came individualism, anti-intellectualism and a sense of duty and service. In particular this new national character was the product of the fusion of two powerful creeds. The first was Evangelical Protestantism, the dominant social ethic of the first half of the nineteenth century. As G. M. Young put it: 'The Evangelicals gave the island a creed which was the basis of its morality and the justification of its wealth and power, and with that creed, the sense of being an elect people.'[16] It was Evangelical activists who civilized a violent, disorderly society by banning the slave trade and public executions, censoring books and plays, outlawing cruel sports like bull-baiting, cock-fighting, dog-fighting, bare-knuckle prize-fighting, by restricting gambling and drinking, by abolishing the national lottery, by seeking to impose a puritanical code of sexual conduct and to inculcate the ideas of duty, service and conscience, thrift, sobriety and per-sonal restraint. Taught in schools and Sunday schools, promoted in literature and enshrined in law, these became the British national values, and the perva-sive Protestantism of Wales and Scotland ensured that they were accepted there as much as in England. It should be emphasized that many of these banned activities did not disappear: they survived but went underground to form the basis of an alternative identity, but one that was not validated by the culture.

At the same time, there was a revival of chivalry, which became all-pervasive in the nineteenth century. Chivalry was deliberately promoted by key figures to pro-vide a code of life for the young, based on the virtues of the gentleman: courtesy, bravery, modesty, purity and compassion, and a sense of responsibility towards women, children, the weak and the helpless. It permeated the literature and paint-ing of the nineteenth century, was advocated by youth organizations, was enshrined in the codes and regulations of sports like football and cricket and was embodied in the public school code, absorbed beyond their boundaries through popular fiction from *Tom Brown's Schooldays* to the Greyfriars stories in the *Magnet*.[17] 'The idea of the gentleman is *not* a class idea', wrote Sir Ernest Barker in 1947, identifying it as a key component of the national identity. 'It is the idea of a type of character . . . a mixture of stoicism with mediaeval lay chivalry, and of both with unconscious national ideals, half Puritan and half secular.'[18] Bernard Crick has recently made the same claim, seeing the idea of the gentleman as an integrative image for the ruling elites of Great Britain which percolated down from the elite to the rest of the population through popular culture.[19]

What these two ideologies had in common was the overwhelming importance of the ideas of personal restraint and concern for others. Merged together, they helped form the national character. One of the facts bedevilling the discussion of national identity is the way in which many people, though not Scots, Welsh or Irish, refer to the British and the English interchangeably. This is because the English as the majority within the British Isles enthusiastically took on the qualities of Britishness. This was confirmed by the great outpouring of books and articles about national identity provoked by the Second World War. There was remarkable unanimity among commentators both left and right. Stanley Baldwin, George Orwell and J. B. Priestley, among others, saw the English as being law-abiding, patriotic, insular, anti-intellectual, good-humoured, stoical, motivated by a sense of tolerance, a sense of service and a sense of fair play: in other words as British. Baldwin spoke of a 'spirit of dauntless decency' and Orwell, characteristically adding class-consciousness, noted that 'the gentleness of English civilization is perhaps its most marked characteristic'. This national persona was faithfully projected in wartime cinema and a wide range of cultural forms.[20] It was a cultural construct, a cultural myth. But as Orwell noted: 'Myths which are believed in tend to become true because they set up a type or persona which the average person will do his best to resemble.'[21] During the Blitz people for the most part behaved exactly as they had been taught British people should behave – with courage, stoicism and good humour. This persona is one of the reasons why the Home Intelligence Unit, set up to monitor national morale, reported in 1941: 'There is at present no evidence that it is possible to defeat the people of Britain by any means other than extermination.'[22]

The worst aspects of Englishness were steadily mitigated by the dominance of an idea of Britishness. The Home Secretary Sir Herbert Samuel said in parliament in 1931, 'We have got rid to a great extent of drunkenness as a national vice.'[23] This can be traced back to the introduction during the First World War of strict licensing hours, reduced-strength alcoholic drinks and the development of counter-attractions to the pub, notably the cinema, where more attractive role models than the boozy and belligerent John Bull were to be found. In 1927 the poet and social commentator Robert Graves wrote: 'Of recent years in England there has been a noticeable decline in swearing, and foul language and this, except at centres of industrial depression, shows every sign of continuing indefinitely until a new shock to our national nervous system . . . may revive the habit of swearing.'[24] Sociologist Geoffrey Gorer wrote in 1955 in his fascinating study *Explaining English Character* (based in part on the replies to 10,000 questionnaires):

> Up until a century ago the English were openly aggressive . . . and took pleasure and pride in their truculence, their readiness to fight and to endure . . . There was little or no guilt about the expression of aggression in the appropriate situations; and there was no doubt . . .that every English man and woman had sufficient aggression for every possible event . . . Today, unless 'one's back is to the wall', almost any overt expression of aggression is fused with guilt. Nearly all the amusements of our forefathers would provoke the greatest indignation; all visible suffering which cannot be avoided must be hidden; any form of childish aggressive behaviour is watched for and punished; and when we think of our faults, we put first, and by a long way, any lapses from our standards of non-aggression, bad temper, nagging, swearing and the like. Public life is more gentle than that reported for any society of comparable size and industrial complexity.[25]

He attributed this state of affairs to the nonconformist conscience, the gradual spread of universal education and the development of what he found to be a widely respected police force.

E. M. Forster wrote in 1920: 'The character of the English is essentially middle class.'[26] But what he calls 'middle class' values were, as Geoffrey Gorer confirmed, shared by a large section of the working classes. Indeed crucial to any understanding of British social and cultural history is the great divide within the working classes between what the Victorians called 'the rough' and the 'respectable'. The 'respectables' cultivated what have been miscalled 'middle class values' but are in fact merely civilized values: self-improvement, education, restraint, thrift and good manners. As Neville Kirk has argued, many in the working class adopted civilized values by their own free will and for their own reasons, and not because of middle-class brain-washing.[27] The 'roughs' lived a life of immediate gratification, particularly in sex, drink and violence. This always provided a potential alternative image for Englishness, but it was largely kept underground until the 1960s when a social and cultural revolution occurred, and a world that had remained substantially Victorian in all its lineaments was overturned by a range of fundamental social, cultural and economic changes of seismic significance: that 'shock to the national nervous system' that Graves predicted.

Since the 1960s almost all the elements that went into making up the British identity have been eroded: Empire has gone, Protestantism is in terminal decline, parliamentary democracy is widely despised. The redevelopment of the old Victorian cities and the destruction of the old urban communities, the continuing decline of organized religion, new educational philosophies based on free expression rather than disciplined instruction combined with a new, all-embracing cultural ideology of individual rights and consumer choice to promote what the sociologist Bernice Martin has dubbed 'the culture of liminality'. The matrix of this was the affluence and materialism of the 1950s and 1960s, which released people from the immediate disciplines of survival and turned their attention to their 'expressive' needs – self-discovery and self-assertion. This had some positive results – the recognition of the rights of minority groups of all kinds, an awakening interest in the Third World and Green issues. But it had a darker side. In this new culture the self was exalted, spontaneity was encouraged and rules, restrictions, conventions and traditions in life and art were ditched, and the old values and old certainties were increasingly derided and rejected. Violence, profanity and sexuality, hitherto rigorously suppressed by a wide-ranging system of censorship, increasingly became prominent both in high culture and low. Personal style, cool, chic, cynical and consumerist became the ideal, immediate gratification the aim, 'I want it now' the watchword.

In the 1960s it became fashionable for the first time in British history to be young and working-class. This emphasis on youth, with its desire to be free from restraint, and on working-class identities of the 'rough' rather than the 'respectable' variety, plus the promotion of the philosophy of self, completely undermined the two shaping creeds of the national character, both of them based on the subordination of the self. Protestantism, in decline since the First World War, is now a minority avocation. Chivalry and sportsmanship were rejected in the 1960s on the grounds that they were expressions of a class-based and patronizing paternalism and patriarchalism.

In the 1960s and 1970s sex, drugs and rock 'n' roll represented the route chosen by the new individualism. But with the recession of the late 1970s, the self took a new direction – the aggressive pursuit of wealth, which came to incorporate a contempt for those who had not got it. This aggressive individualism found its cultural heroes in Rambo, Rocky, Conan the Barbarian, Mike Tyson, Gordon Gecko and Harry Enfield's nouveau riche stereotype 'Loadsa Money'. The cultural validation of swearing loudly and publicly, drinking too much, driving too fast and fighting as an assertion of your masculinity, all aspects of the cult of 'new laddism', was assiduously promoted by a range of 'lads' magazines such as *Loaded* and television programmes like *Men Behaving Badly*. 'Laddism' has always existed but it had never before been so enthusiastically endorsed in the mass media.

Thatcherism was the political expression of this individualist mindset. It was the first dominant ideology in modern times not to have the ideas of selflessness and public service at its heart. It promoted a crude, 'let the people have what they want', lowest-common-denominator populism, let the free market rip and dismantled regulations and restrictions in all areas. It completed the transformation of society and of social and cultural values begun in the 1960s. Its ethos has been reflected in football in the creation of the Premier League in 1991, a development for which there is no justification other than greed, which has undermined and marginalized the Football League, raised admission charges by 300 per cent and sold the rights to televise live football to a satellite television organization, Sky TV, which only reaches 30 per cent of the UK television households.[28]

The erosion of those elements which went to make up Britain – Empire, Protestantism, parliamentary democracy – coincided with the devolution of power to Scotland, Wales and Northern Ireland and with Britain's reluctant entry into and membership of the European Union. This presented no problem in Wales or Scotland, where an alternative Celtic identity is available. Like Britishness, it was a cultural construct, deliberately created, as Malcolm Chapman has shown, to be the opposite of the perceived qualities of Englishness.[29] Where the Englishman was seen as individualist, the Celt was seen as communal. Where the Englishman was prosaic, the Celt was poetic. Where the Englishman was phlegmatic, the Celt was emotional and spontaneous. Where the Englishman was anti-intellectual, the Celt was cultured. This identity, together with widely celebrated national symbols, days, costumes and banners, maintained a Scottish and Welsh identity during the ascendancy of England. But more important is the fact that both Anglo-Saxon and Celt could be and were accommodated within the British Empire, the British Army and the British parliament, making Britishness perfectly compatible with Englishness, Welshness and Scottishness.

As the concept of Britishness has weakened, so that old atavistic Englishness, long lurking in the shadows, has begun to reassert itself: that violent, vandalistic, cruel, drunken, profane, foreigner-hating Englishness. The statistics speak for themselves. A steady rise in recorded crime began in the 1920s, but its largest rise came in the period 1955–91. By 1991 the rate of indictable offences was ten times what it had been in 1955, and forty times the rate in 1901. Although there are still comparatively few murders, there has been a marked increase in reported woundings. They rose from 791 in 1920, to 5,177 in 1930, to 14,142 in 1960, to 95,044 in 1980.[30] There has been a marked increase in drunkenness and drug abuse since the 1960s. Much of this involves young men: by the end of the twentieth century it was statistically more likely that the young British male would die violently than at any other time in the twentieth century during peacetime. So violence and drunkenness are back. So is profanity. In his book *Playpower*, that testament to 1960s radical thinking, Richard Neville called for 'the deflowering of language, making it obscene and useless as part of the structuring of a new age'.[31] The *Lady Chatterley* trial in 1960 established the right of serious novelists to use language hitherto regarded as obscene. The f-word, unheard in the media since the sixteenth century, made a dramatic return. It was heard in films for the first time ever in 1970 and is now ubiquitous in films and television and is heard everywhere. Hatred of foreigners is regularly stirred up by the rabidly xenophobic tabloid press with its rabble-rousing headlines such as 'Hop off, you frogs', 'Up yours, Delors', and 'Achtung, Fritz, for you the war is over', and surfaces in episodes such as the shamelessly racist campaign against asylum seekers, conducted in the popular press and by populist politicians.

Over the past thirty years, with the decline in censorship and the ideological victory of the doctrine of choice, popular culture at all levels, in particular the cinema, has validated and celebrated violence, profanity and macho posturing in such films as *Top Gun, Die Hard, Lethal Weapon* and their many clones and sequels, and in particular in the films of Quentin Tarantino such as *Reservoir Dogs* and *Pulp Fiction*. Tarantino now has an English equivalent in *Lock, Stock and Two Smoking Barrels*, a cockney rip-off of *Pulp Fiction*. It made a star of footballer Vinnie Jones in the role of a tough gangland enforcer and featured various real-life gangland figures such as Lenny 'The Guvnor' Maclean. It launched a taste for what has been dubbed 'geezer chic', manifested in the production of a dozen admiring films about violent London gangsters, such as *Gangster No. 1* and *Essex Boys*, and in the celebration of real-life old-time gangsters. The memoirs of Lenny 'The Guvnor' Maclean, 'Dodgy' Dave Courtney and Big Joey Pile sold in tens of thousands. Reggie Kray wrote a regular column for the laddish *Front* magazine from his prison cell and 'Mad Frankie' Fraser entrances audiences of youthful admirers with tales of how he used to nail people's heads to the floor and extract their teeth with pliers.

Football, as the English national game, can be seen at one level to mirror the national identity. One would expect it to reflect the revival of Englishness, with its characterizing features of violence, drunkenness, profanity and xenophobia. How far can it be seen to have done so? Football, as we know it, emerged in the second half of the nineteenth century, codified, organized and incorporated into an increasingly structured society mainly by middle-class ex-public school-boys. But while the structure of Association football became professional – in England in 1885 and Scotland in 1893 – professionalism was strictly limited by the maximum wage and the ethos remained resolutely amateur, with play-ers able to be punished as they still are for ungentlemanly conduct and bring-ing the game into disrepute.[32]

Football from the 1880s to the 1950s can justly be seen as an expression of the ordered and disciplined society that emerged from the nineteenth century, as the epitome of what Harold Perkin felicitously dubbed 'the structured crowd', who were all 'consciously or unconsciously related in a general way by the bonds of language, inherited ideas and beliefs, and all the common experi-ences of a shared community'.[33] It is visually summed up by the painting of King George V shaking hands with the Huddersfield Town skipper, Alex Jack-son, which adorns the front cover of Dave Russell's excellent book *Football and the English*.[34] Nicholas Fishwick sees football in his period as reflecting a stable, traditional working-class society, neither poor nor rich, male-dominated, cheerful, sociable and patriotic. He called the football stadia in the late 1940s, the era of peak football attendance in Britain, 'the Labour Party at prayer'.[35] Geoffrey Gorer, in *Exploring English Character* (1955), also saw football crowds as an epitome of English life, writing:

> In public life today the English are certainly among the most peaceful, gentle, courteous and orderly populations that the civilized world has ever seen . . . the control of aggression . . . has gone to such remarkable lengths that you hardly ever see a fight in a bar . . . football crowds are as orderly as church meetings . . . all the frustrations and annoyances symbolized by queueing are met with orderliness and good humour.[36]

Perhaps the finest symbol of the structured crowd and the disciplined and ordered society attuned to common values was the singing of *Abide With Me* at the F.A. Cup Final. Introduced in 1927, this hymn was sung annually at the Wembley Cup Final and there were few more moving sounds than to hear 100,000 voices raised in unison in Henry Francis Lyte's words 'Where is death's sting, where grave thy victory, I triumph still if Thou abide with me.' It must have had particular poignancy for those who had lived through the First and Second World Wars. In the 1960s it was shouted down and drowned out by obscene chants and had to be abandoned. Revived later in abbreviated form, it is now an empty and half-hearted ritual. Nothing could be more symptomatic of the death of Protestantism, the fracturing of the structured crowd, and the coarsening and degrading of the public culture which had gone along with the rise of an intrusive and untrammelled tabloid press, the abandonment of Reithian public service broadcasting, the delight in a culture of cruelty and violence, the lowest common denominator populism that has brought us 'dumbed down' television – something admitted in the latest BBC Annual Report – and the 'feel-bad' factor that has led to a 70 per cent increase in male teenage suicide in the past twenty years. Musically this transformation is encapsulated in the superseding of *Abide With Me* by the anthem of the 1998 World Cup *Vindaloo*, recorded by Fat Les: 'Vindaloo-Vindaloo-Vindaloo-Vindaloo na/na: Vindaloo-Vindaloo, we're gonna score one more than you.'

Why do people go to football; have these reasons changed; and if so how and why? First, there is the aesthetic appeal. There is nothing to equal football at its best for beauty, grace, speed, power and control. It is also instant theatre: drama, comedy, tragedy intermingled, complete with heroes and villains. This remains constant.

Second, and perhaps even more importantly, it is a vehicle for belonging. From the late nineteenth century onwards, in a working-class urban and industrial society, it provided a means of expressing civic pride, proclaiming your allegiance to your locality, of identifying with a community larger than the family or the street. This sense of civic pride used to be strong. It was noted by both Orwell and Priestley on their travels. It is part of the reason why local businessmen like Jack Walker at Blackburn, Sir Jack Hayward at Wolves and Sir John Hall at Newcastle have pumped millions into venerable clubs, partly in the interests of reviving civic pride. But more significant is the change that has occurred since the 1960s in football support among the young. It is no coincidence that the 1960s saw the rise of obscene chanting, football violence and the worship of success at any cost. Some of the young, instead of supporting their local team through good times and bad, victories and defeats, transferred their allegiance to those clubs, however far away, who seemed to guarantee permanent victory, clubs like Liverpool and Manchester United. It is now a truth universally acknowledged that there are more Manchester United supporters outside Manchester than in the city.

Why are Londoners now supporting Manchester United when they have half-a-dozen perfectly adequate clubs of their own and it is widely recognized as a truism that Mancunians traditionally hate cockneys? The only reason can be a hunger to identify with success that transcends local loyalty. The development can be dated precisely to 1962 and the demise of the venerable Accrington Stanley. It went out of business in part because it was steadily losing support to more glamorous clubs down the road. Increased social mobility, the creeping Americanization of British society and culture, the rise of an aggressive individualism, the 'losers don't come to dinner' syndrome – a reversal of the traditional British love of the underdog – have all contributed to the erosion of civic pride and identity among the young and its replacement by a mercenary spirit.

Just as some working-class young people have abandoned local loyalties, the middle-class young have sought and found them in football. One of the most interesting phenomena of recent sports writing is the rise of the so-called *soccerati*, educated middle-class young men writing with passion and eloquence about their love of football and of their particular teams.[37] The most famous is of course Nick Hornby, author of the justly praised *Fever Pitch*, which charted his obsession with Arsenal. Among the many insights he offers is this:

> The white south of England middle-class Englishman and woman is the most rootless creature on earth; we would rather belong to any other community in the world. Yorkshiremen, Lancastrians, Scots, Irish, blacks, the rich, the poor, even Americans and Australians have something they can sit in pubs and bars and weep about, songs to sing, things they can grab for and squeeze hard when they feel like it, but we have nothing, or at least nothing we want. Hence the phenomenon of mock belonging, whereby pasts and backgrounds are manufactured and massaged in order to provide some kind of acceptable cultural identity. Who was it that sang 'I Wanna Be Black'? The title says it all, and everybody has met people who really do; in the mid-seventies, young, intelligent and otherwise self-aware white men and women in London began to adopt a Jamaican patois that frankly didn't suit them at all. How we all wished we came from the Chicago Projects, or the Kingston ghettos, or the mean streets of north London or Glasgow! All those aitch-dropping, vowel-mangling punk rockers with a public school education! All those Hampshire girls with grandparents in Liverpool or Brum! All those Pogues fans from Hertfordshire singing Irish rebel songs!! . . . Ever since I have been old enough to understand what it means to be suburban I have wanted to come from somewhere else, preferably north London. I have already dropped as many aitches as I can . . . and I use plural verb forms with a singular subject whenever possible. This was a process that began shortly after my first visits to Highbury, continued throughout my suburban grammar school career and escalated alarmingly when I arrived at university . . . In a way nobody can blame any of us, the Mockneys or the cod Irish, the black wannabees or the pseudo Sloanes . . . we never stood a chance. I blame the eleven-plus. Before the war, maybe, our parents could have scraped the money together to send us to minor public schools and we would . . . have gone to work in a bank; the eleven-plus, designed to create a meritocracy, made state schools safe for nice families again. Post-war grammar school boys and girls stepped into a void; none of the available cultures seemed to belong to us, and we had to pinch one quick.[38]

So, support for a football team, identification with a largely working-class leisure activity, pseudo-proletarianism was the answer. But this is not all. The suburbans had always been attacked and derided – as John Carey demonstrates in *The Intellectuals and the Masses* – but they had remained secure in their own value systems.[39] In the 1960s they swallowed the denigration. The middle class suffered a massive loss of confidence, and culturally self-destructed. They accepted the idea being peddled by deracinated self-loathing intellectuals that they were elitist, paternalist, snobbish, and patronizing and the middle-class young sought to distance themselves from their roots, in the way Hornby describes. It is worth noting that Guy Ritchie, the writer-director of *Lock, Stock* is, like Nick Hornby, a 'mockney'. Educated at public school and raised in a stately home by a knighted stepfather, he has reinvented himself as a 'diamond geezer'. Similarly Tim Westwood, son of the Bishop of Peterborough, presents a rap show on Radio One and speaks in Jamaican patois.

Football's third area of appeal is as an expression of masculinity. Richard Holt in *Sport and the British* argues that football players mirrored the qualities most prized by the working class: grit, loyalty to mates, hardness, stamina and courage. He mentions neither skill nor sportsmanship.[40] Tony Mason argues in *Association Football and English Society* that the sporting code of playing the game, abiding by the rules and fair-mindedness made little headway with the working class crowds who had their own standards of behaviour: virulent partisanship, admiration of toughness and violence, winning at all costs: 'It does not seem an exaggeration to conclude that football does not appear to have been played or watched by working men with that devotion to the ideal of sportsmanship which middle-class people would have liked and which was one of their hopes for the influence of the game.'[41]

This does seem exaggerated. The football crowd has always consisted both of 'roughs' and 'respectables', old and young, and the influence of popular culture in promoting ideas of chivalry and sportsmanship cannot have been lost on at least a section of that crowd. Two of the most important informal influences on the working class young were boys' papers and films.

It was the working class who devoured Frank Richards' stories of public school life in weekly periodicals like *Magnet* and *Gem*. At Greyfriars School, they played not rugby like most public schools but football. Why? Because that is what the working-class readers of the papers would have played and would have identified with, and this sport was played in the highest traditions of chivalry. Robert Roberts, one of the few historians to write from within the working class, spoke of the importance of Frank Richards' *Magnet* stories in his own childhood in the slums of Edwardian Salford and noted that:

> The Famous Five stood for us as young knights *sans peur et sans reproche* . . . With nothing in *our* school that called for love or allegiance, Greyfriars became for some of us our true Alma mater, to whom we felt bound by a dreamlike loyalty . . . Over the years, these simple tales conditioned the thought of a whole generation of boys. The public school ethos, distorted into myth and sold among us weekly in penny numbers for good or ill set ideals and standards . . . In the final estimate, it may well be found that Frank Richards during the first quarter of the twentieth century had more influence on the mind and outlook of young working-class England than any other single person.[42]

The *Magnet* continued to appear until 1940, and after the war Richards' stories returned in books and on television up to his death in 1961. But more significantly, in the wake of the Famous Five in the *Magnet*, Roy of the Rovers, first from 1954 in *Tiger* and then from 1976 in his own comic, maintained the tradition of chivalric sporting heroes. He even gave rise to a commentators' cliché, 'It's real Roy of the Rovers stuff', meaning a heroic victory against the odds by a skilled but unfancied team.[43]

Although there were few films about football – almost all of them bad – chivalry and sportsmanship were consistently promoted in American as well as British films.[44] As John Fraser has written, 'The family of chivalric heroes has been by far the largest and most popular one in twentieth-century culture and its members, in whole or in part, have entered into virtually everyone's consciousness.' He lists them as 'that legion of knightly westerners . . . sired by Owen Wister's The Virginian': Robin Hood, Zorro, the Scarlet Pimpernel, Captain Blood, Beau Geste, Dick Tracy, Dr Kildare, Philip Marlowe, Prince Valiant, Tarzan, Superman, Buck Rogers, Philo Vance, the Saint, gentlemanly English actors like Ronald Colman and George Sanders, gentlemanly American ones like William Powell, Douglas Fairbanks Jr. and Fred Astaire, and 'those immortals Gary Cooper, Spencer Tracy and the rest, who have epitomized native American gallantry and grace'.[45] It is no coincidence that Gary Cooper should have played on the screen Wild Bill Hickock, Beau Geste and Lou Gehrig of the New York Yankees. All were chivalric heroes.

Since the early nineteenth century there have been two rival models of masculinity, the gentleman and the thug. Both of these versions of masculinity co-existed in the working class, the one official and the other unofficial, the one respectable and the other rough, and football provided role models for both. Tony Mason demonstrates this perfectly when he describes Stanley Matthews as the classic footballer of the 1940s and 1950s, a player never cautioned or sent off, a symbol of respectable working-class Englishness – modest, well-behaved, honourable, decent, skilful, cool and sensible, gentlemanly on and off the field.[46]

There has been an apostolic succession of gentleman heroes of football, known for never being cautioned or sent off: Tom Finney, Stanley Matthews, Billy Wright, Bobby Charlton, Bobby Moore, Gary Lineker, who are all characterized in a similar way – as modest, decent, skilful, honourable, in short as gentlemen, demonstrating the truth of Barker's assertion that the idea of a gentleman is classless.[47] The outpourings of national grief at the deaths of Moore, Wright and Matthews reflect in part the feeling that these qualities are vanishing. But the official line of apostolic heroes now has rivals. In the 1960s a new type of player appeared who looked, dressed and behaved like a pop star, and embodied the instant gratification and 'I want it now' ethic, made possible by the abolition of the maximum wage. These became new role models, players like George Best, Rodney Marsh, Stanley Bowles, who drank, gambled, womanized and drove fast cars, 'the bad boys of soccer', who squandered their talent and lived for the moment. This lifestyle, regularly and gleefully headlined in the tabloid press, has led to night-club brawls, drunken orgies, players 'drying out' in clinics and lurid accounts of extra-marital sexual adventures. It also led some football stars (Tony Adams, Duncan Ferguson and Jan Molby among them) to prison. The press began to present the thugs as heroes, including players like Vinnie Jones, who made a video showing the ten best ways to hurt an opponent. There had always been such hard men, the heroes of the 'rough element' on the terraces (Barnsley's Skinner Normanton, Leeds' Norman 'Bites yer legs' Hunter, Chelsea's Ron 'Chopper' Harris and so on). But they were not culturally promoted at the time as role models. Along with the violence and drunkenness, some of the football stars also demonstrate an adherence to the darker side of the new Englishness. Two Leeds stars were prosecuted over an attack on an Asian student, various white players have been accused of racist abuse towards black players, and there has been a sustained homophobic campaign by some fans and some players against Graeme Le Saux who, although not homosexual, was interpreted as being so because he read the *Guardian* and collected antiques. This all-round nastiness does seem peculiarly English. It was refreshing to read that Aston Villa's Portuguese international Fernando Nelson described his favourite leisure activity as 'visiting English stately homes'. Sadly, he did not last very long in the English game. This interest in culture contrasts rather pointedly with Michael Owen, who admitted in an interview that he had never been able to read a book all the way through, even the one he had allegedly written himself.

What of the question of violence? The occasional crowd violence at football matches before the First World War declined markedly afterwards. Football crowds became and remained bywords for peaceful, orderly behaviour and good nature until the early 1960s, when the all-too-familiar upsurge of violence began. The reasons are linked to changes in the game and in society at large.

With the dramatic diminution in audiences for football matches in the 1960s, there was a falling off of attendance by older men and middle-aged family men in particular, and the younger element began to dominate. With increasing affluence and mobility there were greater numbers of travelling away fans. The youngsters colonized the two ends of the ground, forming defined and hostile opposing armies. They were no longer susceptible to the informal discipline that the presence of the older generation had imposed in the days of mass spectatorship. The presence of television at games and the dramatic pictures of violence it carried encouraged imitation and continuation.

But James Walvin, in *Football and the Decline of Britain*, argues that football hooliganism must also be seen in the wider context of recent social and economic history and points to the interrelated structural changes destroying 'the tight codes of discipline, overlapping and mutually reinforcing, in traditional working class communities, within the family, the school and then the workplace'. He correctly indicts the 'redevelopments' which in the 1960s destroyed traditional working-class communities and created in their place bleak and heartless high-rise estates, the failure of the education system and educational philosophies geared to 'short term unstructured hedonism' and the consequences of mass youth unemployment and the decline of apprenticeship. The internal discipline and social sanction imposed on the old working-class communities, by the factory system and the pre-1960s school system, and also by sport, codified and regulated by men who believed in the public school traditions of 'fair play' and 'being a sporting loser', have all broken down.[48] Some elements of the 'rough' working class have always rejected all these agencies and values, but since the 1960s the 'rough' ethic has percolated upwards, infecting the children of the 'respectable' working class and the lower middle class. These have been joining in football hooliganism along with the 'rough' working-class group traditionally providing the recruits to the hooligan gangs.

Working-class male gangs have a long history. Gang conflicts were the way in which young men proved their maleness – displaying their toughness, defending their territory, impressing their peers and potential girlfriends.[49] As Andrew Davies has written, '"Hardness" or toughness was considered a quintessential masculine virtue.'[50] After the dislocations of urban renewal, they found new battlegrounds at football stadiums where the enemy were certain to appear. These relocated football gangs share the values of their precursors: an identification of masculinity with toughness and ability to fight, and an identification of the group within the locality, their own territory or turf. On a larger level, their maleness is equated with whiteness and Englishness, hence the racism and chauvinism which shows itself abroad, in beating up foreigners simply for being foreign and at home, ethnic minorities for being visibly different. This idea of maleness is at the centre of their consciousness and it is equally equated with an active heterosexuality – so they taunt their opponents with their lack of masculinity calling them alternately 'poofs' and 'wankers'.

This violence has been regularly exported for several decades. Jeremy Paxman considered this in *The English*:

> In Turin in the late 1980s, the writer Bill Buford watched with horror as a group of bloated Manchester United football fans staggered off the aircraft that had brought them from England to watch their team play the Italian aces, Juventus. It was not even lunchtime, yet many were so drunk they could scarcely stand. The fans then colonized the town centre, sitting in their tattoos in sidewalk cafés singing 'Fuck the Pope' over and over again, occasionally getting up to piss in the street. And that was when they were being well behaved, and not attacking 'the fuckin eyeties' with sticks, knives or bottles. 'Why do you English behave like this?' an Italian asked Buford, 'Is it because you are an island race? Is it because you don't feel European? Is it because you lost the Empire?' Buford was lost for an answer. The question arose from fear and genuine bafflement. Why *does* a minority of the English population think that the only way to have a good time is to get disgustingly drunk – and I mean *disgustingly* drunk, drunk to the point where the beer and the wine and the spirits have saturated their T-shirts and they are heaving their stomach up into the street – to shout obscenely and to pick a fight? Perhaps all the reasons suggested by the Italian played a part. Certainly, you don't expect to find plane-loads of Italians pouring into the centre of London and behaving in a similar fashion. The only honest answer that Buford could give is that that is how part of the English population have always been. Far from being ashamed of their behaviour they see fighting and drunkenness as part of their birthright. It is the way they proclaim their identity.[51]

The question of football and identity has intensified in recent years, as football has become more and more important. Football stories and stories involving footballers and managers now regularly head news bulletins in the media and provide front page headlines in the papers, in a way which was inconceivable twenty or thirty years ago.

With only about 10 per cent of the population going to church regularly, and both the Archbishop of Canterbury and the Cardinal Archbishop of

Westminster gloomily confirming the marginalization of Christianity, football has become a substitute for that religion. But no single faith transcends all earthly differences, and there is a jostling of rival anthems, such as Liverpool's *You'll never walk alone* and Aston Villa's *Holte Enders in the Sky*. They may be profane in intent, but the imagery is all of heaven, eternity, saints and angels. We see the appropriation of the vocabulary of salvation by a plethora of semi-pagan conventicles whose gods are the star players, who earn their own chants like 'Brian Little walks on water' and 'We all agree Kenny Dalglish is magic'. Hymn tunes have been pressed into service (*Amazing Grace*, for instance, to chant a successful manager's name). There are several well-attested stories of people arranging to have their ashes scattered in the goalmouth of the home supporters' end of their local football ground. Anfield memorably became a shrine of flowers and scarves after the Hillsborough disaster. This has now become a worldwide phenomenon. In 2000 a golden statue of David Beckham was placed in a Buddhist temple in Bangkok and when some worshippers protested, the Buddhist abbot said 'Football is a religion to millions of fans.' As organized religion in Britain has decayed, so the regular Saturday afternoon expression of the faith took the place of Sunday. Recently it has even moved to Sunday itself. But as with many other religions, team worship has its violent acolytes, only too prepared to put to the sword devotees of a rival cult.

It has also become a vehicle for the affirmation of the new national identity, and it is significant that since 1996 England fans have taken to painting their faces with the red cross of St George and waving English flags as opposed to British flags. This face painting gives the idea of football fans as a savage tribe a palpable expression. But some confusion remains, in that these St George's flag-waving English fans were lustily singing the British anthems 'God Save the Queen' and 'Rule Britannia' during Euro 2000 and the World Cup 2002. On an international level, some fans clearly see football as a substitute for war. The regular chanting of 'Two world wars and one world cup' by England fans whenever England faces Germany underlines this equivalence. But England fans do seem to regard all foreigners as the enemy. It has been said that the bad behaviour of English football fans is ironic, parodic or carnivalesque. The Belgians, Swedes, French or Swiss who have regularly had their heads kicked in by the English might not appreciate the ironic nature of their injuries.

The problem stems from the fact that Englishness is *ex*clusive whereas Britishness is inclusive. Until recently Welsh, Scots and Northern Irish could think of themselves and proclaim themselves as Welsh and British, Scots and British, Irish and British – partly a legacy of the two World Wars when Britain as a whole fought against the Germans. Now the evidence suggests that increasingly in Scotland and Wales, the population, especially the young, think of themselves as Scottish and Welsh rather than British. The inclusiveness of Britishness has also been appealing to ethnic minorities in England. Ugandan Asian Yasmin Alibhai Brown has written movingly of how she came to feel British and of her fears that this identity will be taken away, as Britishness is eroded and replaced by an alternative Englishness with which she could not easily identify.[52]

But Gallup published a poll just ahead of St George's Day (*Daily Telegraph* 22 April 2000) asking English people whether they felt more English than British. While 73 per cent said they felt either *more* British than English (17 per cent) or *equally* British and English (56 per cent), only 26 per cent felt more English than British. Asked which of a set of qualities were English, they opted for animal-lovers (85 per cent), tolerant (80 per cent), concerned with fairness (77 per cent), class-conscious (77 per cent), suspicious of foreigners (73 per cent), reserved (71 per cent) – many of these characteristics more associated with Britishness than Englishness. So perhaps there is not a crisis, in that rather than Britishness being relocated – it simply needs to be reasserted; or it may merely be that there is not a crisis yet. Also, the crisis may be a generational one – the young may see themselves increasingly as more English than British. Or it may be that the always existing but long invisible barbarian section of the English has simply become visible.

In all these areas football might help. Arguably the existence of English, Welsh, Scottish and Northern Irish sides has defused tension within the Union by allowing national rivalries to be played out on the football field – the phenomenon identified in Scotland as 'the 90-minute patriots'.[53] But with the narrowing of identities, with the restricting of the once fruitful and enriching concept of multiple identities, the decent values associated with Britishness need to be saved for the nation. The first step could be the creation of a British national team, drawn from the constituent countries of the Union. This has been a unique absence. The Federal Republic of Germany does not have a Prussian, a Saxon and a Bavarian team; it has a German team. The emerging Federal Kingdom of British might do the same. It might help the English fans to learn to behave by mingling with the consistently well behaved Scottish fans, even if Scottish good behaviour is a deliberate attempt to show up the 'auld enemy' as uncivilized thugs.[54] The rival flags, anthems and loyalties could be forgotten and emphasis could be laid on the qualities of Britishness – on tolerance, good humour, decency, stoicism, what Richard Holt rightly calls 'that cheerful modest patriotism in keeping with the sense of solidarity, austerity and respectable socialism of Attlee's Britain', which characterized the post-war soccer crowds.[55] That would be infinitely preferable to the violent and hysterical English jingoism which at both club and national level demeans and degrades the country; and with a British national team, we might actually win something.[56]

Notes

1 Tom Nairn, *The Break-Up of Britain* (London, 1977); Peter Hitchens, *The Abolition of Britain* (London, 1999).

2 Norman Davies, *The Isles* (London, 1999), p. 1053.

3 Dean Peabody, *National Characteristics* (Cambridge, 1985), p. 124.

4 Paul Langford, *Englishness Identified: Manners and Character 1650–1850* (Oxford, 2000).

5 William Brenchley Rye, *England as Seen by Foreigners in the days of Elizabeth and James the First* (London, 1865), p. xliv.

6 Ibid., p. 70.

7 César de Saussure, *A Foreign View of England in 1725–1729* (London,1995), p. 119.

8 Ibid., p. 120.

9 Geoffrey Pearson, *Swearing* (Oxford, 1991), p. 1.

10 Langford, *Englishness Identified*, p. 270.

11 Jeremy Paxman, *The English* (London, 1998), p. 247.

12 Harold Perkin, *The Origins of Modern English Society 1780–1880* (London, 1969), p. 280.

13 Linda Colley, *Britons* (New Haven and London, 1992).

14 Keith Robbins, *Nineteenth Century Britain: Integration and Diversity* (Oxford, 1988).

15 F. M. L . Thompson, *The Rise of Respectable Society* (London, 1989).

16 G. M. Young, *Victorian England: Portrait of an Age* (Oxford, 1989 edn.), pp. 4–5.

17 Mark Girouard, *Return to Camelot: Chivalry and the English Gentleman* (New Haven and London, 1981).

18 Sir Ernest Barker (ed.), *The Character of England* (Oxford, 1947), pp. 566–7.

19 Bernard Crick (ed.), *National Identities* (Oxford, 1991), p. 95

20 Jeffrey Richards, *Films and British National Identity* (Manchester, 1997), pp. 14–18.

21 George Orwell, *Collected Essays, Journalism and Letters*, vol. 3 (Harmondsworth, 1971), p. 21.

22 Richards, *Films and British National Identity*, p. 18.

23 *House of Commons Debates*, vol. 264, pp. 1153–5.

24 Robert Graves, *Lars Porsena* (London, 1927), p. 1.

25 Geoffrey Gorer, *Exploring English Character* (London, 1955), p. 287.

26 E. M. Forster, 'Notes on English character', *Abinger Harvest* (London, 1936), p. 3.

27 Neville Kirk, *The Growth of Working Class Reformism in Mid-Victorian England* (Beckenham, 1985), pp. 174–240.

28 Stefan Szymanski and Tim Kuypers, *Winners and Losers: the Business Strategy of Football* (London, 1999), p. 60.

29 Malcolm Chapman, *The Celts: The Construction of a Myth* (Basingstoke and London, 1992).

30 Gertrude Himmelfarb, *The Demoralization of Society* (London, 1995), pp. 224–6; A. H. Halsey (ed.), *British Social Trends Since 1900* (Basingstoke, 1988), p. 637.

31 Richard Neville, *Playpower* (London, 1971), p. 65.

32 Richard Holt, *Sport and the British* (Oxford, 1989); Tony Mason, *Association Football and English Society* (Brighton, 1980); Dave Russell, *Football and the English* (Preston, 1997).

33 Harold Perkin, *The Structured Crowd* (Brighton, 1981), p. ix.

34 Russell, *Football and the English*, front cover.

35 Nicholas Fishwick, *English Football and Society 1919–1950* (Manchester, 1989), p. 150.

36 Gorer, *Exploring English Character*, p. 13.

37 Peter Davies, *All Played Out* (London, 1990); Ian Hamilton, *Gazza Agonistes* (London, 1993); Harry Lansdown and Alex Spillius (eds.), *Saturday's Boys* (London, 1990).

38 Nick Hornby, *Fever Pitch* (London, 1993), pp. 47–9.

39 John Carey, *The Intellectuals and the Masses* (London, 1992).

40 Holt, *Sport*, p. 173.

41 Mason, *Association Football*, p. 233.

42 Robert Roberts, *The Classic Slum* (Harmondsworth, 1977), pp. 160–1.

43 Alex Leith, *Over the Moon, Brian: The Language of Football* (London, 1998), pp. 181–7.

44 For examples of bad football films, see *Yesterday's Hero* (1970), *When Saturday Comes* (1996), and *Best* (1999).

45 John Fraser, *America and the Patterns of Chivalry* (Cambridge, 1982), pp. 12, 16.

46 Tony Mason, 'Stanley Matthews', in Richard Holt (ed.), *Sport and the Working Class in Modern Britain* (Manchester, 1990), pp. 159–78.

47 In *Finney – a Football Legend* (Preston, 1989), p. 10, Paul Agnew describes Tom Finney as 'the perfect gentleman on and off the field – modest, unassuming and loyal'; and in *Bobby Moore* (London, 1993), p. 268, Jeff Powell describes Moore as 'a gentleman and a gentle man'.

48 James Walvin, *Football and the Decline of Britain* (London, 1986).

49 Steve Humphries, *Hooligans or Rebels?* (Oxford, 1981); Geoffrey Pearson, *Hooligan* (London, 1983); Eric Dunning, Patrick Murphy and John Williams, *The Roots of Football Hooliganism* (London, 1988); Andrew Davies, 'Youth gangs, masculinity and violence in late Victorian Manchester and Salford', *Journal of Social History* 32 (1998), pp. 349–69.

50 Davies, 'Youth gangs', p. 350.

51 Paxman, *The English*, p. 245.

52 Yasmin Alibhai-Brown, *Who Do We Think We Are?* (London, 2000).

53 Grant Jarvie and Graham Walker (eds.), *Scottish Sport in the Making of the Nation: Ninety Minute Patriots?* (Leicester, 1994).

54 Richard Guilianotti, 'Hooligans and carnival fans: Scottish football supporter cultures', in Gary Armstrong and Richard Guilianotti (eds.), *Football Cultures and Identities* (Basingstoke, 1999), p. 36.

55 Holt, *Sport and the British*, p. 278.

56 I am grateful to John K. Walton, Dave Russell, Richard Holt and Andrew Spicer for reading and commenting helpfully on earlier drafts of this chapter.

6

What's happening to England?
Twentieth-century cricket

Charles Barr

A long with David Lean's adaptation of *Great Expectations*, the most cele-brated British film of 1946 remains *A Matter of Life and Death*, written, produced and directed by Michael Powell and Emeric Pressburger. It was chosen in that year for the first Royal Film Performance, and 54 years later a restored print was given the rare honour of a new theatrical release by the British Film Institute. In the course of the film, we hear the reconstruction of a BBC radio cricket commentary of May 1945:

> Well, here we are at Lord's . . . the weather is much more like cricket weather now, it's stopped raining, and the crowd of about 50,000 people have discarded their macs and umbrellas, and have settled down to enjoy the game which to people all over the world is perhaps more truly representative of all that is typically English than anything else . . . And Wally Hammond plays a delightful forcing shot off Miller . . .

This is a commentary on the first in a series of five Victory Test matches between England and Australia – one of the most spectacular popular celebrations of the time, followed not only by huge crowds of spectators but, at a distance, by millions more in Britain and overseas. Eric Midwinter notes that the event was not simply a joyous symbol of the renewal of 'normal' pre-war life, but was marked, however tentatively, by the democratizing process of the 'people's war': 'a civilian [Hammond] and an NCO [the Australian Lindsay Hassett] captained two international sides bristling with commissioned officers'.[1] In the sixth and final unofficial Test of the summer, played likewise at the game's headquarters in North London, Lord's, England would play against the first prominent rep-resentative side to be led by a black cricketer: a Dominions team captained by the West Indian Learie Constantine.

And yet the film uses this passage of radio commentary as a supreme repre-sentation of insular snobbery and decadence. The narrative takes place, as the opening title tells us, 'in the mind of a pilot whose mind has been violently shaped by war', and builds to a trial scene in Heaven where the life of this pilot, played by David Niven, hangs upon the result of a debate between opposing counsels: a British defender and an American prosecutor. The counsels successively deploy anti-British and pro-British (or anti-American) evidence. Exhibit A in the anti-British case is a radio set which relays the passage of cricket commentary transcribed above, introduced sardonically as 'the voice of England in 1945'; the heavenly jury listens to it. Far from offering a defence, Niven's counsel (Roger Livesey) indicates, by a wry smile, that the point is well made, and moves on to counter attack with effective audio evidence of his own, the sound of an American crooner, thus setting up an opposition between the stuffiness of an elite British cultural phenomenon and the vulgarity of an American popular one. The audience, both in heaven and in the cinema, is clearly expected, likewise, to concede the point, and to see cricket as an example of the decadent and reactionary side of British culture.

Why should this case against cricket be seen as, literally, unanswerable? Of the film's two authors, Michael Powell never concealed his dislike for all kinds of sport, but the Hungarian-born Pressburger was a passionate follower of Arsenal, and his love not only of sport but of his adopted country and its traditions might have extended to a little sympathy for the game of cricket.[2] The problem is, perhaps, the portentousness of the (then not uncommon) claim made on behalf of a game 'which to people all over the world is perhaps more truly representative of all that is typically English than anything else', combined with the accent in which it is delivered. The commentator's voice is undeniably pompous and patrician. It sounds rather like E. W. ('Jim') Swanton, a pioneer pre-war radio commentator who would become the establishment 'voice of cricket', via the BBC and the *Daily Telegraph*, for several post-war decades, though at the time of the Victory Tests he was still in a Japanese prisoner-of-war camp.[3] The voice we hear is evidently that of Howard Marshall, whose patrician tones are equally typical of the front presented by the BBC of the time across the full range of announcers and reporters, sporting and otherwise.[4]

One person among the heavenly listeners does not share the general antipathy: David Niven's radio operator, whose presence in heaven is explained by our view, at the start, of his dead body in the blazing plane. He perks up when he hears the commentary, and starts to listen to it eagerly. Robert Coote is typecast here in the role of a genial upper-class idiot, an archetypal 'silly ass' – he complements, at the reception end, the pompous commentator, and is somehow allowed to epitomize, or to outweigh, the 50,000 spectators who we are told are present at the match.[5] The character could have been played by Basil Radford, the popular character-actor who had already come to stand, in British popular cinema, as the prime representative of an enthusiasm for cricket. Radford, and those who used him, must be partly to blame for the common association of the game, at least in Britain, with the old, the dim, and the reactionary; a stereotype which Powell and Pressburger draw upon and reinforce, and which the current Labour government seems likewise to accept: witness the keenness of so many of its members to associate themselves with the 'people's game' of football, and to leave cricket to John Major.[6]

I want to illustrate and interrogate this stereotyping. I am a specialist in British cinema rather than sporting history, but I continue to see a continuity between these two consuming interests. British cinema, English cricket: we can note in passing how the process of naming them immediately connects with a dominant theme of 'Relocating Britishness': the hesitation between the terms English and British. We talk about British cinema, but for most of its history this has been more accurately characterized – as the Scot, Lindsay Anderson, argued in a memorable essay in 1957 – as English, and Southern English at that.[7] For a recent book about the films Alfred Hitchcock directed here before leaving for Hollywood in 1939, I pointedly used the title *English Hitchcock* rather than British.[8] Conversely, the England cricket team might more logically be called Britain, as Robert Croft, an occasional member of the side, argued vigorously in summer 2000, as a native Welsh speaker who plays in the County Championship for Glamorgan. 'England' has actually been captained throughout whole series of Test matches, at different times since 1930, by another Welshman and by two Scots.[9] In the one-day World Cup, played in England in the summer of 1999, Scotland was one of the three minor national teams that competed alongside the nine nations with Test Match status. Their star player was Gavin Hamilton, who plays county cricket for Yorkshire and who made his Test Match debut, a few months later, for England against South Africa. Scotland are not good enough to have a Test team; for the purposes of Test cricket they continue, paradoxically, to be part of England. Both national cinema and national cricket, then, in their different ways, presume, somewhat arrogantly, to equate Britain with England.

'What's happening to England?' – my title is a line of dialogue from *The Lady Vanishes* (1938), the last film but one that Hitchcock made in an English studio before he left for Hollywood. A group of English travellers are stranded overnight by an avalanche in an Alpine inn, and have their homeward journey delayed. Among them are Charters and Caldicott, a bachelor couple, desperate to get back in time to attend the later stages of a Test match in Manchester. When a telephone call is, with some difficulty, put through to London on behalf of another traveller, and the hotel manager goes to fetch him, the phone is surreptitiously appropriated by Charters (Basil Radford), who asks the unknown character at the other end 'What's happening to England?' Told that it is 'blowing a gale', he explodes with impatience, explains he is referring to 'cricket, sir, cricket', and insists that 'you can't be in England and not know the Test score'. When this produces no result, he slams the phone down.

Their single-minded obsession with cricket helped to earn immediate iconic status for this bachelor duo: Charters and Caldicott (played by Naunton Wayne) remain the most widely and affectionately remembered element of this classic film. But it is surely not in itself ridiculous, or unusual, to use 'England' as a shorthand label for 'the England cricket team'. Sport has surely been, and remains, the main context in which we regularly name our country, whatever it may be, and identify ourselves with it – consciously, but without self-consciousness. This factor is central to its cultural significance.

What is absurd about the couple in *The Lady Vanishes* is the narrowness of their obsession, and the way in which, as the film proceeds, it cuts them off from genuine solidarity with their compatriots and thus their country. Because they are so desperate to get home to watch the Test match, they deny having seen the Englishwoman of the title, and thus put her life in danger – if they told the truth, the train might have to be stopped in order to search for her. As the plot develops and the disparate group of English travellers find themselves surrounded by fascist soldiers, Charters and Caldicott remain in their cricket-obsessed cocoon, advising against confrontation, clearly identified with the forces of appeasement: this is a film of 1938. When the bullets start to fly, however, they redeem themselves. Now that there is no alternative, they are able to turn their sporting instincts against a new opponent, a military rather than a cricketing one, and to become part of the cross-class cross-gender solidarity of the train, in a move that anticipates the high-profile incorporation of cricket and cricketers into the war effort, and into its rhetoric.[10] Field-Marshal Montgomery's goal was, famously, to 'hit the enemy for six'.

The same characters reappear in 1940 in a film written by the pair who had scripted *The Lady Vanishes*, Frank Launder and Sidney Gilliat: *Night Train to Munich*, which functions as an informal sequel, though with a different director in Carol Reed. Charters and Caldicott are travelling back by train to England through Germany on the day when war is declared. They find themselves in the same carriage as the film's hero, played by Rex Harrison, a fluent German-speaker who is – as we know but they don't – masquerading as a German officer in order to convey an important scientist and his daughter across the border. Caldicott, however, recognizes the man as an Oxford contemporary of his, Dickie Randall, who used to bowl slow leg-breaks and on one occasion 'played for the Gentlemen'. Charters digests this, and asks, 'You don't think he's working for the Nazis, like that fellow, what's-his-name?' Caldicott: 'Traitor? Hardly, old man. He played for the Gentlemen.' Charters: 'Only once.'

This is the kind of exchange that, as the years go by, stands in increasing need of scholarly annotation, though the film was pitched, successfully, at a popular 1940 audience most of whom will have picked up the allusions. 'Playing for the Gentlemen' refers to the biggest event of the cricket season, other than Test matches: the game at Lord's between the Gentlemen and the Players, the amateurs and the professionals. This was played annually, except in the war years, from the early nineteenth century until 1962: unpaid 'gentleman' cricketers versus paid professionals, on equal terms. In 1962, the formal distinction between amateurs and professionals was abolished, and it soon became normal for those who had played, or would have played, as amateurs, to be paid – men like Colin Cowdrey at the time, and David Gower since. The concept of the unpaid cricketer operating at the top level as late as this may seem anomalous, in comparison to Association football; but we must remember that lawn tennis, athletics and rugby union football were then still, officially, all-amateur sports in all countries at the top level of competition, until, in that order, they went over to professionalism.[11] Test cricketers from other countries were still unpaid, unless they came to England to play in league cricket or, occasionally, for a county.[12] The distinctive thing in English cricket, compared with other sports or with cricket in other countries, was that amateurs and professionals, Gentlemen and Players, played together.

'You don't think he's working for the Nazis, like that fellow, what's-his-name?': the name is William Joyce, popularly known as Lord Haw-Haw, the Irishman with an American passport and an 'English' voice, who regularly broadcast propaganda for the Nazis and who was to be executed as a traitor in 1945. With hindsight, this conjures up the case of P. G. Wodehouse, who was stranded in France when war broke out, interned by the Nazis, and persuaded by them to give a series of cheerful radio talks to the still-neutral United States. Though hardly pro-Nazi in the manner of Joyce, these talks understandably provoked accusations of treachery and collaboration from which Wodehouse's reputation never recovered. Wodehouse had been a top schoolboy sportsman, many of his early novels were centred on public school cricket, and he remained obsessed with the game until, in later life, transferring his allegiance to baseball. Charters is, like his partner Caldicott, a Woosterish figure who surely owes something to Wodehouse's stories in the first place, and the episode of the wartime broadcasts helps to reinforce a strong cluster of associations around the game of cricket: Charters and Caldicott, Wodehouse, upper-class, stupid, sexless, right-wing or worse. Playing for the Gentlemen might not, after all, stop one from sliding into pro-fascism. George Orwell memorably wrote, of the rugby union ethos, that 'a bomb under the West Stand at Twickenham during a big match would put an end to the prospect of fascism in Britain for a generation'. Could the same be said of the Lord's pavilion?

Though Radford, alongside Wayne, exploited the cricket association directly in a lightweight 1949 comedy called *It's Not Cricket*, he made more telling appearances, without Wayne, in two very substantial films of the 1940s, directed by Anthony Asquith from scripts by Terence Rattigan, the playwright who had opened the batting twice at Lord's for Harrow against Eton in the days when this match was a highlight of the social season, played before large crowds. In *The Way to the Stars* (1945), Radford is an RAF officer who has to adjust to sharing the base with a US Air Force squadron. He looks on in alarm at a baseball game, and later attempts to join in, but cannot get the hang of running from base to base rather than towards the pitcher. As a watching American puts it, 'he ought to stick to cricket'. With his cricket goes, as in *The Lady Vanishes*, a complete sexlessness. The John Mills character consults him, as his senior officer, about his love life: is it fair to pursue a courtship with a girl when he might die in action at any time? Radford opts out with the extraordinary line that 'personally, I've never had the old urge'. The same actor was the obvious casting three years later, in the film of Rattigan's play *The Winslow Boy*, for the part of Desmond Curry, disappointed lover of the Winslow boy's elder sister. Introduced to him, the sister's fiancé asks: 'are you any relation of the D. W. H. Curry who used to play for Middlesex?' 'I *am* D. W. H. Curry.' 'You used to be a hero of mine . . .' Hero, once upon a time, in cricket, ineffectual in love; Radford poignantly conveys a sense of one whose post-cricket career as a lawyer has been grey anti-climax.

In none of the films so far referred to, other than *It's Not Cricket*, is the game actually shown. Rattigan and Asquith did, however, later make a cricket-centred film, *The Final Test*, given its premiere in April 1953 in time to take advantage of the intense public interest surrounding the visit of the second post-war Australian touring team. The title of the best book on this series, written by the former Australian test player Jack Fingleton, is evocative: *The Ashes*

Crown the Year.[13] England's first series win over Australia since 1933 became a proud and integral feature of Coronation Year and the putative dawning of a New Elizabethan Age, alongside the climbing of Everest, and the almost equally long-awaited triumphs of popular favourites Gordon Richards in the Derby and Stanley Matthews in the Cup Final. *The Final Test* puts real cricketers on show, notably Len Hutton, who the previous year had become the first professional player to captain England, but does little with them, and its slackly indulgent representation of the game and its culture plays into the hands of hostile critics of the Powell and Pressburger type. Its main representative of cricketing spectatorship, Richard Wattis, comes over as a dim-witted cross between Basil Radford and Robert Coote; the 53-year-old Jack Warner is improbable casting even as a veteran Test batsman; and, partly for this reason, the core scenes of cricket action are lamentably unconvincing.

For a vivid, serious and adult representation of the game, we need to look ahead to the partnership between the playwright Harold Pinter and the exiled American director Joseph Losey. The cricket scenes in *Accident* (1967) and *The Go-Between* (1971) are shaped by Pinter's own inwardness with the game, by Losey's skill in handling space, composition and editing, and by their shared fascination with the English class system. Both films play out social and psychological tensions in terms of cricket: a short but resonant contemporary scene on an Oxford college ground in *Accident* is followed, in *The Go-Between*, by a longer, weightier and more complex sequence set in rural Norfolk in 1900.

The cricket match in *The Go-Between* centres on an intense individual struggle within the wider team contest, a pattern which is the basis of cricket's structure and fascination: the aristocrat, Lord Trimingham, played by Edward Fox, versus the rustic, Ted Burgess, played by Alan Bates. When his side bats first, we see Trimingham play two classically elegant cover drives to the boundary before being bowled. As the match develops after the tea interval, the result comes to hinge on the contest between Trimingham's fast bowling and Burgess' hitting. Despite disparaging remarks by the watching Eton schoolboys about the crudity of his technique, Burgess makes a series of exhilarating cross-bat hits for six, before being caught on the boundary, just short of victory, by one of the boys, Leo, who has come on to field as a substitute.

Trimingham belongs to a classical amateur tradition of batsmanship, forged in the leading public schools, centred on correct style and the straight bat, favouring the offside of the wicket, and associated, at the period in which the film is set, with such men as Archie McLaren (Harrow), C. B. Fry (Repton and Oxford), and Pelham Warner (Rugby and Oxford).[14] But if he is, like them, an archetypal 'Gentleman', where does Burgess fit in? He does not match any comparable model of a professional 'Player'. The professional style was in its own way equally correct, if not more so. They had to perform reliably in order to protect their place in the team and thus their livelihood, and many of them went on to be employed as coaches to the amateur talent at the schools and universities. Ironically, the batsmen to whom Ted Burgess seems closer belong to the 'Gentlemen' side of the divide, for instance W. G. Grace himself and his elder brother E. M., countrymen from Gloucestershire, bearded like Burgess, both of whom caused controversy at the start of their careers by their pragmatic readiness to pull straight balls round to the legside in a manner that had previously been thought to be 'not done', 'not cricket'. Burgess' hitting, from a crouching stance, evokes that of Gilbert Jessop, known as 'The Croucher', the most devastating hitter in the history of the game, who played as an amateur in this same period on either side of 1900, for Cambridge, Gloucestershire and England, and subsequently took a job as secretary of a golf club.[15]

The oppositional Gentleman/Players relationship, as soon as one looks at it in operation, is thus deceptively complex. The opposing styles, correct and transgressive, favouring off-side and leg-side, also represent complementary elements of the amateur tradition. The relation of aristocrat and workman, gentleman and player, can, likewise, be seen as operating in not just an oppositional but also a complementary fashion within county and national sides, and more broadly within the game, and by extension the nation. *The Go-Between* hints at this in its recurrent high-angle shots of the game, setting it in a beautiful rural landscape in the harmonious long-shot manner of a landscape-painting tradition.

Of course this notion of harmony and complementarity is wide open to abuse, and to caricature. Men like Lord Hawke in life and the Basil Radford characters in fiction were extremely happy with an immutable system in which, in cricket and in society, the gentlemen made the rules and gave the orders, and the lower orders knew their place, and meanwhile did most of the hard and unglamorous work. This hardly needs spelling out. In the remainder of this chapter I look at the more positive side.

One of the key popular texts of the inter-war period is J. B. Priestley's *The Good Companions*, which had a huge popular success when published as a novel in 1929 and went on to attract big audiences first in a stage adaptation and then, in 1933, in the more durable form of a film. The Gaumont-British production of *The Good Companions* opens with a map of England, on which are picked out four specific locations: the homes of three of the protagonists, respectively in the industrial North, the rural West Country, and East Anglia (close to Cambridge), and, fourthly, a symbolic Middle England location on which the three of them will converge to form the touring theatrical company of the film's title. The map does not simply provide a conventional initial establishing shot, it is the main focus of the first few minutes of the film. The camera, reinforced by a voice-over commentary, tracks in successively on the appropriate parts of the map to 'reveal' and introduce the characters within it: the differences in region (as well as in gender and in class) are thus firmly underlined. The film's narrative can be seen as a model or template for 'the kind of Second World War propaganda film that pulls together individuals from diverse regions and classes, and forges them into an unselfish collaborative unit'.[16] Diverse regions and classes, from which individuals come together into a touring unit: this is also a very suggestive model for considering the construction, and the national role, of the England cricket team.

The national team continues to represent, and to connect with, the diversity of the nation in a more precise and meaningful way than do other international sporting teams. Note, for a start, the taken-for-granted way in which Test matches cover the country. Twentieth-century England soccer internationals were usually played at Wembley, and Rugby internationals at Twickenham; but there are six Test match grounds, all of which are now used every summer, evenly spread out: two in London, two in the Midlands, and two in the North (with Durham's ground at Chester-le-Street to be added to the list in 2003).[17] The same diversity operates in terms of personnel. Cricketers, or at least most of them, have been until recently more genuinely and recognisably rooted in their own counties than, say, footballers are in the towns and cities that they nominally and often very temporarily represent. The England cricket XI that played the West Indies at Lords in 1933 constitutes the same kind of blend of classes and regions that came together, in the film of the same year, to form the *Good Companions*:

C. F. Walters	c. Barrow b. Martindale	51
Sutcliffe, H.	c. Grant b. Martindale	21
Hammond, W. R.	c. Headley b. Griffith	29
Leyland, M.	c. Barrow b. Griffith	1
D. R. Jardine (capt.)	c. Da Costa b. Achong	21
M. J. Turnbull	c. Barrow b. Achong	28
Ames, L. E. G.	not out	83
G. O. Allen	run out	16

R. W. V. Robins	b. Martindale	8
Verity, H.	c. Achong b. Griffith	21
Macaulay, G. G.	lbw b. Martindale	9
Extras		8
Total		296

The five whose initials are, following the usage of the time, placed before their names are amateur Gentlemen, the other six are professional Players.[18] Sutcliffe, Leyland, Verity and Macaulay are all from Yorkshire, and correspond to the urban working-class Yorkshireman, played by Edmund Gwenn, discovered within the England map at the opening of *The Good Companions*. The West is represented by Hammond of Gloucestershire, Turnbull of Glamorgan, and Walters, formerly of Glamorgan but now of Worcestershire in the West Midlands.[19] The third, East Anglian, element in the film's geographical triangle is more significant in terms of class than of region as such, since it is the location of the boarding-school where the University-educated John Gielgud character teaches; this member of the Companions has his structural equivalent among the public school amateurs, who include the Etonians, Allen and Robins, and the Wykehamist, Jardine; but Robins did, like Turnbull, go on to Cambridge University.[20] Which leaves only one man unaccounted for, the wicket-keeper Ames, from Kent, whose players were often seen as bringing a distinctive 'Garden of England' spirit to the national mix.[21]

It is remarkable how consistently this pattern has been sustained. The England team of summer 2000, again playing the West Indies, included three gritty Yorkshiremen (Gough, Vaughan, White), and two public school/East Anglia men in the captain Hussein (from Essex) and the former captain Atherton (a Lancastrian, but also a Cambridge graduate). It included a new player who in terms of birth, of local roots, of accent, of playing style, and not least of name, radiates an identification with the rural West Country: the Somerset batsman Marcus Trescothick. Though not all the team play for the county or even country of their birth (Hussain himself was born in India, Graeme Hick of Worcestershire is originally from Zimbabwe, Andy Caddick of Somerset from New Zealand), it is very striking that, even in an age of increased movement between counties, every one of this August 2000 team is a one-county man; they have, then, over the years, come to be solidly identified with those parts of the country.

In between these dates, here are two more England cards, the first from the match against Australia at Old Trafford, Manchester, in 1956:

P. E. Richardson	c. Maddocks b. Benaud	104
M. C. Cowdrey	c. Maddocks b. Lindwall	80
Rev. D. S. Sheppard	b. Archer	113
P. B. H. May (capt.)	c. Archer b. Benaud	43
T. E. Bailey	b. Johnson	20
Washbrook, C.	lbw b. Johnson	6
Oakman, A. S. M.	c. Archer b. Johnson	10
Evans, T. G.	st. Maddocks b. Johnson	47
Laker, J. C.	run out	3
Lock, G. A. R.	not out	25
Statham, J. B.	c. Maddocks b. Lindwall	0
Extras		8
Total		459

This was celebrated by conservative critics as a great day for the tradition of amateur batsmanship, with the first five in the batting order earning the right to initials before their name: the same proportion of amateurs as in 1933. The West Country element is only marginal (Peter Richardson, the amateur non-graduate farmer from Worcestershire), and the main emphasis is Southern, but there are still two Northern stalwarts in Washbrook and Statham, both of Lancashire. The most interesting presence is that of the Reverend David Sheppard, future Bishop of Liverpool, on holiday at the time for a few weeks from his ministry in London, and playing well enough for Sussex to force his way back into the Test team. He would return the following year against the West Indies, and again in 1962, when a century in the last Gentleman versus Players match of all earned him a place on the winter tour to Australia; he played in all five Tests there, scoring a match-winning century in the second. After this, his age (thirty-three) and increasing church commitments took him out of the first-class game; and no clergymen now operate in this irregular amateur manner. No longer does a band of schoolmasters, Oxbridge blues, emerge in late July from their summer-term coaching and teaching duties to join their respective counties for the last five or six weeks of the season. A significant number of these, up to the 1950s, were good enough to hold their own, as their figures proved: men like C. H. Knott (Tonbridge-Kent), G. H. Chesterton (Malvern-Worcestershire), Rev. J. R. Bridger (Marlborough-Hampshire), and M. M. Walford (Sherborne-Somerset). Perhaps the most spectacular representative of this band was C. S. Marriott, master in charge of cricket at P. G. Wodehouse's old school, Dulwich College. In the *Good Companions* year of 1933,

Marriott bowled so well in the school holidays for Kent that he was chosen for the final Test against the West Indies, and took eleven wickets in what was to be his only Test match, since in subsequent years no convenient opening appeared in the England team.[22]

One of David Sheppard's team-mates in that final Gentlemen's XI of 1962 was to become almost the last of these part-timers: a Cambridge undergraduate named Michael Brearley, the Cambridge University wicket-keeper. This had for years been the most difficult place in the Gentlemen's team to fill, since all the regular county players were professionals. Brearley went on, after graduation, to play as a batsman for Middlesex, and did well enough to be picked for the MCC party to tour South Africa in 1964–65, without playing in a Test.[23] After that, he pursued an academic career, as a graduate student in America and then a philosophy lecturer at Newcastle, but remained sufficiently interested, and sufficiently in demand for his skills, to return intermittently to the first-class game in the Sheppard manner, mainly by playing for Middlesex in successive University vacations, including that of 1968.

The revolutionary *événements* of May 1968 in Paris had an echo in English cricket, when the startling omission of the Cape Coloured player Basil D'Oliveira from the MCC party to tour South Africa sparked a chain of protests that led, ultimately, to the cancellation of the tour and to the breaking off of official matches while apartheid remained in place.[24] It is no coincidence that the two leading protesters were the last of the prominent top-level part-timers, David Sheppard and Michael Brearley, both unafraid to incur the odium of conservatives within the game.[25] A number of past and former professional players were known to be sympathetic to their position, but reluctant to speak out. This is the other side of the amateur cricketing tradition from the reactionary image associated with the likes of Basil Radford and Lord Hawke: a healthy independence of spirit, able to see the game in a wider social and political perspective, in line with the rhetorical question famously asked by C. L. R. James, 'What do they know of cricket who only cricket know?'[26]

Brearley would no doubt have drifted out of his part-time involvement in the game before long, had he not been persuaded to leave the day job and fill a sudden vacancy as captain of Middlesex in 1971. A few years later, he was picked for England as a batsman, and soon after as captain. But, while a new-model professional in terms both of payment and commitment, he retained the wider interests, in Denis Healey's terms the 'hinterland', of the part-timer.[27] This scorecard is from his final year as England captain: the second England innings of the famous Headingley Test of 1981:

G. A. Gooch	c. Alderman b. Lillee	0
G. Boycott	lbw b. Alderman	46
J. M. Brearley (capt.)	c. Alderman b. Lillee	14
D. I. Gower	c. Border b. Alderman	9
M. W. Gatting	lbw b. Alderman	1
P. Willey	c. Dyson b. Lillee	33
I. T. Botham	not out	149
R. W. Taylor	c. Bright b. Alderman	1
G. R. Dilley	b. Alderman	56
C. M. Old	b. Lawson	29
R. G. D. Willis	c. Border b. Alderman	2
Extras		16
Total		356

The team is a perfect example of the triangular regional structure familiar from Priestley's *Good Companions*. Among a wide mix, the three dominant figures are, from the North, Geoffrey Boycott; from the West, in the great tradition of Grace, Hammond and Jessop, Somerset's Ian Botham; and Brearley himself, filling the John Gielgud role of the intellectual, from public school and Cambridge, as ready as the others to join the national mix and the national project. The video record of this classic series carries some impressive evidence of the mutual help and respect between, in particular, Botham and Brearley.[28] In the course of what becomes a match-winning innings of 149, Botham is seen reaching his 100 exultantly, but then heeding Brearley's signal from the pavilion balcony to get his head down and stay in to increase his score. Afterwards, he pays tribute to Brearley's influence, and the tribute is returned, with equal thought and sincerity. It is a model of a productive, unhierarchical relation between individuals of different backgrounds and regions, and it is not surprizing either that it had such spectacular results on the field, or that the team so strongly captured the imagination of the public.[29]

I end by considering the Marxist writer from Trinidad quoted above, C. L. R. James, who saw no conflict between his politics and his passion for cricket: on the contrary, he saw the game as playing a crucial role both in the development of modern English democracy and in the successful fight for West Indian independence. In 1976, towards the end of his life, I interviewed him for a BBC TV programme inspired by his classic book *Beyond a Boundary*.[30] As we sat in the Long Room of the Lord's pavilion, and the camera panned slowly across portraits of influential figures in the game's history – Jardine, Warner,

Lord Hawke – I asked him this: 'Many of the people whose images preside here, either visually or in spirit, would probably be defined as conservative and even reactionary or philistine figures in a wider context – has that ever bothered you?' 'Not particularly: it hasn't bothered me at all. Because cricket is a game that all people in England at one time were interested in . . .' James went on to recall his first direct exposure to English cricket in the 1930s, when he came from Trinidad to join his friend Learie Constantine, the first West Indian to play as a professional in the Lancashire Leagues. 'The ordinary workers from the mill would come in on Saturday morning at 11 o'clock . . . there was not the slightest taint of aristocracy or superiority there . . . but nevertheless the people who had taught us the game in the Caribbean were the aristocratic planters. Constantine had a tremendous respect and liking for H. B. G. Austin, and so did I.' Austin was the white leader of West Indian sides before they attained Test match status, and for James he stood as a representative figure in the international development of the game as a complex popular phenomenon. He went on to talk about the role in English social history of W. G. Grace. Here are his reflections, in his book, on Grace's achievement of his one hundredth century in 1895:

> On what other occasion, sporting or non-sporting, was there ever such enthusiasm, such an unforced sense of community, of the universal merged in an individual? At the end of a war? A victorious election? With its fears, its hatreds, its violent passions? Scrutinize the list of popular celebrations, the unofficial ones; that is to say, those not organized from above. I have heard of no other that approached this celebration of W.G.'s hundredth century. If this is not social history what is?[31]

'The end of a war, a victorious election . . .' Both were celebrated in the English summer of 1945, and arguably the most intense expression of the emotions of the time came through the playing, before huge crowds, of the Victory Tests. Cricket acted as focus and expression of a celebration that was both national and international; and it was in this summer that Constantine himself became, at Lord's, the first black captain of a representative side – the Dominions against England. In using the game as a negative, Blimpish symbol of English life in 1945, Powell and Pressburger could not have been more wrong.

Notes

1 Eric Midwinter, *The Lost Seasons: Cricket in Wartime 1939–1945* (London, 1987), p. 145.
2 Michael Powell, *A Life in Movies* (London, 1986).

3 E. W. Swanton, *Sort of a Cricket Person* (London, 1972), p. 135. Livesey had previously played the title role in Powell and Pressburger's *The Life and Death of Colonel Blimp* (1943), and the cricket commentary may be seen as carrying Blimpish associations.

4 The *Radio Times* schedule for the opening day of the match, 19 May 1945, refers to passages of running commentary 'from the pavilion at Lord's' by Howard Marshall, an experienced BBC man who had been a war reporter.

5 Lord's has never held as many as 50,000. Present capacity, taking account of new safety regulations, is around 28,000. According to Midwinter (*The Lost Seasons*, p. 145), a total of 70,000 people paid for admission to this game over three days. Though the game began on 19 May, the events of the film are explicitly dated, in an opening voice-over commentary, as beginning on 2 May 1945. This slight liberty with dates can be excused – especially since heaven need not be subject to the tyranny of time.

6 On the day he lost the 1997 General Election, John Major went to relax by watching cricket at the Oval. At the time of writing he is President of Surrey County Cricket Club.

7 Lindsay Anderson, 'Get out and push', in Tom Maschler (ed.), Declaration (St Albans, 1957), p. 157.

8 Charles Barr, *English Hitchcock* (Moffat, 1999).

9 The Welshman is Tony Lewis (1972–73). The Scots are Douglas Jardine (1932–33) and Mike Denness (1974–75).

10 For more detail on *The Lady Vanishes*, see Barr, *English Hitchcock*, chapter 6.

11 Each of these ostensibly amateur sports had problems with covert professionalism, which created growing and finally irresistible pressure to abandon the amateur framework. For W. G. Grace, the Gloucestershire doctor who earned far more in expenses and fees, in a career stretching from the 1860s to beyond 1900, than any professional of his time, see for instance Simon Rae, *W. G. Grace* (Faber, 1998), pp. 103–5. A more common type of cricketing amateur was the Oxford or Cambridge blue who was enabled to play regularly by wealth, or the prospect of it, or, latterly, by the creation of an acceptable cricket-related job like that of Assistant Secretary of a County Club, which might or might not be a sinecure.

12 Frank Keating's obituary of the New Zealand batsman Martin Donnelly recalls a story from his first tour of England at the age of nineteen. 'His first innings was at Old Trafford against Lancashire. Asking the umpire for a guard, he said "Middle-and-leg please, sir". Behind the stumps, George Duckworth [professional, with many England caps] had kittens. "Don't you 'please sir' him, lad. You're the amateur, *he* calls *you* 'sir' in this country."' (Wisden Cricket Monthly, 20 (7) (December 1999), p. 51).

13 Jack Fingleton, *The Ashes Crown the Year: A Coronation Cricket Diary* (London, 1954).

14 Edward Fox, like McLaren and Rattigan, was at Harrow. It is clear that in the film he is executing his own strokes in a thoroughly assured style.

15 E. M. Brodribb, *The Croucher: A Biography of Gilbert Jessop* (London, 1974).

16 Charles Barr, 'Desperate yearnings: Victor Saville and Gainsborough', in Pam Cook (ed.), *Gainsborough Pictures* (London, 1997), p. 57.

17 Lord's and the Oval; Trent Bridge (Nottingham) and Edgbaston (Birmingham); Headingley (Leeds) and Old Trafford (Manchester). Since this was written a Test has been staged at the Riverside, Durham. The obvious gap is in the West Country, though one-day internationals have been staged in Bristol.

18 Scorecards are based on those available from the archive section of the cricinfo website: www-uk.cricket.org

19 The West Country member of the *Good Companions* is a woman, played by Mary Glynne. I am not suggesting any corresponding 'femininity' in West Country cricket or cricketers; more relevant is the mellow 'heritage' iconography of fields and old buildings that the film here draws upon.

20 Looking back to the issue of England/Britain discussed earlier, this list is especially interesting in containing both a Scot in the captain, Jardine, and, in Turnbull, a Welshman who played Rugby for Wales as well as cricket for England.

21 Note in particular players like Colin Blythe, Frank Woolley and Godfrey Evans.

22 Marriott died in 1965, but he had distilled much of his coaching and playing wisdom into a text published posthumously as *The Complete Leg-Break Bowler* (London, 1968).

23 It is an index of the long domination of cricket by the forces of the Gentlemen that, until the late 1970s, representative touring sides were picked by a Committee administered by the Marylebone Cricket Club, and toured Australia and other countries under the name of 'MCC', becoming 'England' only for Test matches.

24 Basil D'Oliveira, *The D'Oliveira Affair* (London, 1969).

25 It was by no means only leftist opinion that supported the Sheppard/Brearley line; Jim Swanton of the *Daily Telegraph* did so strongly, in defiance of his own paper's editorial line and that of most of its readers. See Swanton, *Sort of a Cricket Person*. My own memory of acting as organizer of the extensive protest movement within the MCC confirms my sense that cricketers and cricket followers constitute an extremely 'broad church'.

26 C. L. R. James, *Beyond a Boundary* (London, 1976, first published 1973), p. 11.

27 Denis Healey, former Labour Chancellor, claimed that politicians, to be effective, should have a 'hinterland' of other interests. Brearley himself, in the later stages of his time as a full-time cricketer, trained for a new career as a psychiatrist.

28 *Botham's Ashes*, BBCV 4010, BBC Enterprises, 1981.

29 The scenes of national celebration of three successive spectacular victories over Australia in 1981 were echoed in those of three spectacular victories over the West Indies in 2000, when, as noted above, the rich mix of regions and cultures in the team was still very apparent.

30 *Beyond a Boundary*, produced and directed by Mike Dibb for BBC2, 1976.

31 James, *Beyond a Boundary*, pp. 182–3.

7

From Sherlock Holmes to James Bond: masculinity and national identity in British popular fiction

James Chapman and Matthew Hilton

S ince the late nineteenth century, British masculinity can be presented as experiencing perpetual crisis. In the *fin-de-siècle* metropolis of 1890s London, men's identities were destabilized by the appearance of the assertive new woman and the lurid fascination with homosexuality sensationalized in the Oscar Wilde trial.[1] In the Edwardian period, the crisis of the manliness of youth became a national obsession as the poor quality of Boer War recruits heightened the growing fears over physical deterioration.[2] The First World War literally and metaphorically tore the male apart and prompted a nervous introspection that threatened the sanity of veterans such as Robert Graves and, in fiction, Virginia Woolf's Septimus Warren Smith.[3] At the same time, the alienating and effeminizing nature of mass production and mass society provoked crisis reactions that could, in extreme form, lead to psychological attempts to cover the weakened male body with a hard outer military shell.[4] Society's emasculation of the male is said to have continued into the 1950s as suburbanization stripped the 'organization man' of his individuality.[5] If this was a phenomenon more prominent in the United States than in Britain, it embodied a critique of the lower middle class that stretches back to Pooter and the novels of H. G. Wells.[6] Following the 'death of the salesman', the sexual liberation of the 1960s and the feminist movement of the 1970s finally robbed men of their manhood and traditional role in the family unit. The tortured angst of the 1970s and 1980s 'men's movement' was often led by liberal male academics who pioneered the study of masculinity as a problematic entity. Responding to this latest threat to masculine hegemony, it is no wonder that the crisis narrative has become so predominant in histories of men and gender.[7]

Yet for an identity forever in crisis, definitions and images of British masculinity have proved remarkably resilient since the nineteenth century. This chapter aims to outline some of the continuities and changes in constructions of masculinity and Britishness in commercially successful adventure fiction. 'Popular culture', as Jeffrey Richards observes, 'is one of the ways by which society instructs its members in its prevailing ideas and mores, its dominant role models and legitimate aspirations'.[8] Popular fictions both reflect dominant values and ideologies and serve to construct and reinforce them. One of the primary roles of popular adventure stories, undoubtedly, is to provide solutions to perceived crises within society.[9] Fictional heroes resolve these tensions by promoting idealized types that provide readers with temporary escape from the complexities of their own individual and social identities. However, we do not want to suggest that the popular fictional heroes under discussion arose merely from crises. Rather, they were often cultural expressions of a masculinity and national identity at ease with itself. Issues of patriotism, duty, loyalty, individuality and independence recur as central motifs throughout the novels and stories discussed, suggesting important continuities in images of British masculinity. Popular culture here seems both to have withstood the acute difficulties suggested by conventional histories of masculinity, and to have provided certain continuities that overrode any reformulation of idealized fictional types that would have appeared necessary according to the logic of the crisis narrative.

Historians often draw upon 'middle-brow' literature when exploring questions of identity and representation, especially the works of Dickens, Trollope, Evelyn Waugh, Joseph Conrad and J. B. Priestley. Only relatively recently has popular fiction been given serious attention, with such writers as Wilkie Collins, Mary Elizabeth Braddon, Frank Richards and Agatha Christie receiving sustained historical analysis.[10] Attention is beginning to turn to popular adventure fiction.[11] This chapter contributes to that body of literature by examining two well-known figures (Arthur Conan Doyle's Sherlock Holmes and Ian Fleming's James Bond) together with two less-studied heroes (Sapper's Bulldog Drummond and Leslie Charteris' Simon Templar, 'the Saint'). Issues of masculinity and Britishness could have been explored through a host of other characters. For instance, John Buchan's adventurer, Richard Hannay, is useful for analysing questions of empire, the relationship between London and the countryside and Scotland, as well as the homosocial relations with the bushman Peter Pienaar and the Lawrence-of-Arabia figure Sandy Arbuthnot, and the marital relations between Hannay and his wife Mary who takes an increasingly dominant role in the adventures. Similarly, Dorothy L. Sayers' Lord Peter Wimsey is useful for examining the persistence of an aristocratic ideal in the interwar period, together with the psychological repercussions of the First World War. As with Hannay, Wimsey's masculinity is entirely at ease with women (in the form of the much-pursued and eventually-married Harriet Vane) who are as resourceful, purposeful, independent and intelligent as the male leads. Similar fruitful research could be made of Allan Quatermain, A. J. Raffles, Hercule Poirot and Biggles, although Sax Rohmer's Nayland Smith is rather dull and one-dimensional in comparison to his arch enemy, Fu Manchu.

These characters have been selected principally because they appear at the same time as, and provide the most suitable insights into, four key moments of British cultural and political history. Sherlock Holmes has become an icon of the high Victorian period, the fogs of London that seep into every collection of stories seeming to capture that moment of modernity before Victorian Britain saw clearly into the twentieth century. Bulldog Drummond's arrival in 1920 enables a study of how national and masculine identities responded to the First World War and its immediate aftermath. Similarly, the Saint allows us to tackle issues related to the 1930s and the Depression. Finally, James Bond, the last imperial hero, proves particularly interesting given the political and cultural implications of Britain's 'retreat from Empire' in the aftermath of the Suez Crisis of 1956.

Sherlock Holmes

Sherlock Holmes needs no introduction. His residence at 221B Baker Street, his chronicler Dr Watson, his cocaine habit, his violin, his housekeeper Mrs Hudson and his arch-rival Professor Moriarty are all familiar to us. Although by no means the first literary detective, he has become the most famous and the one to whom all others defer. Indeed, mention of him is made in just about every adventure hero series in the twentieth century. And he has become the hero most critically scrutinized by academics.[12] In the most recent book-length treatment of Conan Doyle's character, Joseph Kestner has argued that the narrative of the crisis in masculinity is the key to understanding Holmes. Kestner provides a host of explanations as to why Britain needed a hero at this time: the fears over Jack the Ripper, the worries resulting from the difficulties in controlling a distant Empire, the rise of the women's rights movements, labour unrest, and the increased economic and military competition from the modern nations of German and the USA. All these factors served to present an image of nation, metropolis and masculinity in crisis.[13]

Kestner argues that Holmes embodied Victorian Christian moral values – 'observation, rationalism, factuality, logic, comradeship, daring and pluck' – and he must be analysed within this context. Holmes 'policed' masculinity. Through imposture and disguise he transgressed boundaries, entering the other, while maintaining his own identity as that of the paradigm of masculinity. Taken together, the sixty stories of the Holmes canon constitute a guidebook on paradigmatic British masculinity, telling the reader about male homosociality, the Empire and school, national and racial differences, gentlemanly behaviour, and the discourses of crime and punishment.

Much of Kestner's analysis convinces. Holmes was all of these things and more. But his character cannot be understood as a straightforward response to crisis. Rather, Conan Doyle used Holmes to celebrate a particular type of masculinity, an assured, confident liberal identity that had little to do with crisis, insecurity or instability. The liberal individual had emerged from the narrow *homo economicus* of political economy and Free Trade, and in the Victorian period was celebrated at a cultural level too. Cultural liberalism manifested itself in a celebration of the twin tenets of its creed: independence and individuality. It is here that the most singular detective was in his element.[14]

Taking one aspect of Holmes's personality, we can see the liberal ideals permeating his every action. Sherlock Holmes was one of the most idiosyncratic smokers of all time. He bought his 'strongest shag tobacco' from a tobacconist named Bradley.[15] He kept his cigars and pipes in the coal scuttle and his tobacco 'in the toe-end of a Persian slipper'.[16] And, as well as his 'everyday' briar pipe, he smoked an 'old and oily clay pipe' and sometimes a 'long cherrywood' when in a 'disputatious rather than a meditative mood'.[17] His smoking habits included the use of a glowing cinder held by a pair of tongs to light his pipes, and the smoking of 'all the plugs and dottles left from his smokes of the day before' for his before-breakfast pipe.[18] Occasionally, he preferred to smoke cigarettes, as when in his 'old nonchalant mood' or when there was a certain rapidity in his conversation.[19] Whilst he never took snuff, he was occasionally inclined to produce a cigar for moments of conviviality or hospitality. He knew everything about his own indulgence and was hardly the passive consumer: indeed, tobaccos and pipes helped him solve numerous cases, and he wrote a 'little monograph on the ashes of 140 different varieties of pipe, cigar, and cigarette tobacco'.[20]

Holmes embodies that pervasive Victorian ethic of manhood which embraced patriotism, amateurism, 'character' and rationality. Although one scholar has noted a hint of republicanism in Holmes's flippant disregard for the fate of Charles I, elsewhere he is seen to support the Queen and hold instead rather disparaging attitudes towards the European aristocracy.[21] And Holmes was hardly an amateur, since he advertized his services as a professional consulting detective. Yet the amateur qualities of Holmes are still apparent: he never trained for his work as a professional might; his talents were inherent rather than acquired; and financial negotiations are hardly ever mentioned in the adventures.[22] Furthermore, Holmes's spare time between cases was filled with that languid *ennui* so typical of Ouida's representations of gentlemanly cavalry officers: the seemingly asexual Holmes avoided the pleasures of the flesh or the town beloved by other bourgeois bachelors and retreated instead to his drawing room sofa to inject cocaine 'as a protest against the monotony of existence'.[23] When energized by the complexities of a case, however, his logical and deductive powers betrayed a hyper-rationality that left his stooge Watson trailing in his intellectual wake.

Holmes's rationality typifies an intellectual strand of histories of modernity, of how the liberal self sought to place order on, and make sense of, a seemingly chaotic and irrational society.[24] The London of Holmes and Watson was not a savoury place: 'that great cesspool into which all the loungers and idlers of the Empire are irresistibly drained' and where any criminal could 'change his name, and vanish in an instant among the four million inhabitants of this great city'.[25] The city represented confusion and danger and was made up of a series of 'whimsical little incidents': 'Amid the action and reaction of so dense a swarm of humanity, every possible combination of events may be expected to take place, and many a little problem will be presented which may be striking and bizarre without being criminal.'[26] To make sense of this disorder required the specific attributes of the rational, liberal British male. Holmes's powers of deductive reasoning are deliberately made clear to Watson in almost every adventure. They inhabit a London of two worlds – chaos and order, crime and respectability, darkness and light – divided by a wall of fog that Holmes would frequently penetrate, often in disguise as though his powers of rationality had to be hidden in the irrational world.

Kestner sees as conclusive proof of the crisis of masculinity thesis, the fact that Robert Baden-Powell made explicit reference to the powers and abilities of Holmes in his *Scouting for Boys*. For Baden-Powell, Holmes's skills in deduction, observation and reasoning were all skills the good scout should learn, to become a better tracker, marksman and soldier of the Empire. The idealized masculinity of the detective was therefore used as a means to help Scouts respond to the current crises of degeneration. But it is Baden-Powell who is in crisis, not Holmes. *Scouting for Boys* appeared in 1908: after the Boer War; after the report of the Committee on Physical Deterioration; after the death of Queen Victoria, the living symbol of the Empire; after the furore over the trial of Wilde; and at a time of political concerns over Europe and the decline of British naval power. Most of the Holmes adventures, and all the defining characteristics of the detective, however, were written before these events – at a time when liberalism was in its ascendancy. Sherlock Holmes epitomized the values of independence and individuality, and these values have continued to mark out British adventure heroes throughout the twentieth century.

Bulldog Drummond

Captain Hugh (Bulldog) Drummond, DSO, MC, late of His Majesty's Royal Loamshires, resident of 60A Half Moon Street, is the hero of a series of novels written by 'Sapper', or Lieutenant-Colonel Herman Cyril McNeile, a professional soldier commissioned in the Royal Engineers in 1907 who fought with the British Expeditionary Force in 1914 and later at Ypres. Drummond is much less fashionable than the other heroes of this chapter, his popularity declining because of his association with fascism and anti-Semitism, especially in the second book of the series, *The Black Gang,* when two Jews were 'flogged within an inch of their lives' for their role in the White Slave Trade.[27] The stories revolve around Drummond, an upper middle-class leader of a gang of perfectly attired urbane latter-day dandies, who enjoy the hunt or the sport of chasing criminals – usually a bunch of hot-headed 'Bolshevists' led by Carl Peterson and his companion Irma who plan to take over Britain.[28]

Drummond shares certain attributes with Holmes. He begins as a bachelor, has a bachelor's residence in Mayfair and is aided by his loyal servant Denny, who serves as a Watson-like stooge. After the first novel, however, Denny falls into the background and he becomes more servile – if not a 'fool', an 'ass' and a 'paralytic idiot'[29] – as he is replaced by Drummond's gang of upper-middle class friends, consisting of his fellow officers from the war: Ted Jerningham, Toby Sinclair, Jerry Seymour, Peter Darrell and Algy Longworth. There is much that is idiosyncratic in Drummond's habits. As in the Holmes adventures, tobacco is used to mark out the hero's character. Drummond always proffers his cigarette case, stating 'Turkish on that side, gaspers on the other'. Although he has the help of his gang, he acts independently, either from the police, the state or from financial reward. He embodies the spirit of the gentlemanly amateur, fighting crime for the sport. When Drummond offers Algy Longworth a job working with him, he only accepts once he sees it as a chase: 'Oh! Not work, dear old boy. Damn it, man – you know me better than that, surely!'[30] Their adventures are motivated by patriotism and contempt for communists and other fanatics who seek to agitate the decent ordinary working class. There is also a touch of bohemianism to Drummond, or at least an urbane flippancy which sees him bored with life, always languid, preferring lounging about in the club drinking cocktails to anything that smacks of real work. Here, Drummond represents a tradition of idealizing the British officer that stretches back to Thackeray's heroes of Waterloo in *Vanity Fair*: lazy in appearance but coming to life whenever there is sport to be had, whether on the field of play or the field of battle.[31]

Drummond was a product of his time and differed in significant ways from either the liberal amateur ideal of Holmes or the effete military ideal of the officer class. Firstly, written during a war which gave little space for hand-to-hand conflict, the novels celebrate Drummond's physicality. At some point, all the novels provide a physical description:

> Slightly under six feet in height, he was broad in proportion. His best friend would not have called him good-looking, but he was the fortunate possessor of that cheerful type of ugliness which inspires immediate confidence in its owner. His nose had never quite recovered from the final one year in the Public Schools Heavy Weights; his mouth was not small. In fact, to be strictly accurate, only his eyes redeemed his face from what is known in the vernacular as the Frozen Limit.[32]

As the novels progress, the stress on his physical attributes seems to increase and he becomes ever larger and stronger. In *The Female of the Species* he was a 'vast individual', with 'two enormous fists' and 'great muscles' that rippled under his sleeves – his observer 'instinctively recoiled a step'.[33] It is his physical rather than mental attributes which lead to success: he had learned from Van Dyck, a Dutch trapper, how to 'move over ground without a single blade of grass rustling' and from Olaki, a Japanese, how to 'kill a man with his bare hands in a second'.[34] Furthermore, he is prepared to use his physical presence and develops such a love of killing that Hans Bertens has argued that Drummond is morally indistinguishable from his supposedly more wicked enemies.[35]

Secondly, while Holmes may have represented a masculine ideal, his idiosyncrasy prevented him from being representative of any other figure or class in society. Drummond, though, was very much a member of the upper middle class, 'a caste which does not aim at, because it essentially is, good form; a caste which knows only one fetish – the absolute repression of all visible emotion; a caste which incidentally pulled considerably more than its own weight in the war'.[36] According to Bertens, Drummond's class is positioned as the natural ruler of society. Its members share an 'old boy' slang and social code, capitalism is acknowledged as the natural organizing principle of society, and wealth is inherited rather than earned.[37] The upper middle classes look down on the lower middle class with outright contempt – 'this crowd of terrible people peering in their asinine way'[38] – though Drummond idealizes the fundamental soundness of the British workman who should be able to withstand the propaganda of the 'wild-eyed, ragged-trousered crowd of revolutionaries' and the 'do-no-work-and-have-all-the-money Brigade'.[39] Drummond worries that the masses will become infected with socialist ideas and seek to overthrow the hierarchies that give him and his friends a natural leading role.

Drummond's class position also accounts for his fierce patriotism, and his values are more stubborn and unthinking than those of Holmes who, in many ways, shares an internationalism that Sapper attributes to the enemies of Britain. Drummond's patriotism, however, is attached only to the nation and not the state. His ruling-class mentality allows him to appeal or resort to a more 'natural' form of justice than that of the state, and he is able to disregard police activities far more contemptuously than Holmes. Scotland Yard was too bureaucratic for Drummond: at one point in *The Black Gang* he even chloroforms the police as they disturb his capture of a gang. Later, when Drummond mercilessly flogs a hunchback with a rhinoceros whip, bayonets his wife's captor and almost strangles Peterson to death in cold blood, his friends acknowledge his right to be above the law: 'They knew their leader, and though they knew not what had happened to cause this dreadful rage they trusted him utterly and implicitly. Whether it was lawful or not was beside the point: it was just or Hugh Drummond would not have done it.'[40]

A third area of differentiation from Holmes is Drummond's avowed anti-intellectualism. Rather than the love of logic and deduction, Drummond's investigations and patriotism were based on sport, the love of battle and the camaraderie of soldiering. 'He had never been a man who beat about the bush', he was 'a man who believed in simplicity' who was 'too obvious for argument'.[41] He was known to dive in head first, worrying about the consequences later, his natural instincts seeing him through the fight. Drummond's physicality instilled agency into the cold, calculating, rational mechanisms of modern warfare and, for him, modern life was improved by the application of the straightforward values of gentlemanly sportsmanship. Rather than individual reason being used to solve a case, Drummond's tactics were very much those of the war from which he had just emerged. He was a leader, but a man who needed a team and he surrounded himself with a 'gang' – a band of like-minded, flippant, immaculately-dressed, cocktail-drinking, fun-loving sophisticates who could also become deadly serious as soon as the battle commenced. They stood in opposition to the enemy on the other side: Peterson too assembled his own gang, consisting of the mysterious girl Irma and an assorted collection of international Bolshevists, Jews and financiers.

Finally, Drummond differs from Holmes in his eventual domestication. By the end of the first book, Drummond is married, and here he parallels Richard Hannay's union with Mary and Lord Peter Wimsey's rather longer pursuit of Harriet. This domestication positions them within a middle-class ideal particularly celebrated in the inter-war period. Drummond may have 'looked the last word in exclusive tailoring' and been a frequent diner at the Carlton Club, but his love of good British beer and his pipe created also a comfortable 'middle-brow' cosiness far removed from his otherwise urbane, officer-class or even Wildean sophistication. Drummond does inherit that tradition of individualism associated with Holmes, and this is no more explicit than in both characters' dislike for the mundane routine of ordinary life: one seeks solace in cocktails, the other in cocaine. But Drummond is never quite so individualist as Holmes. He is a hero for the age of mass society: his physical prowess, his anti-intellectualism, the greater influence of instinct over logic and his love of domestic harmony all provide more egalitarian or accessible virtues than the idiosyncrasies of the most singular Sherlock Holmes. In short, for his readers, Drummond was a figure of identification, rather than of aspiration as with Holmes.

The Saint

The Saint was the most popular and enduring of the gentleman outlaws who enjoyed their golden age during the 1930s. He belongs to a lineage that also includes the likes of Bruce Graeme's Richard Verrell (alias Blackshirt), Berkeley Grey's Norman Conquest (alias 1066), John Creasey's Richard Rollinson (alias the Toff) and Anthony Morton's John Mannering (alias the Baron) – one of the quaint conventions of interwar thriller fiction was the 'alias' which sent shivers through the criminal underworld.[42] The Saint was created by Anglo-Chinese writer Leslie Charteris, who conceived him as 'a rambunctious adventurer . . . who really believed in the old-fashioned romantic ideals and was prepared to lay everything on the line to bring them to life'.[43] The Saint is a self-appointed crusader, who metes out his own brand of justice to those whom he refers to as 'the ungodly' – criminals who have escaped the reaches of the law.[44]

Like Holmes and Drummond, the Saint possesses a rich cultural and ideological currency. His real name is Simon Templar: his Christian name is perhaps an ironic reference to 'Simple Simon' (the Saint of course being anything but simple), while his surname is immediately suggestive of the Knights Templar (the Saint being a crusader against modern-day infidels). One of the early Saint novels, indeed, was entitled *Knight Templar*. Furthermore, like other thriller heroes, the Saint's adventures are tracts for their times. His popularity peaked during the 1930s, when the effects of the Great Depression were keenly felt both in Britain and in the United States. The Saint's enemies include not only the foreign anarchists of the Drummond stories, but also home-grown villains who represent the worst excesses of capitalism – corrupt financiers and business tycoons who exploit their labour forces.

The Saint combines elements of numerous other fictional heroes, including Raffles, the Scarlet Pimpernel, the Four Just Men and Bulldog Drummond. Like E. W. Hornung's 'amateur cracksman' Raffles, the Saint crosses class boundaries insofar as he is equally at home in high society as moving through the metropolitan underworld. Like Baroness Orczy's elusive Scarlet Pimpernel, the Saint disguises his fearless courage and steely determination beneath the languid exterior of an easy-going, slightly foppish man-about-town. He is also sought 'here and there' by policemen such as Chief Inspector Teal of Scotland Yard and Inspector Fernack of the New York Police Department, neither of whom ever succeeds in apprehending the Saint. Like Edgar Wallace's Four Just Men, the Saint (who in some of the early stories led a gang known as the 'Five Kings') takes it upon himself to administer rough justice to criminals who have escaped legal retribution. And, like Drummond, the Saint is physically strong and something of a dandy. His Scotland Yard dossier describes him in terms that recall Drummond:

SIMON TEMPLAR ('The Saint').

DESCRIPTION: Age 31. Height 6 ft. 2 in. Weight 175 lbs. Eyes blue. Hair black, brushed straight back. Complexion tanned. Bullet scar through upper left shoulder; 8-in. scar right forearm.

SPECIAL CHARACTERISTICS: Always immaculately dressed. Luxurious tastes. Lives in most expensive hotels and is connoisseur of food and wine. Carries firearms and is expert knife-thrower. Licensed air pilot. Speaks several languages fluently. Known as 'The Saint' from habit of drawing a skeleton figure with halo on scene of crimes.[45]

While the Saint takes the same pleasure as Drummond in roughing up his enemies – 'We're going to beat you up and do you down, skin you and smash you and scare you off the face of Europe', he tells one early victim. 'We are not bothered about the letter of the Law, we act exactly as we please, we inflict what punishments we think suitable, and no one is going to escape us'[46] – he is a more attractive and humorous character than Drummond and the stories do not exhibit the fascistic overtones that are evident in Sapper. While Drummond was married to Phyllis, a chaste relationship that effectively blocked the possibility of any other romantic involvement, the Saint has a steady (though far from exclusive) girlfriend in Patricia Holm. Jerry Palmer explains the narrative significance of the relationship: 'Clearly their relationship is sexual – that they live together without the benefit of wedlock is heavily stressed; and at the same time she is a companion in the fullest sense of the word, a trusted accomplice who suffers only from that relative incompetence that is the permanent affliction of the back-up team.'[47]

The Saint's ideological currency derives from being a flexible heroic figure who can equally be claimed by the political right and the political left. For the right, the Saint is a super-patriot, a defender of empire and monarchy. At the end of *Knight Templar* (1930), for example, he saves the royal train from being blown up by anarchists and receives a pardon for past crimes. For the left, the Saint is a champion of the oppressed and dispossessed who takes on a corrupt establishment and in the process becomes an outlaw. Charteris likened his hero to an earlier myth-figure – the Saint was often described as 'the Robin Hood of Modern Crime' – who similarly stole from the rich to give to the poor: the Saint donates the proceeds of his private war against the 'ungodly' to charity, keeping back ten per cent for himself as his 'collection fee'.[48]

In his study of the gentleman outlaws of British popular fiction, William Vivian Butler identifies five distinct phases to the Saint's literary career. The first, or Mark I Saint, was the character of the first Simon Templar novel, *Meet the Tiger*, whom Butler describes as 'piratical, romantic, energetic, prone to healthy skipping on beaches, but not considered a major hero, even by his creator'.[49] This version is superseded in the early 1930s by the Mark II Saint: 'the Very English Saint . . . rakehell, impudent, eccentric, outrageously versatile, eternally versifying . . . and the most dazzling stroller along pavements in fiction history'.[50] This is the Saint who appeared in stories for *The Thriller*, where the character of a modern-day Robin Hood took shape. This Saint is nonchalant and witty, regarding crime-fighting as a form of sport, as does Drummond. He combines the bohemian intellectualism of Holmes with the physical strength of Drummond, while like Drummond and Hannay he surrounds himself with a gang of helpers: girlfriend Patricia Holm, faithful valet 'Orace and trusted friend Monty Hayward. He also anticipates James Bond in his expensive lifestyle: 'The Saint, being a man of decidedly luxurious tastes, was the tenant of a flat in Brook Street, Mayfair, which was so far beyond his means that he had long since given up worrying about the imminence of bankruptcy. One might as well be hung for a sheep, the Saint reflected, in his cheerfully reckless way, as for a foot-and-mouth-diseased lamb.'[51]

A turning point came with *The Saint in New York*, published in 1935, which marked the arrival of the Mark III 'Anglo-American Saint' as Templar, like Charteris, gravitated increasingly to America and acquired a new sidekick in the person of dim-witted American gangster Hoppy Uniatz. The Saint lost some of his more flamboyant mannerisms and took on some of the characteristics of the 'hard-boiled' school of American detective fiction represented in the 1930s by Dashiell Hammett's Sam Spade and nameless 'Continental Op'. Thus eccentric English liberal individualism gave way to tough-talking American pragmatism. Butler, for one, regretted the change: 'The new Saint is older in the sense that he is smoother, less flamboyant and (to my personal regret) a lot less outlandish than the old one.'[52] It was in the late 1930s, moreover, that certain tensions began to appear within the narrative ideologies of the Saint stories. Charteris was writing increasingly for the American market, lured by the greater sums paid by American magazines, but found that he had to balance American neutrality with the rise of European dictatorships. The Saint's hatred of fascism is made explicit at the beginning of *Prelude to War* (1938) in which he listens to a ranting speech on his car radio and has a grim, and prophetic, vision of the future:

> He saw the streets swarming with arrogant strangely uniformed militia, the applauding headlines of a disciplined press, the new breed of sycophantic spies . . . neighbour betraying neighbour, the midnight arrests, the third degree, the secret tribunals, the fantastic confessions, the farcical trials, the concentration camps and firing squads.[53]

Thus popular fiction responds to the political climate of the time. A significant difference between the Saint and other fictional heroes of the interwar years, indeed, is that Charteris refused to locate the threats to international peace and security in mythical 'Ruritanian' countries but in real, identifiable geopolitical tensions.

The tension between anti-fascism and American isolationism was resolved by Pearl Harbor and the USA's entry into the Second World War. The Saint, like so many other popular heroes, was pressed into war service for the Allies. However, the wartime Mark IV 'G-Man Saint' worked with the American secret service rather than the British, taking his orders from Washington.[54] This was an aberration for the character, firstly because he lost his familiar companions, and secondly because he became an officially legitimated hero, an 'organization man' who anticipates the professional secret agents of the post-war era. After the war, Charteris found it difficult to rediscover the carefree pre-war Saint – the 'Day of the Desperado', as Butler observes, was over. From *Saint Errant* (1949) there emerged the Mark V 'Cosmopolitan Saint': 'a smooth, relaxed, essentially solitary figure, always on the move around the world, rarely seeming to live anywhere but in hotel rooms'.[55] This version of the Saint, world-weary and lacking the insouciance of his earlier incarnations, marks a signifi-cant ideological shift in the thriller genre. Travelling the world as a lone, freelance troubleshooter, he anticipates the most significant British cultural icon of the post-war period – James Bond.

James Bond

James Bond is a paradox for the cultural historian: he represents a throwback to the 'clubland heroes' of Buchan and Sapper, but is also a product of the post-war period with its greater affluence and changing sense of morality. The idea of Bond as both a Drummond archetype and a modernizing hero is evident in a contemporary review of the first Bond novel, *Casino Royale*, which described it as 'an extremely engaging affair, dealing with espionage in the "Sapper" manner, but with a hero who, although taking a great many cold showers and never letting sex interfere with work, is somewhat more sophisticated'.[56] Bond is as much an individual as his predecessors in the genre, represented by his per-sonalized cigarettes (known as Moorland Specials) and his own recipe for a medium dry vodka martini (shaken, not stirred). And to some extent he recalls both Holmes and Drummond in that he is afflicted by periods of *ennui* between adventures: 'The blubbery arms of the soft life had Bond round the neck and they were slowly strangling him. He was a man of war and when, for a long period, there was no war, his spirit went into decline.'[57] However, he dif-fers from the other heroes discussed here in that he is a professional secret agent who is 'licensed to kill' by the state. Bond is very much the organization man: he has virtually no life outside the secret service. He is also a loner: there is no team of helpers, though he does work fruitfully with CIA agent Felix Leiter on several occasions.

Where Bond differs most significantly from his predecessors, however, is in his frequently indulged sexual appetite. Holmes had been virtually asexual, Drummond and Templar chastely romantic, but Bond is a hedonist who enjoys casual affairs with different girlfriends in each of his adventures.[58] Here, the influence came from America. It is significant, if accidental, that the Bond's first appearance was in 1953, the year that also saw the launch of *Playboy* magazine. Michael Denning argues that 'the James Bond tales can rightly be seen as an important early form of the mass pornography that characterizes the consumer society, the society of spectacle, that emerges in Western Europe and North America in the wake of postwar reconstruction'.[59] The Bond novels reflected the *Playboy* ethos of free, easily available sex. The link between Bond and *Playboy* became institutionalized in the 1960s when the magazine serialized the later stories.

Paul Hoch argues that the cultural history of 'competitive masculinity' has oscillated between two extreme types. There is the puritan, 'hard-working, hard-fighting' and living according to 'a production ethic of duty before pleasure', and the playboy, 'who lives according to an ethic of leisure and self-indulgence'.[60] The puritan dominates in periods of austerity, while the playboy comes to the fore in periods of economic surplus and consumer affluence. Suitably for a hero whose ideological currency was established during the 1950s, conventionally characterized as a decade that saw a shift from austerity to affluence, Bond embodies elements of both the puritan and the playboy. He lives by a code of professional duty, which privileges loyalty to the state, and to the monarchy – made explicit in the title of the eleventh book, *On Her Majesty's Secret Service*. But he also indulges himself (at the state's expense) when on a mission, staying in expensive hotels and enjoying gourmet food and fine wines. Fleming's critics have ridiculed the author's penchant for expensive brand-name goods – Bond wears a Rolex Oyster Perpetual wristwatch and washes his hair with 'that prince among shampoos' Pinaud Elixir – but in the context of a country still emerging from the rationing and austerity regime of the 1940s such trappings were more than mere snob indicators. As Hugh Gaitskell told Fleming: 'The combination of sex, violence, alcohol and – at intervals – good food and nice clothes is, to one who leads such a circumscribed life as I do, irresistible.'[61]

In his structuralist analysis of the Bond stories, Umberto Eco identifies several sets of thematic oppositions within the narratives: between characters (Bond/villain, Bond/girl), between ideologies (Soviet Union/Free World, England/non-Anglo Saxon countries) and between different values (duty/sacrifice, loyalty/disloyalty, comfort/discomfort, excess/moderation).[62] The tension within Bond's character between these different values is most explicitly stated in *Goldfinger* when, during an enforced stayover in Miami, Bond eats 'the most delicious meal he had had in his life' as the guest of an American millionaire, but then, reacting against his companion's statement that 'Mr Bond, I doubt if anywhere in the world a man has eaten as good a dinner as that tonight', is disgusted by his own indulgence:

> Bond thought, I asked for the easy life, the rich life. How do I like it? How do I like eating like a pig and hearing remarks like that? Suddenly the idea of ever having another meal like this, or indeed any other meal with Mr Du Pont, revolted him. He felt momentarily ashamed of his disgust. He had asked and it had been given. It was the puritan in him that couldn't take it. He had made his wish and the wish had not only been granted, it had been stuffed down his throat.[63]

In *Thunderball*, Bond's habits of consumption have reached such excessive levels – sixty cigarettes and half a bottle of spirits a day – that his chief 'M' packs him off to a health farm in order 'to take it easy for two or three weeks on a more abstemious regime'.[64]

Bond's Englishness is problematic. There is a sense that he adopts the veneer of a gentleman hero in order to disguise his tough and ruthless streak. He feels out of place in a gentleman's club:

> And what would the casual observer think of him, 'Commander James Bond, C.M.G., R.N.V.S.R.', also 'something at the Ministry of Defence', the rather saturnine young man in his middle thirties . . .? Something a bit cold and dangerous in that face. . . . Tough-looking customer. Doesn't look the sort of chap one usually sees in Blades.
>
> Bond knew that there was something alien and un-English about himself. He knew that he was a difficult man to cover up. Particularly in England.[65]

The word most frequently used to describe his looks is 'cruel': 'He was good-looking in a dark, rather cruel way and a scar showed whitely down his left cheek.'[66] Yet while his physical appearance is 'alien' and 'un-English', the England that Bond protects is painted in reassuringly traditional terms. At the end of *Dr No*, for example, having survived the requisite trial of his courage and resourcefulness, Bond fondly recalls 'a world of tennis courts and lily ponds and kings and queens' and even longs for 'the douce weather of England'.[67]

The social politics of the Bond novels echo those of Drummond. Bond's England, as Kingsley Amis observes, is 'substantially right of centre'.[68] Bond views social change with scepticism bordering on hostility: on one occasion he takes an intuitive dislike to a taxi-driver whom he considers 'typical of the cheap self-assertiveness of young labour since the war', while on another he opines that lesbianism was 'a direct consequence of giving votes to women and "sex equality"'.[69] David Cannadine argues that the Bond novels are mediations of Britain's 'decline', responding both to moral decline at home (Fleming personally regretted the passing of the public-school ethos of duty, competitiveness and elitism) and to the decline of Britain as a world power. He highlights the (entirely coincidental) significance of the time span of the Bond stories, pointing out that the first, *Casino Royale*, was published in the Coronation year of 1953 – 'a retrospectively unconvincing reaffirmation of Britain's continued great-power status' – whereas the last full novel, *The Man With the Golden Gun*, was published in 1965, the year of Sir Winston Churchill's funeral – 'not only the last rites of the great man himself, but . . . also self-consciously recognized as being a requiem for Britain as a great power'.[70]

On one level, indeed, Bond is something of an anachronism: an imperial hero in an age of decolonization. Written against the background of the Suez Crisis and the retreat from empire, the Bond stories represent the last glorious fling of the British imperial hero who had been such a force in popular fiction since the mid-nineteenth century. As Raymond Durgnat puts it: 'Bond J. is the last man in of the British Empire Superman's XI. Holmes, Hannay, Drummond, Conquest, Templar *et al* have all succumbed to the demon bowlers of the twentieth century, while The Winds of Change make every ball a googlie.'[71] In the Bond novels threats often emanate from outposts of the British Empire, including Jamaica (*Live and Let Die*, *Dr No*, *The Man With the Golden Gun*) and the Bahamas (*Thunderball*), or from traditional British spheres of influence such as the Middle East (Turkey in *From Russia, With Love*). The Bond novels construct an imaginary world in which the Pax Britannica still operates and in which Britain still plays the role of a great power. Britain is in the front line of the Cold War (*From Russia, With Love*) and the war against international terrorism (*Thunderball*). Symbolically, the Anglo-American power relationship is reversed in the Bond narrative, so that Britain becomes the dominant partner in the 'special relationship'.[72]

The decline of British power is referred to most explicitly in *You Only Live Twice*, in which a test of Bond's strength becomes a metaphor for Britain's great-power status. The novel begins with Bond on the verge of a nervous breakdown following the death of his wife Tracy, at the hands of his arch-enemy Blofeld, at the end of the previous novel. At the advice of secret service neurologist Sir James Molony, he is sent on what is considered to be an impossible mission: 'what he needs most of all is a supreme call on his talents, something that'll really make him sweat so that he's simply forced to forget his personal troubles. He's a patriotic sort of chap. Give him something that really matters to his country.'[73] Bond is sent on a mission to Japan, which requires him to perform a favour for the Head of the Japanese secret service, Tiger Tanaka. The Japanese have intelligence secrets that the British want, but

Tanaka is reluctant to release them because he considers Britain has become a third-rate power:

> Now, it is a sad fact that I, and many of us in positions of power in Japan, have formed an unsatisfactory opinion about the British people since the war. You have not only lost a great Empire, you have seemed almost anxious to throw it away with both hands. . . . when you apparently sought to arrest this slide into impotence at Suez, you succeeded only in stage-managing one of the most pitiful bungles in the history of the world, if not the worst. Further, your governments have shown themselves successively incapable of ruling and have handed over effective control of the country to the trade unions, who appear to be dedicated to the principle of doing less and less work for more money. This feather-bedding, this shirking of an honest day's work, is sapping at ever-increasing speed at the moral fibre of the British, a quality the world once so much admired.[74]

Thus the decline of British power is linked to a decline in 'moral fibre' at home. Tanaka presents Bond with a challenge: in return for the intelligence secrets, he must assassinate Dr Shatterhand, an undesirable foreigner living in a medieval castle, whose 'garden of death' full of poisonous plants and animals attracts many Japanese to commit suicide there. The mission becomes personal for Bond when he recognizes that Shatterhand is none other than the hated Blofeld. Bond enters Blofeld's castle, is captured and savagely beaten by the guards, but ultimately vanquishes Blofeld in hand-to-hand combat. Bond is presumed dead and his obituary published in *The Times*; though, as with Sherlock Holmes's apparent 'death' at the Reichenbach Falls, the report is incorrect and Bond is in fact suffering from amnesia following his ordeal. He has also become impotent – the ultimate 'crisis of masculinity' for any male – reflecting Tanaka's taunt about Britain's 'slide into impotence'. But Bond's potency – and, by extension, Britain's – is restored, along with his memory, and he returns to the service of his country in *The Man With the Golden Gun*.

Conclusion

The constructions of masculinity and national identity represented by these four popular fictional heroes respond to the concerns, fears and aspirations of their time. Sherlock Holmes represents the triumph of logic and reason over the chaos and anarchy of urban modernity. Bulldog Drummond reinscribes individual masculine agency for a generation scarred by the inhuman mechanics of the First World War and its consequent social dislocation. The Saint defends Britishness from the threat of political totalitarianism abroad and from the forces of subversion and corruption at home. And James Bond reasserts British leadership and strength during the age of Britain's decline on the world stage.

Yet, as we suggested at the outset, there are sufficient recurrent themes throughout the canon of adventure fiction to suggest that continuity and confidence, rather than the more familiar narrative of perpetual crisis, are more appropriate ways of understanding these cultural representations. The perpetual virtues of patriotism, duty and loyalty are asserted (in remarkably similar terms) through all these fictional heroes. There is also a dislike of the routine, the mundane and the ordinary. This may take the form of intellectual stimulation (Holmes) or the sheer physical excitement of adventure (Drummond, the Saint and Bond). But all these heroes are set apart from the mass through their rejection of the more tedious elements of modern life.

The ideal of British masculinity, as represented through these popular fictions, is based on singularity and difference. Popular culture responds to the perceived crises within society not by offering any radical redefinition of the codes of masculinity, but instead by reaffirming the core values of the British liberal tradition. In examining the transition from Holmes to Bond we detect continuities rather than dislocations as the values of individuality and independence respond to changing historical circumstances. Holmes represents the individuality so typical of Victorian bourgeois liberalism. Drummond shares many of these characteristics, but the experience of war has made him more of a team player (though always the team's captain). The Saint and Bond represent to different degrees the displacement of a notion of British liberal individuality by a more aggressive and very much American notion of assertively masculine individualism. The same traits of individuality and non-conformity (often expressed through a typically British eccentricity which even Bond embodies, with his self-confessed 'old maidish' habits) are to be found throughout the canon of British heroes: Inspectors Morse, Wexford and Rebus are more recent examples of this trend, as are television's Doctor Who and Jonathan Creek. In the realm of popular culture, at least, Britishness and masculinity remain located where they always have been – in the classically liberal codes of individuality and independence.

Notes

1 C. Breward, *The Hidden Consumer: Masculinities, Fashion and City Life 1860–1914* (Manchester, 1999).

2 H. Hendrick, *Images of Youth: Age, Class and the Male Youth Problem* (Oxford, 1990); D. Pick, *Faces of Degeneration: A European Disorder, c.1848–c.1918* (Cambridge, 1989).

3 J. Bourke, *Dismembering the Male: Men's Bodies, Britain and the Great War* (London, 1996); R. Graves, *Goodbye to All That* (London, 1929); V. Woolf, *Mrs Dalloway* (London, 1925).

4 K. Theweleit, *Male Fantasies, Vol. 2. Male Bodies: Psychoanalyzing the White Terror* (Cambridge, 1988).

5 W. H. Whyte, *The Organisation Man* (New York, 1956); M. Roper, *Masculinity and the British Organisation Man Since 1945* (Oxford, 1995).

6 G. Grossmith and W. Grossmith, *The Diary of a Nobody* (1892; Harmondsworth, 1965); H. G. Wells, *The History of Mr. Polly* (1910; London, 1963); idem., *Tono Bungay* (London, 1909); idem., *Kipps* (1905; London, 1952). For a general account of these attitudes, see J. Carey, *The Intellectuals and the Masses: Pride and Prejudice Among the Literary Intelligentsia, 1880–1939* (London, 1992).

7 A. Tolson, *The Limits of Masculinity* (London, 1977); H. Brod (ed.), *The Making of Masculinities: The New Men's Studies* (London, 1987); J. Hearn and D. Morgan (eds.), *Men, Masculinities and Social Theory* (London, 1990); D. Morgan, *Discovering Men* (London, 1992); R. W. Connell, *Masculinities* (Cambridge, 1995).

8 J. Richards, 'Robin Hood on film and television since 1945', *Visual Culture in Britain* 2 (1) (2001), p. 65.

9 M. Denning, *Cover Stories: Narrative and Ideology in the British Spy Thriller* (London, 1987). Denning argues that 'the spy thriller narrates the crises and contradictions in ideologies of nation and Empire and of class and gender' (p. 2).

10 See, for example, P. Gilbert, *Disease, Desire and the Body in Victorian Women's Popular Novels* (Cambridge, 1997), J. Richards, *Happiest Days: The Public School in English Fiction* (Manchester, 1988); A. Light, *Forever England: Femininity, Literature and Conservatism Between the Wars* (London, 1991).

11 See, for example, G. Dawson, *Soldier Heroes: British Empire, Adventure and the Imagining of Masculinity* (London, 1994); M. Paris, *Warrior Nation: Images of War in British Popular Culture* (London, 2000).

12 U. Eco and T. A. Sebeok (eds.), *The Sign of Three* (Bloomington, Indiana, 1983); O. D. Edwards, *The Quest for Sherlock Holmes* (Harmondsworth, 1983); M. Pointer, *The Public Life of Sherlock Holmes* (Newton Abbot, 1975).

13 J. A. Kestner, *Sherlock's Men: Masculinity, Conan Doyle and Cultural History* (Aldershot, 1997).

14 See E. F. Biagini, *Liberty, Retrenchment and Reform: Popular Liberalism in the Age of Gladstone, 1860–80* (Cambridge, 1992).

15 A. Conan Doyle, *The Hound of the Baskervilles* (1901–2; London, 1993), p. 31.

16 'The Adventure of the Mazarin Stone', in A. Conan Doyle, *The Case-Book of Sherlock Holmes* (1921–27; London, 1993), p. 969; 'The Adventure of the Musgrave Ritual' and 'The Adventure of the Naval Treaty', both in A. Conan Doyle, *The Original Illustrated Sherlock Holmes* (Edison, NJ, 1996), pp. 248, 306.

17 'A Case of Identity', in A. Conan Doyle, *The Adventures of Sherlock Holmes* (1892; Harmondsworth, 1994), p. 65.

18 'The Copper Beeches' and 'The Engineer's Thumb', both in ibid., pp. 205, 275.

19 'A Scandal in Bohemia', in ibid., p. 6; 'The Adventure of the Empty House', in
    A. Conan Doyle, *The Return of Sherlock Holmes* (1903–4; London, 1993), p. 126.

20 'The Boscombe Valley Mystery', in Conan Doyle, *The Adventures*, p. 97.

21 See footnotes to p. 44 by O. D. Edwards in A. Conan Doyle, *A Study in Scarlet*
    (1888; Oxford, 1993), p. 173; J. Richards, *Sherlock Holmes, Conan Doyle and the
    British Empire: Musgrave Monograph Number Eight* (Huddersfield, 1997).

22 On the amateur ideal see J. A. Mangan and J. Walvin (eds.), *Manliness and Moral-
    ity: Middle-Class Masculinity in Britain and America, 1800–1940* (Manchester,
    1987).

23 A. Conan Doyle, 'The Adventure of the Yellow Face', in *The Original Illustrated
    Sherlock Holmes*, p. 214; Ouida, *Under Two Flags* (1867; Oxford, 1995); M. Hilton,
    Smoking in British Popular Culture, 1800–2000 (Manchester, 2000), pp. 53–6.

24 D. Harvey, *The Condition of Postmodernity: An Enquiry into the Origins of Cultural
    Change* (Oxford, 1989); M. Berman, *All That is Solid Melts into Air: The Experience
    of Modernity* (London, 1983).

25 Conan Doyle, *A Study in Scarlet*, pp. 6, 64.

26 A. Conan Doyle, 'The Adventure of the Blue Carbuncle', in *The Adventures*, p. 151.

27 Sapper [H. C. McNeile], *The Black Gang* (1922; London, 1950), p. 19.

28 The Drummond adventures consist mainly of four 'rounds' with Carl Peterson:
    Bulldog Drummond (1920); *The Black Gang* (1922); *The Third Round* (1924); and
    The Final Count (1927). Peterson's mistress Irma returns to avenge his death in *The
    Female of the Species* (1928) and *The Return of Bulldog Drummond* (1932). Follow-
    ing Sapper's death in 1937, the series was taken over by Gerald Fairlie.

29 Sapper, *The Black Gang*, pp. 53, 193.

30 Sapper, *Bulldog Drummond* (1920; London, 1929), p. 77.

31 W. M. Thackeray, *Vanity Fair* (1847–48; Oxford, 1983).

32 Sapper, *Bulldog Drummond*, p. 18.

33 Sapper, *The Female of the Species* (London, 1928), p. 21.

34 Sapper, *Bulldog Drummond*, p. 64.

35 H. Bertens, 'A society of murderers run on sound conservative lines: the life and
    times of Sapper's Bulldog Drummond', in C. Bloom (ed.), *Twentieth-Century Sus-
    pense: The Thriller Comes of Age* (Basingstoke, 1990), pp. 51–68.

36 Sapper, *The Black Gang*, p. 105.

37 Bertens, 'Society of murders', pp. 57–8.

38 Sapper, *The Female of the Species*, p. 189.

39 Sapper, *Bulldog Drummond*, pp. 124, 132.

40 Sapper, *The Black Gang*, pp. 20, 186, 296.

41 Sapper, *Bulldog Drummond*, pp. 36, 54, 60.

42 'Anthony Morton' was a pseudonym of the prolific John Creasey.

43 Quoted in the entry on Charteris by Joan Del Fattore in B. Benstock and T. F. Stan-
    ley (eds.), *Dictionary of Literary Biography Volume 77: British Mystery Writers,
    1920–1939* (Detroit, 1989), p. 67.

44 Simon Templar first appeared in *Meet the Tiger* (1929), later republished as *The
    Saint Meets the Tiger*. Charteris' output during the 1930s was prolific: three Saint

titles were published in 1930, four in 1931, two in 1932, two in 1933, three in 1934, one in 1935, one in 1936, two in 1937, two in 1938 and one in 1939. These books included both full-length novels and volumes containing two or three shorter novelettes that had originally been published in the *Thriller* magazine, edited by Charteris' friend Percy Montague Haydon. Although less prolific than in the 1930s, Charteris continued writing new Saint adventures for another thirty years – seven books in the 1940s, six in the 1950s, four in the 1960s – as well as editing *The Saint Magazine* (1953–67). Continuation stories by other writers, supervised and edited by Charteris, continued to be published in the 1970s and 1980s. Charteris died in 1993 at the age of 86. The definitive study of all Charteris' works, and adaptations for other media, is B. Barer, *The Saint: A Complete History in Print, Radio, Film and Television of Leslie Charteris' Robin Hood of Modern Crime, Simon Templar, 1928–1992* (Jefferson, NC, 1993).

45 L. Charteris, *The Saint in New York* (London, 1935; 1984 edn.), p. 3.

46 L. Charteris, *Enter the Saint* (London, 1930; 1983 edn.), p. 32.

47 J. Palmer, *Thrillers: Genesis and Structure of a Popular Genre* (London, 1978), p. 34.

48 It is for this reason that the 1997 Paramount Pictures film of *The Saint* represented a fundamental betrayal of Charteris's character: this Simon Templar (Val Kilmer) hs become a thief whose ambition is to raise $50 million for himself and then retire.

49 W. V. Butler, *The Durable Desperadoes* (London, 1973), p. 177.

50 Ibid.

51 Charteris, *Enter the Saint*, p. 5.

52 Butler, *The Durable Desperadoes*, pp. 177–8.

53 L. Charteris, *Prelude to War* (London, 1938), p. 3.

54 Butler, *The Durable Desperadoes*, p. 211.

55 Ibid, p. 234. It was this post-war Saint who was the basis of the 1960s television series of *The Saint*, starring Roger Moore.

56 'An extremely engaging affair', *The Times Literary Supplement*, 17 April 1953, p. 249.

57 I. Fleming, *From Russia, With Love* (London, 1957), p. 99.

58 The Bond of the novels had a more circumscribed sex life than the Bond of the films, which followed from the early 1960s. As Kingsley Amis observed: 'Bond collects almost exactly [*sic*] one girl per excursion abroad, which total he exceeds only once, by one. This is surely not at all in advance of what any reasonably personable, reasonably well-off bachelor would reckon to acquire on a foreign holiday or a trip for his firm.' K. Amis, *The James Bond Dossier* (London: Pan edn., 1966), p. 46.

59 Denning, *Cover Stories*, pp. 109–10.

60 P. Hoch, *White Hero Black Beast: Racism, Sexism and the Mask of Masculinity* (London, 1979), p. 118.

61 Quoted in J. Pearson, *The Life of Ian Fleming* (London, 1966), p. 304.

62 U. Eco, 'Narrative structure in Fleming', in O. Del Buono and U. Eco (eds.), *The Bond Affair*, trans. R.A. Downie (London, 1966), pp. 35–75.

63 I. Fleming, *Goldfinger* (London, 1959), pp. 30–1.

64 I. Fleming, *Thunderball* (London, 1961), p. 11.

65 I. Fleming, *Moonraker* (London, 1955), p. 40.

66 I. Fleming, *The Spy Who Loved Me* (London, 1962), p. 136.

67 I. Fleming, *Dr No* (London, 1958), p. 247.

68 Amis, *The James Bond Dossier*, p. 96.

69 Fleming, *Thunderball*, p. 16; idem, *Goldfinger*, p. 269.

70 D. Cannadine, 'James Bond and the decline of England', *Encounter* 53/3 (November 1979), p. 46.

71 R. Durgnat, *A Mirror for England: British Movies from Austerity to Affluence* (London, 1970), p. 151.

72 Amis recognized this: 'The point of Felix Leiter, such a nonentity as a piece of characterization, is that he, the American, takes orders from Bond, the Britisher, and that Bond is constantly doing better than he, showing himself, not braver or more devoted, but smarter, wittier, tougher, more resourceful, the incarnation of little old England with her quiet ways and shoe-string budget wiping the eye of great big global-tentacled multi-billion-dollar-appropriating America.' *The James Bond Dossier*, p. 90.

73 I. Fleming, *You Only Live Twice* (London, 1964), pp. 31–2.

74 Ibid., pp. 103–4.

8

'Who dies if England live?' Masculinity, the problematics of 'Englishness' and the image of the ordinary soldier in British war art, c. 1915–28

J. A. Black

The line 'Who dies if England live?' in the title of this chapter is derived from *For All That We Have And Are* by Rudyard Kipling, first published to great acclaim in *The Times* on 2 September 1914. The final stanza reads: 'No easy hope or lies Shall bring us to our goal But Iron sacrifice of Body will and soul. There is but one task for all – One life for each to give. Who stands if freedom fall? Who dies if England live?'[1] The sculptor Charles Sargeant Jagger selected the last ten words of the poem in June 1919 for the inscription on the obelisk which is the main architectural feature for his war memorial at West Kirby on the Wirral peninsula (unveiled December 1922).[2] On either side of the obelisk are two eight-foot-tall bronze figures. One facing west and Wales is of an elongated *Secession*-style female figure representing *Humanity*, and on the other side facing east and England is the bulky, aggressive, glowering *Soldier on Defence* (who has just bayoneted one opponent and is awaiting the next move of others who approach (figure 1)). This figure is also known by the title of *Wipers*, British soldiers' slang for the much fought over Belgian town of Ypres. At the time this soldier was interpreted very much as a reassuring evolution from the figure of 'the old contemptible', part of Kipling's professional long-service British Army whose ranks were decimated during the First Battle of Ypres (October–November 1914).[3] In miniature, this chapter will explore how the image of the British soldier of the First World War developed: firstly through the efforts of painters who were eventually employed by 1917 as official war artists by the Department of Information (upgraded to a Ministry in February 1918); and then as a consequence of figurative sculpture commissioned for numerous war memorials after the end of hostilities. The chapter will focus on the extent to which painters and sculptors with personal experience of life at the front formulated a different image of the ordinary soldier in the British Army from that created by those lacking such immediate visceral

Soldier on Defence, C. S. Jagger
MC, 1921, bronze, Hoylake
and West Kirby Memorial,
West Kirby, Merseyside.
Unveiled 16 December 1922.

exposure to the world of the trenches; and it will probe the variety of often divergent responses to the image of the British soldier in paint, pastel, bronze and stone broadly covering the period *c.*1916–28, and explore how such reactions reveal the deep uncertainty with which middle-class art critics, social commentators and pundits in Britain regarded the figure of the English soldier. My research strongly suggests that such commentators were more comfortable with an image of the English soldier as a well-meaning but rather hapless and inept victim, than as a skilful operator of a wide array of weaponry who in 1918 had played a key role in the defeat of a supposedly more militarily formidable German opponent.

One cannot stress too much the importance of Kipling in moulding popular perceptions of 'Englishness' and of how the English soldier was supposed to behave under stress. He exerted a tremendous grip on the imagination of many of the painters and sculptors I shall mention, such as Jagger, Eric Kennington and Philip Lindsay Clark.[4] In *Plain Tales from the Hills* and *Soldiers Three* (both published in 1888) he imagined the exploits of three archetypal British 'Tommies' or privates serving in the regular infantry in India: the southern Irish catholic Terence Mulvaney, the loquacious Cockney Stanley Ortheris and the dourly silent but savage in battle John Learoyd from Bradford. Kipling's vision of the British Tommy was an immensely influential one; between the early 1890's and 1918 the two series of *Barrack Room Ballads* (1892 and 1896) and *Soldiers Three* sold an average of 30,000 copies a year.[5]

For Kipling England was synonymous with Britain and all that was represented by the British Empire. However, even he appears to have been aware that the essential components of English identity were given a greater degree of coherence by being brought into sharper focus through external observers. Soon after the end of the Great War he reached the conclusion that the concept of Englishness had a peculiarly elusive and nebulous nature. At a dinner of the Royal Society of St George, on St George's Day 1920, he quoted the words of a Scot, Daniel Defoe, writing in 1701, to illustrate the problems the English faced in trying to define themselves: 'A true-born Englishman's a contradiction In speech an irony, in fact a fiction, A metaphor intended to express A man akin to all the universe.'[6]

With the outbreak of the First World War a number of broadsheet newspapers, such as *The Times*, *Daily Telegraph* and *Manchester Guardian*, campaigned to place far greater emphasis than during previous wars on Britain and the British contribution to maintaining the war, rather than describing the British war effort as an English one or referring automatically to troops within the British Army as Englishmen.[7] The media played up the exploits of Highland Scottish and Irish Regiments as part of a deliberate effort to stress how united the peoples of Great Britain were in their support of the war. An important part of this campaign was undertaken by the War Propaganda Bureau based at Wellington House, Hyde Park Gate in London. Among the many writers working for the section were Kipling, Arthur Conan Doyle, Cyril McNeill (who wrote under the pseudonym of 'Sapper' and later created the character of 'snobbery with violence' Bulldog Drummond), John Beith (who used the pseudonym Ian Hay) and John Buchan.[8]

At this time Kipling was deeply uneasy about the apparent martial shortcomings the war had exposed at the heart of English masculinity. As early as 1915 he worried that the English soldiers he had encountered in training seemed too easy-going and lacking in aggression and initiative. They did not seem to hate the enemy enough. In May of 1915 he wrote to his friend C. R. L. Fletcher of how impressed he had been by his first sight of soldiers from the

Dominions, particularly the Australians who struck him as 'the most vindictive haters in the Empire' which he ascribed to 'their heavy meat diet and the unforgiving climate of their native land'.[9]

By spring 1917 some establishment figures in England began to suspect that the efforts of the authorities to foreground the deeds of 'Celtic Heroes' and 'giants from the Dominions' had been only too successful. In March 1917 a reviewer for *The Times Literary Supplement* singled out for praise William Beach Thomas' recent book *With The British on the Somme* because he had

> rightly emphasised the feats of the English soldier . . . as distinct from the Scot, the Irishman or the Colonial. This is as it should be, for the average newspaper reader of late months, even years, has been saturated with epics of different Colonials, Irish regiments and Kilted Companies . . . the plain Thomas Atkins [has been] overlooked to a great extent for far too long.[10]

At this point some statistics would be illuminating. Between 1914 and 1918 just over 5.2 million men served in the British army, of whom just over 4 million enlisted or were conscripted from England (not all of whom necessarily felt themselves to be English: for example, units of Tyneside, Liverpool and London Scottish and Irish were raised in the early days of the war), half a million came from Scotland, a quarter of a million from Wales and surprisingly, given the presence of strong nationalist sentiments, over 134,000 from the whole of Ireland.[11] Such feelings of dissatisfaction with the manner in which the image of the English soldier had hitherto been presented may explain why Eric Kennington's iconic painting of a group of ordinary enlisted men from London on glass, *The Kensingtons at Laventie: Winter 1914*, was accorded such an extraordinarily positive critical reception when it was first exhibited at the Goupil Gallery towards the end of April 1916. Kennington depicts Platoon no. 7, C Company of the 13th battalion of the London Regiment (commonly known as The Kensingtons) who have just served four days and four nights in a fire trench with the temperature twenty degrees below zero. They have struggled through half a mile of communication trench with frozen mud up to their thighs under sporadic shell and sniper fire. The men of the Platoon are forming up prior to a five-mile march back to their billets, beyond the range of German artillery. Kennington served with this unit as a private, and about a month after the scene he depicts he was evacuated from the front after losing a toe to an accidental shot from a friend's rifle.[12] While Kennington includes a reticent portrait of himself in the composition, he literally foregrounds the working class Londoners whom he befriended in the ranks of the Kensingtons and came to admire, such as Corporal J. Kealey, Lance-Corporal H. 'Tug' Wilson and, with his back to us and wearing a bandage around his head, Private A. McCafferty who won the Military Medal for conspicuous bravery in the field, was wounded three times and lived long enough to attend Kennington's own memorial service in May 1960.[13] Kennington has deliberately chosen not to produce a conventional Victorian battle painting with the emphasis firmly on combat and energetic movement. Rather he presents a prosaic episode of stasis, a moment when the elastic of endurance cannot be allowed to relax, with men preserving a façade of resolve and toughness before the gaze of other men despite their collective utter exhaustion.

The chief art critic of *The Times*, Arthur Clutton-Brock, writing in May 1916, was immensely impressed by *The Kensingtons,* and dwelt at length on the innate Englishness of the style and the laudably English characteristics displayed by the men it depicted.

> It is . . . like the best English Pre-Raphaelite pictures and here . . . English art has become itself again. It is a picture of Englishmen and of the manner and spirit in which they fight . . . They are ordinary men, very tired and dirty; there is none of the romance of war as it is commonly painted. No one is enjoying the thought that he is a hero or making history and yet all these soldiers are at one in their common sense of duty and determination to endure . . . These men, if they were not too tired, would make jokes and not speeches. One of them has fallen to the ground exhausted by sickness; one knows that only sickness could have overcome him. Others can only keep on their feet; yet there is nothing merely animal in their weariness . . .[14]

The celebrated war poet Laurence Binyon (1869–1943), author of *For the Fallen*, published in *The Times* of 21 September 1914 and the source of the lines quoted every year on Armistice Day, 'At the going down of the sun and in the morning We will remember them', was equally taken with *The Kensingtons* for the quintessential Englishness the soldiers radiated. In May 1917 Binyon breathlessly described the work as 'one of the finest things in contemporary English painting' with its 'group of young Englishmen . . . tired but masters of the day . . . they stand for no military fanaticism or delusion but for something reassuringly sane and reconstructive in the midst of the horror and the chaos. Theirs is not the hallucination of the machine . . .'[15]

When he made the last remark I am certain Binyon had in mind C. R. W. Nevinson's depiction of British and French soldiers in works exhibited in 1916: the convalescing British 'Tommies' in *When Harry Tate Came Down*[16] exhibited in June 1916 at the Goupil Gallery and on the floor below where *The Kensingtons* was still on display, and the beleaguered French poilu machine gunners in *La Mitrailleuse* exhibited early in March 1916. The latter work was warmly praised when first exhibited, mainly because its style was interpreted as appropriate for depicting French militarized masculinity, men who were allies but still slightly alien and exotic in the eyes of the English. The critic of the *Evening News*, Charles Lewis Hind, writing in March 1916, described the French soldiers using a vocabulary that he never applied when discussing images of the British soldiers, whom he habitually referred to as English, as 'self-sacrificing automata in the clothes of men [who are] as rigid and implacable as their terrible gun . . . They are machines . . . ready to strike, prepared to the ultimate point of efficiency . . . to kill and be killed.'[17] *The Kensingtons*, according to Binyon, moved the spectator by the 'clean and masculine vigour of the design and colouring' which also triumphantly conveys 'the spirit of our splendid new army' composed of 'the civilian soldier . . . the real hero of the war [whose portraits were] the best record we can have of what we fight for'.[18]

Binyon wrote this in May 1917. Seven months later the reaction of censors from the War Office and GHQ in France to an ostensibly inoffensive and innocuous image of what were immediately identified as specifically English soldiers, Nevinson's *A Group of Soldiers*, reveals just how sensitive the issue of the reputation of English soldiers had become in the minds of the authorities. When the War Office censor, a Colonel Foster, first saw the painting late in November 1917, he testily wrote to Nevinson's employers, the Department of Information, that the War Office could neither approve the reproduction nor the exhibition of such an image on the grounds that the men Nevinson depicted were 'questionable types of Englishmen' and if it fell into the hands of the Germans they would surely 'seize upon the picture as evidence of British degeneration'.[19] When he heard what had transpired Nevinson protested hotly that he would not paint 'Castrated Lancelots' for the Government 'though I know this is how Tommies are usually reproduced in illustrated papers . . . high-souled eunuchs looking mild-eyed, unable to melt butter on their tongues and mentally and physically unable of killing a German'. He scornfully asked the War Office to propose a type 'you consider beautiful', and provocatively suggested a contemporary heart-throb of the London stage, the actor-manager George Alexander Samson (1858–1918).[20] He must have known such a model would have been unacceptable to the philistines in authority, as Samson was best known as a faithful supporter of Oscar Wilde and, indeed, had been the very first to perform the role of John Worthing in *The Importance of Being Ernest* in 1895.[21]

Intriguingly, Nevinson concluded his tirade with an assertion that the English public would survive exposure to these 'monstrosities' while 'foreigners in any case think the Englishman's face dull and hairless . . . so you see there's no accounting for taste'. On the whole he thought the War Office and GHQ in France should worry less about what neutrals and foreigners thought of the British army and display more faith in the average Englishman. In the end Nevinson's boss at the Department of Information, C. F. G. Masterman, persuaded the War Office censors to allow the exhibition of *A Group of Soldiers* in Nevinson's solo show as an official war artist held in London in March 1918.[22] The work proved to be highly contentious and provoked an outcry from the more conservative media. A vituperative response appeared in the *Saturday Review*, accusing Nevinson of having represented 'our friends, our sons, our brothers [as] brutalised half-witted . . . hooligans or rather dummy hooligans . . . curiously reminiscent of those semi-idiotic puppets that ventriloquists employ'. The work was a calumny on every Englishman now in uniform and 'lyingly represented . . . the best of British manhood [as] typified by a gang of loutish cretins'.[23] Ironically, one of the few papers to see some worth in the image was a Scottish one, the *Glasgow Herald*, whose critic praised *A Group of Soldiers* for revealing Nevinson to be 'emphatically a realist' who acknowledged, not before time, that it was no longer possible to represent British soldiers as 'pretty or drawn according to the conventional Adonis type used on recruitment placards before the war'. By contrast the Englishmen Nevinson had chosen to paint were 'charged with a sort of uncouth virility'.[24]

In 1918 Nevinson's conception of the English soldier was just uncouth in the eyes of the majority of critics. In July 1918, writing in *The New Statesmen*, Laurence Binyon singled out for approbation Eric Kennington's portraits of The British soldier which had been on display in London the previous month, such as that of a man of the London Rifle Brigade, *The Raider with a Cosh*, though in this case the Department of Information, on the instructions of GHQ, changed the wording of Kennington's catalogue caption. Originally, Kennington indicated that the man had just returned from a successful raid on the German lines somewhere on the Western Front and was cleaning the head of his cosh, presumably removing the remnants of a German's skull. The rewritten caption had the man preparing to embark on a raid.[25] Referring to such pastels Binyon wrote that 'if a foreigner wished to realise the British soldier [the previous year he had written only of Englishmen], he could not do better than see him with Mr. Kennington's eyes. Here he is in his massive, blunt simplicity, with all the qualities of his race written upon him.'[26]

After the war British artists had to tread carefully when depicting the ordinary 'Tommy'. On the one hand if they made him appear too handsome and glamorous, this was widely interpreted as a sign of his innate effeminacy and unsuitability as a soldier. On the other, if a soldier identified as an Englishman was made to appear too self-confident, aggressive, brutal or 'primitive' in phys-iognomy and/or physique this stoked anxieties that such men would become uncontrollable and anti-social in post-war civilian life. It was acceptable to depict Australian and especially Canadian soldiers as hard-bitten professionals with a taste for killing because during the war a certain mythic quality had been allowed to develop around the figure of the Dominion soldier. Writing in 1922, the prominent Liberal journalist, C. E. Montague of the *Manchester Guardian*, gloomily described the English soldiers he recalled encountering at the front as 'battalions of colourless, stunted, half-toothless lads from hot humid Lancashire mills . . . gargoyles out of the tragi-comical-historical-pastoral edifice of modern English life'. In sharp distinction Scottish and Dominion units were composed of men 'startlingly taller, stronger, handsomer, prouder, firmer in nerve, better-schooled, more boldly interested in life, quicker to take means to an end and to parry and counter any new blow of circumstances'. Montague lamented that such men had learned to look upon the English as 'a higher, happier caste perceives a lower and more degraded one'.[27]

In 1920 Philip Gibbs, war correspondent of *The Times*, described Australian and Canadian troops as 'the most fierce in battle, often giving no quarter'. Canadians in particular were notable for their 'tough, hard, fighting spirit' and their talent for 'fierce and scientific slaughter'.[28] So he was tremendously impressed with Kennington's 1920 pictorial tribute to the 16th battalion of the Canadian Expeditionary Force, the Canadian Scottish, which the Canadians exhibited as *The Conquerors* though Kennington changed this later in the year to *The Victims*. Indeed, these Canadian soldiers were described in the official Canadian exhibition programme as 'stern-visaged, war-hardened stormtroop-ers . . . magnificent types of manhood'.[29] When the canvas was exhibited in London, a number of critics thought the soldiers were undoubtedly impressive and yet there was still something alien, menacing and 'un-English' about them. Memories lingered of how Canadian troops awaiting transportation home in 1919 had rioted to relieve the boredom and vent their frustrations, burning down police stations in North Wales, Liverpool, Epsom and Luton and fight-ing pitched battles with British civil and military police.[30] Arthur Clutton-Brock described the Canadian Highlanders as part of a machine that has mastered the will of man and his finer impulses: 'War, the picture says, is that which turns men into machines.' These stormtroopers were part of a 'Franken-stein's monster that will go on trampling and destroying forever, a monster parodying the sense of duty, the sense of fellowship, all the activities of the spirit and perverting them to the task of blind destruction'.[31]

Clutton-Brock, Montague and Gibbs were equally concerned about the prospect of Englishmen returning to civilian from army life having acquired a taste for violence and other socially disruptive habits supposedly characteristic of the Dominion male. Gibbs expressed concern as to what effect the experience of fighting and killing according to 'the ancient code of jungle law' would have on the personalities of millions of hitherto peaceful Englishmen who had survived the war. He grimly predicted that such experience had unleashed 'the primitive barbarism normally overlaid by civilised restraints . . . liberating the brute which has long been chained up by law and the social code of gentle life'.[32]

It is therefore not surprising that Gibbs was decidedly ambivalent in his reaction to memorials which presented the Englishman as a professionally f ormidable, assertive, ruthless and intimidating combatant. Pertinent examples of this type would include Jagger's eight-foot-tall bronze figure of *Soldier on Defence* (figure 2) for West Kirby and Philip Lindsay Clark's bronze of a 'Cockney Colossus' or 'half-pint stormtrooper', as he was described in local newspapers, which he created for the Anglican congregation of St Saviour's Southwark in 1922, and who strides implacably and irresistibly down Borough High Street. *Soldier on Defence* owes its grim and menacing authenticity to the fact that his creator had over a year of combat experience, at Gallipoli in 1915 and then in Flanders in 1918, as an infantry officer who had been awarded the Military Cross for conspicuous bravery in the field. In April 1918 Jagger defended a vital farmhouse against repeated assaults made by German stormtroopers trying to outflank his unit, the 2nd Worcesters. During this action he was wounded in the left shoulder by a machinegun bullet.[33] There is evidence that during this engagement Jagger killed some Germans at close range. Convalescing in a Manchester hospital Jagger wrote to a friend still at the front of having done 'some nifty work with the Lewis [gun] . . . sending some Fritz to Fritz Valhalla'.[34] It would appear that the figure of *Soldier on Defence* was modelled from a certain Private Edwardes who had served in Jagger's company of the 2nd Worcesters and whom the artist later described as 'the black sheep' of his unit, always in trouble for minor military misdemeanors and yet 'a magnificent scrapper'.[35] The aura of primitive and elemental aggression with which Jagger sought to invest the figure of the *Soldier on Defence* was noted by a number of contemporary critics and pundits, whose responses suggest just how sensitive the issue of English masculinity had become. The critic of *The Sunday Times*, Frank Rutter, described the full-sized plaster model on

St Saviour's War Memorial,
Philip Lindsay Clark DSO,
1921, bronze, Borough High
Street, London. Unveiled
16 November 1922.

2

display in the Royal Academy exhibition of May 1921 as guaranteed to lay to rest the figure of the effete Englishman. In his battle rage the soldier appeared to be on the verge of leaping from his plinth to bayonet blasé gallery-goers and gossiping socialites.[36] A writer for the *Aberdeen Free Press* thought the statue depicted 'the Englishman as he is rarely imagined', saturated as he was by an almost tangible 'essence of violence'.[37] It is possible that Jagger looked to a bloodthirsty classic of Anglo-Saxon literature as a source of inspiration for *Soldier on Defence.* A year after the memorial at West Kirby had been unveiled he wrote to a friend, Robert Rattray Tatlock (art critic of the *Daily Telegraph* in the 1930s), that when he wanted to get in the mood for working on a war memorial design he would re-read *Beowulf* (written between the seventh and tenth centuries AD) and especially the passage in which the hero and his warriors are boasting of their martial prowess, while sharpening their swords and battle-axes, prior to getting to grips with *Grendel* and other assorted monsters.[38]

As for Clark, though originally born in Scotland he spent much of his life in south-eastern England and received his sculptural training in London. He had served for two years on the Western Front as a Captain in a Home Counties New Army battalion, the 11th Royal Sussex, and was awarded the Distinguished Service Order for his leadership in October 1917 at Passchendaele.[39] Clark's letters to the Chairman of the St Saviour's war memorial committee show that he identified very strongly with the 'solid English yeoman' he commanded in the 11th Royal Sussex. From the outset he conceived his bronze figure as projecting the spirit of the men he had led at Passchendaele pressing forward remorselessly and more than a match, as Clark put it, for any 'specially trained brute Prussian'. He personally deplored the 'insidious libel' believed by the credulous that the English soldier had been lacking in dash and martial ardour. According to Clark the soldier he had provided for Borough High Street was marching forward to pass last judgment on Prussian militarism and trample it into the dust. He would also serve notice to any foreign passer-by that the English would never shrink from defending their country and Empire with the utmost determination.[40]

Critical reaction to such figures was by no means unanimously favourable, and they represented a minority among the figures of soldiers supplied for war memorials in England. Some thought there was something disturbingly raw and elemental in the soldiers created by Jagger and Clark. For example, soon after discussing the full-size plaster model of *Soldier on Defence*, on display at the Royal Academy in 1921, *The Manchester Guardian* printed a letter from a member of the public describing Jagger's soldier as akin to 'a nightmare revealed for an instant in the white splash of a Verey light . . . on a colossal scale he lacks all sensitivity and no doubt in civilian life he would achieve his ends by the bludgeon and the boot'.[41] Indeed, the sort of soldier Jagger and Clark conceived seems in many ways uncomfortably compatible with the figure of the proto-Fascist stormtrooper imagined by the German writer and Great War veteran of the trenches Ernst Junger in his 1922 book *Battle as Inner Experience*. In a typical passage Junger rapturously described the stormtroopers he commanded in 1918 on the Western Front as

> a whole new race . . . charged with supreme energy. Supple bodies, lean and sinewy, striking features, stone eyes petrified in a thousand terrors beneath their helmets . . . conquerors, men of steel [who] encapsulated the spirit of battle as no other human beings could . . . pioneers of storm, the elect . . . intelligent strong men of will . . . They will be architects building on the ruined foundations of the world.[42]

Prudential Assurance War Memorial, Ferdinand Blundstone, 1921, bronze, High Holborn, London. Unveiled 18 March 1922.

3

My research suggests that most war memorial committees in England, commissioning figures of soldiers, did not want images of men conceived along the lines of Junger and Jagger. Two types of soldier were especially popular for the dead of a commercial concern or a municipality. Falling into the first category is Ferdinand Blundstone's group for the Prudential Assurance Company, Holborn, London, erected in March 1922 with the English soldier/man-from-the-Pru depicted as a bathetic, infantilized victim cradled in the arms of two solicitous and extremely nubile female angels (figure 3). R. Tait McKenzie's *The Homecoming* for Cambridge, erected in July 1922, which presents the tommy as a combination of male fashion model and Apollonian Rupert Brooke clone, is positioned firmly within the second (figure 4). Regarding Tait McKenzie's statue, George Mosse's claim that this sort of soldier was 'representative of a normative manly ideal' and 'in tune with the accepted [British] masculine ideal' is open to challenge.[43] Many contemporaries were deeply dissatisfied with the

The *Homecoming*, Richard Tait
Mckenzie, 1921, bronze,
Cambridge Municipal
War Memorial. Unveiled
4 July 1922.

4

ubiquity of the Tait McKenzie type of soldier. In October 1925, for example, after having unveiled numerous war memorials in England, General Sir Ian Hamilton publicly complained that far too many English sculptors had allowed themselves to accept as models 'young soldiers sent out from the depots [who had not even served in the war] and their commanding officers always showed the best-looking lads with delicate Greek features and smooth cheeks. The result has been, all over England, a sort of bastard Greek sculpture.' He wished war memorial committees had allowed themselves to be more stylistically adventurous and cited the example of Jagger's Royal Artillery memorial unveiled that month on Hyde Park Corner. Hamilton asserted that from his experience of the First World War battlefield, Jagger had created a more truthful image of the Englishman at war, either in stoical repose such as *The Shell-Carrier* (figure 5), or engaged in furious activity and utterly absorbed by the operation of weaponry, such as *The Lewis Gunner*. He described such figures as

The Shell-Carrier, C. S. Jagger
MC, 1923–24, bronze,
Royal Artillery Memorial,
Hyde Park Corner, London.
Unveiled 18 October 1925.   **5**

'the real thing and not only the real thing but the real thing in the rough'.[44] It is intriguing that the model for *The Shell-Carrier*, George Metcalfe, was an ex-soldier from the Division (the 33rd) with which Jagger had served in 1917–18. Jagger ostensibly employed him as a studio assistant but his principal task was apparently to box with Jagger for twenty minutes or so in a rudimentary ring set up inside the studio, as the sculptor released his frustrations concerning the progress of a memorial.[45]

I conclude with a sculptural group conceived by Eric Kennington in the Spring of 1925, and carved from stone between 1927–28, the so-called *Soissons Trinity* of three nine-foot tall figures produced for the Soissons Memorial to the Missing unveiled in July 1928 (figure 6). Although this was a major commission, it received a distinctly muted press reception in Britain. A number of newspaper letter writers wondered whether it had been wise for the Imperial War Graves Commission to spend public money on a sculpture which presented

The Soissons Trinity, E. H. Kennington, 1927–28, Euville Stone, Soissons Memorial to the Missing of the Battles of the Aisne and the Marne, Soissons, France. Unveiled 22 July 1928.

6

English soldiers of the Great War to foreigners, even wartime allies, in such an unflattering and potentially disturbing light.[46] One correspondent from Bournemouth to the right-wing daily *Morning Post* wrote in to agree with Dean Inge of St Paul's cathedral that too many of the younger English sculptors appeared to have fallen under the pernicious and degrading influence of pagan cultures and the 'blasphemous art of South Sea island savages'. This writer accused the soldiers Kennington had carved for Soissons of resembling soulless mechanical puppets, or even worse a group of Aztec tribesmen waiting at the foot of a sacrificial altar for the still-beating heart of some wretched prisoner to land at their feet for them to fall upon and devour.[47]

Hamilton was one of the few prominent public figures to write a defence of Kennington, and then rather tepidly along the lines that the artist had only tried to carve an adequate image of Englishmen under arms 'in our inhuman mechanical age'.[48] French critics and observers noticeably gave Kennington's group a far more positive reception. They uniformly described the three soldiers as looking typically English or Anglo-Saxon in their stockiness, bluntness, emotional restraint and disciplined impassivity. At the unveiling ceremony the Mayor of Soissons declared that the faces of the *Soissons Trinity* bore the stamp of 'calm and impassive' courage so indelibly associated with the English character. The Departmental Sous-Préfet added that the figures were imbued with the 'cold audacity, ferocious resolution and implacable will' of the English once roused to the accomplishment of some great enterprise. Once they had mourned their fallen comrade these men would have proceeded to crush those who took his life, and now victorious they would remain vigilant to ensure 'the enemy from the east' would never again rise to threaten the peace of Europe.[49]

I leave the last word to a friend of Jagger's and a great admirer of Kipling, Graham Seton Hutchison, who possessed his own very distinguished war record. He had come upon the *Soissons Trinity* in 1931 quite by accident, which did not surprise him, since works that celebrated the English soldier were given so little publicity in the British press. Even though the memorial was executed in an unfamiliar style, Hutchison found himself profoundly moved by Kennington's work. This monument could make the example of Kipling's *Soldiers Three* relevant to a new generation of jaded and disenchanted Englishmen. It was worthy of the memory of the English soldiers who 'patient, well-disciplined, stubborn in defence, courageous in attack, fought and won the battles of the Western Front'.[50] Intriguingly, Hutchison said this as a man intensely proud of his Scottish heritage who was convinced that the English could only be fully understood by one 'who is not of them'.[51]

Military (and other) historians have subjected most aspects of the First World War to exhaustive analysis. However, not until the last decade has even a minority argued that the British Army in the First World War became a formidable fighting machine: far more effective in battle, especially during the last year of the war, than has hitherto been recognized.[52] Hutchison would not have been surprised, however, to learn that the significance of the contribution of soldiers from England to the eventual effectiveness of British arms remains hotly contested. Indeed, dominant opinion in England today, like those contemporaries who responded to war memorial designs after 1918, seems more at ease with a perception of its First World War soldiers as passive victims mutely suffering affliction, rather than ordinary men who found themselves capable of extraordinary courage, dedication and fortitude amidst the most appalling conditions in which any soldier has ever been compelled to fight. Much work is needed on the development and diversification of visual constructions of soldiers from the constituent nations of the United Kingdom during and after the First World War. Indeed, as the old certainties that structured this state fall away, amidst the turbulence caused by an accelerating devolutionary momentum, such research appears all the more necessary. As Hutchison hinted as long ago as 1932, an important truth concerning the astonishing powers of endurance and recuperation displayed by the British Army during the First World War will continue to elude us until we can judiciously access the immense contribution of the largely unheralded figure of the English soldier.[53] Furthermore, he believed, as do I, that this enquiry can be undertaken without unwarrantably traducing the memory of his Scottish, Welsh and Irish comrades in arms.

Notes

1 For the full text of the poem see Andrew Lycett, *Rudyard Kipling* (London, 1999), p. 448.

2 Minutes of the Executive Committee of the Hoylake and West Kirby War Memorial Committee, 17 July 1919 and 11 September 1919. 1008 Wirral Archives Service, Birkenhead Public Library.

3 Speech given by F. E. Smith (Lord Birkenhead) at the unveiling of the Hoylake and West Kirby War Memorial, 16 December 1922. *The Birkenhead News*, 20 December 1922, p. 10.

4 In 1918 Kennington hoped Kipling would be available to open his exhibition as an official war artist at the Leicester Galleries, London. Eric Kennington to Alfred Yockney (Ministry of Information), 26 May 1918, Kennington W.W.I File, Department of Art, Imperial War Museum [IWM]. After his death, Jagger's widow recalled that her husband had gone through his entire time in the trenches of Gallipoli and France with a volume of Kipling's poetry in his pack: *The Sheffield Daily Independent*, 17 January 1936. Jagger Archive, Gillian Jagger. Lindsay Clark mentioned in 1922 that he had been terribly disappointed to miss a Kipling public lecture on the British Empire owing to illness. Minutes of St Saviour's Parish Church War Memorial Committee, Southwark Diocesan Archives, Surrey Records Office.

5 For the most recent and informative discussion of *Barrack Room Ballads* see Lycett, *Rudyard Kipling*, pp. 463 and 498.

6 Ibid., p. 502.

7 Gerard J. De Groot, *Blighty: British Society in the Era of the Great War* (London, 1996), p. 51.

8 Niall Ferguson, *The Pity of War* (London, 1998), p. 228.

9 Lycett, *Rudyard Kipling*, p. 454.

10 W. Beach Thomas, *With the British on the Somme*, London 1917, quoted in the *Times Literary Supplement*, 29 March 1917, p. 146.

11 Ian F. W. Beckett and Keith Simpson, *A Nation in Arms: A Social Study of the British Army in the First World War* (Manchester, 1985), p. 11.

12 For details of Kennington's war service see Jonathan Black, *The Graphic Art of Eric Kennington* (London, 2001), pp. 2–3, and Eric Kennington to Alfred Yockney, 11 June 1918, Kennington W.W.I File, Department of Art, IWM.

13 *The Times*, 26 May 1960, p. 18.

14 *The Times*, 20 May 1916, p. 9.

15 *New Statesman*, 12 May 1917. 7311.2C-318 Tate Gallery Archive [TGA].

16 Tate was a popular music hall comedian who frequently toured military hospitals to cheer up the wounded.

17 *Daily Chronicle*, 9 March 1916 and *Evening News*, 16 March 1916, 73112A-142 and 145 TGA.

18 *New Statesman*, 12 May 1917, 7311.2C-318 TGA.

19 Alfred Yockney to Charles Masterman (Head of Visual Propaganda at the Department of Information), 4 December 1917, discussing a conversation with Colonel Foster that afternoon. C. R. W. Nevinson Great War File, 226–A6/129, Department of Art, IWM.

20 C. R. W. Nevinson to Charles Masterman, 25 November 1917, Nevinson Great War File, 226–A6/148–151, Department of Art, IWM.

21 Samson acted under the name of George Alexander and was the actor-manager of the St James's Theatre 1891–1918. He was knighted in 1911. Rupert Hart Davis (ed.), *The Letters of Oscar Wilde* (London, 1962), pp. 282, 308 and 382.

22 Robert Ross, Oscar Wilde's first male lover, bought the painting for the future Imperial War Museum in January 1918 for £100. Robert Ross to Sir Martin Conway, 13 January 1918, Nevinson Great War File, 226–A6/97, Department of Art, IWM.

23 *Saturday Review*, 16 March 1918, 7311.3A-454 TGA.

24 *Glasgow Herald*, 19 March 1918, 7311.3A-466 TGA.

25 *Raider With A Cosh* was passed by the GHQ censor on 19 January 1918. Kennington described the image in a letter to Alfred Yockney, received on 18 February 1918. His description was changed in important respects in the catalogue caption for Kennington's exhibition as an official war artist, *The British Soldier*, Leicester Galleries, London June–July 1918 no. 91 p. 15. WO95–2205, Public Record Office, Kew.

26 *New Statesman*, 13 July 1918. Kennington Press Clippings, IWM.

27 C. E. Montague, *Disenchantment* (London, 1922), p. 152.

28 Philip Gibbs, *Realities of War* (London, 1920), p. 191.

29 Canadian War Memorials Fund [CWMF] exhibition catalogue, July–August 1920 enclosed in a letter from Percy Godenrath to P. G. Konody, 12 October 1920. CWMF File, Beaverbrook Papers, House of Lords Library, London.

30 Eric J. Leed, *No Man's Land: Combat and Identity in World War One* (London, 1979), pp. 201–2.

31 *The Times*, 26 October 1920, Kennington Press Clippings, IWM.

32 Gibbs, *Realities of War*, p. 450.

33 For Jagger's Great War service, see Ann Compton (ed.), *War and Peace Sculpture: Charles Sargeant Jagger* (London 1985), p. 15. War Diary 4th Battalion, Worcestershire Regiment WO95–4312 and War Diary 2nd Battalion, Worcestershire Regiment

WO95–2430, Public Record Office [PRO], Kew. For Jagger's Military Cross, Captain Fitz M. Stacke, *The Worcestershire Regiment in the Great War* (London, 1929), pp. 358 and 529. For his medical record WO330–4591, PRO Kew.

34 Charles Sargeant Jagger to Captain Paul Bennett, *c.* May 1918 (Jagger Archive, courtesy of Gillian Jagger).

35 Mrs Evelyn Jagger interviewed in the *Sketch*, 22 May 1935, Jagger Archive, courtesy of Gillian Jagger. Also article by Marita Ross in *Everybody's Weekly*, 10 December 1938, Jagger Press Clippings, IWM.

36 Press clipping pasted into the Minutes of the Hoylake and West Kirby War Memorial Committee, 1008 Wirral Archives Service, Birkenhead Public Library.

37 *Aberdeen Free Press*, 20 May 1921, Jagger Archive, courtesy of Gillian Jagger.

38 Charles Sargeant Jagger to R. R. Tatlock *c.* October 1923, Jagger Archive.

39 An account of Clark's heroism at Passchendaele appears in Edmund Blunden's *Undertones of War* (London, 1929; 1982 edn.), pp. 214–15.

40 Philip Lindsay Clark to the Chairman of St Saviour's War Memorial Committee, *c.* March–April 1922, Southwark Diocesan Archives, London.

41 Quoted in Jagger's obituary, *Manchester Guardian*, 17 November 1934, Jagger Archive.

42 Klaus Theweleit, *Male Fantasies Volume Two: Male Bodies, Psychoanalyzing the White Terror* (Cambridge, 1989), pp. 159, 161–2.

43 George L. Mosse, *The Image of Man: The Creation of Modern Masculinity* (Oxford, 1996), p. 118.

44 General Sir Ian Hamilton in the *Morning Post*, 19 October 1925, quoted in Major-General Sir Stanley von Donop, *The Royal Artillery Memorial, Hyde Park Corner* (London, 1925), p. 21.

45 *Evening Standard*, 5 February 1924 in PRO RAIL 258/477.

46 The *Daily News*, 9 July 1928, and the *Evening Chronicle* were opposed to the memorial while *The Times*, 10 July 1928, p. 15, was impressed by the figures.

47 *Morning Post*, 14 and 15 July 1928, pp. 10 and 12.

48 General Sir Ian Hamilton to the *Morning Post*, 17 July 1928, p. 10.

49 *L'Argus Soissonnais*, 25 July 1928, pp. 1–3.

50 Graham Seton Hutchison, *Warrior* (London, 1932), p. 92.

51 Graham Seton Hutchison, *Footslogger: An Autobiography* (London, 1931), p. 179.

52 Paddy Griffith, *Battle Tactics of the Western Front: The British Army's Art of Attack 1916–1918* (London, 1994); Gary Sheffield, *Forgotten Victory: The First World War, Myth and Realities* (London, 2001).

53 Hutchison discussed the significance of the English soldier while taking issue with Robert Graves's provocative claims in *Goodbye To All That* that the war exploits of 'the Catholic Irish and the Highland Scots' had been grossly exaggerated. Graves asserted that 'the most dependable British troops were the Midland County regiments, industrial Yorkshire and Lancashire troops and Londoners'. In addition, he identified 'the cleanest troops in the trenches' as 'English and German Protestants'. Robert Graves, *Goodbye To All That* (London, 1929; 1957 edn.), pp. 73 and 162.

9

The 'other war': subversive images of the Second World War in service comedies

Andrew Spicer

Lieutenant Ribstone (Kenneth Fortescue): 'After all, there is a war on.'

Major Poskett (Alfred Marks): 'Not here there isn't.' (*Desert Mice*, 1959)

Pedlar (Sean Connery): 'Don't you believe in the war at all, Pompey?'

Pompey (Alfred Lynch): 'Sure. Sure. I feel sorry for the blokes what get themselves killed. But I look at it this way, most of them didn't have any say about it one way or another.' (*On the Fiddle*, 1961)

In *The Myth of the Blitz*, Angus Calder has shown how an official myth of the Second World War developed, a heroic story of courage, endurance and pulling together which obliterated class divisions and political allegiances, a 'myth of British or English moral pre-eminence'.[1] This myth was particularly active in the 1950s when, amidst a crumbling empire with Britain visibly losing her status as a superpower, a number of prestigious war films – including *Angels One Five* (1952), *The Dam Busters* (1955), *Reach for the Sky* (1956), *Dunkirk* (1958) and *Sink the Bismarck!* (1960) – acted as a consolatory reassertion of national self-esteem through celebrating the heroics of the officer class in winning the war. As with any myth, its hegemony was not absolute, and several war films emerged in the latter part of the decade, such as Hammer's *Yesterday's Enemy* (1959), offering uncompromising accounts of the brutality of combat, its moral ambiguities and how the 'rules' rarely applied, especially in the Far-Eastern theatre of war. The 'Blitz Myth' was also contested by films featuring the maladjusted veteran, the 'damaged man' psychologically and ideologically unfit for peacetime civilian life, depicting the war as a traumatizing experience. This cycle of films flourished in the war's immediate aftermath, including *Mine Own Executioner* (1947) and *Silent Dust* (1949), but continued sporadically throughout the 1950s, culminating in *The League of Gentlemen* (1960).[2]

A third challenge to the myth was provided by a cycle of service comedies which depicted the indignities, arbitrariness and gross inequalities of service life from a lower class perspective (the 'worm's eye' view), mocking the pieties of the 'official' war films. Service comedies were frequently set during the war, but several, including *Reluctant Heroes* (1951) and *Carry on Sergeant* (1958) dealt with National Service, which remained compulsory for all men over eighteen from 1945–63, and helped to universalize the experience of service life amongst adult males during this period. It is no coincidence that the cycle is effectively over by 1963.

This cycle of service comedies – one strand, as discussed below, of a wider cultural corpus that included novels, short stories, plays, comics and radio and television programmes – was highly popular. As service comedy's low cultural status meant that these films were usually only noticed by the trade press and played to suburban and provincial audiences without the benefit of West End showcasing, their box-office success was often based largely on word-of-mouth, making their popularity all the more impressive. Both *Worm's Eye View* (1951) and *Reluctant Heroes* were huge hits, turning Ronald Shiner into a star; and *Private's Progress*, which initiated the second phase, was the third most successful British film released in 1956, while *Carry On Sergeant* also performed extremely well.[3] Their popularity indicates a deep seam of irreverence towards militarism and the myth of the Blitz, a widely shared enjoyment of unofficial, alternative images of bloody-minded and pleasure-seeking lower class representations of Britishness that were suppressed by official discourses. This flowering, or perhaps mushroom growth, of service comedy represents an eruption of a deep-seated tradition of non-conformist, carnivalesque hedonism that constantly struggles against notions of duty, sacrifice and stoicism, a struggle that is central to understanding British national identity.

The significance of these alternative images has yet to be recognized: postwar service comedy has not received any critical analysis, symptomatic of the lack of importance accorded to comedy in conventional British cinema historiography.[4] In what follows I have been necessarily selective from what is a prolific sub-genre with over forty examples, focusing on the later phase (1956–62), and analysing three representative films – *Private's Progress* (1956), *Operation Bullshine* (1959) and *On the Fiddle* (1961) – which are set during the war itself and directly engage with the 'official' myth.

The social context: the 'other war'

John Ellis' classic study, *The Sharp End*, describes the Second World War from the point of view of ordinary Allied front-line soldiers, emphasizing the haphazard induction and training they received, which was often a wholly inadequate preparation for the difficult, hazardous terrain and foul climates in which they had to fight.[5] Ellis quotes James Jones's pithy formulation of the common soldier's mentality: 'I went where I was told to go, and I did what I was told to do, but no more. I was scared shitless just about all the time.'[6] Paul Fussell's *Wartime* argues that ordinary troops were subject to high levels of deprivation and uncertainty about the aims and purpose of the war. For most, boredom was the 'predominant wartime emotion', and they suffered a constant diet of what British troops referred to as 'bullshit', a general purpose term for all those aspects of institutional behaviour that made service life worse than it needed to be. 'Bullshit' included sadism disguised as discipline, verbal humiliations, pulling rank, taking petty regulations to absurd lengths, and frequent and unnecessary inspections. Boredom and bullshit were the seedbed for the constant expressions of verbal subversion and contempt which gave vent to these frustrations and resentments.[7] The following chant, used by the British Expeditionary Force marching to France in 1939, mingled bitterness and contempt with a fantasy of limitless promiscuity through an inverted patriotism:

> I don't want a bayonet up my arsehole
> I don't want my bollocks shot away,
> I'd rather live in England,
> In merry, merry England
> And fornicate my fucking life away.[8]

Boredom, frustration, fear, anger and class-based antagonism about the conduct of the war are the dominant feelings that emerge from Pete Grafton's frank interviews with participants. A young Glaswegian soldier, arrested for something he did not do and then badgered when he tried to explain himself, causing him to lose his temper and strike an officer, concluded that ' "'This army's no what I thought it was." I just folded up my sleeves and said "Right, there's two wars here. Let's get intae it."'[9] This notion of 'two wars' was a powerful metaphor for the deep divisions that remained, indeed were often accentuated, during wartime, and became central to the remembrance of the war itself.

A keen sense of the indignities of service life with its rigid hierarchies was kept alive by the experience of two years' National Service, which also plunged the recruit into a 'total institution' where he was regimented from dawn to dusk. Rather than teaching discipline, fostering patriotism and inculcating team spirit, National Service was, as summarized by B. S. Johnson, 'tedious, belittling, coarsening, brutalizing, unjust and possibly psychologically very harmful'.[10] The result was an insolent rebelliousness: 'The Army taught me how to fight against authority. Only when you have lived within an authoritarian system can you learn how to fight it.'[11] David Morgan recalled that, 'Scarcely a day would pass without some parody of a drill sergeant or some reference to the inherent absurdity of service life as compared to civilian life.'[12] As one overview study notes: 'Not unnaturally, a system based on rigid rules, many of which were palpably absurd . . . [e]ncouraged the art of "skiving".'[13] 'Skiving', as one ex-National Serviceman recalled, 'is an Army tradition. Any soldier spends most of his time working: but what he is working on is evolving means of avoiding work. A good skive always excites admiration.'[14] Occasionally the dream of being billeted in some remote region, or being forgotten altogether, would come true. Such was the case of four airmen stationed at RAF Ferryside in Carmarthen who lived an idyllic life, sharing their rations with the local people 'in return for home-cooked pies and cakes'. Alas, '[i]t was all too good to last and retribution came in the shape of an officer making a casual and unexpected visit while the little group was sitting down to its evening meal.'[15]

Fussell argues that servicemen were convinced that accounts of the 'real war', or what I have termed the 'other war' – stories of boredom, resentment, a dreary nothingness or a life constrained by bullying and sadism – would never find the light of day, such was the power of 'optimistic publicity and euphemism'.[16] However, a vehicle for those emotions was available: service comedy, which, like comedy in general, 'offers both producers and audiences a pleasurable mode of dealing with socially or sexually repressed desires or fears in an acceptable manner, and it safely displaces sensitive social or personal issues into the realm of fantasy by smothering them with laughter'.[17] Memories of the war itself or of National Service frontiers including Kenya and Malaya created a receptive context in which these service comedies could work.

Service comedy and the carnivalesque

Service comedy forms part of a broad tradition of working-class comedy which provides a cultural space for the tribulations of the lower classes and the need to 'look after Number One' in the face of vindictive and petty authority. Its appeal, as Orwell noted, was to 'your unofficial self, the voice of the belly protesting against the soul'. This 'unofficial self' is cowardly, lazy, self-interested, devious and dedicated to bodily pleasures.[18] One archetype was Jaroslav Hasek's *The Good Soldier Schweik* (1921–23), the adventures of the 'little man' battling against pompous authoritarianism whose actions are ambiguously motivated, either stupid or devilishly cunning, which became an international success after it was translated in 1930. But its cultural roots are much deeper, going back at least to Shakespeare's *Henry IV Part 2* and Falstaff's motley band of thieves and drunkards. This notion of an 'unofficial', potentially subversive cultural stratum is best understood through Mikhail Bakhtin's concept of the carnivalesque, a utopian vision of the world seen from below. The carnivalesque is a hybrid, unruly, exuberant world where identity is multiple and mobile. It has a dialectical relationship to official culture, which it inverts or mocks.[19] Bakhtin argued that laughter could undermine the 'fear and piety' audiences experience before 'distanced' (venerated or revered) subject matter by bringing it close up, forming within the everyday, unheroic world 'a zone of crude contact where one can finger it familiarly on all sides'.[20] Applying Bakhtin's ideas, we can understand service comedy as a carnivalesque inversion of the 'official' war films, bringing that epic, distanced world into an over-familiar proximity where it appears ridiculous. Service comedy is therefore best understood as a form of cultural subversion rather than direct social protest.

Service comedy on screen has its roots in the bodily-based visual comedy of music hall sketches and goes back at least to the First World War with *Pimple Enlists* (1914) and *The Better 'Ole or, The Romance of Old Bill* (1918), based on a successful play. In the 1920s and 1930s this tradition was kept alive by popular comedians including Leslie Fuller, who played a burly working-class simpleton in such films as *Kiss Me Sergeant* (1930); Ernie Lotinga, who played an anarchic, anti-authoritarian and belligerent figure, Jimmy Josser, in *Josser Joins the Navy* (1931) and *Josser in the Army* (1932); and Sydney Howard, the put-upon 'little man' who endures humiliations but finally triumphs in *Splinters in the Navy* (1931) and *Splinters in the Air* (1937).[21] During the war Tommy Trinder, Arthur Askey, George Formby and Frank Randle carried on this tradition, poking fun at those absurdities of service life that found no place in exhortatory epics such as *In Which We Serve*, but within the context of broadly patriotic films which celebrated pulling together and seeing it through.[22]

The sub-genre returned, at the same time as the official war films, in the late 1940s with B-features made on shoestring budgets: Hal Monty's *Bless 'Em All* and *Skimpy in the Navy* (both 1949), and *Worm's Eye View* (1951), produced by Byron Films where Ronald Shiner played a quick-witted Cockney spiv in khaki. Films were catching up with popular taste, as R. F. Delderfield's play about a quintet of RAF men billeted at a boarding house on the Lancashire coast during the war had become a West End institution, running continuously for a record five-and-a-half years from December 1945.[23] Byron quickly followed its success with *Reluctant Heroes* (1951), an adaptation of a Whitehall farce which ridiculed National Service, with Shiner playing the barking sergeant. The trade press noted the appeal of the deep familiarity of jokes and situations here given a topical gloss. After a period in which service comedy was displaced by other forms – domestic comedy and the 'Doctor' films – it returned in the late 1950s when *Private's Progress* (1956) was the first of a more vigorous and sustained second cycle. Norman Wisdom's waning popularity revived with his first service comedy, *The Square Peg* (1958), in which the little man triumphs over the Nazis. It is no surprise that the 'Carry On' series was launched on its triumphant way by a service comedy, *Carry on Sergeant*, based on a Delderfield play, *The Bull Boys*.

In addition to the West End stage and novels, screen service comedies drew upon radio, and later television, programmes, including the Goons' *Down Among the Z Men* (1952). The wartime radio show *Mediterranean Merry-Go-Round/Middle East Merry-Go-Round* gave rise to two highly popular series, *Much Binding-in-the-Marsh*, a farce about an RAF station that lasted for six years (1947–53), and *Waterlogged Spa*, depicting a naval shore base at Sinking-in-the-Ooze.[24] Their successor was *The Navy Lark*, set on Boonzey Island, an inshore naval base, another forgotten community of the indolent and the fly, that ran for over eighteen years from 1959–77. Its impact was such that producer Herbert Wilcox sought to buy the rights after the third episode, releasing a film version in October 1959.[25] Granada Television's *The Army Game* (1957–61), set in a transit and surplus ordnance depot at Nether Hopping, was also extremely popular.[26] Hammer's spin-off, *I Only Arsked!*, which retained most of the television cast, was released in 1958. Other television series followed.[27]

As is customary with popular fiction, service comedy uses stock character types and a limited number of scenarios in which the primarily visual humour is leavened with some verbal wit, either in repartee or one-liners. The main types are the Fool and the Rogue: both have a traditional licence to mock constituted authority and were very active in post-war comedy.[28] Fools were well-meaning but accident-prone and idiotic, either working-class 'little men' (Norman Wisdom, Brian Rix or Kenneth Connor), or upper-class 'silly-asses' (David Tomlinson, Leslie Phillips and Jeremy Lloyd). Rogues were almost invariably Cockney wide-boys – Shiner, Richard Attenborough, Alfred Lynch and Harry H. Corbett – always looking for an opportunity to dodge work or make money.

Repeated set-piece scenes, which punctuate the often loose or episodic narratives, included the inept drill or parade; the camp concert (often the vehicle for comedians to display their talents); the catastrophe when some device or piece of equipment blows up or malfunctions; and the unexpected inspection or the premature return of an officer which wrecks elaborate stratagems. Service comedy always constructs an 'alternative community' which protects its members against the ravages of institutional demands. *Up the Creek* (1958) and *The Navy Lark*, for instance, are idyllic fantasies of the forgotten unit fully integrated with the local populace. *Desert Mice* (1959) has an unusual take on this paradigm. Major Poskett's North African paradise, invoked in the first epigraph, is disrupted by the arrival of Sid James's talentless troupe, Chuckles & Co, a skit on the awful intrusiveness of ENSA entertainment.

These types and situations are carnivalesque inversions of their equivalents in the official war films. Some service comedies were direct parodies. In *The Night We Dropped a Clanger* (1959), Brian Rix plays both the pompous officer hero Wing Commander Blenkinsop and the craven Arthur Atwood who has to take his place, a burlesque of *I Was Monty's Double* (1958). *Very Important Person* (1961) is a sustained, often very funny, parody of the POW cycle initiated by *The Wooden Horse* (1950). In order to underline the distance between the official myth and the reality of what actually went on, several service comedies open with a sham paean to wartime unity. Launder and Gilliat's *Joey Boy* (1965), perhaps because it came very late in the cycle, is the most savage. The opening, with its stirring music, stentorian voice-over and montage of actuality footage, evokes the Blitz Myth of a united Britain – 'working together in one supreme self-sacrifice and national effort for victory' – only for this to be instantly subverted by a cut to a well-dressed spiv in a rakish homburg flogging 'nylons, straight from the States'. This ironic and corrosive critique of the official myth is nowhere more explicit than in the film that initiated the second cycle, the Boultings' *Private's Progress*.

Corruption at all levels: *Private's Progress*

Private's Progress' advance publicity trumpeted 'The film THEY didn't want made' and the opening and ending flaunt its iconoclastic status: 'the producers acknowledge the official cooperation of absolutely nobody'; *Private's Progress* is 'respectfully dedicated' to 'all those who got away with it'. The opening uses a mock exhortatory voice-over, with its Churchillian rhetoric and sententious Shakespearean reference: '1942 and Britain is at war. Not only on the battlefield but on the farms, in the factories and in the home, and in the hearts and minds of every one of the men, women and children crowded onto this island, this precious stone set in a silver sea.' This is accompanied not by actuality footage, but by an animated cartoon sequence, provided by the Halas and Batchelor studio, which shows the crushing weight of bureaucracy apparently required to wage 'total war'. The next graphic depicts the largest ever British Army, numbering 1,683,292.5, at which point there is a quizzical voice-over interjection, 'You can't have half a man', before a cut to Stanley Windrush (Ian Carmichael) in his medical parade prior to call-up, the half-man of the statistic, too shy to reveal his bottom half. Stanley, wrenched from his Oxbridge college and admitting he 'never felt less aggressive in my life' is 'not the right type' for military service. Stanley's refined and delicate, 'feminine' sensibility prompts him to report to the MO when 'feeling a little fragile', one of several hilarious scenes that document his woeful ineptitude and lack of conventional manliness. Stanley, the bane of Sergeant Sutton (William Hartnell) who tries to mould him into a fighting man, is a recognisably parodic version of the eager cadet, that key signifier of acceptable young British masculinity in the serious war film. The paradigm example is Donald Sinden in *The Cruel Sea* (1953), who grows to resolute manhood under the stern but watchful eye of his commanding officer, played by Jack Hawkins. Through Hartnell's presence, older members of the audience would recognize the ironic references back to *The Way Ahead* (1944), an official Army recruitment film sponsored by the Ministry of Information, in which a disparate band of men are turned into an effective unit with Hartnell as the hectoring but good-natured sergeant, loyally assisting the benign but effective commanding officer played by David Niven.

Stanley, after failing officer selection, is plunged into the twilight world of the holding unit, recognized as the place where petty bureaucracy and meaningless tasks flourished and boredom and inactivity were the order of the day. Stanley's hut, led by 'Coxie' (Richard Attenborough), the working-class rogue who has worked out every fiddle going, is composed of experienced idlers and loafers whose sole object is to look after Number One. They represent an alternative community, a parody of the varied cross-section of recruits, a nation unified in diversity, which inhabited the official films. The unit's commanding officer, Major Hitchcock (Terry-Thomas), is a well-meaning Blimp, too self-regarding and lazy to do more than occasionally bluster at this 'absolute shower'. In a crucial scene the exasperated Hitchcock slips away from the barracks to see the matinée performance of *In Which We Serve*, that icon of inspirational war films. As he gazes around, he realizes that not only is the audience composed mostly of his men who should be on duty, but that virtually no-one is concentrating. Only the ever-anxious Stanley is watching, puffing furtively on his cigarette, not sure what attitude to assume, uncertain of his real identity in wartime.

The key trope of *Private's Progress* is the link forged between the lower-class wangler Coxie and Stanley's Uncle Bertie, Major Tracepurcel (Dennis Price), the sinister upper class Rogue for whom 'war is a time of opportunity'. Their bond represents the ruthless self-interest that unites all strata of British society. Tracepurcel has devized Operation 'Hatrack', ostensibly to 'rescue' art treasures plundered by the Nazis, but in fact made for private gain and therefore a dark double of the daring raid for a noble purpose beloved of the 'official' war films. Tracepurcel and his driver Cox disappear, faking their own deaths to evade detection. As ever, Stanley is left as the innocent dupe, the khaki Candide, adrift in a corrupt and heartless world. Only the final scene back in his varsity rooms reveals that the authorities have caught up with the reprobate pair.

Private's Progress was based on an established success – Alan Hackney's 1954 novel was already in its sixth reprint – which the trade and popular press understood was based on well-known jokes and scenes that would be 'more recognisable to the vast majority of men in the last war than all those courageous films about raids and parachute drops'.[29] The Boultings' reputation ensured that their service comedy was reviewed extensively in the quality press where it was also welcomed. Derek Granger applauded its

> wholly estimable aim of putting paid to the solemn British war film for ever. Instead of the stiff upper lip and derring-do we are sucked down into that submerged but very recognisable war-time inhabited almost entirely by malingering scroungers in the barrack room and thick-skulled temporary gentlemen in the mess . . . This is a picture which possibly reflects quite a lot of a few people's war and a little bit, surely, of almost everybody's.[30]

Dilys Powell judged it

> the perfect antidote to the high-falutin about war. It is the unheroic record of the hermit-crab combatant, the man who never wanted to have 'much of a war'; nearly eleven years after VE day it is a relief to find this deplorable character celebrated on the British screen, which has given so long an innings to steel nerves and iron jaws. Indeed I wished that *Private's Progress* had gone the whole hog and shown the triumph of the scrounger and the leadswinger.[31]

Private's Progress was the film through which the Boultings aligned their own deracinated middle-class dissidence with popular taste, combining a populist irreverence with a critique of middle-class values. In locating the emergence of anarchic impulses during the war, the dark underbelly of 'our finest hour', the

Boultings prepared the ground for a further six satires, notably *I'm All Right Jack* (1959) where Tracepurcel and Cox were reunited as amoral captains of industry, that subjected other British institutions to the same jaundiced scrutiny, documenting the deep disappointment that the twins felt after post-war hopes for radical change had evaporated.[32] In their view comedy was the 'force most destructive of injustice and ignorance' that could expose the culpability of all classes in this breakdown of moral order.[33]

Khaki sex: *Operation Bullshine*

Operation Bullshine (1959) was, like *Light Up the Sky* (1960), set on a remote battery station during the war. But whereas the later film was a nuanced, tragicomic exploration of the vicissitudes of male comradeship under stress, *Operation Bullshine* is a riotous farce celebrating the fighting female. It also employs an ironic opening in which black and white documentary footage of 1942 and an accompanying voice-over – 'In the darkest days of the Second World War, in her hour of peril and need, Britain prepared to meet the invader with unflinching courage. And who supplied the courage? Who supplied the fighting spirit, the will to win that brought us through the darkness and into the light of hope?' – is interrupted by a sudden cut to a Technicolor shot of a boisterous ATS regiment marching behind its fearsome Commander Maddox (Fabia Drake) with her bulldog mascot. At this point the song 'Girls in Arms' bursts onto the soundtrack: 'It's so exciting to prepare the girls to do the fighting . . . You'll agree, when you see, how they display their charms . . . Those wonderful girls in arms.' This song, and the shot of two squaddies ogling the women through binoculars, might suggest another typical portrayal of women in service comedy as smallminded, well-endowed objects of sexual desire, and there are numerous shots of the women undressing for the male gaze. However, the original screenplay by Anne Burnaby, has, like many of her other scripts for ABPC, a strong feminist undercurrent. *Operation Bullshine*, as Sue Harper argues, is a 'joyful celebration of female bad behaviour'.[34] In particular, Burnaby seems to be intent upon rescuing the image of the ATS, which although commended by Churchill for their contribution to the war effort, had the reputation of being 'Officers' Groundsheets'. 'She'll be wearing Khaki bloomers when she comes' was, according to John Costello, a wartime refrain that, 'loaded with lasciviousness . . . was one of the British soldiers' favourite ways of welcoming the ATS units in the early years of World War II'.[35] In *Operation Bullshine* it is reappropriated by the women themselves, sung lustily in the shower by Ruby Cox (Dora Bryan) as a way of celebrating their youth, freedom and sexual energies. Burnaby's presentation of the ATS comes much closer to the recollections of ATS women themselves who admitted that they 'played dangerously and talked dirty' and who were 'eager to be having as much sex as possible', but on their own terms.[36]

Of course, Burnaby's script is constrained by censorship restrictions and the overall studio policy of ABPC to produce wholesome family entertainment; therefore the sexual encounters are coy rather than frank. The central narrative concerns the efforts of glamorous Private Marge White (Carol Lesley) to get her man, Lieutenant Gordon Brown (Donald Sinden), known as 'Killer' because of his devastating sex appeal. When Marge goes bathing at night knowing that Killer is there and he admonishes her with the standing order that she must be under the supervision of an officer, Marge presses close against his chest, murmuring, 'You're an officer. Come on, supervise me.' A whole world of delicious innuendo is contained in the emphasis placed on 'supervise'. Killer's libido is curbed by the unexpected arrival of his wife Betty (Barbara Murray) at the battery; her presence has to be kept secret because married couples could not serve in the same unit. The battle of the women climaxes in the Browns' London flat, Betty denouncing her husband as a 'khaki Casanova', only for the battery commander, Major Pym (Naunton Wayne), to arrive at the wrong moment and think he has stumbled into a love nest: 'Have you got the rest of the battery in there?' he blusters. In the end the women settle their differences, and, on returning to the camp, join in the desperate manoeuvrings to get ready for the Brigadier's inspection. The final scene, in which both sexes co-operate in the successful shooting down of an enemy fighter, is nicely undercut when the women rush across the field in competition to have first go at the pilot, who surrenders eagerly.

Operation Bullshine was greeted as a light-hearted romp full of 'evergreen gags lightly tinged with sex' and 'wholesome fooling'.[37] However, seen historically, it provided a very different presentation of women from the noble, asexual and self-sacrificing wives and sweethearts of the official films, played by Rosamund John, Celia Johnson or Virginia McKenna. *Bullshine*'s women are as eager as the men to create distractions from dull routines, circumvent petty regulations and have a good time. Their energy and high-spirits are partly derived from their liberation from the dull routines of domestic drudgery – even sensible Betty will not wash dishes because she 'joined up to avoid that sort of thing'. If 819 Battery is not quite the fantasy of 'merry England' where everyone can 'fornicate their fucking lives away', it is a carnivalesque world that uses comedy to register some important truths about what went on in the war and who helped to win it.

The rogue as anti-hero: *On the Fiddle*

On the Fiddle (1961) was adapted from another Delderfield service comedy, *Stop at a Winner*, which, like *Worm's Eye View*, celebrated the triumph of the chameleon rogue who can mould his identity to any circumstances. However, in this instance, Delderfield, who provided the screen treatment of his own novel, retains its broad canvas rather than concentrating all the action in one enclosed community. *On the Fiddle* charts the picaresque wartime adventures of two outsiders, Pedlar Pascoe (Sean Connery) the muscular, slow-witted gypsy who has volunteered as he regards the RAF as a place where you get 'regular grub and a place to sleep', and Cockney wide-boy Horace Pope – 'Pompey' (Alfred Lynch) – who, after being enlisted accidentally, feels that he's been 'shanghaied'. As a slum child Horace feels no loyalty to King and Country – 'Suppose Hitler don't win the war. We might be stuck here for years and years' – but consoles himself by adapting his entrepreneurial skills to a new context. Pompey has no illusions about how the war is being fought: 'Everybody's watching out for himself . . . It's only honest if you make money out of it. Everyone's on the fiddle.'

In each new situation – the Non-Effective Pool at Blackrock where airmen who are not being trained for combat are assigned general duties, a transit camp, a maintenance station at Craddock Wood, active service in Northern France – Pompey's fertile brain devises an imaginative scheme to avoid danger and turn a profit. At Craddock Wood, the pair enter what is a ready-made 'alternative' community, a 'snide's holiday'. Corporal Gittens (Bill Owen), his feet on the desk, looks up lazily from his Western comic to explain to the new 'erks' that the CO is 'courting a rich widow at the big house and only looks in Tuesdays and Thursdays', the Adjutant is training to be a parson and therefore buried in his books, the Sergeant is a snooker champion and only leaves the NAAFI once a week, 'and on top of that there's two judys to every erk on the strength'. The one area where Pompey and Pedlar can make their mark is to improve the food, for a price, and the pair set to work in the cookhouse. The only problem is the 'unnecessary' and officious inspections of staff officer Flora McNaughton (Eleanor Summerfield). Having decided her problem is sexual frustration – 'all high-strung and unhappy' – Pompey sets Pedlar to work. In a beautifully played scene he seduces the reluctant yet eager Flora and the pair get extended leave passes.

Pompey's most accomplished fiddle, of which he is justly proud, is to renovate the pub near their next posting. Complete with raunchy barmaids (including

Barbara Windsor) brought down from London, it becomes a money-spinning Mecca for British and American servicemen. Its success ensures Pompey's come-uppance in the form of his American rival – Sergeant Buzzer (Alan King) – who, unhappy about the competition, gets the pair posted overseas. Pompey, in an impassioned moment of patriotism, remarks bitterly: 'There's Yanks for you. It was our war wasn't it? Ours and the Jerries. Why did the Yanks horn in?' But Pompey again works the situation to their advantage as he and Pedlar sell scarce commodities to an adoring local populace in the Ardennes.

After they stray behind enemy lines, the comic tone alters. Rather than the sardonic farce of *Private's Progress'* Operation Hatrack, encountering the enemy in *On the Fiddle* becomes the occasion for the brutal realities of combat to intrude. Pompey, who, as the epigraph quotation shows, believes not in patri-otism but natural justice, kills a German who has just shot an American soldier and is immediately sick. Pedlar, who always wanted to fight the enemy, seizes the moment and displays great courage and skill in defending their position. He is proud of their achievement, but Pompey is disconsolate that 'three years' capital' has gone up in smoke when their lorry is incinerated. The tone light-ens again when the pair are decorated by the Americans for bravery – forcing the British to ignore their list of misdemeanours and 'chip in a gong' – and sent home as war heroes. They return to the pub which Pompey has sized up as his future, telling the biddable owner (Wilfrid Hyde White), that it just needs a local attraction to bring in the punters: 'We'll search the neighbourhood for some Roman ruins. In fact I know a bloke in London who makes 'em.' Pedlar, anxious that it should be a proper home and that no-one suffers, returns with Iris (Ann Beach) and Pompey's illegitimate child, the by-product of a liaison forged during an earlier dodge selling 'surplus' RAF meat to Iris' father the local butcher (Stanley Holloway). 'Gawd love a duck', mutters the quondam bache-lor as he is handed his son in the expectation that he will now lead a conven-tionally respectable life. This was a neat ending, perhaps at the suggestion of the censor, but it lacks the picaresque punch of Delderfield's novel. Here, demor-alized by demobilization, which means that they will have to pay for things, the pair decamp to America, 'a Fiddler's Paradise' in Pompey's view, all expenses paid by a still grateful US government.[38]

On the Fiddle was one of the rare examples of service comedy to be reviewed positively by the *Monthly Film Bulletin*: 'Lynch takes the trouble to create a real character not a caricature . . . Connery is almost equally believable. His slow, conscience-ridden and rather gormless Pascoe is the ideal foil for Pope's quick-wittedness.'[39] Their engaging performances create an inverted image of the 'brains and brawn' exalted in *The First of the Few* (1942), representing a carnivalesque underclass which emerges in the extraordinary conditions of wartime. Rather than the relentless cynicism of *Private's Progress* about the conduct of the war, *On the Fiddle* was Delderfield's celebration of the resourcefulness of the dispossessed classes for whom the war is indeed a 'time of opportunity'. In the great tradition of working-class Rogues, nobody is really harmed by their schemes, which usually have the effect of allowing ordinary people to have a better time. As the central figure, Pompey emerges as an attractive, vibrant and likeable anti-hero. Adaptable, knowing, unencumbered with much ethical baggage, he is a man for the new age of consumerism, dedicated to giving the punters what they want. Pompey, like Joe Lampton in *Room at the Top* (1959), was not part of the officers' war, but their brains and energy have been sharpened by their wartime experiences and both now want to inherit the peace.

As Vincent Porter has argued, the most successful 1950s comedies mocked established rule-bound institutions and their 'imposition of unreasoning and unreasonable authority', calling for a more flexible way of operating which could be seen to be in the interest of the working and lower-middle classes rather than the old guard.[40] Service comedies were an important part of this process, attacking British society's most antiquated, hide-bound and authoritarian institutions. Even more importantly, through their inversion and mockery of the official war film, they undermined the partial and flattering version 'official' films constructed of the Second World War as the triumph of a virtuous middle class. Service comedy could critique this myth in its entirety (*Private's Progress*), but it could also celebrate those who had been excluded from that myth: the 'liberated' woman (*Operation Bullshine*) or the underclass Rogue (*On the Fiddle*). Thus the sub-genre provided an important space for alternative images of the British at war, which refused to allow working-class attitudes and experiences to be entirely written out from the dominant discourses and included a whole range of 'unacceptable' masculine types, centrally the Fool and the Rogue, but others that I have not had space to examine, the censorious intellectual and the fey 'gay fool', played by Kenneth Williams and Charles Hawtrey respectively in *Carry on Sergeant*.

The relationship between service comedy and the 'official' war films was clearly symbiotic: both were popular during the 1950s and declined in the 1960s. This relationship demonstrates the existence of 'two wars', the real war experienced by ordinary servicemen and the one promoted in official discourses. The popularity of both cycles of films showed that there was a profound need for both: the desire for a comforting, uplifting and victorious image of the war, but an equal desire for an alternative image that celebrated the largely lower-class arts of anti-authoritarian rebelliousness and individual hedonism. This struggle over the meaning of the war was absolutely central to this phase of British national identity, and should encourage a re-examination of the 1950s as a contest between these antithetical forces rather than the decade of dull conformity and consensus that has, for too long, dominated conventional accounts.

Notes

1 Angus Calder, *The Myth of the Blitz* (London, 1991), p. 2 and passim.

2 Andrew Spicer, *Typical Men: The Representation of Masculinity in Popular British Cinema* (London, 2001), pp. 161–77.

3 See the annual round-ups of 'Box Office Winners' in *Kinematograph Weekly*, 20 December 1951, p. 5; 13 December 1956, p. 6; 4 December 1958, p. 17.

4 One or two individual films – notably *Private's Progress* – have been discussed, but not in the context of this sub-genre. John Ramsden briefly touches on their existence in his excellent 'Refocusing "The people's war": British war films of the 1950s', *Journal of Contemporary History* 33 (1998), pp. 60–2.

5 John Ellis, *The Sharp End: The Fighting Man in World War II* (London, 1993).

6 James Jones, *World War II* (London, 1975), quoted in Ellis, *The Sharp End*, p. 102.

7 Paul Fussell, *Wartime: Understanding and Behaviour in the Second World War* (New York and Oxford, 1989), pp. 79–95, 129, 139, 195–207, 263–8, 291.

8 Quoted in John Costello, *Love, Sex and War: Changing Values 1939–1945* (London, 1986), p. 121.

9 Young Glaswegian man, quoted in Pete Grafton, *You, You & You! The People Out of Step with World War II* (London, 1981), p. 44.

10 B. S. Johnson, 'Introduction', in B. S. Johnson (ed.), *All Bull: The National Servicemen* (London, 1973), p. 14.

11 Bill Hodsworth in ibid., p. 92.

12 David Morgan, '"It Will Make a Man of You": notes on national service, masculinity and autobiography', *Studies in Sexual Politics* 17 (Manchester, 1987), p. 38.

13 Trevor Royle, *The Best Years of Their Lives: the National Service Experience 1945–63* (London, 1986), p. 111. See also the recollections in Peter Chambers and Amy Landreth (eds.), *Called Up: The Personal Experiences of Sixteen National Servicemen, Told By Themselves* (London, 1955), David Baxter, *Two Years To Do* (London, 1958), Mike Baker, *The Last Intake* (London, 1995), E. G. Barraclough, *National Service: An Insider's Story* (London, 2001) and David Findlay Clark, *Stand by Your Beds! A Wry Look at National Service* (Dunfermline, 2001).

14 Trev Leggett, in Johnson, *All Bull*, p. 274.

15 Royle, *The Best Years*, p. 112.

16 Fussell, *Wartime*, pp. 267–8.

17 Vincent Porter, 'The hegemonic turn: film comedies in 1950s Britain', *Journal of Popular British Cinema* 4 (2001), p. 81.

18 George Orwell, 'The art of Donald McGill', in *Collected Essays* (London, 1961), pp. 167–78.

19 M. M. Bakhtin, *Rabelais and His World*, trans. Hélène Iswolsky (Bloomington, 1984). For informative discussion of Bakhtin's ideas see Peter Stallybrass and Allon White, *The Politics and Poetics of Transgression* (London, 1986), pp. 1–26 and *passim*.

20 M. M. Bakhtin, *The Dialogic Imagination: Four Essays*, ed. M. Holquist, trans. C. Emerson and M. Holquist (Austin, 1981), p. 23, quoted in David Sutton, *A Chorus of Raspberries: British Film Comedy 1929–1939* (Exeter, 2000), p. 31.

21 See Sutton, *A Chorus of Raspberries*, pp. 104–17.

22 For a recent analysis of wartime comedies see Robert Murphy, *British Cinema and the Second World War* (London, 2000), pp. 33–53.

23 R. F. Delderfield, *Overture for Beginners* (London, 1970), pp. 218–19.

24 Andy Foster and Steve Furst, *Radio Comedy 1938–1968* (London: Virgin, 1996), pp. 78–85. Michael Paris has shown how popular comics in the 1950s retained a powerful strand of anti-authoritarianism in their depiction of working-class heroes such as 'Ticker' Turner, the Army's champion 'wangler' and scrounger, in *Victor*, or Sergeant-Pilot Matt Braddock in *Rover*: see his *Warrior Nation: Images of War in British Popular Culture, 1850–2000* (London, 2000), pp. 234–5.

25 Denis Gifford, *The Golden Age of Radio* (London, 1985), pp. 189, 225.

26 Jane Harbord and Jeff Wright, *40 Years of British Television* (London, 1992), pp. 14, 17, 20, 23, 26.

27 Stephen Wagg, '"At Ease, Corporal": social class and the situation comedy in British television, from the 1950s to the 1990s', in S. Wagg (ed.), *Because I Tell a Joke or Two: Comedy, Politics and Social Difference* (London, 1998), pp. 1–31. One of the best radio parodies was 'Hancock's War', first broadcast in May 1958.

28 Spicer, *Typical Men*, pp. 102–25.

29 Milton Shulman, *Sunday Express*, 19 February 1956; see also *Today's Cinema*, 15 February 1956.

30 *Financial Times*, 20 February 1956.

31 *The Sunday Times*, 19 February 1956. Only right-wing critics, like Campbell Dixon in the *Daily Telegraph* (18 February 1956), a staunch champion of the 'official' war film, demurred.

32 Interview with Stanley Price, 'The lion has two heads', *Man About Town* (December 1960), p. 53.

33 Interview in *Films and Filming* (February 1957), p. 7.

34 Sue Harper, *Women in British Cinema: Mad, Bad and Dangerous to Know* (London, 2000), pp. 85–6, 182.

35 Costello, *Love, Sex and War*, pp. 40–6, 79–98.

36 Quoted in ibid., pp. 87, 91.

37 *Kinematograph Weekly*, 13 August 1959, p. 24.

38 Delderfield, *Stop at a Winner* (London, 1961), pp. 249–56.

39 *Monthly Film Bulletin* (Autumn 1961), p. 157.

40 Porter, 'The hegemonic turn', p. 91.

10

Regional identity: a gendered heritage?
Reading women in 1990s fiction

Val Williamson

A discussion in the *Manchester Evening News* on 22 February 1926 quoted a library assistant's advice: 'If a woman is taken up with the house all day, she doesn't want tales about married problems or misunderstood wives – she knows enough about these already . . . what she enjoys is something possible, but outside her experience.'[1] How, three quarters of a century later, are we to explain that those subjects are exactly what 'a woman' wants to read about today? Could it be that, by the end of the twentieth century, the woman reader had largely escaped the domestic context within which her identity was previously confined, and that that historical identity is now sufficiently remote from her own experience for her to discover pleasure in reading about it? Q. D. Leavis insists that 'It is essential to recollect that the past can only be estimated through the present, and that its significance is given to us through the present.'[2] I suggest that a significantly large group of woman readers, and writers, has now embarked on a quest to interrogate that past identity, especially but not exclusively through fiction, and to locate it within a regional history. 'The fictional space of Liverpool is increasingly being used to interrogate the past', Nickianne Moody suggests. 'Liverpool is used as a point of connection between the fictional past and the readers' present.'[3] This chapter examines this distinctive phenomenon of the relocation of a gendered past, within wider conceptions of Britishness, at a local and regional level; and the discussion will demonstrate that not only Liverpool, but also several other towns and cities in north-west England, provide locations for just such points of connection.

But we must consider why the north-western working-class woman's domestic heritage is being sought in the pages of popular fiction rather than at locations where such historical evidence is 'officially' displayed. The Liverpool sagas published between 1974 and 1999 are the focus of a research project into the cultural practice of writing popular fiction. Methodology includes comparing fact with fiction (history with fantasy), frequent contact with practising authors, surveying the writers' press, reading 'how-to' books and articles written by fiction authors, attending talks by authors to writers and to readers, and various specific author surveys.[4] The project thereby becomes informed about the remarkable input of personal and cultural memory into saga fictions.

Through the prolonged and prolific career of Dame Catherine Cookson (d. 1998), a strong perception of a north-eastern English identity in working-class saga fiction has emerged, but there are now many north-west authors and sagas. Representing Liverpool, by 1999 twelve authors had written books in that category, nine on at least an annual basis, with two others producing occasional fast-sellers. Some Liverpool authors also write sagas set in other Lancashire locations. My research suggests that each title by the top-selling authors of Liverpool and Lancashire sagas may sell two or three times as many copies as the working-class publishing sensation of the 1990s, *Trainspotting*, in the year that its high-profile film version came out (1996).

Saga novels, with their long-term sales pattern of reprints and repackaging, most often constitute Escarpit's 'steady-sellers' (for example, HarperCollins reprinted Helen Forrester's *Twopence to Cross the Mersey* (1974) 24 times between 1981 and 1995), but Alex Hamilton's annual charts of the fastest selling 100 books (*Bookseller, Guardian*) throughout the 1990s nevertheless provide a useful market context for sagas. In 1999, the first full year after Cookson's death, 139 titles exceeded Hamilton's required 100,000 sales, and 6 north-west working-class sagas were named in the chart. Josephine Cox titles reached 27 and 29, Audrey Howard 83 and 92, Lyn Andrews 89 and Ruth Hamilton 91. This represents sales of over £3 million for Cox alone (approximately 750,000 copies sold), the overall figure for north-west working-class regional sagas in 1999 being *c.* £7 million. (1.2 million copies). These north-west saga authors sign book club contracts for mail order and are offered supermarket deals, and their sagas are likely to become available on audio-cassette and in large print editions; some are under offer for film, television or video production. Liverpool titles generally attain the same Public Lending Right ranking as those by Catherine Cookson.

We must ask why British regional sagas sell so phenomenally: I suggest that it is because sagas address a lack of official accounts of aspects of working-class life. Bernice Martin states, 'We simply do not possess systematic ethnographic data on British life-styles such as anthropologists would habitually collect for more exotic tribes.'[5] Working-class people and their activities have habitually been given low priority in the protocols of public representation, and women even lower. What we discover with saga writers *and* readers (reciprocity is an important dynamic of the process) is a strong impetus to tell the stories of north-west working-class women: an impetus aptly located as part of the national trend to nostalgia Cannadine identified, demonstrated by the periods chosen for the settings of sagas (the 1870s–1890s and 1920s–1940s), and the strongest market impulses toward developing the genre, from the 1970s to the 1990s.[6]

Hewison expresses abhorrence of this impulse to nostalgia, and seems heavily critical of the movement towards establishing preserved accounts of working-class history and its associated industrial landscape conservation.[7] He is particularly sceptical about the 'The Way We Were' exhibition at Wigan Pier, which presents facets of working-class north-west history, and especially sceptical of its use of photograph and simulacrum. Yet there clearly is a demand for opportunities to revisit the north-west's working past, and rather small evidence offered of individual endeavour within it. Consequently, we must consider what motivations prevailed when Josephine Cox returned to Blackburn for a signing of her first local saga and found a waiting queue over a quarter of a mile long. 'In the January cold and snow six hundred people were queuing down the street. The signing took four and a half hours. My old friends and teachers had come to see me after thirty five years, and I had used actual names and stories in my book!' From this response, we must consider that her fictionalized memory may be representative of the Blackburn community in ways that nothing else is. We may deduce from the extreme popularity of British regional working-class sagas that they represent aspects of working-class life that remain unrepresented in other readily accessible texts. In visual representation especially, domestic life is missing. Photographers and film-makers encapsulating urban, industrialized Britain preferred to document men's work themes, external scenes and machinery; when museums accept photographic and filmic evidence in place of artefacts (of which the poor left very few) working-class domestic work remains isolated and under-represented.[8] Even now, the 'hegemony of one class over another in representing public history . . . offers us "memories" of social life through TV and newspho-tos . . . paralleled in [amateur photographic practice] by this dominance of one version of family history [as fun] which represses much lived experience'.[9]

Regional sagas fill a lack by offering fictional representations of lived domestic experience framed by considerations of class and gender, so specifically based in fact that the writing of them has become a type of cultural practice, books written in a specific way to answer a need felt by local readerships who read them in a specific way. This readership was originally created by Cookson, a writer who from 1950–70 became her own category, which was then set up for plagiarism, or very close imitation, the first step toward genre-ization, by publishers searching for her 'successor'. Joan Eadington reports that she answered 'an advert in the Society of Authors Journal for people to write saga novels'. Eadington, as Joan Eadith, published seven Manchester sagas with Warner (paperback imprint of Little, Brown) between 1992 and 1998, all promoted on the success of the first one's offering of an entirely working-class setting and heroine. I suggest that the importance of locale rather than region was not clearly understood in publishing in the 1980s, and that publishers perceived (non-domestic) workplace and inter-class relations, rather than a specific sense of community defined through class, as the desired elements. In Cookson-like fictions set 'not in the north-east', looking at industries, examining women's relationships with men, the topography of sagas became the category: 'Scottish saga', 'Swansea saga', 'Cornish saga'. That the story of the enterprising independent working-class woman was an essential ingredient of the regional saga was not understood until Barbara Taylor Bradford's *A Woman of Substance* (1979) was imported from the USA. It sold on the author's northern English connections and the Granada TV series (1980). That such a woman could be a heroine and yet remain in, and even aspire to, the domestic domain only became clear in the 1990s. Themes relating 'heritage' to class had been thoroughly exploited by then in television series, but the enterprising, independent, single, working-class heroine was new.[10] By 1979 Helen Forrester had become established as an important Liverpool chronicler, but it was not until the mid-1980s that the region began to offer textualizable versions of its varying locales with the ensuing sense of heterogeneity of women's experience. My recent enquiry demonstrates that the use of personal memory and local archives has enabled a number of north-west working-class women to become professional authors by rendering 'truthful' fictions of the twentieth century lives of working-class women in this region.[11] We must further consider what regional and local cultural resonances may have brought this about.

Caunce explains that 'In northern England identity tends to be more the property of ordinary people than elite groups, which drastically limits the sources available to most historical researchers.'[12] Yet, Giles suggests, feminist historians and fiction writers alike are drawing attention to lived working-class female experience, 'areas of the past that remain uncharted, beyond history, visible only in the memories of those who survive'.[13] An important aspect of saga narratives is that they offer a heterogeneous range of identities to women who are normally spoken of in official discourses as part of a mass or group. Working-class women may assume the identity of their paid work, 'tobacco packers' or 'canteen cooks', for instance, but the blanket definition 'housewife' homogenizes women's experience, denying even differing experience of class and locale. Giles brings methods of textual analysis normally applied to fiction to oral narratives of self, to recover a variety of meanings from a previously unrecorded female 'hidden' history.[14] She discovers differences in the significance of domestic experience for women of different classes, and in the status attached to domestic labour, differences that may be implicated in the creation of a cultural impetus to the British regional saga. The domestic aspect of the working-class female 'self-story' has been problematic given that feminism finds it unsatisfactory, a situation that 'runs the danger of excluding and alienating those whose livelihood and/or sense of worth are closely tied to their domestic skills'.[15] Among the working-class women Elizabeth Roberts interviewed in Barrow, Lancaster and Preston, she found that 'The influence of the domestic idyll of the wife staying at home managing the home and family . . . was very strong. So too was the idea that a woman staying at home was more respected than one going out to work.'[16] Giles further points out that 'Accepting that historical reconstruction has a story-telling and mythic function does not mean . . . dispensing with "verifiable, fact-based truth"' but acceptance that '"there are better and worse pieces of history"'.[17]

The fictional histories of north-west working-class women are based in specific locations, lying, like Barbara Taylor's Bradford, mainly along the Leeds and Liverpool Canal. Most of the authors have been promoted as 'the new/next Catherine Cookson'; several also now write for the well-established Liverpool market. Blackburn still features in most novels by Cookson's actual successor (on the basis of sales), Josephine Cox (Headline). The successor promoted by Cookson's publisher, Corgi, Ruth Hamilton, made her reputation on Bolton fictions but now writes for the more lucrative Liverpool readership. Audrey Howard (Arrow, Hodder) explores historical and economic relationships between Lancashire and Liverpool to produce sagas for both markets. While Maisie Mosco (Hodder, HarperCollins) wrote some working-class historical fictions of Manchester in the 1980s, these have a different narratological profile from the next decade's 'gritty nostalgia' or 'clogs and shawls' working-class sagas. It was to address a lack of Manchester working-class women's saga fictions (illustrated by the large numbers of Liverpool sagas available in Manchester libraries and book shops) that Freda Lightfoot (Hodder) began her new series based in the Ancoats district as Joan Eadith departed from Warner. In addition, the prime site of recreation for the Lancashire working-class, Blackpool (Margaret Thornton, Headline) and a northern location of the rural idyll, the Lake District (Freda Lightfoot, Hodder) feature in saga fictions of the 1990s.

Non-fictional representation of the history of north-west working-class women, especially of their domestic experience, could be expected to be available both in museums, particularly those devoted to working-class or labour history, and in socio/historical projects and reports. The 'official' record seems fragmentary: for example women's concerns are not the focus of publications from the Mass-Observation 'Worktown' project (Bolton 1937–49), nor a feature of the cataloguing of this massive archive, whose Sussex location makes access very difficult for working-class Lancashire authors with domestic commitments. This group also finds it difficult to access most relevant work by academic historians. A tour of north-western heritage museums reveals that domestic labour at home rather than at paid work is represented by lack. 'When cleaning is successful, it produces lack as value, but this value frequently does not accrue to the one who does the cleaning.'[18] Conversely, Fowler observes of Cookson's sagas,

> the theme of 'redundant women' is largely absent. Rather, her perspective depends on a comparison between the craft work done by men and that done domestically by women, in terms of their equivalent resilience, skill and resourcefulness. Minute detail is included of women's domestic labour, so as to enhance its use-value.[19]

This is an important aspect of regional saga fiction, which often focuses on the evolution of working-class domestic aspiration and practice. Giles's study of women's domestic role from 1918–50 suggests reasons why this should be so, in that she 'investigates working-class women's consciousness of their domestic role at a specific moment when that role was in the process of reformulation'.[20] It is through the working-class woman's domestic role, whose past is accessed above all by listening to older people, that Liverpool sagas posit perceptions and analyses that more nostalgic and simplistic accounts of back-street domestic life preclude. It is an active role, revealing the emotional effects of deprivation, the sense of lack (frustrated desire, envy), rather than the passivity Steedman detects in Seabrook and Hoggart's accounts of working-class women in their domestic role.[21]

Much of the internal action in sagas, the protagonist's thought, is concentrated on devising strategies for defeating poverty, working-class woman's identity and sense of status shown to be dependant on her ability to follow strategies for 'making do' and 'getting by', central rubrics of all married working-class women's lives between the wars.[22] According to Moody, 'The themes of the family saga . . . are not romance, but action in the face of adversity . . . for example, good housekeeping and domestic management; the acquisition of education and skills leading to [paid] work, security and respectability as well as a general bettering oneself.'[23] In actuality, the sense of self-worth gained from the sense of purpose which the years of wage-earning work gave women before marriage was often eroded by the drudgery of an impossible struggle into 'feelings of guilt, shame and fear in wives, who bore the responsibility for balancing the household budget'.[24] Saga authors (recently Katie Flynn) note that readers often quietly tell them details of their own past difficulties and do not mind seeing their recollections repeated in print.[25] Giles speaks of a previously unrecorded female 'hidden' history, which sagas enable to 'come out'. I do not want to construct a victim position for north-west working-class women, or assist nostalgic fiction's effect of falsely constructing the opposite 'creating quasi-myths'.[26] Women are already either excluded by official accounts or positioned as victims within them, at the very moment when the last remnants of the history of housewifery are still available for collection and display.

Heritage Museums are locations of popular memory as well as representations of that memory. Visitors to cotton mill museums in Lancashire include those who grew up in the industry, who remember the surrounding valleys before the hundreds of mills were demolished, and the sound of 100,000 looms chattering into action each day.[27] Machine operators in the mills are also people who once did the job as manufacturers rather than as curators. At each site it is the machinery that has been restored and displayed. This is the problem for women in the home, for not only have they left too few artefacts to be representative, the pre-war working-class housewife was not afforded the gadgets which make excellent relics and curiosities, and focal points prompting 'active reminiscing'. In north-west heritage museums displaying preserved domestic interiors, however, it is not uncommon to find visitors, aged apparently in their fifties or later, gathered in the 1930s/40s/50s kitchen around the mangle, each with a tale to tell about how their grandmother and mother had used one. Clogs and shawls seem seldom represented in museums as aspects of women's lives, but they are not a fictional cliché, they were worn late into the 1960s, and provide symbolic 'points of departure' for personal histories.[28] Helen Forrester portrays 1930s women wearing shawls instead of coats in several of her Liverpool books; Freda Lightfoot's father was a cobbler in Oswaldtwistle, making and repairing clogs, including the ones his daughter wore to primary school in the 1950s.

Given that domestic support was essential to the effective workforce, somewhere in the heritage text domestic life should be represented. Most often it is via the reconstructed 'living room', a fireplace, or a narrowboat cabin, cosy images of home and hearth, a doll's house encapsulation of an idealized sense of home, where no work harder than pouring tea is located. Even in university libraries, it is difficult to locate the required visual evidence of the history of housewifery, of the work of the home. In museums, simulacra and drama are often used in an attempt to fill omissions; female volunteers wearing Victorian costume tend the fires, roll pastry, or make bread, and may teach you how to push in a latch-hook to make a rag rug. How these constituted survival strategies in a culture of deprivation and economic exploitation is not explained. Dramas often emphasize the victim position of working-class housewives, portraying them as lacking in agency, and their economic strategies, especially pawning, as evidence of failure. They seem unable to represent the centrality or the powers and pleasures of these women's domestic role at all. Twentieth century housewifery is not even being inscribed as middle-class consumerism; for instance the collection of ephemera at *Opie's Museum of Memory* (1998) at Wigan Pier, is scarcely representative of women at all after the 1940s display, which reflects that during the war there was a national interest invested in women skilfully 'making do and mending', exercising their skills as housewives. Afterwards, apparently, this role disappeared from print, giving way to the more decorative magazine 'cover girls'.

Two of my recent strategies to locate evidence of north-west woman's twentieth-century identity as housewife led me to the Lancashire Schools Museum Service, and to the Pump House Museum in Manchester, a branch of the National Museum of Labour History. At the Lancashire Schools Museum Service, boxes of 'evidence', whether real or simulacral, are supplied to educators; the usual way to compile historically accurate boxes is to seek visual evidence from books. At my request, the curator supplied pictorial evidence to inform a project on working-class domestic life and women's homemaking /housekeeping work before the Welfare State. Evidence was compiled from the existing archive at the Museum of Lancashire, all taken from the same book by Frank Atkinson.[29] Only one shows the interior of a typical 'saga' home, revealing its poverty-stricken shabbiness, but positioning the woman on a fireside chair (a typical cooking position). We see its range, kettle (on the hob) and cooking utensils, a low fire and washing drying on the oven/boiler door, all evidence of the woman's work. Gas lamps hang on the wall above fresh candles in holders on the mantelpiece, ready to be taken to other rooms later, further evidence of her agency as housekeeper. A mirror is carefully positioned for both usefulness and safety, suggesting attention to the need to keep up appearances. Yet Atkinson's caption reads: 'Depressed to the point of inactivity, this poor woman in a rotting house . . . sits before her tiny fire, surrounded by damp walls, with inadequate food and without the will to do anything about it. These conditions were not uncommon in the 1930s, when this picture was recorded as part of a move towards slum clearance.'[30] This woman's agency within 'the rotting house' and her political analysis of who or what is the cause of her difficulties are more adequately portrayed in British regional working-class saga fictions.[31] Other pictures of interiors show women pouring tea or knitting. Only two pictures show women engaged in obvious domestic work: a girl of fifteen in Yorkshire in 1945, sitting outside on the step, cleaning seventeen pairs of leather clogs; and a mature woman, half out of the doorway, scrubbing the pavement beyond her doorstep.[32]

At the Manchester Pump House branch of the National Museum of Labour History I found a direct juxtaposition between representations of active Trades Unionism and different styles of fireplace. Home is represented by hearths and tables lacking dirt or dust, furniture lacking clutter and floors lacking footprints, i.e. clean, as after domestic labour. There is no representation of that labour, the 'house work' itself, or the range of tools, skills and important life-/health-preserving strategies involved in successfully controlling the domestic sphere. There were milk checks/tokens on the counter from a Co-op store, but no explanation as to how these became part of the housewife's survival strategy, or of how their enrichment contrasted with the economic deprivations of those foregrounded earlier periods where Trades Union support extended to widows' pensions. However, from May to October 2000, the Pump House hosted an interesting two-floor temporary artistic project, *Every Street* (the name of a street in Manchester's Ancoats district) which chronicled and visually represented the everyday, including domestic, life of the community in the mid-twentieth century. Here I found family washing hanging on a line (fabrics authentic to the period, the 1960s–70s) and a representation of ironing, including iron and board, if not the person doing the work. Two aspects of the Every Street project particularly endorse what is known about the saga's function as representational of actuality. First, like saga authors, this artist, Bill Longshaw, is gathering evidence from relocated residents because the locale is now demolished and this evidence is not recorded elsewhere. Second, the resulting testimonies are revealing an overwhelmingly domestic experience, and Longshaw is striving to devise means to attain representation of that. 'There were once many streets within metropolitan centres where communities made their own worlds', the Foreword to the exhibition brochure declares. 'People who lived in Every Street made the *Every Street* exhibition. Bill Longshaw, its curator, collected their stories. He is, in the tradition of documentary artists, a sensitive observer and he is also, like every good neighbour, a great listener.'[33]

A particularly emotive display in Bill Longshaw's *Every Street* is of notes from mothers to teachers explaining their children's absences from school, a rich text for analysis and interpretation revealing actual housekeeping and child rearing skills and strategies. Significantly, the identities claimed in the signatures in these notes (undated, but probably 1960s) are invariably those of wife, 'Mrs –'. To some extent, they also voice a local system of behavioural values that are relevant in the analysis of meaning within north-west regional saga fictions. Rather than 'Hoggart's endless streets of little houses' or Seabrook's "cradling and comforting' ritual', Steedman prefers to speak of 'the terraced houses [of Burnley]' as a 'map that my mother brought [South] with her to use as a yardstick for our own childhood in the post-War years'.[34] A 'map' symbolic of a set of values or controls, since Martin propounds that a [pre-war Lancashire working-class] 'culture of control offered the only hope of creating human dignity and a modicum of self-determination against all the odds'. This is reflected in saga fictions, which amply demonstrate awareness of how

> the price of relaxing any of the boundaries and controls was very high. It made the difference between respectability and degradation, between coping and debt, between survival and starvation, independence and the workhouse. The crucial difference between the rough and the respectable was that the rough refused the disciplines of boundary and control.[35]

Good quality housework and the striving toward effective domestic management strategies are shown in saga fictions as central to that identity of respectability, and respectable survival, even in times of supreme hardship such as the northern economic depressions of the 1930s.

Before the Second World War many a working-class north-western woman accepted domestic power in place of sexual fulfilment, making the recording of her history as a housewife even more significant to her. Fowler mentions positively that 'sexual vitality is attributed by Cookson to lower-class women' but also describes the 1930s ethos that 'paramount moral virtue in a woman is her exemplary practice of pre-marital and extramarital chastity'.[36] Giles suggests passion as at best a vicarious experience for working-class women (via magazines and films), and the choosing of a marriage partner as a commonsensical matter.[37] Nella Last records stoical acceptance of her husband's dismissive treatment in her 1940s Mass-Observation journal of her life as a Barrow-in-Furness housewife.[38]

What the working-class woman in sagas does, includes all the detail of domestic and social skill missing from heritage texts and found in oral testimonies.

Equally significantly, the saga includes fictionalized 'case studies' of typically 1990s problems, such as mothers coping alone without a husband (easily rendered believable in fictions of a seafaring culture like Liverpool's, or through fictions of women on the 'home front' in wartime). Moody points out how, in Helen Forrester's *The Liverpool Basque* (1993) for instance, 'the fictional space is being used . . . to actively explore the change in culture experienced over a lifetime . . . written in hindsight . . . set in the context of contemporary life and experience'.[39] These are in fact expositions and comparisons of the ways that women have now escaped the past, as their mothers and grandmothers could not. The saga heroine is no helpless victim 'depressed to the point of inactivity . . . without the will to do anything about it',[40] losing the battle for health and cleanliness or pawning her family's possessions because she is a 'bad manager'. When such iniquities are inflicted on her they are described in terms of anger and political analysis, a standpoint important to readers,[41] filling another lack noticed by Steedman, that working-class women are not officially ascribed a psychology or any ability at political analysis.[42]

That women readers seek education in their fiction is well established. Janice Radway's research into reader reception in America revealed 'readers . . . believe that reading of any kind is, by nature, educational. They insist accordingly that they also read to learn.'[43] Fowler's research into women readers of Catherine Cookson shows, 'many women stressed this element of learning through fiction in which the genre elements of happy ending and contrived plot developments became merely formal elements subordinated to the novels' representation of history'.[44] My argument is that women readers of north-west regional sagas seek a specific history, that of their mothers' and grandmothers' private and communal but largely domestic negotiation of the vagaries of post-colonial capitalism. Josephine Cox states that, 'If you take an ordinary family in an ordinary house in an ordinary street, you have got a full novel just there. In my stories, there are always one or two families.'[45] Within a British sense of the family, through most of the twentieth century, remains the notion of 'the housewife' at its centre. Cox told the Romantic Novelists Association (in July 1998) that authenticity comes from knowing that 'you paid the rag 'n' bone shop 3d. for false teeth or specs' and that being away from home for a time leaves 'your dishcloth as stiff as buggery!' This turn of phrase instantly locates the fictional family within a specific regional and class setting, as well as highlighting the central pleasure of north-west readers in consuming saga fictions: that they display, in an entertaining way, a range of specialist local women's knowledge and an appreciation of working-class women's gendered identities that would otherwise be lost in the past. They give expression, as Ken Worpole suggests popular fiction increasingly does, to what working people 'do know [and] the value . . . of their experience and knowledge.'[46]

As Freda Lightfoot says,

> My family have been weavers (or websters as they were once called) for generations on both sides of the Pennines, and I have vivid memories of my own grandmother black-leading her range and donkey-stoning her doorstep. You could have eaten your dinner off her stone flag floors for although she was poor, she was clean. Therein lay her dignity. . . . If the telling of this country's history cannot include women like her, then it will be a poorer place.[47]

Notes

1 Q. D. Leavis, *Fiction and the Reading Public* (London, 1932), p. 8.

2 Ibid., p. xv.

3 N. Moody, 'The leaving of Liverpool: popular fiction in context', in G. Norquay and G. Smyth (eds.), *Space and Place: the Geographies of Literature* (Liverpool, 1997), pp. 312–15.

4 V. Williamson, 'The role of the librarian in the reconfiguration of gender and class in relation to professional authorship', in E. Kerslake and N. Moody (eds.), *Gendering Library History* (Liverpool, 2000), pp. 163–78.

5 B. Martin, 'Symbols, codes and cultures', in Patrick Joyce (ed.), *Class: A Reader* (Oxford, 1995), p. 251.

6 D. Cannadine, *The Pleasures of the Past* (Glasgow, 1990).

7 R. Hewison, *The Heritage Industry* (London, 1987).

8 G. Porter, 'Putting your house in order: representations of women and domestic life', in R. Lumley (ed.), *The Museum Time Machine* (London, 1988), pp. 102–27; A. Mellor, 'Whose heritage?', *North-West Labour History* 14 (1989/90), pp. 1–13; S. Marwick, 'Learning from each other: museums and older members of the community', in E. Hooper-Greenhill (ed.), *Museum, Media, Message* (London, 1995), pp. 140–50.

9 J. Williamson, *Consuming Passions: The Dynamics of Popular Culture* (London, 1987), pp. 115–26.

10 R. Bromley, *Lost Narratives: Popular Fictions, Politics and Recent History* (London, 1988).

11 Williamson, 'Role of the librarian'.

12 S. A. Caunce, 'Regional identity in Lancashire and Yorkshire', *Journal of Regional and Local Studies* 20 (1999), p. 28.

13 J. Giles, *Women, Identity and Private Life in Britain, 1900–1950* (London, 1995), p. 8.

14 Ibid., pp. 8–14.

15 J. Giles, 'A home of one's own: women and domesticity in England 1918–1950', *Women's Studies International Forum* 16 (1993), pp. 239–40.

16 E. Roberts, *A Woman's Place: an Oral History of Working-Class Women 1890–1940* (Oxford, 1984), p. 230.

17 Giles, *Women, Identity and Private Life*, pp. 9–10.

18 K. McHugh, 'One cleans, the other doesn't', *Cultural Studies* 11 (1997), pp. 17–39.

19 B. Fowler, *The Alienated Reader: Women and Popular Romantic Literature in the Twentieth Century* (London, 1991), p. 94.

20 Giles, 'A home of one's own', p. 239.

21 C. Steedman, *Landscape for a Good Woman* (London, 1986), p. 11.

22 M. Tebbutt, *Making Ends Meet: Pawnbroking and Working-Class Credit* (Leicester, 1983); Giles, *Women, Identity and Private Life*.

23 Moody, 'Leaving of Liverpool', pp. 314–15.

24 J. Lewis, *Women in England, 1870–1950* (London, 1984), p. 66; P. Ayers and J. Lambertz, 'Marriage relations, money and domestic violence in working-class Liverpool, 1919–39', in J. Lewis (ed.), *Labour and Love* (London, 1984), p. 196.

25 V. Williamson, 'Consuming poverty: saga fiction in the 1990s', in J. Hallam and N. Moody (eds.), *Consuming for Pleasure: Selected Essays on Popular Fiction* (Liverpool, 2000), pp. 268–86.

26 Giles, *Women, Identity and Private Life*, pp. 8–14.

27 A. Mellor, 'Enterprise and heritage in the dock', in J. Corner and S. Harvey (eds.), *Enterprise and Heritage* (London, 1991), p. 100.

28 Mellor, 'Whose heritage?'

29 F. Atkinson, *Pictures from the Past: Northern Life* (London, 1993), pp. 14–15, 23–9.

30 Ibid., p. 15.

31 Williamson, 'Consuming poverty'.

32 Atkinson, *Pictures*, pp. 23, 28.

33 L. Purbrick, 'Foreword', in Bill Longshaw, *Every Street: An Artist's View* (Manchester, 2000).

34 Steedman, *Landscape*, pp. 6–11, 121.

35 Martin, 'Symbols', p. 256.

36 Fowler, *Alienated Reader*, pp. 57, 82.

37 Giles, *Women, Identity and Private Life*, p. 125.

38 R. Broad and R. Fleming, *Nella Last's War* (Bristol, 1981).

39 Moody, 'Leaving of Liverpool', p. 318.

40 Atkinson, *Pictures*, p. 15.

41 Williamson, 'Consuming poverty'.

42 Steedman, *Landscape*, pp. 6–11.

43 J. Radway, 'Women read the romance', *Feminist Studies* 9 (1983), p. 59.

44 Fowler, *Alienated Reader*, p. 151.

45 J. Spelman, 'The Judith Spelman interview: Josephine Cox', *Writers' News*, May 2000, pp. 15–16.

46 K. Worpole, *Dockers and Detectives* (London: Verso, 1983), p. 23.

47 F. Lightfoot, 'In praise of the saga', *RNA News*, January 2001, pp. 8–9.

11

Welsh national identity and the British political process

Carwyn Fowler

This chapter emphasizes the dynamic role of the political process as a central feature of national identity in Wales. Many authors (including Welsh nationalists) have consigned Welsh identity to a set of somewhat 'static' criteria, as if inexorably and exclusively bound to, say, the economy or the Welsh language.[1] Here, it is argued that the development of national identity in Wales is the result of a reciprocal interaction between territorial institutions and mobilized political actors. This process is essentially 'modern' in its timing: its origins should be attributed to economic, social and political developments beginning no earlier than the second half of the nineteenth century. More generally, developments in Wales should be understood within the context of a wider Western European 'discourse' of nationalism that could only have evolved after 1789.[2]

An understanding of 'Britishness', and specifically the territorial aspects of the UK state, is crucial to any understanding of contemporary national identity in Wales. Hitherto, British nation-state identity has, whether consciously or not, been popularly accepted both at home and abroad as a 'given', 'rational', 'natural' or 'historic' national identity. Schulze includes France, Spain, Russia, Sweden, Germany and Italy in a list of national identities that widely impart a similar sense of the 'historic' or of 'given-ness' (regardless of whether or not these nationalities can point to a strictly unbroken national state tradition in fact).[3]

The UK, in its present territorial form, dates from only 1922. Yet British identity has been able to reproduce and duplicate a powerful sense of 'given-ness' on a daily basis through its media and institutions, often in almost imperceptible or 'banal' ways.[4] Peripheral challenges to the central English-British hegemony therefore face an immediate difficulty. They have often been portrayed as 'irrational' or 'illiberal', 'unhistoric' or 'artificial'.[5] Herein lies a clue as to why Welsh sports fans are invariably frustrated into supporting 'Wales, and whoever is playing against England'.[6]

A second and perhaps more tangible effect of 'Britishness' on the Welsh identity has been the political function of the UK state. It is within this institutional context that agents of Welsh national identity have had to operate. However, this 'political opportunity structure' is not set in stone. Indeed, UK attitudes towards territorial policy have proved to be remarkably 'open' for a nominally unitary state. Policies towards the component UK territories have been malleable and subject to temporal change. This chapter aims to demonstrate how a variable, ad hoc British institutional context has helped produce a multi-dimensional national movement in Wales, characterized by a broad range of demands and strategies. The Welsh Language campaign is included within this study of Welsh nationalism, as the history and philosophy of both national and language campaigns have often overlapped. Indeed, language campaigners have perhaps come closest to encapsulating, in Wales, the principal difference between 'Welshness' (and 'Scottishness') and their 'Britishness' counterpart: namely, the location of sovereignty in the people and their culture as opposed to the symbols of the 'crown in parliament' doctrine.[7]

Nationalism and the 'new regionalism' in Western Europe

Until the late 1960s, the concept of the territorial nation-state appeared unassailable, not only as the main unit of analysis within political studies, but as the pre-eminent unit of human organisation itself. The prevailing stream of nationalist discourse of this period is summarized by Max Weber: 'a nation is a community of sentiment which would adequately manifest itself in a state of its own; hence, a nation is a community which normally tends to produce a state of its own'.[8]

More recently, such uncompromising definitions of nations and nationalism have been challenged from several directions. For example, the problem of self-determination and the question of 'who' is entitled to become a nation;[9] nationalism's attendant problems of sovereignty;[10] the cultural determinism of certain 'modernist' definitions of nationalism;[11] the converse unworkable aspects of 'primordial' theoretical heritage;[12] the normative quandary of whether nationalism is to be defined as an inherently 'good' or, more often than not, a 'bad' ideology;[13] the possible connections (or otherwise) between nationalism and other ideologies;[14] and the interminable debate as to whether nationalism itself can in fact be counted as an ideology.[15]

For all of these difficulties, the dominant paradigm of the territorial organisation of governmental power will remain for the foreseeable future. Yet the classic theoretical connection between 'nation' and 'state' is becoming far more nebulous than orthodox nationalist theory would allow. Recent research in Europe focuses upon those developments within the 'sub-state' or 'meso' levels of regional mobilisation within the EU, and has become known as 'new region-alism' literature.[16] A related theme within this literature is the trend towards 'multi-level governance' within the EU.[17]

The inherent attraction of the 'new regionalism' literature is that, compared to 'nationalism', 'regionalism' is defined by fairly technical criteria and, as such, does not carry the same historical baggage as 'nationalism'. In other words, it is an inherently 'value-free' concept. 'New regionalism' emphasizes the contin-gent and contested nature of regions across space and time. We may identify three main stimuli behind the 'new regionalism' in the EU. First, a series of changes in the economic, political, social and cultural nature of the European nation-state.[18] Second, the impact of 'globalisation', in multi-faceted ways, upon sub-state regional economies.[19] Third, the process of European Union, with a territorial dispersion of (domestic) competencies away from national states to sub-national and supranational authorities.[20]

A 'political opportunity structure' for the Welsh identity

Kitschelt defined the concept of 'political opportunity structures' as 'specific configurations of resources, institutional arrangements and historical prece-dents for social mobilisation, which facilitate the development of protest move-ments in some instances and constrain them in others'.[21] During the past thirty years, the concept of political opportunity has, according to McAdam, 'become a staple in social movement inquiry'.[22] With few exceptions, however, the con-cept has been restricted to the study of 'new social movements', ranging from feminist campaigns to anti-nuclear mobilisation.[23] Only rarely has the concept been applied on a territorial basis.[24] Recently, however, Marks and McAdam have made an explicit link between the changes in territorial governance within the EU, and the consequential policy process or 'political opportunity' impacts of this upon social mobilisation (including sub-state regionalism) in western Europe:

> Our general argument is straightforward; to the extent that European integration results in the replacement, or, more likely, the decline in the importance of the nation-state as the exclusive seat of formal political power, we can expect attendant changes in those forms of interest aggregation/articulation historically linked to the state.[25]

An emerging EU political framework is, therefore, crucial for any current analysis of Welsh national identity and the future of Welsh nationalism is closely linked to the continuing process of European unity.

It would be premature, however, to discount the role of the British policy process in the 'political opportunity structure' of Welsh national identity. For the foreseeable future, the British context will continue to be a key factor. Yet it would be wrong to view the UK as a monolithic, oppressive entity, committed since the 1536 Act of Union to the suppression of Welsh identity in all its forms. What is remarkable about the UK political context is the ad hoc nature of territorial policy that has evolved within its various component parts. This has rendered the UK a 'union state', open to various degrees of regional autonomy, as opposed to a 'unitary state' that would be committed to complete standardisation of territorial policy within the state boundaries.[26] We may also note that the British policy process has been characterized by a comparatively 'open' policy style in comparison to other countries that might have a more entrenched or 'closed' process.[27]

Accounts such as these help explain the process of 'asymmetric devolution' that has occurred in the UK as a result of separate referenda since 1997 in Wales, Northern Ireland and Scotland.[28] The creation of a Greater London Authority (GLA) in 1999 continued this trend.[29] In Wales, the Labour government decided upon a course of executive, rather than legislative, devolution.[30] Perceptions of a 'weaker' form of devolution, at least in comparison with Scotland, were underscored by the 'corporate' status of the National Assembly for Wales, thus embodying a local government rather than a parliamentary ethos.[31] The comparison with local government is exemplified by the role of the committees, which are intended to carry out both policy-making and scrutinizing roles.[32] Financially, the National Assembly funds will be allocated largely by means of a block grant from the UK treasury, in the same manner as the Welsh Office prior to 1997.[33] Thus, any reference to a Welsh 'national' policy process cannot be made without referring to the constraints placed upon it by processes of British governance.

Nevertheless, the National Assembly for Wales brings with it significant changes in the 'political opportunity structure' for Welsh national identity within the current British and European frameworks. Indeed, there are clear signs that the prescribed *de jure* legislative constraints of the 1998 Government of Wales Act are, de facto, being cast aside.[34] For example, the realities of party politics have apparently put paid to any lingering notions of 'corporate' or 'inclusive' government. A 'parliamentary' style of organisation has effectively been assumed during the course of the National Assembly's first term.[35] This shift is symbolized, in turn, by the assembly committees' trend towards a parliamentary 'select committee' style, moving towards scrutiny of the executive rather than policy development.[36] More fundamentally, the continued development of the national assembly's legislative and functional scope is now widely regarded as both practical and desirable.[37] This trend indicates that the ad hoc and 'open' UK territorial policy style in Wales is alive and well.

Devolution opens new avenues in terms of the various relationships that exist between the Wales level and other levels of governance and identity. Not least of these is the relationship between the National Assembly and the localities and regions of Wales.[38] A key development in this relationship might arise with the possible introduction of proportional representation to local government in Wales, and the subsequent ending of entrenched monolithic party blocs in several counties of Wales. Elsewhere, the relationship between Cardiff and Westminster will continue to evolve. Current debate focuses on the role of ad hoc concordats as the current basis of a working relationship between the two levels of governance.[39] Of further significance is the increasingly direct relationship between Wales and the European Union. For example, Wales' formal channels of influence have recently been accentuated by the development of an informal lobby of sub-state 'constitutional regions', involving Wales, Bavaria, Catalunya, North Rhine Westphalia, Piedmont, Salzburg, Tyrol, Tuscany, Flanders and Wallonia.[40]

Another major change to the 'Political Opportunity Structure' of Welsh nationalism was the establishment of a new 'Additional Member System' electoral system (AMS) for the National Assembly for Wales.[41] Again, the new system reflects the *ad hoc* style of "Britishness" with regard to its component territories: there are now different electoral systems for the National Assembly for Wales; the Scottish Parliament; the Northern Ireland Assembly; the GLA; European Parliamentary elections; and UK General Elections. In Wales, the main impact of the new system in 1999 was to deny Labour its expected majority in the new National Assembly. The second impact of fresh 'Welsh' elections was to assist Plaid Cymru (the Party of Wales) in attaining its highest ever share of the vote in Wales, an event which is discussed in more detail below. Suffice to say that these outcomes had different and profound impacts upon the Labour party in Wales;[42] the 'dynamic' of the opposition parties in Wales;[43] the composition and character of assembly committees[44] and, as discussed above, on the character of the National Assembly as a working institution. The electoral process is a key element in any study of the political configurations that affect a given social movement.[45] With these observations in mind, we turn to an overview of multiple agents of 'Welshness' which have sought to express their political demands within an institutional climate governed by a tailored, 'union-state' form of 'Britishness'.

The national movement in Wales

It was noted that traditional accounts of nationalism sit rather uncomfortably with contemporary processes of sub-state regional or national mobilisation, at least within the context of the European Union. Wales is no exception: there are very good grounds for arguing that the general philosophy of Welsh nationalism runs contrary to the demands set out by the orthodox theories, and has been characterized by a marked responsiveness to ideas such as: shared sovereignty; dissenting non-conformist religion; and left-libertarian political thought.[46] The Welsh experience of nationalism may be closer to what Anthony Smith – probably the most prolific author in nationalism studies – defined as 'national identity':

> 'national' identity involves some sort of political community, however tenuous. A political community in turn implies at least some common institutions and a single code of rights and duties for all the members of the community. It also suggests a definite social space, a fairly well demarcated and bounded territory, with which the members identify and to which they feel they belong.[47]

Reference to Smith, however, invites assumptions of agreement with his 'primordial' stance, and with the role of pre-national *ethnie* in relation to the development of nations. I therefore reiterate my belief that the development of modern European regions and nations is temporally contingent; it is related to the post-1789 discourse and is bound up with issues of political process. Perhaps J. Snicker provides a more accurate synopsis for our purposes:

> The idea of Wales and the Welsh has been transformed during the 1980s and 1990s, a process with significant implications for the British constitutional settlement. Such transformations depend on the ability of social and political actors to define, refine, produce and reproduce identity in the course of interaction. Nationalism is not an adequate descriptor for this process.[48]

The importance of situational factors is vital when we examine the range of mobilisation strategies that have been deployed on behalf of the Welsh national identity. In line with 'political opportunity structure' theory, we may argue that the ad hoc nature of British political opportunities has given rise to an ad hoc national movement in Wales in terms of its demands and strategies. We now turn to this wide range of multiple actors. For the sake of clarity, the following analysis deals in turn with both 'political demands' and 'campaigns for the Welsh language'.

Political demands

According to Hans Kohn, the stateless national movement is, by definition, a temporary concept that 'satisfies itself with some form of autonomy or pre-state organization which, however, always tends at a given moment, the moment of "liberation", to develop into a sovereign state. Nationalism demands the nation-state; the creation of the nation-state strengthens nationalism.'[49]

If we accept this definition, we may state confidently that Welsh 'nationalism' is not a nationalism at all in the classic sense. What follows will demonstrate that the political demands of Welsh identity have been variable. The Welsh case may be contrasted with Scotland and Northern Ireland, where both 'unionist' and 'nationalist' political parties have emphasized populist ultimate positions, along the lines of classic nation-state theory. Thus we regularly hear talk of 'Scottish independence', 'united Ireland' and 'unity of the UK'. In comparison, both the rhetoric and practice of Welsh nationalism has fallen far short of an 'ultimate' aim, or a 'moment of liberation' of the kind that Kohn demanded. For example, the central Welsh political demand of the early twentieth century, as espoused by the Liberal Party in Wales, was not legal-political 'independence', but a more amorphous demand for cultural and religious 'freedom', through the disestablishment of the Church in Wales.

Similarly, Plaid Cymru's short-term demands have not focused on an irredentist position of 'independence' for Wales. Instead, they have aimed consistently at securing an intermediate position for Wales within the prevailing international order of the day: the British Empire; the British Commonwealth; and subsequently the European Union. The ad hoc nature of the National Assembly for Wales – outlined above – means that Welsh nationalism is set to continue on this gradualist course for the foreseeable future. Bolstered by a new electoral configuration, the establishment of primary legislative powers, or 'parity with Scotland' within the UK, appears to be a logical and attainable step for a broad national movement, currently embodied by elected Labour, Plaid Cymru and Liberal Democrat members of the National Assembly for Wales.

The first 'catch-all' party? The Liberal Party in Wales

The Liberal Party could legitimately claim to be the first 'Party of Wales', almost a century before Plaid Cymru and Labour began their bitter tussle for this disputed crown. The Liberals won a comfortable majority in every election in Wales from 1868 until 1922.[50] The party gained its popularity through campaigning on a wide range of issues, such as land reform, working conditions and, of great symbolic importance, for the Disestablishment of the Church in Wales. Inspired by the Irish home-rule movement, younger members of the Welsh Liberals founded a pressure group for home rule, Cymru Fydd (literally 'The Wales that will be'), within the Liberal Party. Principal actors included Tom Ellis, MP for Meirionnydd, and the young David Lloyd George, MP for Caernarfon.

An understanding of religious sentiment in Wales is important. Here, the various shades of dissenting non-conformist Protestantism accounted for around two-thirds of worshippers, with the official Anglican church in an historic minority. By the beginning of the twentieth century, non-conformism had become synonymous with Welsh nationhood, to the extent that it could be claimed that 'The Nonconformists of Wales are the people of Wales.' This was exaggerated; yet the nonconformist influence upon Welsh politics and national identity, at least in the period 1870–1920, remained unmistakable.[51]

The attempt to achieve religious dignity for Welsh people in the eyes of the British state succeeded in galvanizing far more support, from both rural and industrialized areas of Wales, than the seemingly complex political and legal manoeuvrings required to secure a Welsh parliament. However, disestablishment in 1920 met the main Welsh national demand. Calls for 'Home Rule all round' fell on increasingly deaf ears, and demands based on national or cultural factors gave way to an economic cleavage, with Labour inheriting the working-class vote of industrial Wales from the Liberals. Yet the Liberal years in Wales were important in establishing a political ethos for civic national identity. This also explains why Welsh Nonconformity, despite the pressing evidence for its modern decline and decay, still constitutes an important aspect of Welsh national identity.[52]

Campaigns within the Liberal Party, including those of Cymru Fydd, were never intended to undermine the ultimate authority of UK structures, either of the Liberal Party or of the UK Parliament as a whole. The tactical influence of Parnell's Irish home-rule party was certainly evident. However, Welsh Liberals of the period never countenanced secession from the UK, as was advocated by

Sinn Féin in Ireland. This aspect is clearly illustrated by the political rise of David Lloyd George. After the eventual failure of Cymru Fydd to force a Home Rule act for Wales on to the statute book, Lloyd George turned his attentions to UK matters and ultimately rose to be Prime Minister.

Plaid Cymru: An 'independent' or 'independence' strategy?

Plaid Genedlaethol Cymru (The National Party of Wales) was founded in 1925, by a group of activists frustrated by the failed attempts to gain political home rule through the Liberal Party in Wales. It is perhaps indicative of the party's future philosophy that the word 'national' was eventually dropped from its official title. Although its founders had been inspired by the success of Sinn Féin in gaining an Irish Free State, they declined to use the term 'independence' to describe Plaid Cymru's constitutional aim. Rather, they have tended to call for variations on the theme of 'full self-government', a term which has prevailed to this day, despite the comparative success of the SNP – at least until 1999 – in campaigning on a platform of 'independence' for Scotland.

Plaid Cymru's founding president, Saunders Lewis, was determined that the dominance of the centralist state, witnessed in the UK, should not be replicated in a self-governing Wales. Furthermore, Plaid Cymru acknowledged from its inception the concept of shared or pooled sovereignty. The immediate aim was for 'Dominion Status', on a par with the self-governing territories within the British Empire. Saunders Lewis rejected the word 'independence' out of hand in the party's first pamphlet, *Egwyddorion Cenedlaetholdeb* ('Principles of Nationalism'), published in 1926. Over seventy years later, when challenged on the issue of separatism prior to the 1999 National Assembly elections, Plaid Cymru president Dafydd Wigley was able to point out that Plaid had *'never, ever'* advocated independence.[53] As Thomas D. Combs summarizes:

> Plaid Cymru's concept of political freedom for Wales does not connotate [sic] either a self-imposed isolation or complete economic separation from England. The Party's spokesmen since 1925 have carefully differentiated between the goal of national freedom and what others have labelled a quest for independence. To men like Saunders Lewis . . . freedom connotes a spiritual, moral and individual-istic quality that the word independence lacks.[54]

A further distinction between Plaid Cymru and their Scottish counterparts, or indeed other 'classic modernist' European nationalist movements, has been Plaid Cymru's greater willingness to propose interim constitutional options short of full self-government. As noted above, the first manifesto in 1925 argued for 'Dominion Status' for Wales within the British Empire. The party was at the fore of a cross-party 'Parliament for Wales' campaign in the 1950s, which called for a legislative parliament, but again firmly within the UK context. Plaid Cymru reluctantly supported the 'Yes' campaign for the 1979 Wales Act. This proposed a (fairly weak) form of executive devolution. Whilst the Act was a product of the Callaghan Labour administration, several prominent Labour MPs in Wales opposed it vigorously, with Neil Kinnock at the forefront. The proposals were heavily defeated, by a 4:1 ratio, in the all-Wales referendum on St David's Day, 1 March 1979. Similarly, in 1997, Plaid Cymru backed Labour's devolution proposals, despite their falling far short of Plaid's call for 'Parity with Scotland' through a legislative parliament with tax-varying powers. These proposals were narrowly accepted in the referendum of September 1997.

Until 1999, Plaid Cymru's electoral performance had rendered Welsh nationalism, from an external viewpoint, a somewhat poor relation of its Scottish counterpart.[55] In the period 1945–97, Plaid Cymru advanced from 1.1 per cent to 9.9 per cent of the Welsh vote in UK General Elections, and from 0 to 4 parliamentary seats. The party's highest vote share, 11.5 per cent, came in the 1970 General Election. Plaid did record some spectacular by-election performances in Labour's South Wales strongholds. However, their Westminster representation has continued to consist of various permutations of five rural, predominantly Welsh-speaking constituencies in the west and north-west.[56] This area is commonly referred to in socio-political terms as '*Y Fro Gymraeg*' ('Welsh-speaking heartland').[57]

As we saw above, the establishment of the National Assembly for Wales brought with it a new electoral system, entailing a significant cultural change in Welsh politics. Balsom sums up the importance of this change in 'political opportunity structure': 'The election to select the administration, and therefore which party leader was to become First Secretary and de facto Prime Minister, was now of enormous importance. In the new constitutional framework that now applies to Wales, this was to be the first Welsh general election.'[58]

The overriding theme of 1999 was the success of Plaid Cymru in gaining support in Welsh-identifying, but non-Welsh-speaking parts of Wales. Plaid Cymru captured three of the most symbolic of the south Wales seats: Llanelli, with its strong traditions of tinplate and rugby, and the only remaining example of a largely Welsh-speaking industrial town; Rhondda Valley, formerly the hub of the Welsh coal industry; and probably the most audacious of the Plaid Cymru successes came in Islwyn, the traditional mining constituency of former Labour Party leader Neil Kinnock, where Labour had secured a 65.8

per cent majority in the 1997 General Election. Furthermore, this was achieved without alienating their core support in *Y Fro Gymraeg*. Indeed, their grip on this region was considerably strengthened. Throughout Wales, Plaid Cymru secured 30 per cent of the Welsh vote. This was higher than the SNP vote share in the first elections to the Scottish Parliament on the same day in May 1999.

There had been speculation among psephologists as to whether the 1999 elections would merely constitute a 'second order' election, with voters expressing their satisfaction (or otherwise) with 'mid-term' Westminster developments.[59] Several characteristics of a second order election could be observed. For example, there was perhaps 'less at stake' in the sense that the National Assembly is not a legislative body in the UK or even Scottish sense. Thus turnout was low, at 48 per cent. An opposition party (Plaid Cymru) made large percentage gains in all areas of Wales. The governing party (Labour) suffered dramatic losses. However, and crucially for the 'second order election' thesis, poll evidence suggests that these factors were not due to perceptions of party performance at Westminster. We should turn instead to the view that Welsh national identity reacts in different ways to different political contexts. When Labour defectors to Plaid Cymru were asked for their reasons for switching, the evidence is compelling: 'By far the largest group claimed, in an unprompted, spontaneous response, that the Assembly election was a Welsh, rather than a British election and that Plaid Cymru, as a party, were more concerned for Wales.'[60]

Plaid Cymru's electoral approach as an independent political party has been an important strategy for the broad national movement in Wales. It has been strongest when the party has harnessed favourable political contexts. In this sense, the electoral opportunities offered by the creation of a national assembly are hugely significant for the party. It can now try to achieve its constitutional objectives on a sustainable basis, aided by potential allies within the Labour, Liberal Democrat (and even Conservative) parties in Wales. However, Plaid's major situational strength has an axiomatic weakness, namely, that voters will continue to view the party as comparatively irrelevant in terms of Westminster elections, electing a cabinet and selecting a Prime Minister. Plaid 's support fell back to 14 per cent in the 2001 UK General Election. Welsh nationalism is therefore viewed as a useful mechanism for promoting Wales' domestic interests, yet 'Britishness' reigns supreme in the minds of Welsh voters when the 'high politics' of state are concerned.

Campaigns for the Welsh language

Campaigns for the Welsh language can be viewed as an important part of the Welsh national movement. There has been a cross-fertilisation both in terms of ethos and personnel between the various political and language campaigns.[61] Early campaigns bore the hallmarks of the non-conformist influence. By invoking the egalitarian tradition of non-conformism, campaigners sought to confer upon the language an inherent moral value. As such, the Welsh language should be regarded as inviolable and protected from the interference of the bureaucratic (British) state.

Cymdeithas yr Iaith Gymraeg (the Welsh Language Society) was linked to non-conformism in an interesting way. Some notable activists were 'sons of the manse', seeking a more explicitly political campaign for the language.[62] The movement perceived itself as an ally of the 'new' social movements that appeared throughout western democracies during the 1960s and 1970s. As such, we may view Cymdeithas yr Iaith Gymraeg within the context of 'left-libertarian' traditions of continental Europe. Nevertheless, the society retained a 'Welsh national' outlook in that it campaigned for bilingualism within the public sector throughout Wales.

A more recent development is the establishment of the Cymuned (Community) pressure group, whose ideological emphasis has been to emphasize the existence of different 'ethno-linguistic groups' in Wales. Whilst its members have endorsed non-violent direct action as a possible avenue, Cymuned's early strategy has focused upon political lobbying, with a focus on influencing the deliberations of the National Assembly committees on culture and housing.[63] Significantly, the leadership of this new group have engaged in a forthright critique of the civic nationalist movement in Wales, including Plaid Cymru. The group's variable and unorthodox early ideological publications mark a significant theoretical shift away from the civic nationalist tradition, as embodied by Plaid Cymru and, at an earlier time, the Liberal Party in Wales. First, we may briefly note some ideological premises of early language campaigners, which date to a particular incident in 1936.

State sovereignty vs. 'moral law': the Penyberth incident

In 1936 Saunders Lewis, along with two other eminent Plaid Cymru figures, D. J. Williams and Rev. Lewis Valentine, set fire to an RAF training range in Penyberth, North Wales. Their political aim was a pacifist protest against the

British state's preparations for war. In addition, they wished to draw attention to the Anglicisation of a predominantly Welsh-speaking area of Wales that the RAF development would bring in its wake. The following is an extract from Saunders Lewis' defence speech in court:

'Remember that the God who created men ordained nations', said Emrys ap Iwan, and the moral law recognises the family and the nation to be moral persons. They have the qualities and the natural rights of persons. And by the law of God the essential rights of the family and the nation, and especially their right to live, are prior to the rights of any state. It is part also of the moral law that no state . . . has a right to seek national advantages which would mean genuine harm to any other nation. All that is universal Christian tradition . . . We saw the English state preparing mortal danger to the moral person of the Welsh nation . . .You cannot calculate in figures the irreparable loss of a language, of purity of idiom, of a home of literature, of a tradition of rural Welsh civilisation stretching back fourteen hundred years . . .We were compelled, therefore, to do serious damage to the bombing school buildings . . . in a last desperate and vital effort to bring the immorality of the Government's action before the judgement of Christian Wales.[64]

Several factors, then, have inspired the inclusion of language and culture within the campaigns for an institutionalized Welsh identity. And certain perceptions of 'Britishness' in the inter-war era are crucial. In Saunders Lewis' speech, we learn of the sense of political opposition to a centralized state. This is regarded as alien to the distinct historic, cultural and linguistic traditions of Wales. The inherent value of the spoken language and written literature itself cannot be ignored. Finally there is a moral argument, that Wales is a pre-ordained community founded upon Christian ideals, and that the imposition of foreign law and customs upon Wales is wrong according to 'moral law'.

A 'left-libertarian' approach: Cymdeithas yr Iaith Gymraeg

At first glance, it might seem incongruous to link Welsh nationalism with a concept which has recently evolved in the so-called 'post-materialist' political culture of countries such as Germany, Belgium and the Netherlands. Left-libertarianism might usually be associated with the development of ecological, feminist and anti-nuclear 'new social movements' in those countries during the 1960s and 1970s. More recently, the progress of Green and other third parties across the European continent has led to the concept being extended to political parties: 'They are "left" because they share with traditional socialism a mistrust of the marketplace, of private investment, and of the achievement ethic, and a commitment to egalitarian distribution. They are "libertarian" because they reject the authority of private or public bureaucracies to regulate individual and collective conduct.'[65]

Cymdeithas yr Iaith Gymraeg (The Welsh Language Society) is the nearest Welsh approximation to a continental European 'new social movement'.[66] It drew inspiration from other civil rights movements of the period, such as those of the USA, Northern Ireland and the European continent. The society's most visible campaigns were mounted during the 1970s. They aimed at securing bilingual road signs within Wales. Campaigns were also targeted at such bodies as the Post Office, Welsh Office and Local Government. During the early 1980s, the campaign for a Welsh Language Television Channel reached its peak, and a channel was eventually established in 1982. In 1993 a Welsh Language Act established new provisions for the Welsh language within the public sector in Wales.

The group's strategies and methods were directly comparable to any other 'new social movement' of the period, not least in an explicit renunciation of physical violence. Rucht notes that 'old' movements of previous centuries would have tended to use physical violence as a political strategy. However, 'new' social movements have tended to opt for non-violent civil disobedience, not only for moral, but also for several practical and strategic reasons. Certainly, Cymdeithas yr Iaith Gymraeg would appear to have adhered to the following strategy:

> These acts allow the venting of specific and intense criticism without necessarily aiming at a general transformation of society. Moreover, civil disobedience as an act with a highly symbolic and expressive component requires an audience to whom the actor can appeal. Unlike revolutionary or terrorist acts . . . civil disobedience must take account of public opinion – and the dependence of power-holders on that opinion . . . Obviously, the presence of modern mass-media enhances the efficacy of civil disobedience.[67]

An 'ethno-linguistic' approach: Cymuned

Cymdeithas yr Iaith had initially been rallied by a BBC radio speech, *Tynged yr Iaith* (Fate of the Language), in which Saunders Lewis argued that unless drastic political action was taken, the language would be extinct early in the twenty-first century: Maybe the language will bring self-government in its wake; I don't know. The language is more important than self-government. In my opinion, if any form of self-government for Wales was gained before restoring and using Welsh as an official language in the entire administration of local and national government in the Welsh speaking regions of our country, it would not be an official language at all, and its decline would be quicker than its decline will be under England's government.[68] In its campaigns, however, Cymdeithas yr Iaith rarely forced the dichotomy of 'language v. self-government'. Indeed, it can be argued that the society assisted the self-government movement by 'taking care' of language issues across the whole of Wales, thus letting Plaid Cymru deal with the everyday political concerns of party politics, along with the constitutional issue of Wales' national future. Since 2001, however, the politics of the Welsh language has taken another twist, with the formation of the Cymuned pressure group and an entirely new set of ideological perspectives.

First, the group's principle spokesperson, Simon Brooks, has asserted a dichotomy between civic and cultural nationalism.[69] Essentially, such a dichotomy recalls the statement of Saunders Lewis that 'the language is more important than self-government' as a Welsh nationalist aim. In the same article, Brooks argues that the idea of a Welsh civil society, in its present manifestation, militates against the continuation of a Welsh speaking ethno-linguistic group. Furthermore, it is claimed that during the course of the centuries, the Welsh-speaking group within Wales has suffered a systematic campaign of 'ethnocide' on the part of the British state.[70] Most recently, Brooks has suggested that Welsh speakers might consider opposing further measures of constitutional reform for Wales (i.e. further legislative powers for the National Assembly for Wales) unless certain guarantees can be made about the status of Welsh speakers as an 'ethno-linguistic' minority within Wales.[71] The group's current slogan on housing policy is 'No to Colonisation'. The group has provided a more detailed breakdown of their understanding of the colonisation concept, and its possible relevance to Wales.[72]

These demands run against hitherto prevailing conceptions of Welsh identity, which would note the 'unity in diversity' of the several geo-political areas of Wales and were promulgated in turn by the Welsh Liberals, Plaid Cymru and elements of the Labour Party in Wales.[73] The 1997 devolution referendum result was an expression, *par excellence*, of the Welsh civic national identity: Welsh-speaking (agri)culture combining with destitute south Wales mining valleys to deliver a decisive verdict on what effectively became a referendum on the Thatcher-Redwood effect on their areas of Wales. The subsequent electoral success of Plaid Cymru in the south Wales valleys added a further dimension to this political configuration, which has its roots in a distinctive social and economic history. By contrast, Cymuned's opening gambit countenances a de facto – if not *de jure* – dichotomy (including, presumably, further divergence in electoral priorities) between *Y Fro Gymraeg* and the former south Wales coalfield.[74]

These recent developments are also relevant in that they shed light upon the often overlooked 'Britishness' of the Labour Party. However implicitly, the territorial unity of the United Kingdom is at least as much a fundamental platform for Labour as it is for the more overtly expressed 'Britishness' of the Conservatives. The staunchly Labour *Welsh Mirror* (a Welsh edition of the *Daily Mirror*) has responded to Cymuned's agenda with a series of vitriolic attacks upon language campaigners within both Cymuned and Plaid Cymru. These attacks are characterized by the worst kind of tabloid excess. Yet they are nevertheless written with one, very rational, aim in mind: to unsettle 'soft' voters in coalfield Plaid-Labour marginal seats. Nationalists have (fairly justifiably) reacted with anger at the *Mirror's* tactics.[75] Yet political logic suggests that Labour and its media supporters would not passively concede three-quarters of a century of political hegemony in the valleys to Plaid. The occasionally injudicious remarks of language campaigners have given the *Welsh Mirror* an opportunity to seize a clear agenda, with the ultimate intention of assisting Labour in turning the political tables on Plaid in South Wales at the 2003 National Assembly elections. Cymuned's apparent disregard for the electoral process means that there remains perhaps a grain of truth in the *Welsh Mirror's* taunt: 'Get used to it, Plaid . . . It's Politics.'[76]

It is too early to gauge the long-term political impact of Cymuned. Yet there is at least some intrigue surrounding its ideology, strategy and, most importantly, the group's ultimate impact upon language policy in post-devolution Wales. Thus far, we may summarize that Cymuned has pursued a two-fold aim during its first months of existence. First, an effective, pro-active and highly professional articulation of Welsh language demands within the context of the new National Assembly policy arena. Second, and as Plaid Cymru's electoral star has risen in anglicized south-east Wales, a more dubious agenda of maintaining the internal ideological influence of cultural nationalists within Welsh nationalism.

Conclusions

During the course of this book, various contributors have accorded the concept of 'Britishness' a widely differing theoretical treatment. For the purposes of this chapter, 'Britishness' is assumed to be a set of values that have, by a process of convention, or 'unwritten law', become embodied through the political institutions and processes of the UK state. As one of Europe's 'given' national identities,

'Britishness' has sometimes assumed a seemingly timeless and unending quality that aspirant national identities, such as in Scotland and Wales, can only envy.

Yet it is in the very 'unwritten' nature of 'Britishness' that we find a threat to its existence, at least as a static, hegemonic entity. As the 'union state' model suggests, the process of territorial integration has always remained incomplete within the UK. Territorial policy has been characterized by an ad hoc and reciprocal interplay between peripheral demands and central response. Never at any point has there been a sustained attempt to achieve an entrenched settlement by means of a written constitution.[77] The situation is underscored by the reluctance, or perhaps nervousness, of the UK state to attach any formal political significance either to England or its component regions.[78]

It is in relation to this very 'open' style of British territorial policy – a direct product of 'Britishness' – that we may conceptualize the campaigns of the national movement in Wales. This is not to deny the Welsh national movement its own endogenous qualities. We have noted the distinctively Welsh inputs (in comparison to dominant English trends) of a sense of popular sovereignty, along with more 'objective' factors such as the role of non-conformist religion, combined with a distinct Welsh territory, language and economic profile. However, the political saliency of these issues only becomes clear when they are applied within a certain context of values and processes.

(Un)fortunately, for the entirety of its 'political' existence, Wales happens to have adjoined what is arguably the most powerful value system on earth, within just a few dozen miles of that system's main population centres – where the values and symbols of 'Britishness' are constantly being reproduced. It is for these reasons that 'Britishness' will continue to be an important player in Wales for the foreseeable future, and why Wales' growing clarity on Europe's political map constitutes a daily minor miracle.

Notes

1 For the economic aspects of UK territorial politics, see M. Hechter, *Internal Colonialism: The Celtic Fringe in British National Development, 1536–1966* (London, 1975); T. Nairn, *The Break-Up of Britain: Crisis and Neo-Nationalism* (London, 1977). Early language-based accounts of Welsh national identity are summarized by D. Phillips in his *Trwy Ddulliau Chwyldro. . .?* (Llandysul, 1998).

2 C. Calhoun, *Nationalism* (Buckingham, 1997).

3 H. Schulze, *States, Nations and Nationalism*, trans. W. E. Yuill (Oxford, 1996).

4 M. Billig, *Banal Nationalism* (London, 1995).

5 For example, E. J. Hobsbawm, *Nations and Nationalism Since 1780* (Cambridge, 1990).

6 To Nanny, with love from her 'treacherous grandson'.

7 C. Fowler, *Analysing the Welsh Identity: Welsh Governance Centre Working Paper IV* (Cardiff, 2001); N. McEwen, 'state welfare nationalism: the territorial impact of welfare state development in Scotland', *Regional and Federal Studies* 12 (2002), pp. 84–5.

8 *Essays in Sociology* (London, 1970), p. 176.

9 The work of one particular author, Margaret Moore, might be read in the following order: M. Moore, 'On national self-determination', *Political Studies* 45 (1997), pp. 900–13; M. Moore (ed.), *National Self-Determination and Secession* (Oxford, 1998); M. Moore, *The Ethics of Nationalism* (Oxford, 2000).

10 J. Camilleri and J. Falk, *The End of Sovereignty?* (Aldershot, 1992).

11 C. Geertz, *The Interpretation of Cultures: Selected Essays* (London, 2nd edn., 1993).

12 E. Shils, 'Primordial, personal, sacred and civil ties', *British Journal of Sociology* 8 (1957), pp. 131–44.

13 K. R. Minogue, *Nationalism* (London, 1967).

14 For example, Y. Tamir, *Liberal Nationalism* (Princeton, NJ, 1993).

15 M. Freeden, 'Is nationalism a distinct ideology?', *Political Studies* 46 (1998), pp. 748–65.

16 M. Keating and J. Loughlin (eds.), *The Political Economy of Regionalism* (London, 1997); M. Keating, *The New Regionalism in Western Europe* (Cheltenham, 1998).

17 G. Marks, 'Structural policy and multilevel governance in the European Union', in A. Cafruny and G. Rosenthal (eds.), *The State of the European Community: The Maastricht Debates and Beyond* (Boulder, 1993), pp. 391–407.

18 J. Loughlin, 'Regional autonomy and state paradigm shifts in Western Europe', *Rgional and Federal Studies* 10 (2000), pp. 10–33.

19 J. Loughlin, 'Introduction: The Transformation of the Democratic State in Western Europe', in idem (ed.), *Subnational Democracy in the European Union* (Oxford, 2001).

20 G. Marks, 'An actor-centred approach to multi-level governance', *Regional and Federal Studies* 6 (1996), pp. 20–38.

21 H. Kitschelt, 'Political opportunity structures and political protest: anti-nuclear movements in four democracies', *British Journal of Political Science* 16 (1986), pp. 57–85.

22 D. McAdam, 'Conceptual origins, current problems, future directions', in D. McAdam, J. McCarthy and M. Zald (eds.), *Comparative Perspectives on Social Movements* (Cambridge, 1996).

23 For example, A. Costain, *Inviting Women's Rebellion: A Political Process Interpretation of the Women's Movement* (Baltimore, MD, 1992); L. Overby, 'West European peace movements: an application of Kitschelt's political opportunity structures thesis', *West European Politics* 13 (1990), pp. 1–11; W. Rüdig, 'Peace and ecology movements in Western Europe', *West European Politics* 11 (1998), pp. 26–39.

24 N. Vladisavljevi_, 'Nationalism, Social movement theory and the grass roots movement of Kosovo Serbs, 1985–1988', *Europe-Asia Studies* 54 (2002).

25 G. Marks and D. McAdam, 'Social movements and the changing structure of political opportunity in the European Union', *West European Politics* 19 (1996), pp. 249–78.

26 S. Rokkan and D. Urwin, 'Introduction: centres and peripheries in Western Europe', in idem (eds.), *The Politics of Territorial Identity* (London, 1982), p. 11; S. Rokkan and D. Urwin, *Economy Territory Identity* (London, 1983), p. 181; J. Mitchell, 'Conservatives and the changing meaning of Union', *Regional and Federal Studies*, 6 (1996), pp. 30–44.

27 G. Jordan and J. Richardson, 'The British policy style or the logic of negotiation?', in J. Richardson (ed.) *Policy Styles in Western Europe* (London, 1982).

28 M. Keating, 'What's wrong with asymmetrical government?', *Regional and Federal Studies* 8 (1998), pp. 195–218.

29 J. Tomaney, 'The governance of London', in R. Hazell (ed.), *The State and the Nations* (Thorverton, 2000), pp. 241–67.

30 A. Cole and A. Storer, 'Political dynamics in the assembly: an emerging policy community', in J. B. Jones and J. Osmond (eds.), *Building a Civic Culture* (Cardiff, 2002), pp. 257–70.

31 K. Patchett, 'The New Welsh Constitution: The Government of Wales Act 1998', in J. B. Jones and D. Balsom (eds) *The Road to the National Assembly for Wales* (Cardiff, 2000), pp. 229–64.

32 J. Osmond, 'Carving out a distinctive position: the future of the subject committees in the National Assembly', in J. B. Jones and J. Osmond (eds.), *Inclusive Government and Party Management* (Cardiff, 2001), pp. 157–73.

33 G. Bristow and A. Kay, 'Spending autonomy in Wales: setting the National Assembly budget within the framework of the Barnett formula', in Jones and Osmond (eds.), *Building a Civic Culture*, pp. 83–97.

34 J. Osmond, 'The enigma of the corporate body: relations between the committees and the administration', in Jones and Osmond (eds.) *Inclusive Government and Party Management*, pp. 1–23.

35 J. Osmond, 'Introduction: emergence of the assembly government', in Jones and Osmond (eds.), *Building a Civic Culture*, pp. xvii–xxiii.

36 J. B. Jones, 'Politics and crisis management: the Agriculture and Rural Development Committee', in Jones and Osmond (eds.), *Building a Civic Culture*, pp. 155–64.

37 J. Williams, 'The Assembly as a legislature', in Jones and Osmond (eds.), *Building a Civic Culture*, pp. 1–16.

38 A. Thomas, 'Relations between the Assembly and local government', in Jones and Osmond (eds.), *Building a Civic Culture*, pp. 17–32.

39 K. Patchett, 'The central relationship: the Assembly's engagement with Westminster and Whitehall', in Jones and Osmond (eds.), *Building a Civic Culture*, pp. 17–32.

40 J. B. Jones, 'Wales in Europe: developing a relationship', in Jones and Osmond (eds.), *Building a Civic Culture*, pp. 57–66.

41 D. Balsom, 'The first elections', in Osmond (ed.), *The National Assembly Agenda*, pp. 17–27.

42 J. B. Jones and D. Balsom, 'Aftershock', in Jones and Balsom (eds.), *The Road to the National Assembly for Wales*, pp. 265–74.

43 M. Lang, 'A lack of direction: the Local Government and Housing Committee', in Jones and Osmond (eds.), *Building a Civic Culture*, pp. 165–74.

44 S. Burnett, 'Finding a way through the forest: the Health and Social Services Committee', in Jones and Osmond (eds.), *Inclusive Government and Party Management*, pp. 108–25.

45 D. McAdam, J. McCarthy and M. Zald, 'Introduction', in McAdam, McCarthy and Zald (eds.), *Comparative Perspectives on Social Movements*, pp. 1–20.

46 Fowler, *Analysing the Welsh Identity*.

47 A. Smith, *National Identity* (London, 1991), p. 9.

48 J. Snicker, 'Strategies of autonomist agencies in Wales', *Regional and Federal Studies* 8 (1998), pp. 140–57.

49 H. Kohn, *The Idea of Nationalism* (New York, 1945), p. 19.

50 J. Davies, *A History of Wales* (London, 1993), chapter 8.

51 Ibid., p. 507.

52 A. Butt-Philip, *The Welsh Question* (Cardiff, 1975), p. 54.

53 *Western Mail*, 13 April 1999.

54 T. Combs, 'The Party of Wales, Plaid Cymru', unpublished Ph.D. thesis.

55 B. Jones, 'Poliical ideas: themes and fringes', in idem (ed.), *Politics UK* (Hemel Hempstead, 1998), p. 110.

56 L. McAllister, *Plaid Cymru: The Emergence of a Political Party* (Bridgend, 2001).

57 D. Balsom, 'The three-Wales model', in J. Osmond (ed.), *The National Question Again* (Llandysul, 1985), pp. 1–16.

58 D. Balsom, 'The first Welsh General Election', in Jones and Balsom (eds.), *The Road to the National Assembly for Wales*, pp. 212–28.

59 A. Heath, 'Were the Welsh and Scottish Referendums second-order elections?', in B. Taylor and K. Thomson (eds.), *Scotland and Wales: Nations Again?* (Cardiff, 1999), pp. 149–68.

60 Balsom, 'The first Welsh General Election', pp. 219–25.

61 Phillips, *Trwy Ddulliau Chwyldro. . .?*, pp. 58–60.

62 Ibid., p. 27.

63 'Submission by Cymuned to the Culture Committee', Cymuned, 2001: www.penllyn.com/cymuned/papurau/cym2.html#; 'Presentation by Cymuned to the Local Government and Housing Committee', Cymuned, 2001: www.penllyn.com/cymuned/papurau/t2.html.

64 D. Jenkins (ed.), *Tân yn Llyn* (Aberystwyth, 1937), pp. 136–40.

65 H. Kitschelt, 'New social movements and the decline of party organisation', in R. Dalton and M. Kuechler (eds.), *Challenging the Political Order* (Cambridge, 1990), pp. 179–208.

66 Phillips, *Trwy Ddulliau Chwyldro. . .?*, pp. 18–24.

67 D. Rucht, 'The Strategies and Action Repertoires of New Movemnts', in Dalton and Kuechler (eds.), *Challenging the Political Order*.

68 S. Lewis, *Tynged Yr Iaith* (London, 1962), p. 30.

69 S. Brooks, 'Hawl Foesol i Oroesi', *Barn* 463 (2001), pp. 6–8.

70 S. Brooks, 'The Living Dead', *Agenda*, spring edition, 2002, pp. 10–12.

71 S. Brooks, 'Sensoriaeth', *Barn* 472 (2002), pp. 6–11.

72 T. Webb, 'Colonization, colonialism and anti-colonialism: the ethical basis for

Cymuned' (Cymuned,2001). www.penllyn.com/cymuned/papurau/colonization.html.

73 D. Williams, 'Darlun o Dop Dowlais', *Taliesin* 115 (2002), pp. 148–54.

74 Cymuned, 'Submission by Cymuned to the Culture Committee' (Section 12), 2001: www.cymuned.org.

75 S. Brooks, 'Drych y Gymru Newydd', *Barn* 474–5 (2002), pp. 6–9.

76 *Welsh Mirror*, 12 July 2002, cited in Brooks, 'Drych y Gymru Newydd', pp. 6–9.

77 I. Holliday, 'Territorial politics', in P. Dunleavy, A. Gamble, I. Holliday and G. Peele (eds.), *Developments in British Politics* 5 (Basingstoke, 1997), pp. 220–40.

78 J. Tomaney, 'The regional governance of England', in Hazell (ed.), *The State and The Nations*, pp. 117–48.

12

The Orange Order and representations of Britishness

Christine Kinealy

Northern Ireland, Mrs Thatcher said, was as British as Finchley. We hoped, at least for the sake of Finchley, that she was wrong. (John Hume)[1]

The current crisis in British identity has been precipitated by the demand for devolution, the disappearance of Empire, the problems of the monarchy, the death of Protestantism as a signifier of Britishness, a distrust of parliamentary democracy and a concurrent rise in football hooliganism. Fear of the United Kingdom's imminent demize contributed to the mobilization of the UK Independence Party and the British National Party in the General Election of 2001 and the local elections of 2002. Northern Ireland is an exception to aspects of this trend. In the six counties, devotion to the monarchy, Protestantism and British identity continues to be vehemently asserted, at least by one section of the community. The majority of the Protestant population also desires to remain within the United Kingdom. Significantly, none of the far right parties organized in Northern Ireland during the General Election of 2001, despite allegations of links between these groups and some Protestant paramilitaries.[2] The Democratic Unionist Party, however, under the leadership of Ian Paisley, attempted to organize branches in areas outside Northern Ireland with traditions of sectarian politics, including Liverpool and Glasgow.[3]

In Northern Ireland, national identity is frequently defined on religious lines, with the Protestant community claiming British identity. When the Northern Ireland State was created in 1920, its borders were chosen to ensure a Protestant majority and, despite having an independent parliament in Belfast, it remained within the United Kingdom. Protestant identity, in turn, has been formed from having 'a particular history in Ireland and Ulster, a sense of being British in an Irish context, a sense of identifying with the reformed faith as opposed to Roman Catholicism, and a political identification with the United Kingdom particularly as a country with a Protestant monarchy'.[4] However, as the context has changed, so also has the relationship with Britain, and Protestant identity has been shaped as much by disagreement and divergence as by professions of loyalty. Moreover, few people elsewhere in Britain would recognize the variety of Britishness presented by Unionists in Northern Ireland, and even fewer would identify with it.

This chapter looks at the Orange Order in Northern Ireland as an organization that has invented a distinctive tradition of Britishness. The significance of parades to supporters of the Orange Order, especially the annual 12 July parades, which have become a symbol of British and Protestant identity in Northern Ireland, is also examined. The parades, in turn, are based on a set of practices that 'seek to inculcate certain values and norms of behaviour by repetition, which automatically implies continuity with the past'.[5] Yet, despite assertions of loyalty to many British institutions, to what or to whom is the Orange Order loyal? How British, therefore, is the Orange Order?

The Orange Order's allegiance to the United Kingdom allegedly has its roots in a body of rights that were won in the late seventeenth century, before parliamentary ratification of the Acts of Union with either Scotland or Ireland.[6] Its view of Britishness has been modified, in response to changing external economic and political pressures: not least, disillusionment with the actions of successive British governments. A key factor in the emergence and growth of Orangeism, however, has been the fear of Catholics attaining political power. The Orange Order's view of Britishness, therefore, has been based on a defensive, reactive ideology. Also, despite claiming historical continuity with the past, many of the traditions of the Orange Order are of recent origin, and have been used to create a coherent Protestant history in which British identity is claimed to be paramount.

The origins of the Orange Order

The Orange Order emerged from the European political turmoil of the end of the eighteenth century. At this time, Protestants within Ireland formed an Ascendancy class, even though they accounted for less than 15 per cent of the population. The majority of landowners were Protestant, and the Irish parliament based in Dublin was exclusively Protestant. Moreover, the Penal Laws, a body of repressive legislation introduced during the reign of William of Orange, had ensured that Catholics remained economically and politically subordinate. At the end of the eighteenth century, however (mainly in response to events in America and France), much of the penal legislation was removed, granting Catholics the right to vote, own land, enter various professions and carry weapons, although they were still prohibited from becoming members of parliament. Many Protestants viewed the relaxation of the penal laws as a threat to their traditional religious, political and economic domination.[7] Protestant fears intensified after 1791 when a new radical nationalist group was formed, the United Irishmen, led by Wolfe Tone, who argued that Irish identity rather than religious affiliation should define their political allegiance.

The Orange Order was founded in County Armagh in 1795, following a clash between Protestant and Catholic secret societies in which over thirty Catholics were killed.[8] The triumphant Protestants decided to form a permanent defence organization that was exclusively Protestant and dedicated to the memory of William of Orange. The Orange Order, therefore, offered a conservative alternative for Irish Protestants at a time of increasing religious integration. Its appearance also coincided with the emergence of a coherent British identity within Britain, in which Protestantism was the key identifier.[9] Orangeism espoused a Protestant version of history dating back to the seventeenth century, in which the victory of William of Orange at the Boyne had guaranteed their civil rights and religious identity.

From the outset, the Order was dedicated to sustaining 'the glorious and immortal' memory of William of Orange, and the anniversary of the Battle of the Boyne was chosen as the key commemoration within the Orange calendar. Before his adoption by the Orange Order, William had been widely admired as a liberal monarch.[10] However, the Orange Order appropriated William and recast him as the conservative defender of Protestant values and civil liberties. Yet William was an unlikely Protestant or British icon. He was Dutch and never mastered the English language. Although a Protestant himself, he had been personally tolerant of all religions and his campaign in Ireland had received the blessing of the Pope.[11] Also, unlike the heroic and dashing representation on white horseback, beloved of Protestant imagery and based on seventeenth-century Dutch propaganda, he was short, pock-marked and rode a brown horse.[12] More significantly, William had no lasting interest in Irish politics or internal squabbles: he used the constitutional crisis in England and the war in Ireland to pursue his wider European ambitions. William had never been in Ireland before 1690 and he stayed for only two months, taking in the Battle of the Boyne and then departing never to return to the country. Nonetheless, he became the British monarch most associated with Irish affairs. In the eighteenth century William's birthday (4 November) and to a lesser extent, the date of his landing in England (5 November, which coincided with the anniversary of the Gunpowder Plot) were celebrated by the state in both Britain and Ireland, but the Orange Order chose the date of Boyne as their key commemoration, thus honouring the military victory over Catholic aspirations. Prior to his death in 1702 a statue was erected in College Green, outside Trinity College in Dublin (commissioned by Dublin corporation), but three Protestant students from Trinity defaced it in 1706, apparently on the grounds that the rear of the horse faced the college gates. They were expelled from the university, fined £100 each, imprisoned for six months and made to stand in front of the statue bearing placards admitting their offence.[13] In 1830, the statue was blown up but reassembled. An IRA bomb finally destroyed it in 1929.[14] Regardless of William's significance in Belfast history, no public statue was erected in that city, although an equestrian statue of him adorned the Orange Hall, built in 1889.[15]

The Orange Order had instant appeal to Protestants in Ireland, helped by the general political instability throughout Europe. In 1796, the first 12 July parades took place in various locations throughout Armagh. The Orangemen marched in military formation, carrying weapons. The burning of Catholic homes and their forcible removal from the area followed the parades. Posters were displayed warning, 'Go to hell or Connaught. If you do not, we are all haters of the papists and we will destroy you.' The local magistrates, and officials in Dublin Castle, refused to intervene. An estimated 7,000 Catholics were forced from their homes.[16] The 12 July commemorations quickly spread throughout Ulster and in 1798 the Grand Orange Lodge was established in Dublin. By the same year, 330 lodges had been established throughout the country, the majority in the counties Tyrone, Armagh and Down.[17]

The Orange Order was able to take advantage of the political insecurity of the late 1790s by offering Irish Protestants a conservative, sectarian alternative to the radical non-denominational politics of the United Irishmen. Both the Protestant gentry and the British government realized their potential as a counter-revolutionary movement, the latter issuing them with weapons and ammunition during the 1798 uprising.[18] The government, in particular, viewed the Orange Order as a valuable mechanism for defending British interests in Ireland, especially against the nationalist challenge.[19]

In 1798, with the aid of troops from France, the United Irishmen led a republican uprising in Ireland. It was brutally put down, with the help of the newly-formed Orange Order, which thus demonstrated its value as a counter-insurgency force. Orangemen also started to write a Protestant version of history in which the rebellion had been an act of Catholic disloyalty, even though many leaders of the uprising had been Protestant and the aim had been to establish a non-sectarian republic. Following the uprising, the British government no longer trusted the Irish parliament to manage Irish affairs and rushed an Act of Union through parliament. Ireland thus lost its own parliament in Dublin and the United Kingdom of Great Britain and Ireland was created. Consequently Ireland was joined to a British state, which was already united by internal trade, a shared monarch, adherence to Protestantism, a common land mass and traditional enmity against France.[20]

Following the Act of Union, the Orange Order was still seen as a safeguard against the threat of invasion by Napoleon, and many of its members joined the Yeomanry, which was overwhelmingly Protestant.[21] The Yeomanry was also used for policing duties, despite its association with sectarian violence.[22] The allegiance of the Orange Order to the British government, however, was selective. They opposed the Act of Union of 1800, which created the United Kingdom, fearing that Catholics might gain more rights from a British rather than from an Irish parliament. Members of the Orange Order therefore campaigned to preserve the 'Protestant Constitution'.[23] Within a few years, however, they had changed their position, seeing the Union as their best defence against Catholic advancements, as it made them part of a Protestant majority rather than remaining a minority within Ireland. The Act of Union copper-fastened and legitimized for Protestants their British identity.[24] Within a few decades, as the north-east corner of Ireland benefited from the economic fruits of being part of the British Empire, Protestant allegiance to the Union became even more firmly cemented.

The attitude of successive British governments to the Orange Order became increasingly ambivalent after 1805, as the threat of a republican uprising or invasion by France diminished. The government also distanced itself from William of Orange and, in 1806, the state commemoration of his birthday ceased. The disappearance of the republican threat did not mark an end to Orangeism or to the annual celebration of the Boyne anniversary, which continued to spread throughout Ireland. The association of the parades with sectarian violence resulted in an attempt to proscribe the Orange Order and other political associations in 1824. Although the Grand Orange Lodge told its members to comply with this legislation, the grassroots members ignored it and the Boyne anniversary continued to be observed with parades.[25]

Protestants of all classes regarded the granting of Catholic Emancipation in 1829, which permitted Catholics to become members of the British parliament, as a threat to their political supremacy. Anglicans and Presbyterians, directed by the gentry, united to form a Protestant alliance to resist the legislation.[26] The Orange Order, despite the ban on its activities, organized a number of parades that triggered attacks on Catholics. Portentously, in continuing to march the Orange Order showed itself willing to defy the law when it felt that its interests were being threatened. The government responded by passing more stringent legislation in 1832 banning political processions.[27] The opposition to Catholic Emancipation was significant for uniting Irish Protestants, the common bond being not only religious identity, but also political objectives.[28] At the same time, the Grand Orange Lodge issued a declaration claiming to have always supported law and order and helped to put down rebellions in order to maintain 'the integrity of the Empire'.[29] In 1834 Orangemen were advised to 'be alert' as they might 'soon, very soon, be called on to exert out best energies either in a political or real contest for our hearths and altars'.[30] Although marches were banned, the number of local Orange lodges continued to grow and membership spread into the gentry and professional classes. The granting of Catholic Emancipation also meant that while the defence of Protestantism still remained the main aim of the Orange Order, the British government was no longer perceived as an ally. The wariness of the British government towards Orangeism was demonstrated following a parliamentary enquiry into the activities of the Order in 1835. The report was largely critical, noting that Orange members had successfully infiltrated the army, police force and judiciary in both Ireland and Britain. A number of high-ranking officials were also Orangemen, including the Duke of Cumberland, the king's brother, who was Grand Master of the Orange Lodge, and the Lord Bishop of Salisbury, who was its Prelate. The enquiry also found that the 12 July parades were being used by Orangemen to provoke Catholics, as the routes were deliberately chosen to go through Catholic areas.[31] Although the Grand Lodge disbanded in the wake of the report, the local lodges remained active.

The onset of the Great Famine in 1845 was accompanied by an evangelical revival in Ireland and renewed attempts at proselytizing by the Protestant churches. It also coincided with a period of nationalist agitation in Ireland, which the British government attempted to undermine with a mixture of coercion and conciliation. To appease Irish Protestants, the Prime Minister, Sir Robert Peel, decided not to renew the 1832 legislation banning political marches. The immediate consequence was that Orange marches resumed, on a larger scale than before. The Orange Order believed that a show of strength was necessary because the current nationalist activity was a threat to the interests of Protestants in Ireland. More significantly, they felt let down by successive

British governments and unable to rely on them for support. In 1848 the Grand Lodge in Dublin warned its followers that:

> The present disorganized and deplorable state of Ireland can only be attributed to the base policy of statesmen who have treacherously betrayed the trust confided to them by Protestants, in granting unjustifiable concessions to Popery, and that no attempt to remedy existing evils will be successful until the Romish Emancipation Bill, the Maynooth Endowment Bill, and all such measures are entirely repealed, and the Constitution restored to its original integrity.[32]

The revolution in France in February 1848 increased the concerns both of the British government and of Protestants in Ireland that an uprising was imminent. As in 1798, various Orange lodges offered their services as a counter-insurgency force and a number of them started to practise military manoeuvres. Some even asked the government to send them armaments, the Castlewellan Lodge explaining that they had 'about 80 steady, able, determined men ready and willing to take the field at any time to die, if need be, for their beloved queen and constitution'.[33] Some members of the British government wanted to use the Orange Order in this way, but the Prime Minister, Lord John Russell, decided not to. However, the Lord Lieutenant, the Earl of Clarendon, advised that while the Orangemen 'must not be encouraged . . . yet they ought not to be too much snubbed, for many of these people mean well to the institutions of the country, though hostility to the Catholics is doubtless their moving principle'.[34] Moreover, despite the official policy, Clarendon secretly funded the purchase of arms for the Orange Order and held talks with its leaders.[35]

During the late 1840s, therefore, the Orange Order again presented itself as a counter-insurgency force and defender of British interests in Ireland. This representation was juxtaposed against the disloyalty of Irish Catholics to the Union with Britain and conveniently ignored the fact that when an uprising actually took place, many of its leaders were Protestant. The 1848 uprising, therefore, despite being small and easily overcome by the constabulary, was used by Orangemen to remind the British government of their loyalty and to portray themselves as 'a native, unpaid garrison'.[36] Moreover, in the wake of the uprising the number of Orange lodges within Ulster grew rapidly and loyalty to Britain increasingly became associated with this province. Hence, in the second half of the nineteenth century, the Orange Order was able to present itself as the loyal defender of Britishness in Ireland.

By 1849 the revolutionary threat had passed, but the Orange Order used the Boyne commemorations in July as an opportunity to demonstrate not only their loyalty to the Union but their continuing supremacy within Ireland. Dozens of parades took place throughout Ulster, which were more numerous and better attended than in preceding years.[37] The previous year's insurrection had also infused the marches in 1849 with deeper political and sectarian significance. Government officials based in Dublin Castle were aware of heightened tensions and the likelihood of armed conflict in several areas. From early July, they started to deploy troops and extra constabulary to perceived sectarian flashpoints.[38] However, it was the Rathfriland Orange Lodge's decision to march through the small Catholic village of Dolly's Brae in County Down that triggered a bitter conflict.[39] The route through Dolly's Brae was neither traditional nor direct, and the mountain road was in poor condition. The Orangemen had clearly come prepared for conflict: the commander of the troops described them as being 'armed to the teeth' with each man carrying an estimated forty rounds of ammunition.[40] In the ensuing conflict four Catholics were killed in their own homes, including Hugh King, a ten-year-old boy who died of gunshot wounds, and Anne Taylor, aged eighty-five, whose skull had been struck repeatedly with a blunt instrument.[41]

Following the conflict, thirty-five Catholics were arrested, but no Orangemen. An inquest held four days later acquitted the Orangemen of any wrongdoing and described the deaths as 'justifiable homicide'.[42] However, a government enquiry held a month later criticized the actions of the Orange Order, the local police and the magistracy, with three of the latter being dismissed.[43] In the wake of Dolly's Brae, the government introduced the Party Processions Act, which again banned political marches in Ireland. Moreover, this legislation, unlike earlier bans, was meant to be permanent.[44] The Lord Lieutenant of Ireland, the Earl of Clarendon, was optimistic that the outcome of the collision at Dolly's Brae would be 'the extinction of Orangeism'.[45] He was wrong. The incident at Dolly's Brae became embedded in unionist mythology as a significant victory of Protestantism over Catholicism.[46] The 'victory' was commemorated in oral tradition, and various 'Orange' songs and banners depicting the conflict were carried on 12 July parades.[47] For the Orange Order, Dolly's Brae was viewed as an important signifier not only of identity, but also of Protestant domination. The action of the government in banning marches angered many Orangemen, who saw it as an additional example of indulgence towards Irish Catholics. A further outcome of Dolly's Brae, therefore, was to weaken the relationship between government and Orangemen, although the latter's adherence to their version of Britishness appeared undiminished.

Playing the Orange card

The Party Procession Act had limited success and a reduced number of annual marches continued, some resulting in violence. In 1857, ten days of rioting followed the 12 July parade in Belfast, and there were similar clashes in 1864 and 1867. The fact that the government rarely intervened to stop the parades, regardless of their illegality, demonstrated that it was reluctant to alienate the Orange Order. The Act was flagrantly ignored by a leading Orangeman, William Johnston, who had founded the Down Protestant Association in 1854, for the purpose of removing all concessions that had been made to Catholics.[48] In 1867 he led a procession of Orangemen from Newtownards to Bangor. The day ended with sectarian fighting. Although Johnston was arrested, he left prison a hero. Shortly afterwards he was elected MP for Belfast as an independent Orange candidate and, in this role, he was instrumental in having the Act banning marches removed in 1872.[49] Initially, the Liberal government was reluctant to remove this legislation, ineffective though it was, but gave in following a militant campaign by Orangemen, which included threats to attempt to repeal the Act of Union.[50]

As Home Rule agitation developed in Ireland in the late nineteenth century, the Orange Order and 12 July marches revived. Reaction to the growth and success of the Home Rule movement forged new links between the Orange Order and militant unionism, with the Orange Order as clear beneficiaries. Protestant gentry and ministers also began to rejoin the Order, seeing it as a bulwark against nationalist and Catholic encroachments. During the late nineteenth century the appearance of Orange marches changed, as some of their more militaristic aspects were subsumed beneath pageantry. Union Jacks became more numerous, with sashes, flute bands, bowler hats and Lambeg drums being other additions, each of which helped to reinforce an impression of tradition and respectability.[51] Elaborate banners depicting Protestant victories over Catholics were carried in order to reinforce 'political solidarity'.[52] The banners united all Protestants against Home Rule and suggested that their unity was long-standing. Thus the 12 July parades, especially the display of Union Jacks, became a visible sign of British allegiance and, increasingly, of Protestant separateness within Ireland. British identity in Ireland also became associated with place, that is, Ulster. Yet, despite professions of loyalty to Britain, the loyalty of most Ulster Protestants was based on self-interest, namely, that Ulster should remain part of the United Kingdom, rather than concern with wider British or imperial matters.[53]

In the 1880s links between the Irish Unionist Party, the Conservative Party and the Orange Order were also established. The value of the Orange Order in maintaining the Union with Britain was recognized by the British politician, Lord Randolph Churchill, who coined the phrase 'playing the Orange card' in response to the Home Rule crisis. But for Gladstone and others, Irish independence was not exclusive of British nationality, as they believed that dependence on Westminster and links with the Empire would continue.[54] The influence and distinctive brand of loyalty articulated remained confined to Ireland; but since the beginning of the nineteenth century Orange lodges had been formed throughout Britain and in other parts of the British Empire, transported by emigrants and members of the British army. By the end of the nineteenth century, the Orange Order had firmly established itself within British society, leading one historian to claim that 'Orangeism became the very symbol of British patriotism; once appropriated by the Tories, it recruited strongly among Protestant workers in Liverpool with no Ulster or Irish connections'.[55]

The successful passage through the House of Commons of the Home Rule Bill of 1912 resulted in a period of militant activity by the Orange Order. In 1912 an Ulster Covenant was signed by over half a million Irish Protestants, and in the following year the Ulster Volunteer Force was formed and immediately began practicing military manoeuvres. The threat of the end of the Union with Britain led to a reappraisal of Protestant identity in which Britishness was no longer a critical ingredient, but allegiance to Ulster and Protestantism remained crucial. Moreover, Irish Protestants appeared to be willing to fight in order to preserve this identity. Loyalty to Britain became subordinate to the need to maintain a Protestant ascendancy. Both Irish nationalists and British politicians repeatedly failed to address the fears of Irish Protestants even when conflict appeared inevitable. The British Prime Minister, for example, sought to minimize differences within Ireland averring, on the eve of the Boyne commemorations in 1913, that 'the fundamental unity underlying the differences of race, creed and political faith in Ireland will suffice to ensure Ireland's peaceable acceptance of Home Rule'.[56] Ulster politicians responded by saying they were willing to use unconstitutional means to maintain the Union.[57] The agitation, in which Ireland appeared to be on the brink of a civil war, was only brought to an end by the outbreak of the First World War. The support of the Orange Order for the First World War and the actions of some of their members, notably the 36th Ulster Regiment – the 'Shankhill Boys' – who suffered heavy losses on the first day of fighting at the Battle of the Somme, was contrasted with the disloyalty of Catholic nationalists who led the Easter Rising in the same year. The fact that nationalists, encouraged by the Irish Parliamentary Party, had joined the British army was ignored; and Irish Protestants, particularly Orangemen, were able to portray themselves as selfless defenders of British and Imperial interests. The sacrifices made by the 36th Regiment at the Somme and other battles had, in the eyes of Protestants, 'sealed the Union with blood'.[58] The fact that only two years earlier they had been willing to wage war on the British government was forgotten.

Partition and the 'Troubles'

The partition of Ireland in 1921 created two parliaments in Ireland and a border that had neither precedent nor popular support.[59] The new state of Northern Ireland remained within the United Kingdom, enabling the population to regard themselves as retaining British nationality. The British parliament, however, showed little interest in internal politics within Northern Ireland, until forced to do so after 1969. The new, overwhelmingly Unionist Northern government declared itself to be 'an Orange state'. The political outlook was exemplified by the first Prime Minister, Sir James Craig, who stated 'I have always said that I am an Orangeman first and a politician and a member of parliament afterwards . . . All I boast is that we are a Protestant parliament and a Protestant state.'[60] Clearly Protestantism rather than Britishness was the key identifier. The political authority of the Orange Order increased in the state. Between 1921 and 1968, 138 out of the 149 Unionist MPs were members of the Orange Order, as were all the Prime Ministers.[61] Popular attachment to the British monarchy remained strong among Protestants in Northern Ireland, although it was not always reciprocated. Queen Victoria in 1849 was the first monarch to visit Belfast since William of Orange in 1690, and she annoyed some Protestants by her refusal to visit any sectarian establishment.[62] Edward VIII tried to exclude Northern Ireland from his planned Coronation tour of the United Kingdom.[63] Nonetheless, the allegiance to William of Orange remained strong and his iconic presence was helped by the use of murals, in which he appeared regularly imploring on-lookers to 'Remember 1690'.[64] In 1925 the Unionist government decided that 12 July should be recognized formally as a public holiday, although many Catholic or nationalist parades continued to be banned.[65] The significance of the day was reinforced by Unionist politicians using it as for important political statements. Despite Northern Ireland's self-proclaimed status as an 'Orange state' sectarian conflicts continued to mark the anniversary.[66] Following a violent clash in Belfast in 1935 in which eight Protestants and five Catholics were killed, and 200 Catholic families were burnt out of their houses, the Northern Ireland government attempted to outlaw the marches. Like the British government prior to 1920, the Unionist government was unsuccessful in preventing marches, and it backed down in the face of determined opposition led by the Orange Order.[67] Throughout the 1950s, a number of Orange marches were deliberately re-routed to pass through Catholic areas. Clearly, the parades were being again used as a symbol of Protestant ascendancy. The proliferating murals, depicting William riding into battle at the Boyne, became a further way for Protestants in Northern Ireland to assert their version of history, their dominance and their allegiance to the British monarchy.

In the decades following the creation of Northern Ireland, British identity was partly replaced by an Ulster Unionist identity. The gap between Catholics and Protestants also widened and by the 1960s, politicians were referring to Ulster Catholics as being distinct from Ulster Protestants.[68] In a poll carried out in 1968, 39 per cent of Protestants identified their national identity as British, whilst 32 per cent chose an Ulster identity. The allegiance of Catholics within Northern Ireland was different; only 15 per cent accepted British nationality and over half of those who did admitted their dissatisfaction with existing constitutional arrangements.[69] The commencement of the 'Troubles' in 1969 forced the British government to take a renewed interest in the affairs of Northern Ireland. The British government's attempt in 1974 to introduce a power-sharing government – which was forcefully opposed by Protestants – demonstrated again that British interests were different from those of Protestants in Northern Ireland.

After 1969, the marching season became more significant because, as Protestant political and economic power was being eroded, visible symbols, such as the annual marches, became important signifiers of supremacy and union with Britain. The number of marches grew: in 1985 there were fewer than 2,000 annual loyalist marches, but by 1995 there were 2,600.[70] The 12 July parades, which were part of the so-called 'marching season', became a microcosm of other conflicts and tensions between nationalists and unionists in Northern Ireland. The conflict over the right to march, especially along routes that were claimed to be 'traditional', had exposed deeper issues about loyalty, allegiance and identity. The Orange Order justifies the parades by claiming that they are an important way of celebrating their Protestant – and British – identity. They also claim that they are maintaining an essential civil right, which was guaranteed by William's victory at the Boyne. At the same time, the Order denies the sectarian and political nature of such marches. Instead, they describe the various parades as 'a colourful cultural tradition', 'neither triumphalist nor sectarian – instead we see them as the legitimate expression of the culture of the Orange tradition in Northern Ireland'.[71]

In the 1990s the Orange Order gained international notoriety due to the conflict at Drumcree, a small village near Portadown in County Armagh.[72] Because of its historic associations with militant Protestantism, this area gained the sobriquet 'the Vatican of Orangeism'. In 1995, the Portadown Orange Lodge commenced a protest in this village, ostensibly over the denial of their right to march along the nearby Garvaghy Road on 12 July. The Orange Order laid great emphasis on the idea of tradition and longevity, claiming that the Garvaghy Road in Drumcree was the traditional route along which their ancestors marched.[73] But this interpretation was historically incorrect. The Garvaghy Road was chosen as a route only in 1985. Like the route that preceded it, was occupied almost exclusively by Catholics who opposed the march.[74] The attempt to provide this and other Orange parades with historical continuity and respectability was part of a wider move in the 1990s to reinvent the Orange Order as part of a cultural, rather than political, tradition.[75] To defend what the Orange Order regarded as their civil right to march down the Garvaghy Road, a radical loyalist group known as 'The Spirit of Drumcree' was created. Defence of identity, never precisely defined, was central to its creation. Its founder, Joel Patton, explained the symbolic significance for Protestants in Northern Ireland of marching down this road, and others inhabited by Catholics, saying:

> In many ways it is not about 800 Orangemen marching down a road. It's about the survival of a culture, of an identity, of a way of life. It's about our ability to still hold on to parts of the country . . . [Northern Protestants] believe intensely that if it's taken away from them there, then there isn't anywhere in Ulster that will be safe. If they're beaten in Portadown, then they believe that they can be beaten anywhere, and that's why I don't think they're about to give in.[76]

The ending of the IRA ceasefire at the beginning of 1996 increased tensions during the marching season. On 6 July 1996 the RUC announced that the 12 July parade in Drumcree was to be re-routed away from the Garvaghy Road. The Orange Order ignored this directive, and within two days 10,000 supporters were protesting in Drumcree. Although the RUC responded by sending in 2,000 police dressed in riot gear to the village and erecting barbed wire fences, with support from the British army, the Orange Order were allowed to amass in Drumcree despite the illegality of the march.[77] The Orange Order also orchestrated other acts of civil disorder throughout Northern Ireland, including roadblocks and closing the international airport in Belfast. A Catholic taxi-driver was killed in nearby Lurgan. After four-and-a-half days, the RUC reversed its decision and announced that it was allowing the march to go ahead. The police and the troops were then deployed to contain the nearby nationalist population, and in doing so used 7,000 plastic bullets.[78] Clearly this amounted to a breakdown in law and order, yet the British government refused to intervene, again playing a passive role when the Orange Order was involved in conflict. In 1999 Rosemary Nelson, the legal adviser to the Garvaghy Road residents and solicitor for Robert Hamill (a Catholic who had been murdered in a sectarian attack in Portadown), was killed by a car bomb. Her death shocked public opinion, but was celebrated by local Orange lodges.[79]

The events at Drumcree illustrate the Orange Order's continuing defiance of the British government when it believes that its interests are not being supported. The majority of Orange members of the Ulster Unionist Council opposed the Good Friday Agreement in 1998, thus bringing themselves into direct opposition to the British government, yet many of them believe that they are fighting to maintain a British identity. In 1998, when a one-year ban was placed on the march in Drumcree, Ian Paisley, the leader of the Democratic Unionist Party, described the decision as 'a sell out to the IRA': it was 'an indication that all through the marching season the Unionist and British identity will be sold on the altar of political expediency by government authorities'.[80] David Dunseith, who since 1989 has presented the radio show with the largest audience in Northern Ireland, in 2000 explained the bitterness of Protestants towards the British government thus:

> Protestants are an embattled minority. They see that Britain was willing to send a task force to defend the concept of Britishness in the Falkland Islands away off near Argentina. They see the way Britain fights to keep Gibraltar from Spain. And then they listen to the British political leadership saying that they have no strategic interest in remaining in Northern Ireland . . . They feel they are losing everything. It almost reaches hysteria. The sense of identity among Catholics is much stronger.[81]

Despite the long history of associated violence, Unionists have attempted to re-invent the parades as colourful pageants historically devoid of political or sectarian overtones; thus, according to the historian and journalist Ruth Dudley Edwards, they were 'a jolly family day out . . . with scones and a cup of tea at the end'.[82] The ambivalence of the British government to the Orange Order and their parades has also continued. In 1998, the Labour government recognized the centrality of the parades to a resolution of the Troubles with the appointment of a Parades Commission, whose the Grand Orange Lodge refused to acknowledge. In the same year, the Prime Minister, Tony Blair, on the eve of the Drumcree parade, attempted a positive interpretation of the tradition, saying 'we are looking at ways of helping to show the wider world the positive continuation to British culture that the Orange Order and other loyal institutions have made, both locally and internationally . . . While the loyal institutions have also been a force for stability and community cohesiveness. And no one could doubt their commitment to their country.'[83] However, events in Drumcree and elsewhere made it difficult to sustain this viewpoint, especially the sectarian murder of the Catholic Quinn brothers (aged ten, nine and eight) in Ballymoney on the morning of 12 July 1998.[84]

The conflict in Drumcree took place in a highly charged political atmosphere and, not for the first time, Protestants in Northern Ireland felt under threat from the Catholic community. It also caused an open rift with the British government, and it was condemned both by the RUC and the Anglican Church in Ireland: institutions that were traditionally allies of the Orange Order. Senior members of the Order, including David Trimble, the local Unionist MP, also distanced themselves from events in Drumcree. In 2000, Trimble precipitated division within his party by suggesting that the influence of the Orange Order in the Ulster Unionist Council should be ended, thus breaking the historic link between the Orange Order and the Unionist Party.[85] The crisis within Orangeism was reflected in the decline of members: in 1972 the membership was 60,000, in 1997 it was 43,000, and by 2001 it had fallen to 38,000.[86] In the wake of Drumcree some Protestants started to reject the assumption that within Northern Ireland 'Protestant culture is Orange'.[87]

The standoff at Drumcree has become a symptom of deep-rooted tensions between the nationalist and unionist communities within Northern Ireland. It also has clear precedents. Moreover, recent attempts to ban the marches in Northern Ireland have been met with the same defiance that has characterized the Orange Order since its inception.[88] A casualty of the recent conflict over the right to march, however, is Protestant allegiance to various British institutions and, consequently, their British identity. Yet, the history of the Orange Order demonstrates that, despite claims of continuity and tradition, the allegiance of the Order to Britishness has frequently been tenuous. In the late nineteenth century, Orangeism was sufficiently powerful to subvert the granting of Home Rule to Ireland, and after 1920 it was a significant force in moulding the political ideology of the new Northern Ireland state.

The constitutional changes made to the United Kingdom since 1998 have given political recognition to the unravelling of British identity.[89] In Northern Ireland, however, allegiance to British identity was the bedrock upon which the state was forged. Nonetheless, as the history of the Orange Order demonstrates, allegiance to British identity amongst Irish Protestants has always been conditional, in contrast to allegiance to Protestantism and to place (Ulster), which has remained constant and unconditional. Even allegiance to the British Crown has remained conditional on it continuing to be Protestant; in the early nineteenth century all Orangemen swore an oath that:

> I will be faithful and bear true allegiance to His Majesty the King; and that I will to the utmost of my power support and maintain the laws and constitution of the United Kingdom of Great Britain and Ireland, as established by William the Third of glorious memory, and the succession to the throne in His Majesty's illustrious house, being Protestant.[90]

Following the accession of Queen Elizabeth in 1952, Orangemen swore an oath to be 'faithful and bear true allegiance to Her Majesty Queen Elizabeth II, and to her Protestant successors'.[91] During her Golden Jubilee celebrations in 2002, Queen Elizabeth referred to the United Kingdom as a multi-faith and multi-cultural state.[92] What are the implications of the secularization of society, the ecumenicalism of monarchy and devolution for Protestants in Northern Ireland? What will replace Britishness, or even what David Trimble refers to as 'Ulster-Britishness'?[93] As the United Kingdom breaks down into its constituent parts and even the Britishness of Finchley is in doubt, what are the implications for the Orange Order and the British identity of its supporters? The Orange Order has adapted to many changes throughout its history, but the situation at Drumcree has revealed that its particular representation of Britishness has little support, even amongst the groups it claims to uphold. The decline in membership is a manifestation of the internal crisis.[94] The Orange Order's political influence both in Britain and in Northern Ireland has consequently declined. As Britishness seeks to redefine itself and accommodate the political uncertainties of the twenty-first century, Orangeism will have to do the same.

Notes

1 John Hume, *Personal Views of Politics, Peace and Reconciliation* (Dublin, 1996), p. 80.

2 Nick Lowles, *White Riot. The Violent Story of Combat 18* (London, 2001).

3 *Guardian*, 12 January 1999.

4 Dominic Bryan, *Orange Parades. The Politics of Ritual, Tradition and Control* (London, 2000), p. 12.

5 Eric Hobsbawm and T. Ranger (eds.), *The Invention of Tradition* (Cambridge, 1993), p. 1.

6 Christine Kinealy, *A Disunited Kingdom. England, Ireland, Scotland and Wales 1800–1949* (Cambridge, 1999), chapter 1.

7 Hereward Senior, *Orangeism in Ireland and Britain 1795–1836* (London, 1966), pp. 3–4.

8 Jonathan Bardon, *History of Ulster* (Belfast, 1992), pp. 224–6.

9 Linda Colley, *Britons. Forging the Nation* (London, 1992), p. 20.

10 Jacqueline Hill, 'National Festivals, the state and "Protestant ascendancy" in Ireland 1790–1829', *Irish Historical Studies* 93 (1984), pp. 30–1.

11 William III and Pope Innocent XI shared a common hostility towards Louis XIV of France: see Kevin Haddick-Flynn, *Orangeism: The Making of a Tradition* (Dublin, 1999), p. 427.

12 Bill Rolston, *Politics and Painting: Murals and Conflict in Northern Ireland* (London, 1991), pp. 15–17.

13 Haddick-Flynn, *Orangeism*, pp. 95–6.

14 Rolston, *Politics*, p. 28.

15 C. E. B. Brett, *Buildings of Belfast* (Belfast, 1985), p. 56.

16 Bardon, *Ulster*, pp. 226–8.

17 Haddick-Flynn, *Orangeism*, p. 411.

18 Jim Smyth, 'The men of no popery: the origins of the Orange Order', *History Ireland* (1995), p. 52.

19 R. B. McDowell, 'Revolution and the Union', in T. Moody and W. E. Vaughan (eds.), *A New History of Ireland* vol. IV (Oxford, 1984), p. 347.

20 In *Britons* Linda Colley argues persuasively that France was the 'other' and war against France served to cement British identity, but it could also be argued that Ireland represented the other 'other' and in the nineteenth century remained far more troublesome than France.

21 Bardon, *Ulster*, p. 244.

22 S. J. Connolly, *Oxford Companion to Irish History* (Oxford, 1988), pp. 601–2.

23 Bardon, *Ulster*, p. 239

24 James Loughlin, *Ulster Unionism and British National Identity since 1885* (London, 1995), p. 27.

25 *Northern Whig*, 14 July 1825.

26 Proceedings of Grand Orange Lodge of Ireland, Beresford Papers, ms2288a, Trinity College Dublin (TCD), 19 January 1832.

27 Brian Walker, *Dancing to History's Tune: History, Myth and Politics in Ireland* (Belfast, 1996), p. 93.

28 Bryan, *Orange Parades*, p. 179.

29 Resolution of Grand Orange Lodge, Beresford Papers, ms2319, TCD, 21 January 1832.

30 Ibid., 12 November 1834.

31 Report of the Select Committee to Inquire into the Nature, Character, Extent and Tendency of Orange Lodges, Parliamentary Papers, 1835, xv.

32 *Belfast Protestant Journal,* 18 March 1848. The Maynooth Endowment bill referred to a grant made to Maynooth College, a seminary for training Catholic priests, by the British government in 1845.

33 Resolution of Orange lodges, Outrage Papers, County Down, National Archives Dublin (NAD), 29 July 1848.

34 Clarendon to Russell, Clarendon Papers, Bodleian Library, 15 March 1848.

35 Donal Kerr, *A Nation of Beggars?* (Oxford, 1994), p. 201.

36 Loyal Address of Inhabitants of Belfast to Lord Lieutenant, Public Record Office, Kew, HO45 2488, 20 April 1848.

37 *Armagh Guardian,* 16 July 1849.

38 John Groves, R.M. to Lord Lieutenant, Outrage Papers for County Antrim, NAD, 17 July 1849.

39 *The Times,* 18 July 1849.

40 Ibid.

41 *Armagh Guardian,* 16 July 1849; *The Times,* 18 July 1849; *Warden,* 21 July 1849.

42 *Freeman's Journal,* 17 July 1849.

43 *The Times,* 8 April 1850.

44 An Act to Restrain Party Processions in Ireland, 12 March 1850.

45 Kerr, *Nation of Beggars,* p. 202.

46 Jonathan Bardon, *A History of Ulster* (Belfast, 1992), pp. 303–4; S. Connolly (ed.) *The Oxford Companion to Irish History* (Oxford, 1998), p. 152.

47 Unofficial Orange Order web page, http://river.tay.ac.uk/~c95gb/12 July/parades. htm.

48 Haddick-Flynn, *Orangeism,* p. 281.

49 Walker, *Dancing to History,* pp. 93–4.

50 Haddick-Flynn, *Orangeism,* p. 284.

51 Walker, *Dancing to History,* p. 94.

52 Rolston, *Politics and painting,* p. 17.

53 Alvin Jackson, *Ulster Unionists: Irish Unionists in the House of Commons 1885–1911* (Oxford, 1989), p. 120, contested by Loughlin who argues that in the late nineteenth century local self-interest and British identity were not incompatible (*Ulster Unionism,* p. 37). Loughlin may understate the extent to which the narrow sectarianism associated with the Orange Order had largely disappeared from politics elsewhere in Britain, largely due to the decline of popular Protestantism, while allegiance based on class or economic status was becoming more significant.

54 Loughlin, *Ulster Unionism,* p. 60.

55 Donald M. MacRaild (ed.) *The Great Famine and Beyond: Irish Migrants in Britain in the Nineteenth and Twentieth Centuries* (Dublin, 2000), p. 142.

56 *The Times,* 12 July 1913.

57 Ibid.

58 Keith Jeffrey (ed.) *'An Irish Empire': Aspects of Ireland and the British Empire* (Manchester, 1996), p. 99.

59 Kinealy, *A Disunited Kingdom,* p. 97.

60 Haddick-Flynn, *Orangeism,* p. 331.

61 Ibid.

62 For more see C. Kinealy and G. MacAtasney, *The Forgotten Famine: Hunger, Poverty and Sectarianism in Belfast* (London, 2000), pp. 177–8.

63 Loughlin, *Ulster Unionism*, p. 113.

64 Rolston, *Politics and Painting*, pp. 15–17.

65 Bryan, *Orange Parades*, p. 61.

66 Michael Farrell, *Northern Ireland: The Orange State* (London, 1976).

67 Bardon, *History of Ulster*, pp. 608–9.

68 Loughlin, *Ulster Unionism*, p. 182.

69 Richard Rose, *Governing without Consensus* (1971), quoted in Loughlin, *Ulster Unionism*, p. 183.

70 *Belfast Telegraph*, 14 August 1996.

71 Orange Marches Web Site, www.geocities.com/CapitolHill/1684/orange.html.

72 For example, the *Economist* on 13 July 1996 dedicated its front cover and a number of internal articles to the issue.

73 Ruth Dudley Edwards in the *Daily Telegraph*, 7 July 1997.

74 Peter Taylor, *Loyalists* (London, 1999), p. 179.

75 This approach has been most clearly exemplified in the work of Dudley-Edwards. See also Hobsbawm, *Invention of Tradition*, pp. 5–8.

76 Joel Patton quoted in Taylor, *Loyalists*, pp. 239–40.

77 Human Rights Watch (Helsinki), *To Serve Without Favour: Policing, Human Rights and Accountability in Northern Ireland* (New York, 1997), p. 76.

78 Human Rights Watch says this figure is an underestimate. Ibid., p. 57.

79 Chris Ryder and Vincent Kerney, *Drumcree: The Orange Order's Last Stand* (London, 1988), pp. 293–4.

80 Decision by Parades Commission in Relation to Drumcree March, 1998, *Determination in Relation to Portadown District LOL No. 1 Church Parade on 5 July 1998*, available at www55.pair.com.iowc/1998/parades/decision.html – the ban was for one year only; for reaction see 'Statement by Dr Ian Paisley, MP, MEP on the Parades' Commission on Drumcree, 1998', in which he described the decision as 'a sell-out to the IRA', available at: wyswyg://10/http://cain.ulst.ac.uk/issues/parade/docs/ip29698.htm.

81 Susan McKay, *Northern Protestants: An Unsettled People* (Belfast, 2000), p. 26.

82 *Telegraph*, 7 July 1997.

83 Dudley Edwards, *Faithful Tribe*, p. 433.

84 *Irish Times*, 14 July 1998.

85 The Orange Order had 120 seats on the 860-member council, and they consistently voted against the Peace Agreement. *Irish Times*, 17 April 2000.

86 Ryder, *Drumcree*, p. 333.

87 McKay, *Northern Protestants*, p. 23.

88 *Belfast Telegraph*, 21 June 2000.

89 Richard Weight, *National Identity in Britain 1940–2000* (Macmillan, 2002).

90 Declaration of An Orangeman, Rules of Society in 1834, PP, *Report of Select Committee*, Appendix 3.

91 Quoted in Bryan, *Orange Parades*, p. 107.

92 Queen's Speech, 30 April 2002, *Guardian*, 1 May 2002.

93 David Trimble in Maurna Crozier (ed.) *Cultural Traditions in Northern Ireland. Varieties of Irishness* (Belfast, 1989), pp. 45–50. He also draws distinctions between what he refers to as the 'Ulster-British and the Gaelic/Catholic cultures'. Protestants in Northern Ireland are describing their identity variously as Northern Protestants, Ulster Protestants, Ulster Scots, Northern Irish Protestants, or Ulster British.

94 Ryder, *Drumcree*, p. 333.

13

Filmic representations of the British–Irish conflict since the ceasefires of 1994

Cahal McLaughlin

Introduction

After twenty-five years of political violence on the question of the constitutional status of the North of Ireland, the 1993 Downing Street Declaration, which acknowledged the right of those living in Ireland to 'self-determination', and the paramilitary ceasefires of 1994 encouraged a sense that we may be in the endgame of the 'Troubles'.[1] It also opened the way for a small wave of Irish-directed films which attempted to engage with themes that had previously been too politically sensitive to be financially supportable by either the broadcasting market or state agency. Up until then these had been the most likely sources of production money for Irish filmmakers.

The short-lived Irish Film Board in the South had been abolished by the government in 1987 in preference to an industrial model funded by tax incentives and did not re-emerge until 1993. There had been no local support for filmmaking in the North, except for small grants from the Arts Council of Northern Ireland for films about artists.[2] The establishment of the Northern Ireland Film Council in 1989 finally helped establish a financial and cultural space for independent filmmaking.[3]

Broadcast television, especially Channel 4 and, later, BBC Northern Ireland, had offered small if sustained support for local films, but these were obviously aimed at television audiences, for example John Davies' *Acceptable Levels* (1984) and Margot Harkin's *Hush-a-Bye* (1989).

The political pressures had been even more restrictive. In 1972 the Irish government had sacked the entire state television's Radio Telefís Eireann Authority because of a broadcast television interview with the then IRA Chief of Staff. The Irish Broadcasting Act, Section 31, was henceforth interpreted as denying republican representatives any access to the airwaves – television or radio.[4] The political space in the North, which already had an almost inevitable bias in favour of the state,[5] limited its representation of all sides of the conflict even more when the British government introduced broadcasting restrictions, prohibiting the use of actual 'spoken words' by republican representatives. This resulted in subtitling not only of republicans but also those who tried to explain their ideas and actions.[6] These legislative censorship conditions added to the atmosphere of self-censorship where those working in the media often decided not to deal with an issue, rather than risk the wrath of their bosses or funders. There was a resultant tendency to create an unchallenging and conformist body of work.[7]

While these pressures operated primarily on journalists and drama directors in television, they also reflected the stereotypes and paradigms which John Hill has identified as dominating mainstream films about Ireland, primarily made, for financial reasons, by British and American producers and directors.[8] He suggested two main categories, the romantic and heroic, preferred by US filmmakers, and the dark and endemically violent, preferred by their British counterparts. Martin McLoone was later to place these attitudes in a more political context, referring to the colonial relationship between Britain and Ireland and the large-scale emigration from Ireland to the USA in the last two centuries.[9] There was nevertheless a liberal consensus underpinning these stereotypes which portrayed political violence as restricted to those outside of the state, an aberration, linked to the past, opposed to liberal democracy and to be condemned. Violence by the state, however, was reactive, legitimate and necessary, if unfortunate.

I suggest that challenges to these censorial and stereotypical representations began to emerge hesitantly as a result of the combination of the political impact of the peace process and the re-emergence of film support agencies in the mid-1990s in Ireland. The sudden economic growth in the southern state, dubbed the 'Celtic Tiger', coincided with the Anglo Irish political developments and made 'Irishness' more acceptable. British popular culture was able to replace the stereotype of violent drunkard with the vogue for theme pubs and the Riverdance phenomenon. British Prime Minister Tony Blair even felt magnanimous enough to apologise for Britain's role in the Irish famine of the mid-nineteenth century, when the population had been sharply and enduringly reduced by death and emigration.[10] While shining a spotlight on the neglected cinematic area of competing nationalisms, where opportunities have been taken to develop a more innovative approach to self-representation, I also wish to reveal the limitations of this hesitancy, which have resulted in some continued reliance on stereotypes of character, metaphor and narrative.

The main films discussed here have substantial Irish creative input in the form of screenwriter/director credits. I will reference others as Irish because of a combination of their themes and other inputs such as production company and/or screenwriting credits.[11] I will look primarily at four films which were produced in the mid-1990s, a period when there was a combination of political and filmic optimism.[12] The first three films are Neil Jordan's *Michael Collins*,[13] Ireland's first indigenous 'epic', which mapped the war of independence earlier in the twentieth century; Thaddeus O'Sullivan's *Nothing Personal*,[14] which sought to foreground the loyalist paramilitary, an absent figure in 'Troubles' cinema; and Terry George's *Some Mother's Son*,[15] centred on the republican hunger-strikes. In contrast, Stephen Burke, the director of a planned trilogy of short films which spans the conflict,[16] attempts to challenge such stereotypes. His second film, *'81*,[17] follows a fictional French camera crew who are profiling two families from either side of the 'peace wall' at a time of heightened tension during the republican hunger strikes of 1981 and interrogates with humour and insight notions of news' impartiality.[18]

These four films are not 'representative' as such, but were released in a two-year period immediately following the 1994 ceasefires, directly engaged with the 'Troubles' and offer a range of subject and approach which hopefully will illuminate the issues I want to address.

Michael Collins

In *Michael Collins* the 1916 Easter Rising against British rule is defeated, the leaders are executed, and a guerrilla war ensues, led by Michael Collins. The Irish Republican Army responds in kind to each new British offensive. A truce is called and a treaty signed. But as it offers only independence within the empire and to twenty-six of the thirty-two counties, a civil war follows. The personal and the political merge as old comrades shoot it out.

Much has been written in the British press about *Michael Collins*. Its accuracy has been critiqued (there were no car bombs at the time), Adam Sweeting accused it of 'stoking up of republican violence'[19] and Paul Bew described it as having a romantic view of violence and as being 'neo-fascist art'.[20] But I wish here to concentrate on its representation of the earlier British–Irish conflict and the ensuing conflict within the Irish side as a mirror of the more recent conflict.

As Ireland's first 'epic' by an Irish director,[21] dealing with the foundation of the state, it has set a filmic standard for understanding those relationships. Britain is portrayed as the originator of violence when the G Men, the Black and Tans, and later a British intelligence elite squad each take new counter-insurgency initiatives. Despite Jordan's claim that '*Michael Collins* is innocent

with regard to contemporary politics'[22] the press reaction, accusing it of justify-
ing or at least explaining republican violence, is probably not wide of the mark.
The film clearly sets out a scenario where the British are militarily in occupa-
tion of Ireland, the Irish resist, and after many differences over tactics, achieve
a sort of independence, although leading to a civil war. That this is also a narrative of more recent republican violence in the north cannot be easily dismissed. For example, Jordan has Collins claiming at a cabinet meeting, 'Force
is the only thing the British understand.' Although it may be argued that the
Loyalist military campaign in the 1980s and 1990s forced the republican
movement to negotiate, it could just as convincingly be argued that the IRA
and the British army fought each other to a stalemate and that this led to negotiations.[23] The British government and IRA began secret talks shortly after the
hunger strikes of 1981, counter to the government's public position which held
that negotiations could not be considered until IRA violence had stopped.[24]

The significance of *Michael Collins* for Irish and British cinema is that it portrays Irish resistance to British rule as justified, as fought by sympathetic
people, and as capable of promoting identification with the cause and therefore
support for it. This tendency runs counter to the prevailing and persistent
stereotypes of atavistic murderers with inexplicable motives identified by Hill,
McLoone and Bennett.[25]

However, while *Michael Collins* breaks through the liberal consensus around
violence, the film's funding from the USA and the targeting of its primary mass
audience in that country (the world's most lucrative market) seems to force it
along well-trodden grooves of two-dimensional characterisation and narrative
simplicity. There is a consequent omission of social context, with all its attendant tensions. In the narrative necessity to personify the historical conflict in
the difference between two men, Collins and DeValera, the political forces at
work – namely class, gender and the rural/urban, reform/revolution splits –
become sidelined if not completely omitted.[26] The men's differences are represented as much by their egos as by their politics. For example, one is portrayed
as devious, the other well-meaning and straightforward. And, in a subplot, the
break-up of the Boland/Collins friendship is predicated as much on their competition for Kathleen as on their political differences. The Civil War which followed the Treaty-signing is shown as an unfortunate case of misunderstanding
at best, and at worst as manipulation by DeValera who appears to resent
Collins' popularity. The economic and political forces become marginalised.[27]

While narrative drive and character identification are imperatives of feature
filmmaking, complexities of social contradictions need not be excluded. Gillo

Pontecorvo in *Battle of Algiers* (1965), John Sayles in *Matawan* (1987) and Ken Loach in *Land and Freedom* (1995) all achieved the representation of historical conflict through fairly sophisticated characterisation and plot devices. Jordan comes to rely too heavily on one character, Collins, and his 'other', DeValera, to convey the contradictions in the independence movement. Titles at the end of the film reinforce this simplification when the text, after archive footage of Collins' funeral, includes 'He had fought the British to a standstill'.

Jordan has stated that he watched *Battle of Algiers* (1965) shortly before making *Michael Collins*.[28] Another director who is influenced by Pontecorvo is Thaddeus O'Sullivan, who acknowledges the same film in text at the beginning of his *Nothing Personal*, the portrayal of a loyalist paramilitary group in Belfast. What both Irish films have in common with Pontecorvo's film is an attempt to offer representation of violent political conflict. Although influence is claimed, there is little evidence of the radical style of filmmaking characteristic of *Battle of Algiers* in either Irish film. However, with *Michael Collins* it has to be acknowledged that there is an attempt at understanding the motives of those who practice political violence, a radical departure in terms of content. But with *Nothing Personal* the case is more difficult to argue.

If Irish nationalists have felt misrepresented by filmmakers until fairly recently,[29] then unionists and loyalists can feel underrepresented. Television plays have been more generous here, especially if one looks at the output of Graham Reid, in particular his *Billy* trilogy,[30] and I would contest Brian McIlroy's contention that even television has written unionists out of history, particularly as he merely mentions the above trilogy in passing and fails to offer it the detailed analyses reserved for other productions.[31] Reid's insightful examination of loyalist working class masculinity has rarely been emulated, even by himself. O'Sullivan, a filmmaker from the South of Ireland, had previously directed the acclaimed *December Bride* (1990) on the sexual tensions within a rural Protestant community in the Ards Peninsula. Other attempts at representing the loyalist include Marc Evans' *Resurrection Man* (1998) and the theatrical work of Gary Mitchell, whose plays, including *As the Beast Sleeps*[32] for television, have come out of his experiences in that community. *Nothing Personal* was the first to appear cinematically, and later films can be measured against it.

Nothing Personal

Whereas there have been sympathetic portrayals of IRA volunteers, albeit usually reluctant ones, in such films as Neil Jordan's *Crying Game* (1992) and in

TV plays such as the Ronan Bennett-scripted *Love Lies Bleeding*,[33] the loyalist paramilitary has not caught the imagination in the same way. This may be because their cause is less romantic, they are seen to identify with the status quo, they are not regarded as the underdogs and their attacks have been characterised as indiscriminate.[34]

In *Nothing Personal* Liam, a Catholic father, is kidnapped by a loyalist gang, who torture and threaten to shoot him. Kenny, the leader of the gang, is caught between the moderate leadership and the more extremist members of his gang, especially Ginger. Kenny releases Liam and it is suggested that this is connected with their previous boyhood friendship, referencing pre-1968 Belfast when housing was less segregated.[35] In a blazing finale, Ginger attempts to kill Liam but is shot in the leg by Kenny. Liam's daughter, Kathleen, is accidentally shot dead by her young friend in his attempt to shoot Kenny. As they attempt to escape, Kenny and his gang are killed by British soldiers.

While the other feature films I discuss suggest that Britishness is the 'other' and that Irishness is defined in opposition to it, with *Nothing Personal* we get close to what Britishness means to loyalists. 'For the sake of the country' is a refrain from Kenny the gang's leader, but is deliberately ambiguous, referring in loyalist lexicon to the UK, but also to the six counties of Ulster, if it seems that the UK government is not looking after loyalist interests or, at worst, threatening the union.

For loyalists, their self-definition obviously has its other, nominally the IRA, but as Ginger says, any Catholic can be included. In a confrontation with Kenny, he says, 'We have to make life so miserable for them that they have to get down on their hands and knees and crawl across the fucking border. In my wee book that makes one Catholic as good as another.' The film subverts stereo-typical notions of paramilitaries as godfathers, psychopaths or those addicted to bloodlust, but although the characters articulate their motives in limited ways, sometimes as asides, allowing them a political motive, O'Sullivan fails to develop this challenge to the dominant trend. To show how far O'Sullivan has gone in his limited way, it is only necessary to see Marc Evans's later *Resurrection Man*, where the loyalist gang leader is portrayed as erotically sadistic and although some allusion is made to the awkward relationship with his adoring mother and silent father, the sexual mysticism drowns out political motive and we are once again left with the bloodlust of psychotic killers.

An important tension within the loyalist community is the contradictory relationship with the British state. Their 'loyalty' has always been conditional. They have links with the British military and intelligence sources in a joint battle against republicanism, as evidenced by the Brian Nelson case,[36] and yet they are also subject to assassination and imprisonment by that state, if they are caught or if it is expedient. This relationship is not explored in *Nothing Personal*. By minimising Britishness and the British state (who in a reversal of roles in the real world are literally called upon by the loyalist leader to kill the maverick gang) an opportunity is lost to the director. O'Sullivan subsumes the subject matter of 'Nothing Personal', the loyalist paramilitary, to the narrative of a young girl, Kathleen, who looks after her younger brother and searches for her kidnapped father. This notion of innocence is foregrounded in the film's opening titles with a quote from W. B. Yeats –

> The ceremony of innocence is drowned:
> The best lack all conviction, while the worst
> Are full of passionate intensity.

O'Sullivan states elsewhere of Kathleen, 'She carries the real burden of pain . . . She represents the thing we kill in people. Innocence. Hope . . . if she wasn't in the film I wouldn't be making it.'[37] But it is just as convincing to argue that the innocence of the child is a metaphor which the director uses to avoid having to look any deeper into the heart of militant loyalism.

Kenny is torn between his boss, who has negotiated a ceasefire with the IRA and declares that Protestants want peace, and the extremist Ginger, who wants not only to kill the 'other' but admonishes Kenny who had shot a rioter just after Ginger had set him on fire: 'Why didn't you let him suffer?' These tensions are reasonably handled, but by being inward-looking and avoiding referencing the role of the British state, they reinforce the stereotype of a tribal war, where two sides of the community battle for supremacy. The *mise-en-scène* claustrophobia of the streets adds to this tribal atmosphere of the conflict. We, and presumably the loyalists, never see outside their district, never have a world view, and so have no context for this conflict. The tribal view is again confirmed when we see the IRA seeking a ceasefire with the loyalists although in reality it is the British whom they claim to be fighting, and with whom, historically, ceasefires have been negotiated.

Meanwhile, Kathleen's search for her father has taken her through the peace wall. Kenny's separated wife, Ann, an ex-nurse, tends to the injured Liam, who finds refuge in her house. These female characters suggest that women, as carers, can cross divides and literally and metaphorically heal the wounds of those divides. But this also suggests that women do not inhabit a political space, a common assumption in many Troubles films.[38]

Some Mother's Son

Not so in *Some Mother's Son*, Terry George's directorial debut, which makes up the second of his collaborative trilogy with Jim Sheridan, the first being *In the Name of the Father* (1993) and the last *The Boxer* (1997). *Some Mother's Son* is also a first of another sort. In 1981 ten Republican prisoners died on hunger striker for political status and, by creating the conditions for Sinn Fein to stand in and win Westminster elections, encouraged a more political, and less military, path for the republican movement. Secret negotiations between the republican movement and the British government were later to lead to the ceasefires of 1994 and the subesquent peace process.[39] These prison protests have been the theme of many unfulfilled film treatments, one involving the Hollywood actor Mickey Rourke.[40] The political sensitivity of the time, when the British state was at war with the IRA and apparent sympathy for the hunger strike was met with allegations of IRA propaganda, probably explains their unfulfilled status.[41] Recently, the ex-hunger striker Lawrence McKeown scripted *H3*,[42] a story of the notorious prison wing in Long Kesh, where most of the hunger strikers came from. Directed by Les Blair, the film is an intimate portrayal of the circum-stances which lead these young prisoners to embark on the anti-criminalisation campaign which culminated in ten deaths. Although the hunger strike appar-ently ended in defeat for the prisoners, within two years they had attained almost all of their demands.[43]

In *Some Mother's Son* Gerard is arrested for IRA activity and joins a prison hunger strike against the British government's policy of criminalisation of republican prisoners. His mother Kathleen reluctantly joins the support cam-paign but is torn between violent republicanism and her own liberal pacifism. After witnessing other strikers die, she intervenes after Gerard lapses into a coma, and consents to him being fed.

Despite the obvious political nature of the subject, George, himself a former republican prisoner, is keen to point out, 'You are telling the story about women and not some horror picture about what went on in the Maze'.[44] Kathleen is drawn into the conflict between the British state and the republican movement. The state is portrayed as having two factions, the hard-line Thatcher govern-ment which wants to defeat the protest by head-on confrontation and the more subtle diplomatic/intelligence services, which want to reach a compromise in order to defuse the tension.

Kathleen is Everywoman, whose conversion, struggle and reversion consti-tute the driving narrative that we, the audience, are asked to identify with. She is a teacher, raising three children on her own, and opposed to violence. Her ally and to some extent her 'other' in the film is Annie. While Kathleen is a professional, Annie works a small farm. Kathleen drives a car and Annie rides a bike. Kathleen drinks easily in a Protestant bar, Annie refuses to sit under a portrait of the Queen. Kathleen is liberal, Annie is republican.

Their journey from being merely mothers to political activists, as a result of the hunger strikes, drives the story forward. But the conversion plot has a twist at the end. Kathleen, who also becomes caught between the apparent dogma of Sinn Fein and the moralising of the Catholic Church, eventually signs her son off the hunger strike. Annie's son dies and when Kathleen offers her sympathy, Annie replies, 'At least you had a choice', implying that her own politics deny her choice. Because of the liberalism of the project Kathleen's decision is an individual, moral one. As Everywoman, she takes the decision to save her son. By implication, if Annie was to have a choice she too would save her son. What mother would not? And yet in reality ten mothers did allow their sons to die. This tension between saving a life and allowing a son to die is played out between the two women, one a liberal and the other a republican. One has a choice; the other does not. However, if the tension had been played out within one person, who did have a choice and who did let her son die, the intimate texture of the drama would have been heightened and the film would have become a radical critique of not only British rule but of republican resistance. Because George projects the conflict onto two 'others', ambiguity and contradiction are safely handled as character traits and plot devices and not complex tensions in the characters', and so the audience's, personal and political lives.

The storyline of the film, US-funded and -targeted, repeats the formula of the individual against the might of the state, adding as foe the employer who disapproves of her electioneering. This approach still has much mileage in it, but George's contempt for any other filmmaking tradition can be gauged from his remark, 'The European syndrome of filmmaking, which was well described once as directors putting their personal anxieties and angst up on the screen, is a problem in Ireland . . . I don't think that's entertainment by any definition of the word'.[45] Apart from George's rejection of the idea that cinema can be a place where art and entertainment meet, he seems to be unaware that if a representation of the hunger strikes was to produce any emotions they would probably include 'anxiety' and 'angst'.

Kathleen's growing confidence in her own identity, both in her politicisation in supporting her son, and then making the decision to take him off the hunger strike, is mirrored by the gradual silencing of Annie. Annie begins the film strongly, challenging the British army and having the last word, and continues by challenging the school's Mother Superior, alleging that she has hit her daughter, only to fade as an individual as the hunger strike takes hold. We see her on protests, but only as part of a crowd. She is silent when they visit the British parliament, with Kathleen doing the talking. She is the fundamentalist republican foil to Kathleen's stoic liberal individualism. Kathleen's son survives, Annie's dies.

The representation of contradictions within the British establishment between reaction and reform attempts to reflect tensions within the Thatcher government, and although it could be claimed that the characterization is two dimensional, it does capture the frustration of the regime at reconciling short term defeat of the enemy with the risk of creating martyrs and increasing resistance. The 1990s ceasefires, resulting from the bringing of Sinn Fein into the parliamentary fold, would suggest that, in the long run, the reformers within the British state have won out.

'81

The hunger strikes are also the theme for *'81*, Stephen Burke's second short film. A French film crew visits two working-class families on either side of the peace line during the prison protests of 1981. We see their daily routine, mothers cooking and children playing in the street, and the incongruity of being close yet so separate. The political divisions and social sameness are refracted through the increasing political tensions of the hunger strikes and the death of the first hunger striker, Bobby Sands, who had been elected a Westminster Member of Parliament during his protest.

This is probably the film which most self-reflexively deals with representation of the 'Troubles'. It is the second in his trilogy. The first, *After 68*,[46] tells the story of a teenager coming of age during the period of the civil rights protests in Derry in 1969, and the third, in development at the time of writing, deals with the post-ceasefire period.

Unlike the other films that I have discussed this short film (22 minutes), which was funded by the Irish Film Board and the national television station, RTE, challenges form as well as content. The film takes as its reference point the margins. The two families, one republican, one loyalist, live next to the peace wall, at the edges of their communities and next to the 'other'. The families are also on the edges of the republican and loyalist movements, either having been involved previously or having relatives imprisoned. The film is ostensibly a documentary shot by a French film crew, which offers a view at two removes – the television camera, and a foreign nationality.

'*81* comments on broadcast news' requirement for 'balance'[47] by emphasizing otherwise banal similarities and differences through devices such as one of the women enquiring about the other's cooker. It also subverts the notion of dour Protestantism by exploiting the outsiders' gullibility when the Protestant woman, Sarah, plays a practical joke on the film crew. This also reverses the normal power relations of crew and subject, and this theme is revisited when the Catholic woman, Clodagh, at one point asks not to be interviewed.

When the camera crew enter the Catholic home, that point of slight embarrassment when introductions are over and no one is sure who should begin the conversation is replicated in the Protestant home, so the joke becomes funnier because it is told a second time. It also reminds us that what is left out is often as important as what is left in at the shooting and editing stage.

The paralleling of stories is stretched most when Bobby Sands' funeral is compared with the funeral of Kenny's mother. Actual archive footage of Sands' funeral is blended with drama to produce an emotionally and politically powerful sequence, where those on the margins make choices and take sides. Kenny comments, 'Another republican martyr. That's all we need', before going off to his mother's funeral. But despite his and his son's cynicism, we are never pushed out of the orbit of empathy with them. His own grief draws us in and enables us to both disagree and sympathise.

We see the family and peer conditions which may lead to young people on either side of the peace line joining paramilitaries. The youngest boy is no 'innocent'. He does not act as a conduit for another character's agenda. He is independent, opinionated, takes sides and even acts as a guide for the film crew. At one point he even stages his own short-lived hunger strike.

Archive material, as in Burke's previous *After '68*, is interwoven into the narrative, and we are made aware of how representation is constructed in both documentary and drama. This short film, almost more than any other, also offers up concise and unapologetic reasons why people take up arms. Kenny reads out a letter from his son, Kenny jnr.: 'I became involved in paramilitary activity when I saw that the British government were not prepared to take on the IRA.' In another sequence, Tommy counters, 'Sure the IRA killed innocent people. The difference between us and them is that they target innocent people. Any Catholic will do.'

'*81* was probably the most overtly political fiction film to have been produced during the recent conflict, with only Joe Comerford's *High Boot*

Benny[48] coming close in attempting to ask why young people join paramilitaries. Comerford was to delay the release of his film because of the initial press reaction to his apparent sympathy with republicanism.[49] Yet although *'81* wears its politics on its sleeve, its awareness of the patterns of film and television coverage and its empathy for the unionist community lifts it above most other examples and suggests possibilities for stories which avoid stereotypical characterisation, narrative mimicry and liberal balance in favour of an open, independent and critical cinema, which the peace process might yet allow.

Conclusion

The political developments which both resulted in and came out of the ceasefires of 1994 have helped create a space for Irish screenwriters and directors to cinematically portray aspects of the Anglo-Irish conflict. The previous twenty-five years of political violence had limited the scope of such representation because of its censorious climate, which was both legislative and cultural. The independent film production funding base, apart from television money, had been almost non-existent in the North until the Northern Ireland Film Council was established in 1989, with money not available until the early 1990s. In the South the Irish Film Board was not re-established until 1993 after a six-year gap.

The films which emerged at this time and whose intentions were to address the consequences of competing nationalisms opened new territories in representation but at the same time carried some of the baggage of previous stereotypes of character and narrative. These stereotypes were produced primarily by US and British directors who were best placed to benefit from their countries' funding opportunities and the relationships which those countries had with Ireland. The representations of the Irish who were engaged in political violence are best described by John Hill as heroic, if flawed, as viewed by US directors and endemic, as viewed by British directors, at least up until the end of the 1980s.[50]

The four films under discussion can now be seen in retrospect as staging posts for a later body of more original work, which directly addresses some of the issues of the previous three decades. While television has always been able to seek out more voices, primarily because of lower production costs, films such as *H3* finally give us a previously unavailable cinematic insight into an aspect of the 'Troubles'. Not all recent Irish films benefit from this approach and many of the stereotypes persist, but new possibilities are opening up and are to be welcomed as antidotes to the more mainstream and inflexible representations.

It remains to be seen whether British- and US-directed movies can catch up with an approach which is more sensitive to the realities and experiences of those who have lived through this traumatic period.

Notes

1 Martin Mansergh, 'The background to the Irish peace process', in Michael Cox, Adrian Guelke and Fiona Stephen (eds), *A Farewell To Arms? From Long War to Long Peace in Northern Ireland* (Manchester, 2000), p. 22. The Irish Republican Army ceasefire broke down temporarily in 1997 but was reinstated and has since held fast, despite unionist accusations of breaches. The Ulster Volunteer Force and the Irish National Liberation Army are still on ceasefire at the time of writing. The Ulster Defence Association has since been described by the Secretary of State for Northern Ireland as not being on ceasefire because of breaches. The organisation claims that it is still on ceasefire. Smaller paramilitaries, having split from the main groups, are not on ceasefire and include the Loyalist Volunteer Force and the Real IRA.

2 Independent Film, Video and Photography Association, *Fast Forward: Report on the Funding of Grant-Aided Film and Video in the North of Ireland* (Belfast, 1988).

3 Lance Pettitt, *Screening Ireland: Film and Television Representation* (Manchester, 2000).

4 Liz Curtis, *Ireland and the Propaganda War: the British Media and the Battle for Hearts and Minds* (London, 1984).

5 Ibid.

6 Pettitt, *Screening Ireland.*

7 Curtis, *Ireland and the Propaganda War.*

8 Luke Gibbons, John Hill and Kevin Rockett, *Cinema and Ireland* (London, 1988).

9 Martin McLoone, *Irish Film: The Emergence of a Contemporary Cinema* (London, 2000).

10 Although the potato crop failure was ostensibly to blame, it has been convincingly argued that the economic and social policies of the occupying British government can be held primarily responsible. See Christine Kinealy, *A Death-Dealing Famine: The Great Hunger in Ireland* (London, 1997).

11 I wish to establish as inclusive a definition as possible. It is clear however that certain films, such as Alan J. Pakula's *The Devil's Own* (1997), which have little or no Irish input but which deal in Irish themes, should not be classified as Irish.

12 Although some of the films discussed were distributed after the ceasefires, they were produced during a period when expectations were at an all-time high that such political developments were imminent.

13 Neil Jordan, *Michael Collins,* 1996, Geffen Pictures.

14 Thaddeus O'Sullivan, *Nothing Personal,* 1995, Little Bird Productions.

15 Terry George, *Some Mother's Son,* 1996, Castle Rock Entertainment.

16 Stephen Burke has more recently been commissioned to write screenplays for RTE, the Irish state broadcaster.

17 Stephen Burke, *'81*, 1995, Mammoth Films.

18 Remarkably, neither Lance Pettitt nor Martin McLoone, despite their welcome coverage of short films in Ireland, refer to Burke's films.

19 Adam Sweeting, *Guardian*, 28 October 1996.

20 Paul Bew, *The Sunday Times*, 10 Novemeber 1996.

21 *Michael Collins* was funded by US money and followed Jordan's surprise hit, *The Crying Game*.

22 Neil Jordan, *Independent*, 7 November 1996.

23 Mansergh, 'Background'.

24 Mark Ryan, *War and Peace in Ireland: Britain and the IRA in the New World Order* (London, 1994).

25 Ronan Bennett, 'Don't mention the war', in David Miller (ed.), *Rethinking Northern Ireland* (London, 1998), pp. 200–1.

26 Conor Kostick, *Revolution in Ireland: Popular Militancy 1917 to 1923* (London, 1996), pp. 1–2.

27 In an example of the social forces at work, although the anti-Treaty forces initially outnumbered the Treaty forces by more than three to one, the victorious Treaty forces tellingly had big business, the press and the dominant Catholic Church on their side (see Kostick, *Revolution*).

28 Neil Jordan, *Michael Collins: Screenplay and Film Diary* (London, 1996), p. 30.

29 Independent Film, Video and Photography Association, *Fast Forward*.

30 Graham Reid, *Too Late to Talk to Billy* (1982), *A Matter of Choice for Billy* (1983) and *A Coming to Terms for Billy* (1984), BBC Northern Ireland.

31 Brian McIlroy, *Shooting to Kill: Filmmaking and the 'Troubles' in Northern Ireland* (Trowbridge, 1998).

32 Harry Bradbeer, *As the Beast Sleeps*, 2002, BBC2.

33 Michael Winterbottom, *Love Lies Bleeding*, 1993, C4.

34 Susan McKay, *Northern Protestants: An Unsettled People* (Belfast, 2000).

35 Michael Farrell, *Northern Ireland: The Orange State* (London, 1976), p. 229. It is important to note that while the 1960s may have offered new opportunities for integration because of changes in higher education and inward investment, it must also be seen in the context of the previous forty years of low-level political violence in a one-party state.

36 Brian Nelson was an ex-British Army serviceman who was recruited by the military intelligence unit, Force Research Unit. He penetrated the largest loyalist paramilitary group, the UDA, becoming its chief intelligence officer. BBC's two-part Panorama Special (19 June and 26 June 2002) has alleged that he was used not only to gather counter-intelligence, but to target republicans and others from the nationalist community.

37 Thaddeus O'Sullivan, Film Ireland.

38 Sarah Edge, 'Representing gender and national identity', in Miller (ed.), *Rethinking*.

39 Ryan, *War and Peace*.

40 Rourke was involved in negotiations over the rights to the story of one of the ten hunger strikers who died.

41 Curtis, *Propaganda War*.

42 Les Blair, *H3,* 2001, Metropolitan Films.

43 David Beresford, *Ten Men Dead: The Story of the 1981 Irish Hunger Strike* (London, 1987).

44 Significantly, George describes the prison as the Maze, the name change given to Long Kesh by the British Government, in order to deflect the bad publicity that it was receiving.

45 *Film West* 25 (1996), p. 17.

46 Stephen Burke, *After 68*, 1994, Mammoth Films.

47 Curtis, *Propaganda War*.

48 Joe Comerford, *High Boot Benny*, 1993, Sandy Films.

49 David Butler, 'High Boot Benny', in *Film Ireland* 38, December/January 1993/94.

50 John Davies' Channel 4-funded *Acceptable Levels* (1983), about a British TV crew covering the shooting dead by plastic bullet of a girl in the Divis Flats, Belfast, was a welcome challenge of these stereotypes.

14

From *Z Cars* (1962) to *The Cops* (1998): the northern television police series

Susan Sydney-Smith

If, as Benedict Anderson has argued, we may best understand the nation in terms of other nations, the same may be said of that diverse but distinctive form of popular entertainment, the television police series.[1] But whereas in Britain we are thoroughly familiar with the American police procedural, from *Dragnet* (1951), *Highway Patrol* (1955), through *Hill Street* and *NYPD Blues* (1981, 1995), right up to *CSI: Crime Scene Investigation* (2001), the same does not hold true the other way around.[2] Indeed, evidence at the British Broadcasting Corporation's (BBC's) Written Archive at Caversham shows that attempts to market *Dixon of Dock Green* (BBC, 1955), the earliest example of the British police series to remain solid in the popular imagination, met with failure largely due to the essentially parochial nature of its concerns.[3] American audiences would have experienced even more difficulties with its *Z Cars* (BBC, 1962), famous for its 'gritty' documentary realism and vernacular 'authenticity'.

The British television crime product that finds perennial favour in the US is the 'golden age' literary adaptation, from the earliest BBC production of *Sherlock Holmes* (BBC, 1954), up to, and including, *Agatha Christie's Poirot* (LWT – Carnival Films, ITV, 1989) – notwithstanding the latter protagonist's Belgian nationality. Nor has the transatlantic traffic flowed one way. Sheldon Reynolds' Public Broadcast Service (PBS) series, *Sherlock Holmes* (1980), made by Guild Films in Poland, with Geoffrey Whitehead as Holmes and Donald Pickering as Watson, shows how a highly selective projection of Britishness early became not only a transnational, but a 'global' commodity.[4] Such representations tended to portray a repertoire of received images of an 'old country'. As has been noted, the linking of so-called 'heritage' values to those of enterprise is part of the currency of the British film and television export trade.[5] Hence, in police series terms, it is little wonder that the nostalgic *Heartbeat* (Yorkshire Television, 1992), also set in the North of England and deeply embedded in a heritage discourse, and unlike *Z Cars* or its successor *The Cops* (BBC, 1998), has sold extremely well both to the United States and elsewhere.

How does this brief comparison help towards understanding our own national popular generic product? It tells us that US audiences have become acculturated to a certain projection of Britishness – or, often, Englishness – which has rendered 'authentic' representations less intelligible (as in the case of *Z Cars*) than those whose concerns are to purvey a more picturesque image of national identity. J. B. Priestley, in his famous *English Journey* (1934), identified three Englands: 'Old England', characterized as essentially bucolic, 'the country of the cathedrals and ministers and manor houses and inns, of parson and squire; guidebook and quaint highways and byways'.[6] Set against this 'heritage' version of national identity are Priestley's other two Englands: 'the nineteenth-century England, the industrial England of coal, iron, steel, cotton, wool, railways' and modern England, 'the England of arterial and bypass roads, of filling stations and factories'.[7] As Dave Russell explains, writers on 'the North' before the 1950s (and sometimes later) have referred to the pastoral version as the 'True North' and set it against the industrial waste of 'Black England'.[8] This essay suggests that, like the novel before it, the television series has been articulated around very different 'norths', based not only on a rural–urban divide but also upon their relationship to reality. As it aims to show, the earliest version of what may identified as the Northern television police series *reversed* the literary hierarchy, which favoured the pastoral version. Placing emphasis upon a grim, 'gritty' urban North, and in dialogue with their sound broadcasting precursors during the 1930s, including Geoffrey Bridson's early documentary 'features', British television producers endeavored to extend – in line with new wave cinema and kitchen sink drama – a new 'documentary' realism, exemplified by *Z Cars*.[9] It is not until the 1990s with the production of *Heartbeat* that the 'gritty version' of the northern police series, shifts to a more idealized, less referential version of both policing and representations of national identity.

What can we make of these contradictions and reversals? In furthering their understanding, this chapter charts the emergence of the northern police series and the way it defines itself away from that distinctive sub-genre of the metropolitan police series, famously incarnated by *Dixon of Dock Green* (1955) and arguably continued in today's *The Bill* (1984).[10] It focuses primarily on two formative periods: that between the 1950s and 1960s, and that between the 1990s and the present day. The first period commences with an examination of *Z Cars*' story-documentary precursors. This looks closely at a trilogy set in 'the North': *Tearaway* (1957), *Who Me?* (1959), and the four-part *Jacks and Knaves*

(1961), before analysing *Z Cars* itself. During what may be regarded as the Northern police series' second cycle, the essay concentrates on the shift towards pastoral versions, including *Juliet Bravo* (BBC 1980) and *Heartbeat*, culminating in an authentic realist 'return', most fully exemplified by *The Cops* (1998). The analysis takes place within a profoundly changing broadcasting landscape, as British television moves away from a protective, monopolistic system towards a deregulated market economy. In order to contextualize the foundational form of the British television story-documentary in generic terms, it is worth looking briefly at its early appearance in British television.

Dramatized reconstructions in the studio, story or drama documentaries formed the original spine of most workplace narratives, including the police series.[11] They responded to a need to expand the new medium of television within the repressive conditions of postwar British broadcasting. As John Caughie argues, during the 1940s, 1950s and early 1960s 'they were accepted as part of its social responsibility to inform and educate a democratic citizenry'.[12] By being seen to fulfil this remit, they legitimated television's own abilities to dramatize events, taking it on from its perception as a second-hand relayer of events, towards that of an independent, story-telling entity. Although these programmes are said to have appeared regularly on BBC until the end of 1962 and then to have disappeared, that is because they become absorbed into the line of 'isolated events of considerable importance', including the seminal *Cathy Come Home* which appeared in the Wednesday Play series and the television series itself, including *Z Cars*.[13] They arguably informed the discourse of 'the angry young man', supposedly predicated upon John Osborne's play, *Look Back in Anger* (1956).[14] The story-documentary's 'angry' or new wave link is clearly seen in a brief analysis of the previously mentioned *Tearaway, Who Me?* and the *Jacks and Knaves* series. All three programmes were the work of the BBC writer-producer team (a term taken from radio), of Gilchrist Calder and Liverpool-born Colin Morris, and may be seen as direct precursors of *Z Cars*. Each production was set in an undisclosed but deprived area of the north: Liverpool is indicated but often the directions merely state 'a northern city'. In evaluating their relationship to documentary methods, it is worth noting that the narrative interests and characterization were founded on Detective Sergeant Bill Prendergast, a renowned and contemporary Liverpudlian policeman: a redoubtable character described by the *Radio Times* as 'a man with a talent for acting and more than a touch of psychology, of whom it was said that when he had interrogated a thief, the prisoner would leap into the dock and shout: "GUILTY"'.[15] After the notorious cases of the Birmingham Six and Guildford

Four, such interrogatory policing methods are profoundly disturbing. The 'acting' caveat confirms, rather than averts, our suspicions, and the certainty with which Prendergast is promoted over the production's fictional characters (consecutively, those of DS Bulliver and DS Hitchins), confuses the programme's narrative status (is it drama, or documentary?). The *Radio Times* entry carries the confusion further, describing *Tearaway* – in a significant reversal of terms – as a 'documentary drama showing how certain people remain silent when threatened with violence'. Writing earlier of a preference for dramatization over documentary Morris stated that, whereas 'the documentary camera can only record what is at once visible; it cannot explain what brought the situation about. I approach a subject not with any social conscience, but simply with curiosity . . . What I want to know is why and how.'[16]

Although *Tearaway* abandons the 'voice of god' technique of the earlier story documentary, it retains the familiar detective-film trope of inserting extra information into the diegesis via printed newspaper headlines. The camera picks up the words 'Gangs Stalk the City' as it pans into a close-up of a newspaper stand, upturned by the eponymous protagonist. It next cuts to the interior of a police station, where we meet Detective Inspector Hall, framed in medium close-up, mulling over the same report:

> Gangs, what Gangs? One night Paddy's drinking with Alf and that's another gang. Another night Len's having a mojo, drunk with Billy and that's another gang (taps paper). This sort of journalism makes the subject more important than it really is. It's not bad because it gives muscle men ideas – They don't read anyhow! It's bad because it tends to make the public nervous. The one thing this country's got left – and it hasn't got much is its justice. And the police are part of British justice. Their reputation grew up over many years on the good temper, the integrity and the fairness of the man on the beat.[17]

It is hard at this juncture to decipher who is the narrator: the playwright, the police, or the BBC? As can be seen, the emergent form and shifting terms of the dramatized documentary tended to result in a confusion of the programme's ideological and emotional registers: on the one hand, its informative function seems to place it within the category of a 'documentary' public service narrative, whilst on the other, its affective dimension secures it a place within progressive 'new wave' television drama. *Tearaway's* narrative line is about what happens when two tearaways decide to pick on a victim named Tommy Baxter, beat him up, and the witnesses – Tam, Mrs Molden, and First Neighbour – are too scared to come forward. It portrays the grimness of life in a Victorian slum setting, and the script indicates an attempt at vernacular authenticity.

Next in the trilogy, *Who Me?* is a programme about three men held for questioning over a shop theft – and involves even more dubious interrogative methods than previously. In yet another incarnation of Prendergast Detective Superintendent Hitchins, played by Lee Montague, takes the lead in a narrative whose action is set entirely inside a police station. As with the Bulliver characterization in *Tearaway*, Hitchins is representative of the modernising tough new policeman. As he tells the potential suspects, 'Before the night's over, we'll be close as brothers.' Despite, or perhaps because of, these brutal methods, the Audience Reaction Index for the programme was as high as that for 'the more sensational crime story-documentary' of *Tearaway* at 71.[18] But, lest any should find the portrayal of the police at all reprehensible, the BBC was keen to explain away the narrative as premised on 'exceptional conditions'. A copy-letter on file from Gilchrist Calder hastens to reassure a correspondent that 'the people being interrogated in the programme were, if you remember, already criminals with bad records. The methods used would obviously not be used in normal circumstances.'[19]

A need for BBC television to discover more popular forms, and methods of rationalized production, became paramount with the arrival of Independent Television (ITV), whose filmed series formed the backbone of its popular entertainment. The four-part *Jacks and Knaves* was a deliberate attempt at both a regional representation to match that of *Coronation Street* (1960), and a shift into series production. It was advertized in the *Radio Times* as:

> four self-contained 45-minute programmes which spring directly from the experience and the success of *Who Me?* concerning the lighter side of CID work in the North of England . . . In Liverpool they call a detective a 'Jack' – and one of the most colourful Jacks who ever nobbled a knave in that windy city was Detective Sergeant William Prendergast . . . Liverpudlians, who nicknamed him 'Ace', still swap stories about his exploits.[20]

The programmes, once again located in the 'Liverpool area', are about the work of the same uninhibited detective sergeant, who 'doesn't so much break the rules as bend them'. 'The Master Mind', 'The Interrogation', 'The Great Art Robbery' and 'It was Doing Nothing' were transmitted at weekly intervals from mid-November to early December 1961. According to pre-publicity on file, the stories:

> involve the theft of a church gate and a church wall (this is not a mistake – some splendid demolition characters are careering around the city knocking down anything they think looks useless); the theft – accidental for the most part – of a painting, the value of which is not even suspected by the thieves who are really after *lead*; a case of shop-lifting which gets very complicated indeed because it leads to the recovery of other goods stolen more belligerently.[21]

While *Tearaway* had shown crime as socially conditioned, *Who, Me?* was conditioned by humour.[22] By the time the producer-writer team arrived at *Jacks and Knaves*, they had resorted to slapstick. 'The Great Art Robbery' commences with an especially filmed song sequence featuring the Frankie and Johnny ballad, together with mouth-organ accompaniment. The script details the use of filmed inserts telecined into the live performance, giving actors time to change between scenes and expanding the diegetic space beyond the studio. Maurice Wiggin, writing in *The Sunday Times* about the second programme 'The Interrogation', described the series as 'the most enjoyable item in my week ... It never for one moment flagged; there was never a pointed pause for laughs; the writing was fluent, economical, and precisely keyed to every image and nuance of character.'[23]

Just as in the case of *Tearaway*, according to the BBC Audience Reports, perceptions differed as to the degree of its 'authenticity'.[24] Some respondents thought the Liverpool accents badly done, the police officers played with an unlikely casualness, and the thieves poorly characterized.[25] Others felt the programme 'showed the police in an unfortunate light, making them out to be fools lacking in discipline'.[26] Fed up with their increasingly acrimonious exchanges with the authorities over minor procedural details, Gilchrist and Calder decided to quit.

Z Cars was both a response to the 1954 Television Act, which required that television programme companies should be of a regional nature, and a natural extension of its precursors. Troy Kennedy Martin and John McGrath, the *Z Cars'* series' first writer and director, were fascinated by the American police procedurals shown on ITV and aimed 'to use a *Highway Patrol* format, but to use the cops as a key or way of getting into a whole society'.[27] The seemingly impossible task of reproducing the aesthetics of film in a studio situation was achieved by the use of cars mounted on rollers, back projections and the use of the (by now standard) filmed inserts telecined into the performance: all to produce a sense of extra-diegetic space.[28] In creating a cast of six main characters, as well as a combination of plain-clothes and uniformed policemen, *Z Cars* also opened up more narrative opportunities than had occurred in the *Dixon of Dock Green* series. Its regular plain-clothes cast included the bad-tempered Detective Inspector Barlow, played by Stratford Johns, and a gentler Detective Sergeant John Watt, played by Frank Windsor, in a variant American 'buddy' theme. The first episode, 'Four of a Kind', is predicated upon the death of PC Reginald Farrow, 'shot down in the course of his duty'. Its elegiac mood is a direct homage to *The Blue Lamp* film in which the eponymous Dixon arose, only to meet his death at the hands of a lawless young Dirk Bogarde.[29] But whereas, in the spin-off television series, crime tends to be treated as in such episodes as *The Rotten Apple* as apart from society, in *Z Cars* there is a strong sense that crime is endemic. The soulless new towns are full of 'rogues and tear-aways' (Barlow to Watt) and there are few community values. As Janey tells her husband Steel, the bruise he has administered gives her more credibility with the neighbours, than 'a stretch in Strangeways'. The *Radio Times* described the series' environment: 'fraught with danger for policemen in the North of England overspill estate called Newtown. Here a mixed community displaced from larger towns because of slum clearance has been brought together and housed on an estate without amenities and without community feeling.'[30]

This critique of the new sink estates, with their lack of community and sense of anomie, cuts right across so-called 'progressive' 1960s slum clearance discourses: its social concerns perform a dialogue between Priestley's 'nineteenth century England, the industrial England of coal, iron, steel, cotton, wool, railways' and the modern England, 'the England of arterial and bypass roads, of filling stations and factories that look like exhibition buildings'. Of the first thirteen *Z Cars* scripts (constituting a season), three were based directly on casebook material from the prolific Prendergast; the rest were 'improvised' from the experiences of the scriptwriter and director, out on patrol with the Lancashire police force. The police collaborated throughout, specifically briefing the producers to present their Force as 'tough but not as yobbish', not, as one police spokesman put it, 'with straw in our heads'. So disgusted was the Lancashire Constabulary after *Z Cars'* first episode was transmitted it is now television folklore that the Chief Constable marched into the office of Stuart Hood, then Television Controller, and demanded that the programme be taken off air. Although the series remained, its reception was generally marked by national and local criticism. In terms of the first, remarks by an anonymous senior police officer from Lancashire in the *Guardian* were typical:

> You can say there have been heated arguments . . . It was awful. We all thought it made us look fools. And our wives thought it made them look fools too, it, I mean it made it look as though we're always running into each other's houses, eating each other's dinners. We never meet each other's wives. No, never. Things aren't like that at all.[31]

Letters to the *Lancashire Evening Post* expressed extreme indignation. For the fact was that although *Z Cars* producers may have specifically aimed to create 'a kind of documentary about people's lives in these areas, and the cops were incidental', local people did not see it like that at all.[32] One reader, disputing the BBC's claims that viewers' reactions were 'one hundred per cent favourable', opined:

> It is evident that he did not make any inquiries in Preston. Dozens of people here are disgusted with this BBC presentation. . . . If I had any say at the BBC all future instalments of Z Cars would be stopped at once, the producer given a month's salary, a minute's notice, and appoint a new producer to portray the Lancashire Constabulary as they really are – a fine body of reasonably educated, decently spoken men.[33]

Although such anger was partly a result of viewers' failure to grasp the difference between fiction as represented by BBC television and reality, it nonetheless raises questions about accountability. Complaints were made by Kirkby's Urban Council about the ease with which members of the public were able to identify Kirkby with Newtown, especially since a great deal of trouble had been taken to improve the more run-down areas of the borough.[34]

Kennedy Martin states that there was a 'whittling away of class attitudes. The crime patrol began with a firmly working class crew . . . There was some pressure to make them £1,000 a-year men. One week Sergeant Watt got a shiny new raincoat. Another, Janey, the policeman's wife, got a snazzy new cooker to replace the old stove.' Frustrated at what he increasingly saw as a failure to produce a desired agitational left-wing content and avant-garde style, he left after the first series.[35]

Just as writers and producers used 'the North' more as an imaginative space for their own solipsistic projections rather than as a real space, so too vernacular dialects were equally inauthentic, being derived from a diverse array of 'the North' and elsewhere. Alan Plater, one of Z Cars' earliest writers, describes how:

> The original streetwise coppers in Z Cars were played by Jimmy Ellis from Ireland, Joe Brady from Scotland and the Yorkshiremen, Brian Blessed and Jeremy Kemp. Their immediate superior, Sergeant Watt, was played by Frank Windsor from the Midlands, and his superior, Inspector Barlow, by Stratford Johns, who was born in South Africa.[36]

In other words, they were a motley crew of different regional and (in the case of Johns) national origins. As Stuart Laing indicates, there was a softening of the characters because after the actors arrived, their mismatch with those originally researched became evident. For example, Fancy Smith's sub-Sillitoe character, who liked 'a crafty kip after his lunchtime pint' and was famed for 'the Italian cut of his civilian gear', as played by Brian Blessed did not suit Kennedy Martin's creation.[37] There was also a notable tendency towards creating gender and racial stereotypes although the 'strong women' in Granada's *Coronation Street*, such as Ena Sharples, were conspicuous by their absence. Indeed, female characters were sometimes literally written out of their parts. After her function in demonstrating her coordinating role had been established, Virginia Stride's part as Katie Hoskins, the radio-control operator, shrank to nothing.[38] Barlow and Watt's respective wives were despatched from the start. During the first episode, we hear Watt discussing the fact that his wife Mary has headed for the bright lights of the swinging metropolis: 'She won't come back, not from London!'

After its first three seasons, despite its multiple storylines and protagonists, *Z Cars* began to contract. Nonetheless, the series continued unabated in its original form for four years, until the arrival of *Softly, Softly* (1966), which saw Barlow and Watt relocated to a fictional Wyvern, near Bristol, in the southwest. The relocation was precipitated by the producers' desire to explore new terrain and narrative themes, in particular, that of the regional police force. However, the southern recuperation was by no means absolute. During the 1960s, what may be seen as alternative productions of the genre I have identified as the northern police series were made. For example *Cluff* (1964), set in Yorkshire in the small fictional town of Gunnarshaw, centred on the activities of the eponymous local police constable, who lived alone but for his dog. He wore tweed suits, brown boots, broad ties, and smoked a pipe: setting an unusually nostalgic sartorial trend for the sixties. 'Cluff' was played by Leslie Sands (who had previous police experience as Superintendent Miller in *Z Cars*), and the series featured a more pastoral version of the North than *Z Cars*.

Cluff's somewhat sleepy village motif was continued during the 1980s with a second series, *Juliet Bravo*. This series was set in the small, supposedly Lancashire-based village of Hartley, where there was very little crime. Such incidents as did occur were dealt with by officer Joe Beck and his fellow sergeant, George Parrish, their very names indicative of the series' bucolic setting. Narrative interest was gently stimulated by the role reversal between Inspector Jean Darblay, senior police officer and housewife (played by Stephanie Turner), and her husband Tom. Darblay's appointment as a uniformed female Inspector highlighted many of the problems and prejudices faced by a woman arriving to take charge at a male stronghold.[39] Tom was a Southerner – thereby referencing the North/South divide – forced on occasion to take second place within the marriage. For all its parochialism, *Juliet Bravo* was nationally popular, running on into six seasons.[40]

During the 1990s, often seen as a re-visitation of the 1960s, there have been, in northern police series terms, numerous generic 'returns'. *Heartbeat*, presented by Yorkshire Television, was undoubtedly based, in part, upon its pastoral precursors. Set in the idyllic 'picturesque' rural community of Aidensfield deep in the North Yorkshire Moors, *Heartbeat* shifts right away from the documentary realism that characterizes the mainstream northern police series. Seen through a veil of nostalgia, with its rolling verdant hills, small stone villages, inns and air of timelessness, it provides an alternative version of the North to *Z Cars*, one that is much closer to Priestley's 'Old England'. Unlike *Cluff* and *Juliet Bravo*, as Robin Nelson argues, the series negotiates a new relationship away from referential reality.[41] Set in the 1960s the production, at the same time, possesses elements of the 1950s. However, Nick Berry, fresh from his role as Wicksy in the soap opera, *EastEnders* (BBC, 1982), brings the production into the near present. *Heartbeat* is no longer set in 'real' time, nor does it attempt to 'reflect' the real: rather, the programme is the product of intensive market research, the result of exigencies brought about by the multi-channel environment and consequently fragmented audience. The original *Heartbeat* series was shown on Friday nights at 9.20 pm and drew an audience in the region of 10–13 million, the biggest ever Friday night audience for a drama series in the UK. During the second series (Autumn 1992), it was scheduled on Sunday night, in the primetime 7.30 pm slot, and its audience reached, and eventually surpassed, the 10 million mark.[42] *Heartbeat* is a manifest demonstration in programme terms of what has happened in the development away from the BBC's 'brute force of monopoly' to an increasingly deregulated broadcasting economy. At the same time, it exemplifies the way in which the relationship between television and its audience has altered. *Heartbeat* offers us a form of virtual cultural tourism connected to a repertoire of other 1970s and 1980s locational attractions, including *Emmerdale* (Yorkshire TV, 1972). *All Creatures Great and Small* (ITV 1977) and *A Country Practice* (ITV 1988). What this programme, its precursors and successors construct, is that 'deep' mythology previously assigned to the South, a process, with spin-offs to the tourist industry. All of these programmes are examples of cultural rationalization in an expanding market, evoking picturesque versions of a regional England little changed by modernity, let alone post-modernity: a 'deep North'.

Despite *Heartbeat*'s shift away from the realism of the Northern police series most fully realized by *Z Cars*, there have been some generic reprises of the 'line' of agitational contemporary enquiry the latter set in motion, beginning with *City Central* (1997), and the ongoing *Merseybeat* (2001) (set in Manchester and Liverpool respectively). The apotheosis of this contemporary revival is undoubtedly *The Cops*, produced by Tony Garnett and set in fictional Stanton (the fact that Garnett played a policeman in *Z Cars* is hardly coincidental). The first episode – simply called *Episode 1* – opens, as did its precursor, with news

of a police death, but here is no elegy. We learn of the passing of Detective
Sergeant Pool; and the accession of Detective Superintendent Edward Giffen
provides a narrative opportunity to usher in a new, contemporary form of
policing, one that is resisted at every level. When Jazz, the Asian policeman, is
singled out for special treatment as a potentially 'ethnically compatible officer',
he tells top brass Chief Inspector Newland that he doesn't want to be presented
as a paid-up minority group fixture: 'I'm not a minority. My father was born in
India. I am British.' Roy, a self-confessed old-style beat copper who was taken
to task in the first episode for physically attacking Vince, an old-fashioned 'tearaway' whom he sees as responsible for the death of Giffen's predecessor, is puz-
zled by being thwarted for the administration of what he sees as a rough but
necessary form of justice. Such Prendergast-like methods, it is suggested, are
strictly out of bounds in the 1990s.

As with *Z Cars*, *The Cops* had the Lancashire constabulary up in arms. *The
Preston Citizen* described the new series as an 'unrelentingly depressing and
negative' portrayal of every policing routine. Gillian Radcliffe, Corporate
Communications Manager of the Lancashire Constabulary, stated that
although a minority of officers in the police service may behave badly and fail
to meet the standards that the public expect: 'To put so many together in one
place and have them all behaving so shockingly over one eight-hour shift is the
ultimate in dramatic license. It would be laughable if there wasn't a risk some
viewers would fear it is realistic.'[43]

What especially riled the police was that, just as in the case of *Z Cars*, they
had collaborated with the new series – shot predominantly in Bolton – allowing the cameras to shadow the police's every move. An added insult was the way
the BBC appeared to be manipulating the controversy for the sake of its own
publicity. On a *Radio Times* cover feature, entitled 'Shock Tactics: *The Cops*:
Breaking New Ground or Breaking the Rules?', Chief Constable Pauline Clare
(twenty-seven years on Merseyside) stated:

> there are things in *The Cops* which I felt, 'Yes, they could happen,' 'Yes, that hap-
> pened' and 'Yes, I know people like that.' But they are things that happen rarely.
> There is another side; there are good things which go on. We are working very hard
> to build up relationships with the public to help them to trust us and to make them
> realise that we are professional people who will take their complaints seriously.[44]

The argument ran on, as did the programme, just like its *Z Cars* predecessor,
shorn of its police acknowledgement. Although *The Cops* undoubtedly represents
some sort of a 'return', we by now are aware that in television's multi-choice
world, it does not in itself represent any definitive version. What is of interest,

however, is that amid the post-modern world of pastiche and parody exemplified by *Heartbeat*, realist television drama with that distinctive northern focus not only survives, but still packs a powerful political punch, at home if not abroad. Its dominant forms have changed over time, in step with broader changes in the representation of northern England within Britishness, but its power to attract attention and stir controversy remains as potent as ever.

Notes

1 Benedict Anderson, *Imagined Communities: Reflections on the Origins and Spread of Nationalism* (London, 1983).
2 The first British television police series to be exported was *The Sweeney*, syndicated n the United States in 1976. *Highway Patrol* was shown in the London ITV region as early as 1956.
3 *Dixon of Dock Green* was produced live and was not initially conceived with an eye to the export market. An especially filmed early episode was turned down by Australia and destroyed.
4 For 'heritage television' as a relevant concept see Charlotte Brunsdon, 'The structure of anxiety: recent British television crime fiction', in Edward Buscombe (ed.), *British Television: A Reader* (Oxford and New York, 2000), p. 202.
5 John Corner and Sylvia Harvey (eds.), *Enterprise and Heritage: Crosscurrents of National Culture* (London, 1991), p 1.
6 J. B. Priestley, *English Journey* (London, 1997, first published 1934), p. 321.
7 Ibid., pp. 322–5.
8 Dave Russell, *The North in the National Imagination: England 1850–2000* (Manchester, 2003).
9 Bridson produced *Steel* (1937) as part of a trilogy. See Paddy Scannell, 'The stuff of radio', in John Corner (ed.), *Documentary and the Mass Media* (London, 1986), p. 8.
10 For *Dixon of Dock Green*, see Susan Sydney-Smith, *Beyond Dixon of Dock Green: Early British Police Series* (London, 2002), pp. 103–17.
11 Ibid., pp. 55–86.
12 John Caughie, *Television Drama: Realism, Modernism and British Culture* (Oxford, 2000), pp. 104–5.
13 Ibid.
14 See Michael Barry, *From the Palace to the Grove* (London, 1992), p. 71.
15 *Radio Times*, 9 November 1957, p. 47.
16 Cited in Stuart Laing, *Representations of Working Class Life, 1957–1964* (Basingstoke, 1986), p. 130.
17 Playscript, *Tearaway* by Colin Morris, BBC Written Archives, Caversham (WAC), TX 1950.
18 For the Audience Reaction Index, see Robert Silvey, *Who's Listening? The Story of BBC Audience Research* (London, 1974).
19 Letter from Gilchrist Calder, dated 17 October 1959, WAC T5/2428.

20 Cited in *Radio Times*, 9 November 1961.

21 BBC WAC T5/2121/5.

22 These programmes were consecutively transmitted on 16 November 1961 ('The Master Mind'), 23 November 1961 ('The Interrogation'), 7 December 1961 ('It was Doing Nothing'), 30 January 1962 ('The Great Art Robbery').

23 Maurice Wiggin, 'Swinging a very pretty pick', *The Sunday Times*, 26 November 1961.

24 Whereas a letter from a CID Training Officer of Cornwall County Constabulary praised Tearaway as 'really live education by any standards', in the north-west, once again according to the BBC Written Archives, it was found 'sordid' with 'far too much bad language': WAC T5/2428.

25 BBC Audience Report, 4 December 1961. *Jacks and Knaves*, 'The Master Mind', WAC T5/2122.

26 WAC, BBC Secretariat to Nicholas Ridley MP, in reply to a copy of a constituent's letter complaining about *Jacks and Knaves*. See Sydney-Smith, *Beyond Dixon of Dock Green*.

27 J. McGrath, 'Better a bad night in Bootle', *Theatre Quarterly* 5, no. 19 (1975), pp. 42–3.

28 Around eight film inserts per programme was the 'norm' for *Z Cars*' production. See Jason Jacobs, *The Intimate Screen: Early British Television Drama* (Oxford, 2000), p. 139.

29 Only to be resurrected five years later in *Dixon of Dock Green* (1955): Sydney-Smith, *Beyond Dixon of Dock Green*, and Jeffrey Richards, 'The thin blue line: *The Blue Lamp*', in A. Aldgate and J. Richards (eds.), *Best of British: Cinema and Society from 1930 to the Present* (London, 1999), p. 125.

30 *Radio Times*, 28 December 1961.

31 '*Z Cars* limelight declined: BBC to drop police', *Guardian*, 5 January 1962.

32 McGrath, 'Bad night in Bootle'.

33 *Lancashire Evening Post*, 9 January 1962.

34 H. E. Legg, Chief Constable, Lancashire Constabulary, to David Rose, dated 10 November 1961, WAC T5/22449/1.

35 See Troy Kennedy Martin, 'Nats go home: first statement of a new drama for television', *Encore* 48 March/April 1964), pp. 21–33.

36 Alan Plater, 'The drama of the north east', in R. Colls and B. Lancaster (eds.), *Geordies* (Edinburgh, 1992).

37 'Allan Prior and John Hopkins talking about the Z Cars series', *Screen Education* 21 (September/October 1963), p. 10, cited in Laing, 'Banging in some reality', in Corner (ed.), *Popular Television in Britain*, p. 141.

38 Sydney-Smith, *Beyond Dixon of Dock Green*, pp. 181–202.

39 Inspector Kate Longton, played by Anna Carteret, took over after three seasons.

40 *Juliet Bravo* was created by Ian Kennedy Martin. It ran from 30 August to 13 December 1980, and continued a yearly pattern until Season 6, which ran from 7 September to 21 December 1985.

41 Robin Nelson, 'Signs of the times? *Heartbeat* and *Baywatch*', in his *TV Drama in Transition*, p. 73.

42 Ibid., p 74.
43 *Preston Citizen*, 26 November 1999.
44 *Radio Times*, 20 November 1999.

Index